AN ANNOTATED BIBLIOGRAPHY OF ERIC BIBLIOGRAPHIES, 1966–1980

Compiled by JOSEPH GERALD DRAZAN

Greenwood Press
WESTPORT, CONNECTICUT • LONDON, ENGLAND

Library of Congress Cataloging in Publication Data

Drazan, Joseph Gerald, 1943-
  An annotated bibliography of ERIC bibliographies,
1966-1980.

  Includes indexes.
  1. Bibliography—Bibliography—Education. 2. Education—
Bibliography.   I. Educational Resources Information
Center.   I. Title.
Z5811.D73   016.01637   82-6151
[LB1025.2]   AACR2
ISBN 0-313-22688-1 (lib. bdg.)

Library of Congress Catalog Card Number: 82-6151
ISBN: 0-313-22688-1

First published in 1982

Greenwood Press
A division of Congressional Information Service, Inc.
88 Post Road West, Westport, Connecticut 06881

Printed in the United States of America

10 9 8 7 6 5 4 3 2 1

Contents

Introduction

This bibliography is a comprehensive collection of over thirty-two hundred individual bibliographies, which are permanently stored and always available for reproduction in the ERIC system's microfiche files. They are indexed by the monthly abstract journal *Resources in Education* from which this bibliography was compiled and briefly annotated.

ERIC is the acronym for the Educational Resources Information Center, an information system in existence since 1966 that specializes in non-copyrighted and unpublished documents, which could be labeled fugitive literature. The primary purpose of this book is to make a select portion of these resources more widely known and available. ERIC is currently sponsored by the National Institute of Education within the Department of Education. It is designed to provide users with ready access to English-language literature dealing with education and related topics. It does this through a variety of products and services, most notably *Current Index to Journals in Education* (CIJE), and *Resources in Education* (RIE).

Early in 1981 I had published *The Unknown ERIC: A selection of documents for the general library* (Scarecrow, 1981), in which I wanted to make widely known over five hundred general-interest titles that should be of use to a larger audience. While I was involved in that project I began to notice the numerous bibliographies that should also have a general appeal, or were on subjects not at all related to education. The initial thought was to compile only those several hundred. However, when I began the actual gathering of bibliographies for this book, it seemed most appropriate to collect all of them in order to provide a comprehensive reference work of permanent and lasting value. Probably three-fourths of the citations here are directly related to aspects of education at all levels, the others only remotely or not at all.

The ERIC organization is quite remarkable among information systems in that it provides for the availability of reproductions of the documents that it indexes and abstracts. The entries in this bibliography are all for sale in full text from the ERIC Document Reproduction Service (EDRS), either in paper copy or microfiche. Those ED numbers in the bibliographic citations that are followed by (MF) are available in microfiche only; all others are available in either format.

Further availability is provided for by the fact that about seven hundred organizations now subscribe to the ERIC microfiche collection, which contained over 203,000 documents at the end of 1981. A *Directory of ERIC Microfiche Collections* can be obtained free from the ERIC Processing and Reference Facility, 4833 Rugby Avenue, Suite 303, Bethesda, MD, 20014.

The method for compiling this book was relatively straightforward. The subject index of every issue of RIE, from its inception in 1966 to September 1980, was searched under three headings: bibliographies, annotated bibliographies, and reference materials. In addition, scanning the Information Resources Clearinghouse sections (IR) picked up many more. In mid-1980 an obvious difficulty presented itself; the subject index no longer always contained the necessary terms. It seemed an appropriate place to halt the search and put the list in order.

The citations were arranged in about six hundred broad and narrow subject categories and further indexed by subject terms and keywords to bring out multiple aspects of many of the bibliographies. Cross references will be found throughout for additional assistance.

Many of the bibliographic entries are anonymous. All give full title, an imprint if present, the number of pages, and the ED accession number, which is the key for referral to RIE or a microfiche collection. The imprint often refers to where the bibliography was compiled, but usually implies sponsorship if not actual publication. If desired, other contract information and descriptors, and the full abstract, can be easily located in RIE by using the ED number provided for each.

The annotations presented here are intentionally brief. If the title is self-explanatory, often only the scope of the work is added. If the title is unclear or meaningless, an explanatory annotation is given.

ERIC states that it would like the opportunity to examine virtually any document dealing with or related to aspects of education. The ERIC audience is very broad, encompassing teachers, administrators, supervisors, librarians, researchers, media specialists, counselors, students, and others; it must collect a wide variety of documentation to satisfy its users. Bibliographies, annotated or not, are listed as desirable items. RIE is distributed in five thousand copies, and the ERIC data system is on-line through BRS, SDC, and Lockheed's DIALOG.

Currently there are sixteen ERIC Clearinghouses in addition to the Processing and Reference Facility at Bethesda. The bibliographies in this book were drawn from all of them. They are:

Adult, Career, and Vocational Education
Counseling and Personnel Services
Educational Management
Elementary and Early Childhood
Handicapped and Gifted Children
Higher Education
Information Resources
Junior Colleges
Languages and Linguistics
Reading and Communication Skills
Rural Education and Small Schools
Science, Mathematics, and Environmental Education
Social Studies/Social Science Education
Teacher Education
Tests, Measurement, and Evaluation
Urban Education

The addresses of each can be found in any issue of RIE.

Many fine bibliographies on an array of topics are found in this compilation. My goal was to lift these thirty-two hundred documents from their relative obscurity among 200,000 others and have them displayed and distributed in a manner that could be useful to virtually every library anywhere.

Joseph Drazan
Whitman College
Walla Walla, Washington

December 1981

How to Order A Bibliography from ERIC

Order from:

ERIC Document Reproduction Service (EDRS)
PO Box 190
Arlington, VA 22210

EDRS will invoice and add a 50¢ service charge for each document ordered, plus the cost of postage.

As of December 1981, prices for paper copy and microfiche reproductions can be computed from this chart. Like any other price schedule, it too is subject to change.

PAPER COPY/HARD COPY

PAGINATION	PRICE
1- 25	$2.00
26- 50	3.65
51- 75	5.30
76-100	6.95
101-125	8.60
126-150	10.25
151-175	11.90
176-200	13.55
201-225	15.20

PAPER COPY/HARD COPY

PAGINATION	PRICE
226-250	16.85
251-275	18.50
276-300	20.15
301-325	21.80
326-350	23.45
351-375	25.10
376-400	26.75
401-425	28.40
426-450	30.05
451-475	31.70
476-500	33.35

ADD $1.65 FOR EACH ADDITIONAL 25 PAGES, OR FRACTION THEREOF

MICROFICHE

PAGINATION	NUMBER OF FICHE	PRICE
1-480	1-5	$.91
481-576	6	1.10
577-672	7	1.29
673-768	8	1.48
769-864	9	1.67
865-960	10	1.86

ADD $0.19 FOR EACH ADDITIONAL MICROFICHE (1-96 PAGES)

AN ANNOTATED BIBLIOGRAPHY OF ERIC BIBLIOGRAPHIES, 1966–1980

The Bibliography

ACCOUNTABILITY

1. <u>Accountability: related bibliographies</u>. Tallahassee, Florida State Department of Education, 1975. 163p. ED 116 339 (MF)

> Areas include: criterion-referenced tests, educational accountability, evaluation criteria, methods, and techniques, functional literacy/illiteracy, performance criteria and specifications, and program effectiveness. All references are from a complete search of RIE and CIJE.

2. Hanson, Gordon. <u>Accountability: the state of the knowledge</u>. Madison, State Department of Education, 1972. 12p. ED 070146.

> Contains 144 articles, documents, and books. Forty ERIC documents are listed separately.

3. Tucker, Ellis E. <u>Accountability in education: a bibliography</u>. 1971. 21p. ED 055990.

> This annotated list contains 120 citations of journal articles, most of them published in 1970 and 1971, which deal with various aspects of the subject.

4. Browder, Lesley H. <u>Who's afraid of educational accountability?</u> Denver, Colorado State Department of Education, 1975. 66p. ED 108343.

> An unannotated representative review of the literature.

5. Saretsky, Gary. <u>Accountability: a bibliography</u>. Bloomington, ERIC Clearinghouse on Reading, Indiana University, 1971. 16p. ED 055757.

> 225 unannotated citations of books, journal articles, and conference proceedings are listed. Subdivided into: general, technical assistance, needs assessment, management systems, change strategies, performance objectives, per-

formance budgeting, staff development, comprehensive evaluation, program auditing, community involvement, and cost
effectiveness. Most of the titles were published from 1965
to 1971.

ACCREDITATION

6. Mills, Gladys H. Accreditation, licensure, certification,
and public accountability. Denver, Education Commission of
the States, 1972. 7p. ED 096902.

57 unannotated citations, some of which are ERIC items.

7. Accountability: review of literature and recommendations
for implementation. Raleigh, North Carolina Department of
Public Instruction, 1972. 168p. ED 066826.

Emphasis: accountability for accreditation outlining the
North Carolina plan.

8. Brandon, George L. Research visibility; evaluation and
accreditation. 1969. 16p.   ED 029155.

Eleven reviews organized under Cost Analysis, Follow-up
Studies, and Behavioral Analysis. The bibliography lists
39 additional items on these topics. Unannotated.

ACHIEVEMENT

9. Hanson, Gordon. Predictors of achievement: a bibliography. Denver, Colorado State Department of Education, 1973.
99p. ED 084629.

In a series of reports dealing with accountability, this
bibliography provides an overview of the literature, from
theoretical model design to the effects of specific factors such as student's self-concept, reinforcement, socioeconomic status, etc. It covers the literature on school
characteristics and student characteristics.

10. Bibliography on achievement. Cambridge, Harvard University, 1966. 7p. ED 011310.

40 unannotated references dating from 1952 to 1965 include
books, journal articles, and report materials. Subjects
included are behavior tests, achievement behavior, academic achievement, and social class background. ED 011311 is
a nine page supplement with 60 references dating from 1961
to 1966. Its additional subjects are motivation, underachievers, and probability estimates.

11. Harris, Chester W. Achievement test items: methods of
study. UCLA, Center for the Study of Evaluation, 1977. 157p.
ED 156718.

Contains an annotated list of over 100 selected journal

articles plus a list of additional references.

ACOUSTICS

12. Quindry, Thomas L. <u>Standards on noise measurements, rating schemes, and definitions: a compilation</u>. Washington, DC, National Bureau of Standards, 1976. 88p. ED 146689 (MF)

   Annotated list of documents covering measurement techniques calibration methods, definitions, rating schemes, and equipment, and product specifications concerned with acoustics.

ADMINISTRATION   See Also MANAGEMENT

13. <u>Administration: a selective bibliography</u>. Arlington, VA, Council for Exceptional Children, 1972. 23p. ED 069067.

   66 abstracts dated 1961 to 1971 dealing with administration relating to handicapped and exceptional children.

14. <u>The Best of the best of ERIC</u>. University of Oregon, ERIC Clearinghouse on Educational Management, 1977. 114p. ED 136 325.

   This annotated bibliography is intended for use by educational administrators. It contains 321 documents and journal articles from the ERIC system, subdivided under 20 headings. ED 163620 is a 123 page Volume 2 (1979).

15. Goldhammer, Keith. <u>Issues and problems in contemporary educational administration: a review of related literature</u>. Eugene, University of Oregon, 1967. 63p. ED 015538.

   Annotated. 138 articles, research reports, and unpublished items, dating from 1953 to 1966, contributed to the development of a rationale for a major study of problems facing public school superintendents.

16. Gillespie, Bonnie J. <u>A Selected bibliography for public administrators in minority settings</u>. Monticello, IL, Council of Planning Librarians, 1974. 18p. ED 103566.

   Concerns Black, Native, Spanish speaking, and women, and includes a subsection of films, filmstrips, tapes, records, games, and other media.

17. Saunders, Nancy and Bill Franklin. <u>Departments and department chairs: organizational and administrative influences on undergraduate teaching: an annotated bibliography on teaching undergraduate sociology</u>. Washington, American Sociological Association, 1977. 21p. ED 140701.

   Contains 35 references, from 1958 to 1975, to articles, books, dissertations that focus on the organization and administration of departments/divisions in colleges.

18. Stone, Franklin D. International perspective: a bibliography of educational administration. 1974. 34p. ED 098716

    Emphasizes primary and secondary education in Australia,
    Canada, Great Britain, New Zealand, and the United States.

ADMINISTRATORS   See Also PRINCIPALS and PRESIDENTS

19. Piele, Philip K. New programs for training school administrators: analysis of literature and selected bibliography.
University of Oregon, ERIC Clearinghouse on Educational Administration, 1970. 18p. ED 043119.

    This review analyzes current trends in the literature con-
    cerned with the training of school administrators. A 69
    item bibliography is included.

20. Selected bibliography on evaluation of administrators.
Eugene, University of Oregon, 1968. 9p. ED 018853.

    Contains 88 unannotated citations.

21. Piele, Philip K. Annotated bibliography on educational
administrator programs. University of Oregon, ERIC Clearinghouse on Educational Administration, 1968. 9p. ED 023198.

    Dated 1962 to 1968, a collection of more significant liter-
    ature describing or proposing programs for the inservice or
    preservice preparation of educational administrators for
    public and private educational organizations at the elemen-
    tary, secondary, and higher education levels. The 36 docu-
    ments included deal with such topics as the influence of
    the social sciences and the humanities on the preparation
    of the educational administrator, the writing of case study
    materials, and the use of simulation.

22. Stauffer, Thomas M. A Reference guide to important books
for academic administrators. Washington, American Council on
Education, 1975. 23p. ED 121181.

    400 unannotated items, most published after 1968. Topics
    include: the sociology of organizations, management, aca-
    demic organization and administration, history of higher
    education and comparative higher education, goals and pur-
    poses, higher education's environment, impact of post-sec-
    ondary education, and special reports.

23. Administrator evaluation: the best of ERIC. University
of Oregon, ERIC Clearinghouse on Educational Administration,
1974. 4p. ED 094451.

    From RIE and CIJE, 23 unannotated items covering overviews
    of current philosophy and practice, manuals and guides for
    the evaluation of the performance of principals and super-
    intendents.

ADOLESCENT LITERATURE   See Also CHILDRENS LITERATURE

24. Willard, Charles B. Your Reading: a book list for junior high schools. National Council of Teachers of English, 1966. 197p. ED 079762.

   Approximately 1300 books are grouped under 13 main headings: adventure, home & family, problems of youth, the arts,
   just for fun, folklore and legend, animals, sports, science,
   vocations and avocations, people worth knowing and knowing
   about, our country, and the world.

25. Walker, Jerry L. Your reading: a booklist for junior high students. Fifth edition. National Council of Teachers of English, 1975. 424p. ED 112425.

   Contains annotations for over 1500 fiction and non-fiction
   items. Most entries have been published in the past few
   years, though well-written older books are also included.

26. Donelson, Kenneth L. Books for you: a booklist for senior high students. Sixth edition. National Council of Teachers of English, 1976. 490p. ED 130270.

   The annotated list has 43 categories, and includes author
   and title indexes.

27. Books for the teenage. New York Public Library, 1977. 70p. ED 135005.

   1250 annotated books are listed that vary greatly in depth
   and difficulty. They were selected by a committee of librarians who work with teenagers. The titles are under 92 subject headings.

ADULT EDUCATION

28. Charters, Alexander N. and Donald Holmwood. Resources for educators of adults: professional development for educators of adults: a bibliography. ERIC Clearinghouse of Resources for Educators of Adults, 1978. 115p. ED 159438.

   Subjects include: accreditation, administration, agencies,
   communications, counseling, evaluation, philosophy, futures,
   history, instruction methods, legislation, public relations,
   research, and resources. Unannotated.

29. Charters, Alexander N. Resources for educators of adults. Acquisition list, pamphlet file at E. S. Bird Library. Syracuse University, 1978. 109p. ED 162671.

   Unannotated subject list.

30. Charters, Alexander N. Resources for educators of adults.

The Paul Hoy Helms Library in liberal adult education, Syracuse
University, 1978.   57p.   ED 162672.

An unannotated list of books chosen by faculty and students
with the intention of furthering adult education and independent study.

31.   DeCrow, Roger and Karen.   University adult education: a
selected bibliography: review and topical index. Syracuse University, Libary of Continuing Education, 1967.   111p.   ED 045
926.

This 144 item annotated bibliography represents the work of
evening colleges and general extension divisions, with some
references from junior college and Cooperative Extension
Service literature.

32.   Thomas, Myra H.   Books related to adult basic education
and teaching English to speakers of other languages. Washington, DC, National Center for Educational Communication, 1970.
25p.   ED 043850. (MF)

Includes textbooks and professional resources   received
between 1968 and mid-1970.

33.   Berenson, Gail.   A Bibliography of instructional and professional materials for adult basic education. Portland, ME,
Urban Adult Learning Center, 1977.   108p.   ED 143856.

The instructional materials listing comprises about 90%
of the bibliography. Unannotated.

34.   Kulich, Jindra.   Annotated bibliography on program evaluation in residential adult education. Silver Spring, MD, National University Extension Association, 1970.   67p.   ED 038578.

These 29 books, articles, and book chapters have been
chosen for practical application of theoretical significance to the evaluation of program design and content and
of learning within programs.

35.   D'Antoni, Susan.   Continuing education in the professions:
a selected bibliography.   Toronto, Ontario Institute for Studies
in Education, 1970.   19p.   ED 052465.

150 unannotated citations are listed for works dealing
with adult education in professional fields.

36.   Residential adult education.   Syracuse University, ERIC
Clearinghouse on Adult Education, 1969.   47p.   ED 032449.

This annotated bibliography contains 113 entries, mainly
1964 or later, and most with abstracts covering the residential method, historical reviews, and bibliographies on
instructional methods and techniques. Also included are
programs and learning resources, conference planning and

administration. Program descriptions are from such areas
as professional education, management training, inservice
training, sensitivity training, labor education, family
life education, and the contemporary folk schools.

37. Smith, Edwin H. and Weldon Bradtmueller. A Selected annotated bibliography of instructional literacy materials for
adult basic education. Tallahassee, Florida State Department
of Education, 1968. 52p. ED030831.

Divided among three stages of prevocational or adult basic
education: introductory, elementary, and intermediate.
Areas covered include English as a second language, language arts in general, reading instruction, practical mathematics and money management, citizenship, social studies,
and prevocational orientation.

38. Mezirow, J. D. and Dorothea Berry. The Literature of liberal adult education, 1945-1957. Brookline, Mass., Center for
the Study of Liberal Education for Adults, 1960. 317p. ED 030
791.

A comprehensive guide to books, articles, government publications, and pamphlets in the US, Great Britain, and Canada.
The 1027 entries are categorized as follows: educational
philosophy and trends, research and bibliography, the roles
of colleges and universities, adult education conducted by
public schools, business, industry, and labor and other
agencies. Partially annotated with indexes.

39. Adult basic education. Syracuse University, ERIC Clearinghouse on Adult Education, 1970. 89p. ED 035777.

Annotated. Contains 261 entries, most published since 1965.

40. Dickinson, Gary. Research related to adult education conducted at the University of British Columbia. 1968. 69p.
ED 028364.

Annotated list of 232 items including 32 abstracts of dissertations and theses. Topics: agricultural extension, literacy education, community development, leadership training,
evening classes, correspondence study, vocational education,
age differences in adult learning, and educational methodology. Author index.

41. Ohliger, John. The Mass media in adult education: a review of recent literature. Syracuse University, ERIC Clearinghouse on Adult Education, 1968. 130p. ED 024907.

The references in the text comprise the bibliography of
120 items.

42. Watt, Lois B. and Sidney Murphy. Adult basic education:
a bibliography from the educational materials center. Washington, DC, Office of Education, 1968. 19p. ED 025737 (MF)

Unannotated. Materials range up to eighth grade level.

43. Kreps, Juanita and Ralph Laws. Training and retraining older workers: an annotated bibliography. New York, National Council on the Aging, 1965. 30p. ED 026472.

123 documents published 1943 through 1964 organized under headings of general references and government.

44. Methods and techniques of adult training. Syracuse University, ERIC Clearinghouse on Adult Education, 1967. 19p. ED 013429.

35 annotated items in such areas as military training, management development, and vocational education and retraining.

45. Training of adult education personnel. Syracuse University, ERIC Clearinghouse on Adult Education, 1967. 27p. ED 014 670.

Annotated. Contains 44 indexed entries.

46. Charters, Alexander N. Resources for Educators of adults: abstracts of dissertations and theses. Syracuse University, Publications Program in Continuing Education, 1979. 101p. ED 183168.

Contains abstracts of all doctoral research studies which were planned and supervised in the adult education area of Syracuse University between 1958 and 1979.

47. Higher adult education: current information sources. Syracuse University, ERIC Clearinghouse on Adult Education, 1967. 24p. ED 014031.

The 41 items abstracted deal with fine arts education, urban extension, community development, leadership training, managerial and professional education, and vocational training.

48. Knox, Alan B. Adult basic education. New York, Columbia University Teachers College, 1967. 58p. ED 015392.

This report contains abstracts of research reports and evaluation conducted in the US and Canada.

49. Community education for adults. Syracuse University, ERIC Clearinghouse on Adult Education, 1967. 19p. ED 014025

30 annotated entries on community development in the US and abroad, manpower development and leadership, and professional training, educational and information needs, dynamics of social change, community planning and action, and urban and rural university extension services.

50. Television and radio in adult education. Syracuse University, ERIC Clearinghouse on Adult Education, 1967. 19p. ED

014032.

Annotated. Contains 32 items on aspects of educational and instructional radio and television, particularly viewing habits, motivation, public television, and media technology. Many entries are related to needs of developing countries.

51. Evening college education: basic information sources. Syracuse University, ERIC Clearinghouse on Adult Education, 1967. 27p. ED 014023.

A selected, annotated bibliography with five sections including: periodicals and indexes, research and enrollment data sources, and program reviews.

52. Alexander-Frutschi, Marian. Special education. Stanford Research Institute, 1963. 52p. ED023021.

References are annotated and date from 1949 to 1961. Entries include literacy education, community development, cooperative education, extension work, rural education, management education, and vocational education.

53. Schulz, Harriette. Survey of adult education programs for the disadvantaged. Kansas City, Institute for Community Studies, 1975. 132p. ED 117360.

An annotated bibliography of 47 pages follows the survey.

54. Public school adult education: current information sources. Washington, DC, National Association for Public School Adult Education, 1968. 27p. ED 023992.

Concerns training and retraining adults and out of school youth. 36 annotated entries date from 1965 to 1968, and include program descriptions and statistics.

55. Askov, Eunice N. and Joyce Lee. An annotated bibliography of adult basic education instructional materials. Pennsylvania State University, College of Education, 1974. 77p. ED 123610.

Subjects are communication skills, English as a second language,computation skills, and testing.

56. A Bibliography of materials: adult basic education. Cheyenne, Wyoming State Department of Education, 1966. 172p. ED 107919.

Annotated entries are under 38 subject headings indexed by author and title.

57. DeCrow, Roger and Nehume Loague. Adult education dissertation abstracts, 1963-1967. Syracuse University, ERIC Clearinghouse on Adult Education, 1971. 309p. ED 044537.

505 annotated entries under broad subject headings.

58. <u>Adult basic education: a bibliography of materials</u>. Lansing, Michigan State Department of Education, 1969. 168p. ED 044599.

   Subjects: reading, spelling, writing skills, English grammar, English as a second language, math skills, science, social studies, testing and evaluation.

59. Carter, Nancy B. <u>Adult basic education annotated bibliography</u>. Saint Louis, MO, Public Library System, 1969. 142p. ED 034142.

   Areas covered are: reading, English, grammar, handwriting, mathematics, science, social science, job orientation materials, family life and daily living, and tests.

60. White, Sally. <u>Physical criteria for adult learning environments</u>. Washington, DC, Adult Education Association, 1972. 30p. ED 080882.

   A 54 item annotated list of books, articles, and reports, and a six item listing of bibliographies on educational environments supplement the text.

61. Ohliger, John and Joel Rosenberg. <u>Compulsory adult education</u>. Ohio State University, College of Education, 1973. 41p. ED 079572.

   231 annotated entries are given; includes career education and professional education.

62. Milne, Terry L. <u>Continuing adult education: an annotated bibliography</u>. 1974. 117p. ED 109393.

   Includes 75 books, articles, and reports dealing with history, philosophy, needs, purposes, methods, and institutions.

63. Draper, James A. and Jeffrey Field. <u>Canadian theses in adult education: a look at the '70's</u>. Toronto, Ontario Institute for Studies in Education, 1974. 16p. ED 109490. (MF)

   163 theses on adult education and community development submitted to Canadian universities since 1970.

64. <u>Adult education and staff development bibliography</u>. College Park, University of Maryland, 1973. 178p. ED 109494.

   Basic books and journal articles to assist in the development of adult education. Unannotated.

65. Draper, James A. <u>University of Toronto theses research relating to adult education: an interdisciplinary analysis, 1900–1970</u>. Toronto, Ontario Institute for Studies in Education, 1974. 78p. ED 107901.

   Annotations of 62 theses conducted mainly in the humanities. These are examples of research from other disciplines from which adult education might benefit.

66. An Analysis of selected issues in adult education. Final report. Washington, DC, E. J. Kirschner and Associates, 1976. 151p. ED 122045.

This final volume of a set of three comprises an annotated bibliography and a selective bibliography of references consulted in the study. Abstracted are 100 items that mention roles, policies, and/or strategies for Federal involvment in adult education.

67. Ohliger, John. Radical ideas in adult education. 1976. 21p. ED 121979.

81 annotated references are included.

68. Grabowski, Stanley M. Adult education dissertation abstracts: 1935-1962. Syracuse University, ERIC Clearinghouse on Adult Education, 1973. 448p. ED 069967.

69. Warner, Larry S. and Renae Humburg. Teaching adult vocational education learners: annotated and selected bibliography. Greeley, University of Northern Colorado, College of Education, 1977. 107p. ED 154140.

Contains 83 books, reports, guides, papers, and articles.

70. Personnel development in adult education: current information sources. Syracuse University, ERIC Clearinghouse on Adult Education, 1970. 101p. ED 041244.

This annotated bibliography contains 192 items on program planning, educational trends, legislation, and other matters within or relevant to the preparation of adult educators.

71. Campbell, Boyd P. and Harold Williams. Continuing education film survey: a national survey of 16mm films. Albany, State University of New York, 1968. 23p. ED 019615.

A Selective, annotated list of 162 films in the area, including citizenship, vocational education, family life, personal development, and general education.

72. Mezirow, Jack and David Epley. Adult education in developing countries: a bibliography. University of Pittsburgh, School of Education, 1965. 128p. ED 022086.

Forty sources listed at the end of this document were used to compile this comprehensive bibliography which includes references for Africa, the Near East, South and Southeast Asia, the Far East and Oceania, and Latin America. It is not annotated.

73. Sheffield, Sherman B. and John H. Buskey. Annotated bib-

liography on residential adult education. Minneapolis, National University Extension Association, 1968.   25p.   ED 021182.

The 49 entries deal with procedures and methods, university extension, historical reviews, objectives, programs and registration data, administrator roles and attitudes, and student morale.

74.   Adult education in Africa. Syracuse University, ERIC Clearinghouse on Adult Education, 1968.   17p.   ED 019565.

23 annotated items published from 1962 to 1967.

75.   Adult education in Asia, Australia, and New Zealand. Syracuse University, ERIC Clearinghouse on Adult Education, 1968.   34p.   ED 018705.

Arranged by geographic location, the 45 items were published between 1963 and 1967. Annotated.

76.   Crew, Vernon. Bibliography of Australian adult education, 1835-1965. Melbourne, Australian Association of Adult Education, 1968.   114p.   ED 023024.

868 annotated entries are grouped under subject headings and arranged chronologically within sections. Includes indexes.

77.   A Bibliography for use in the preparation of materials for adult literacy education in Brazil. Tallahassee, Florida State University, 1967.   26p.   ED 019550.

Annotated. Includes commercial and UNESCO publications dated 1942 through 1965.

78.   Kidd, J. R. Adult education in Canada. Toronto, Canadian Association for Adult Education, 1950.   262p.   ED 024875.

An unannotated bibliography is appended to this report.

79.   Kulich, Jindra. Adult educaion in continental Europe: an annotated bibliography of English language materials, 1945-1969. University of British Columbia, Center for Continuing Education, 1971.   225p.   ED 057321.

Organized by country with a section on Europe and one on Scandinavia, a total of 25 countries are covered. 857 items. ED 117444 is a 167 page supplement covering 1970-1974. It has 556 items.

80.   Savicky, I. European selective bibliography on adult education, 1966-1971. Prague, European Center for Leisure and Education, 1973.   105p.   ED 080836.

Sixteen countries are covered in this annotated list of 165 books, articles, and bibliographies.

81.   Schadt, Armin L. Adult education in Germany: bibliography.

Syracuse University, ERIC Clearinghouse on Adult Education, 1969. 49p. ED 029167.

 Lists 100 German language documents, some with abstracts, arranged in three historical periods, and a supplement of 13 English language documents.

82. Marquardt, William F. Review of contemporary research on literacy and adult education in Latin America. 1967. 26p. ED 015396.

 Includes a selected bibliography of about 190 references. Unannotated.

ADULT LEARNING

83. Adult learning characteristics: current information sources. Syracuse University, ERIC Clearinghouse on Adult Education, 1968. 49p. ED 024014.

 82 annotated entries arranged under: mental and perceptual abilities, personality and social role factors, and general bibliographies.

84. Kuhlen, Raymond G. Learning and cognitive performance in adults: bibliography. Syracuse University, 1967. 106p. ED 015413.

 Over 1500 unannotated items largely devoted to conditioning, skill learning, discrimination, verbal learning, problem solving, complex behavior, memory, and verbal behavior.

85. Rosen, Pamela. Tests of basic learning for adults: an annotated bibliography. Princeton, NJ, ERIC Clearinghouse on Tests, Measurement, and Evaluation, 1971. 21p. ED 058274.

 Information given for each includes the purpose of the instrument, the nature of the materials, groups for which it is intended, and information on administering, scoring, and interpreting.

ADULT LITERACY

86. Nazzaro, Lois B. Annotated bibliography. Free Library of Philadelphia, 1971. 79p. ED 054783.

 The 610 references are designed to aid under-educated adults and young adults in overcoming the educational, cultural, and economic deficiencies in their lives.

ADVERTISING

87. Children and advertising: a bibliography. New York, Council of Better Business Bureaus, 1976. 22p. ED 131850.

    248 unannotated books, articles, speeches, statements, and
    testimonies concerning the effects of television advertis-
    ing on children are listed. All were published from 1945 to
    1975 with the majority published in the 1970's.

ADVISORY COMMITTEES

88. Advisory Committees: the best of ERIC. University of Oregon, ERIC Clearinghouse on Educational Management, 1975. 5p.
ED 099954.

    Seventeen annotated items consider the roles of such groups
    in student involvment, citizen participation, community co-
    operation, and school-community relationships.

89. Advisory Committees: the best of ERIC. University of Oregon, ERIC Clearinghouse on Educational Management, 1977. 5p.
ED 144204.

    Eleven more documents and journal articles examine the
    issue of the extent to which citizens and parents should
    be allowed to participate in school decision making pro-
    cesses through advisory committees.

AEROSPACE TECHNOLOGY

90. Aerospace bibliography. Fifth edition. Washington, DC,
National Aerospace Education Council, 1970. 103p. ED 040882.
(MF)

    For elementary and secondary school teachers.

AFFIRMATIVE ACTION   See Also SEX DISCRIMINATION

91. Guide to resources for equal employment opportunity and
affirmative action. Washington, DC, Equal Employment Opportunity Commission, 1976. 61p. ED 127722.

    Lists over 200 annotated items that may be helpful for
    developing equal employment and affirmative action prorams.
    Many entries are produced by private organizations.

92. Mickey, Melissa. Developing a plan for affirmative action:
human rights bibliography. Chicago, Medical Library Association, 1973. 58p. ED 136763.

    Unannotated. Includes books and articles on methods of
    laboratory education which are used to reduce racial pre-

judice; literature on the case method of training personnel
managers; materials describing the specific problems of su-
pervising minority group employees and the general problems
of minority employment; and books on the promotion of interracial sensitivity.

93. Pemberton, S. M. Research reports on affirmative action
programs in colleges and universities: an annotated bibliography. Washington, DC, Office of Education, 1977. 16p. ED 147
247.

Provides narrative summaries of 31 articles and books that
appeared between 1972 and 1977.

AFRICA

94. Anderson, Teresa. Rural development in Africa: a bibliography. Madison, University of Wisconsin, Land Tenure Center,
1971. 86p. ED 068251 (MF)

List approximately 1950 books, journal articles, and unpublished manuscripts. Unannotated. Subjects are; agriculture,
law, economics, population, finance, trade and commerce,
politics and government, transport, and communications.
ED 138385 is a 107 page supplement done in 1973 that contains over 1000 items by country, and ED 067213 is a 91
page supplement that has about 940 items that date between
1953 and 1971. The two supplements are available in hard-
copy in addition to fiche.

95. Schmidt, Nancy. Selected bibliographies for teaching children about Subsaharan Africa. Urbana, IL, ERIC Clearinghouse
on Early Childhood Education, 1975. 50p. ED 115377.

An annotated list for elementary and secondary teachers.

96. Case, John H. Annotated bibliography on science and
mathematics education in Subsaharan Africa. Paris, UNESCO,
1969. 231p. ED 052949.

Intended to be comprehensive up to 1967; covers all levels
from elementary to post-graduate.

97. Garland, William E. Traditional African religion: a resource unit. Pittsburgh, Carnegie-Mellon University, 1970.
73p. ED 037586.

Part 1 is an annotated list of selected sources, and part
2 is a model teaching unit of two weeks duration.

98. Schmidt, Nancy. Resources for teaching children about
Africa. Urbana, IL, ERIC Clearinghouse on Early Childhood Education, 1976. 65p. ED 131953.

Includes bibliographies as well as African games.

99. Bown, Lalage. African adult education: a bibliography.
Lusaka, Zambia University, 1966. 128p. ED 010857.

Unannotated list of materials in English and French. Most
English sources are non-American

100. Brembeck, Cole S. and John P. Keith. Education in emer-
ging Africa: a select and annotated bibliography. East Lansing,
Michigan State University, College of Education, 1962. 156p.
ED 028349.

Most of the sources are from the 1950's on: administration
and control, education and change, educational planning,
teachers, teaching, and students, vocational and special
education, and bibliographies.

101. Molnos, Angela. Sources for the study of East African
cultures and development. Nairobi, East African Research Information Centre, 1969. 64p. ED 029295 (MF)

The subtitle of this bibliography is: "A bibliography of
social scientific bibliographies, abstracts, reference
works, catalogues, directories, writings on archives, bibliographies, book production, libraries, and museums, with
special reference to Kenya, Tanzania, and Uganda 1946-1968"
It has 796 unannotated listings.

102. Jumba-Masagazi, A. African socialism: a bibliography
and a short summary. Nairobi, East African Academy, 1970.
75p. ED 054990.

Concentrates on Africa South of the Sahara, and provides
a somewhat complete listing of items published from 1948
to 1970. Unannotated.

103. Ehrman, Edith and Ward Morehouse. Preliminary bibliography on Africa South of the Sahara for undergraduate libraries.
SUNY, Foreign Area Materials Center, 1967. 328p. ED 031254.

Classified and unannotated.

104. Near East and North Africa: a selected functional and
country bibliography. Washington, DC, Foreign Service Institute, 1971. 45p. ED 076488.

Topics: history, politics, international relations, Islam
and the Islamic world, the Arabs, geography, art, literature, education, sociocultural patterns, economics, labor,
and oil. Unannotated.

105. Africa Subsahara: a selected functional and country bibliography. Washington, DC, Foreign Service Institute, 1972.
34p. ED076489.

500 unannotated citations. Topics: communism, urbanization,
politics, labor, military, colonialism, art, literature,
religion, agriculture, and history.

106. Off the African shelf: an annotated bibliography on society and education. Boulder, CO, ERIC Clearinghouse for Social Studies/Social Science Education, 1970. 39p. ED 044349.

   39 items that are taken from RIE and CIJE focus on teaching guides and curriculum materials, bibliographies, resource guides, and reports dealing with the institution of
   education in Africa, the purpose and structure of an African studies in the curriculum, and information about Africa.

107. Johnson, G. Wesley. Francophone African elites: a selective bibliography. Washington, DC Institute of International
Studies, 1971. 14p. ED 057645.

   Unannotated. Lists over 340 books and articles written between 1920 and 1970. Includes literature by and about the
   elites.

108. Molnos, Angela. Language problems in Africa: a bibliography and summary of the present situation with special reference to Kenya, Tanzania, and Uganda. Nairobi, East African
Research Information Centre, 1969. 68p. ED 030862 (MF)

   Includes African, European, British, and American publications dated from 1946 to 1967.

AFRICAN LITERATURE

109. Afro writers: bibliography of recent works in French.
New York, French and European Publications, 1972. 35p. ED
069197.

   Includes books only on historical and cultural background,
   economic and social development, religion, the arts, and
   language. Literature is the second major category.

110. Amosu, Margaret. A Preliminary bibliography of creative
African writing in the European languages. Ibadan University
(Nigeria), Institute of African Studies, 1964. 41p. ED 159
933 (MF)

   Includes about 250 authors and 650 titles of creative
   writing by Africans in English, French, and Portuguese.
   Not annotated.

111. Redd, Virginia P. African literature: the bonds of tra-
dition versus the winds of change. A critical review and selective bibliography. Paper presented at the National Council of
Teachers of English annual meeting, 1973. 24p. ED 089279.

   The annotated bibliography cites works that articulate the
   stratification of African society into "haves" and "have-
   nots", and the incipient class conflict that resulted from
   a European inspired elitism. Most of the citations are actual literary works.

AGED   See   GERONTOLOGY

AGRICULTURAL EDUCATION

112. A Description and source listing of curriculum materials
in agricultural education. Washington, DC, American Vocational Association, 1973. 38p. ED 085501.

> 246 annotated items in such topics as: field crops, soils,
> forestry, animal science, horticulture, diseases and pests,
> and agricultural engineering. Earlier lists for 1963 to
> 1971 are available as ED 013880, 027400, 028273, 038507.

113. Thomas, Willie H. Agricultural education instructional
materials from "Abstracts of Instructional and Research Materials in Vocational and Technical Education", 1972-1975. Ohio
State University, Center for Vocational Education, 1976. 264p.
ED 130141.

> The first collection of resumes from 1967 to 1971 is a-
> vailable as ED 062571. Annotated.

114. Carpenter, Earl T. and John H. Rodgers. Review and synthesis of research in agricultural education. Second edition.
Ohio State University, Center for Vocational and Technical Education, 1970. 90p. ED 040275.

> About 500 studies were reviewed since 1966. A similar
> document covering research prior to 1966 is available as
> ED 011562.

115. Lambert, Roger H. A Bibliography of free loan materials
for agricultural education. Madison, University of Wisconsin,
Vocational Studies Center, 1976. 40p. ED 132279.

> Annotated.

116. Ellis, Willie T. and A. L. Berkey. Bibliography of summer programs in agricultural education. Ithaca, State University of New York, 1968. 16p. ED 020404.

> 160 annotated professional books and articles for use in
> planning and conducting summer programs.

117. Ellis, Willie T. and David G. Craig. An Annotated bibliography for young adult farmer education. Ithaca, State
University of New York, 1965. 17p. ED 010793.

> Unannotated articles from the Agricultural Education Maga-
> zine (1959-1965) are arranged by topics.

118. Frelund, William. Indexes and abstracts of research completed in the field of agricultural education from 1951-1965
at Iowa State University. Des Moines, Iowa State Department
of Public Instruction, 1966. 177p. ED 014536.

Annotated list of 103 master's theses and 19 doctoral dissertations.

119. Moore, Eddie A. Student performance objectives and selected references for teaching agricultural production. East Lansing, Michigan State University, College of Agriculture, 1976. 401p. ED 159356 (MF)

This is the first of a three volume set. The other two, ED 159357 and ED 159358, cover agricultural mechanics and ornamental horticulture, respectively.

120. Moore, Eddie A. Student performance objectives and selected references for teaching agricultural mechanics. 1976. 175p. ED 159357 (MF)

AGRICULTURAL LABORERS See Also MIGRANT LABOR

121. Ruesink, David C. and T. Brice Batson. Bibliography relating to agricultural labor. Texas A&M University, Agricultural Experiment Station, 1969. 96p. ED 028886.

Over 1000 bibliographies, books, dissertations, proceedings, bulletins, government documents, and periodicals are listed. Mostly includes material from the five years prior to publication. Unannotated.

122. Fujimoto,Isao and Jo Clare Schieffer. Guide to sources on agricultural labor. University of California (Davis), Department of Applied Behavioral Sciences, 1967. 45p. ED 026152

Contains 85 annotated items to provide an overview on agricultural labor in general and California farm labor in particular.

AGRICULTURE

123. Agriculture and agronomy: a dissertation bibliography. Ann Arbor, MI, University Microfilms, 1978. 69p. ED 161666 (MF)

3386 unannotated doctoral dissertations are cited from the years 1973-1976.

124. Morrison, Denton E. Farmers' organizations and movements: research needs and a bibliography of the United States and Canada. East Lansing, MI, Michigan State University, Agricultural Experiment Station, 1969. 117p. ED 051930.

Part two is the bibliography consisting of 998 unannotated items published between 1846 and 1969.

125. Neville-Rolfe, Edmund. Economic aspects of agricultural

<u>development in Africa: a selective annotated reading list of</u>
<u>reports and studies concerning 40 African countries during the</u>
<u>period 1960-1969</u>. Oxford University, Agricultural Economics
Research Institute, 1969. 267p. ED 039051.

1394 research studies arranged by country.

AIR CONDITIONING

126. <u>Bibliography of training aids</u>. Second Edition. Arlington, VA, Air Conditioning & Refrigeration Institute, 1970.
112p. ED 047154.

Over 160 training aids are listed. The annotated list includes films and other visual aids available from 34 member companies for use in air conditioning and refrigeration training programs.

AIR POLLUTION

127. <u>Mercury and air pollution: a bibliography with abstracts</u>.
Environmental Protection Agency, 1972. 65p. ED 072965.

Categories include: emission sources, control methods,
measurement methods, atmospheric interaction, effects on
humans, plants, and livestock, standards and criteria,
legal and social aspects.

128. <u>Hydrocarbons and air pollution: an annotated bibliogra-</u>
<u>phy</u>. National Air Pollution Control Administration, 1970.
1183p. ED 059099 (MF)

2300 documents published from 1959 to 1970 are listed in
13 categories. Indexed by geographical location, in addition to author, title, and subject.

ALASKA

129. Hubbard, Terry E. <u>Alaska. Part I: bibliographies, his-</u>
<u>tory, and natural sciences</u>. Fairbanks, University of Alaska
Library, 1978. 29p. ED 163936.

No fiction or childrens' material is included in this guide
to the Alaskana collection of the Rasmuson Library at the
University of Alaska.

130. Symons, Ann. <u>Alaska wilderness: a bibliography for sec-</u>
<u>ondary students on marine vertebrates, birds, small or fur</u>
<u>bearing mammals and game animals of Alaska</u>. Juneau, Alaska
State Department of Education, 1978. 13p. ED162893.

Some entries are fiction in this annotated list of 53 items.

ALASKA NATIVES

131. McGary, Jane. Bibliography of educational publications for Alaska native languages. Juneau, Alaska State Department of Education, 1978. 153p. ED 180197.

Includes general works, reference works, and materials on bilingual education. Languages covered are: Tlingit, Haida, Tsimshian, Athabaskan, Aleut, Yupik Eskimo, and others.

ALBANIA

132. Albania area studies: bibliography arranged by topics. Monterey, CA, Defense Language Institute, 1974. 38p. ED 176 563.

Includes language, history, culture, geography, natural resources, communication, transportation, demography, public utilities, industry, and agriculture. Also poetry, linguistics, psychology, and children's books. The works listed are in Albanian, English, Italian, English, and French; some are annotated.

ALCOHOLISM

133. Guthrie, P. D. Measures pertaining to health education: Alcohol: an annotated bibliography. Princeton, NJ, ERIC Clearinghouse on Tests, Measurement, and Evaluation, 1972. 55p. ED 068570.

Instruments for the alcoholic and the general population designed to assess attitudes, behaviors, practices, knowledge, and correlations are described.

134. Cameron, Colin. Alcoholism in employment: bibliography and references with selected annotations. Madison, WI, Contemporary Bibliographical Services, 1972. 89p. ED 080683.

Focuses on the culture of industrial alcoholism, and the alcoholic worker's environment. The books and articles were published from 1960 to 1972.

ALTERNATIVE EDUCATION   See Also CHANGE and INNOVATIONS IN ED.

135. Esp, Barbara. Program evaluation in alternative education: an annotated bibliography. University of Indiana, School of Education, 1976. 12p. ED 128312.

In two parts, it covers evaluation issues and methods, and studies of alternative environments.

136. Dobson, Catherine. Non-traditional education: a bibliography. Ann Arbor, University of Michigan Libraries, 1973.
8p. ED 086635.

Over 100 books appropriate for use by educators, parents,
and community groups date from 1967 through 1972.

137. Natriello, Gary and Thomas J. Alternative education:
books and films: an annotated bibliography. Trenton, New Jersey State Department of Education, 1974. 23p. ED 098665.

Includes critical literature, reform literature, experimental literature, directories and manuals.

138. The Basics controversy; the best of ERIC. Eugene, OR,
ERIC Clearinghouse on Educational Management, 1978. 5p. ED
153302.

Ten journal articles and documents annotated in this bibliography cover several aspects of the controversy pro-
voked by the emergence of the back-to-basics movement.

ALTERNATIVE SCHOOLS

139. Alternative education: the best of ERIC. University of
Oregon, ERIC Clearinghouse on Educational Management, 1975.
5p. ED 111052.

Annotated.

140. Selected bibliography on optional alternative public
schools, 1972-1974. University of Indiana, School of Education, 1974. 17p. ED 100041.

Brief annotations describing possible alternatives to the
traditional form of American public elementary and secondary education.

141. Alternative schools: the best of ERIC. University of
Oregon, ERIC Clearinghouse on Educational Management, 1976.
5p. ED 128876.

Twelve annotated articles and documents range from analyses of what is wrong with alternative schools to procedures for their development.

142. Jayatilleke, Raja. Alternative schooling. Columbia
University, ERIC Clearinghouse on the Urban Disadvantaged,
1976. 27p. ED 128495.

On community schools, educational alternatives, educational innovation, and experimental schools. Annotated.

143. Vollbrecht, Michele T. Evaluation of alternative schools:
an annotated ERIC bibliography. Princeton, NJ, ERIC Clearing-

house on Tests, Measurement, and Evaluation, 1977. 39p. ED 142583.

62 references cover both the elementary and secondary level.

AMERICAN INDIANS See also specific Tribal Names

144. Good words: notable books on the American Indian. Chicago, American Library Association, 1973. 11p. ED 092953.

50 annotated titles published from 1967 to 1972 that reflect realistic and honest images of the American Indian. Emphasis is on the Plains Indians.

145. Cane, Suzanne S. Selected media about the American Indian for young children, K-3. Boston, Massachusetts State Department of Education, 1970. 31p. ED 048949.

Every item was evaluated for its usefulness in refuting stereotypes. Some of the annotated references are to Canadian Indians.

146. Fehr, Helen. Bibliography for professional development. Saskatoon, University of Saskatchewan, Indian and Northern Curriculum Resources Centre, 1972. 76p. ED 085129.

Publications between 1953 and 1970 on the American Indian are included in this annotated bibliography designed to aid professional development in the field of education. Topics: culture, education, ethnology, folklore, art, housing, history, language, social conditions, wars, and nativistic movements.

147. The North American Indian and the Eskimo. San Francisco, Unified School District, 1972. 26p. ED 085454.

All items are audio-visual materials including 16mm films, filmstrips, prints, and models.

148. Annotated bibliography of articles pertaining to native North Americans. Saskatoon, University of Saskatchewan, Indian and Northern Curriculum Resources Centre, 1972. 53p. ED 085167.

Includes Metis and Eskimos. The books, journal, and newspaper articles were printed from 1959 to 1971. 335 items.

149. Anderson, Sue Ellen. North American Indians: an annotated resource guide for the elementary teacher. Tempe, Arizona State University, Indian Education Center, 1972. 119p. ED 085156.

600 listings dating from 1926 to 1972 include materials prepared by Indians and non-Indians for all children. Audiovisuals account for a large portion of the document.

150. <u>American Indian reference book</u>. 1976. 307p. ED 134391

Includes periodicals, 575 books, films, filmloops, and
filmstrips, records, tapes.

151. Revai, Loretta Z. <u>An Annotated bibliography of selected</u>
<u>books about American Indians for elementary through high school</u>
<u>students</u>. Columbia University, ERIC Clearinghouse on the Urban
Disadvantaged, 1972. 73p. ED 065642.

300 books, many written by Indians, which are considered
to represent the Indian point of view. Pre-Columbian
through modern.

152. McDonald, David R. <u>Native American fishing/hunting</u>
<u>rights: an annotated bibliography</u>. 1977. 21p. ED 136994.

37 citations from 1915 to 1975 include law journals,
books, and government documents.

153. <u>About Indians: a listing of books</u>. 4th edition. Toronto, Department of Indian Affairs and Northern Development,
1977. 351p. ED 157644.

Includes North and South America, but specifically points
out books of Canadian interest. The 1452 annotated books
are classified according to interest level, Kindergarten
through adult.

154. Tahushasha, W. <u>Bibliography on the native American</u>
<u>experience</u>. Springfield, Illinois State Commission on Human
Relations, 1973. 28p. ED 080271.

Written by native Americans, there are 120 entries dating
from 1942 to 1972. Includes reading for elementary school
children, teachers, and parents on general history, Indian nations, biographies, autobiographies, drama, fiction,
poetry, and photography.

155. <u>Current North American Indian periodicals</u>. Revised ed.
Washington, DC, Smithsonian Institution, Information Systems
Division, 1972. 23p. ED 065253.

218 newspapers, newsletters, and other periodicals by,
for, or about the American Indian are briefly annotated.

156. <u>American Indians: an annotated bibliography of recom-</u>
<u>mended resource materials: elementary grades</u>. San Jacinto,
CA, Unified School District, 1971. 36p. ED 056798.

Prepared by Indians of many tribes throughout California.
Contains 257 books published between 1884 and 1971. Also
includes films, records, workbooks, and teacher guides.

157. Tyler, S. Lyman. <u>The Ute people: a bibliographical</u>
<u>checklist</u>. Provo, Brignam Young University, Institute of Amer-
ican Indian Studies, 1964. 125p. ED 059004.

Categorized by: bibliographies and guides, manuscript
material from the Spanish and Mexican periods, US Government documents, Utah Territorial documents, newspapers,
and periodicals.

158. Indian bibliography of BIA Instructional Service Center
with addendum. Washington, DC, Bureau of Indian Affairs, 1970.
48p. ED 059815.

Includes more than 600 documents published between 1893
and 1970. Many have annotations.

159. Crutchfield, Regina K. and Charles Worsley. Focus on
people - the Native American: a multimedia bibliography, K-12.
Rockville, MD, Montgomery County Public Schools, 1978. 137p.
ED 182076.

Books, records, cassettes, transparencies, kits, charts,
maps, filmstrips, slides, and games that provide an accurate portrayal of Indian heritage. 383 items, plus an annotated bibliography of bibliographies that has 50 citations.

160. Harkins, Arthur M. Modern Native Americans: a selected
bibliography. Minneapolis, University of Minnesota, 1971.
131p. ED 054890.

Unannotated. 1500 books and articles published from 1927
to 1970.

161. Sheldon, Dorothy L. and Victoria J. Sitter. A Selective
bibliography of American Indian literature, history, and culture. Minneapolis, University of Minnesota, General College,
1968. 20p. ED 030526.

160 annotated books written between 1825 and 1967. Areas
include autobiography and biography, fiction, and art.

162. Books about Indians and reference material. Boise, Idaho
State Department of Education, 1968. 22p. ED 030531.

Over 500 entries include books, films, and filmstrips.

163. Wax, Rosalie H. Rosalie H. Wax: a list of her publications. 1966. 2p. ED 019146.

Her major publications and unpublished essays are listed
for 1942 to 1966. Subject matter includes sociology with
with special emphasis on the American Indian.

164. Wax, Murray L. Murray L. Wax: a list of his publications.
1966. 2p. ED 019147.

His major publications and unpublished essays from 1947 to
1966. Subject matter is scociology with a special emphasis
on the American Indian.

165. Kellerhouse, Kenneth. The Iroquois: a bibliography of

audio-visual materials. Oneonta, State University of New York, 1967. 9p. ED 018324.

Unannotated. 25 sources pertaining to the Iroquois and other northeastern tribes.

166. Native American resources annotated bibliography of print and non-print materials: a model program in multi-ethnic heritage studies. Mankato State College, 1975. 120p. ED 115634.

167. Index to bibliographies and resource materials: project MEDIA. Minneapolis, National Indian Education Association, 1975. 225p. ED 118341.

Includes descriptions of print and non-print media by, for, and about native Americans. 84 individual bibliographies are listed.

168. North American Indians: a comprehensive annotated bibliography for the secondary teacher. Tempe, Arizona State University, Indian Education Center, 1973. 126p. ED 084067.

1490 books and articles published between 1871 and 1971.

169. American Indians: an annotated bibliography of selected library resources. St. Paul, Minnesota State Department of Education, 1970. 171p. ED 040004.

Over 500 entries evaluated from an Indian point of view include books, articles, pamphlets, films, maps, slides, and records. Most published since 1960.

170. Books about Indians and reference material. Boise, Idaho State Department of Education, 1971. 177p. ED 052887.

Over 1500 books are annotated that were published from 1911 to 1971. This document is an expanded version of ED 030531.

171. Harkins, Arthur M. A Bibliography of urban Indians in the United States. Minneapolis, University of Minnesota, Center for Urban and Regional Affairs, 1971. 44p. ED 052871.

Unannotated. 450 citations, most published since 1960. The emphasis is on relocation, problems of rural-urban transition, and adjustment to the urban environment.

172. Willis, Cecelia A. and M. E. Travis. Significant literature by and about native Americans. 1973. 126p. ED 071 837.

Over 850 books, articles, and documents on antiquities, captives, culture, education, economic conditions, history, medicine, government relations, religion, and tribes.

173. A Bibliography of materials on the American Indian and the Spanish speaking. Lansing, Michigan State Department of

Education, 1975. 49p. ED 122985.

An annotated list of 447 books, periodicals, records,
filmstrips, and slides published between 1950 and 1974.
Topics: art, poetry, language, cultural differences, customs, history, folk culture, and literature.

174. Anderson, Bernard F. Urban-rural cross cultural adjustment problems of Indians and Mexican Americans: a survey of
literature. 1970. 392p. ED 119893.

The American Indian section cites 344 books, 310 articles,
and 423 master's and doctoral theses which were written
between 1902 and 1969. The section on Chicanos cites 405
books, 624 articles, and 382 theses, plus 168 other unpublished items. Topics are education, health, socioeconomic influences, culture, housing, employment, language,
history, politics, civil rights, and migration.

175. Jarrett, Gladys W. The American Indian, then and now:
a bibliography. Jamaica, NY, CUNY, York College, 1975. 98p.
ED 103183.

Annotated. Lists 996 books and articles published between
1672 and 1974.

176. The North American Indian: a bibliography of community
development. Washington, DC, Department of Housing and Urban
Development, 1975. 69p. ED 107443.

403 annotated citations published between 1969 and 1974
on government relations, legal aspects, demographic distribution, economic conditions, education, health, housing, and problems of urbanization. Part 2 is a special
section of 365 citations on planning.

177. Snodgrass, Marjorie P. Economic development of American
Indians and Eskimos 1930 through 1967: a bibliography. Wash-
ington, DC, Bureau of Indian Affairs, 1968. 272p. ED 037259
(MF)

1595 annotated references are divided into 15 subject
areas which are indexed by Indian reservation.

178. Harvey, Cecil L. Agriculture of the American Indian: a
select bibliography. Washington, DC, Department of Agriculture, 1979. 63p. ED 182099.

In addition to agriculture, this also covers technology,
settlement patterns, economics, family organization, and
religious ritual as they relate to the main topic. Includes children's books, dissertations, articles, books,
scientific reports, and government documents dating from
1940 to 1977.

179. Wheelbarger, Johnny J. Native American archaeological
sites: an annotated bibliography relating to Indian archaeo-

logical sites in the Southeastern United States. 1974. 41p.
ED 111592.

Cited are 36 sites in Alabama, Florida, Georgia, Kentucky,
North Carolina, and Tennessee.

180. Native American arts and crafts of the United States:
bibliography. Washington, DC, Indian Arts and Crafts Board,
1971. 6p. ED 071831.

Organized by culture area, 118 documents dated from 1941
to 1971 cover the subject from prehistoric to modern day.

181. Bibliography of contemporary American Indian and Eskimo
arts and crafts. Minneapolis, Public Schools Task Force on
Ethnic Studies, 1968. 6p. ED 077782.

Includes seventy annotated references.

182. Books for teachers and children. Toronto, Department
of Indian Affairs and Northern Development, 1970. 28p.
ED 037266.

Books and periodicals published between 1951 and 1969 are
listed in this 108 item annotated bibliography of materials on general research in education, on programs affecting social change, and on the backgrounds of Indian people
of Canada.

183. Byler, Mary. American Indian authors for young readers:
a selected bibliography. New York, Association on American
Indian Affairs, 1973. 26p. ED 086420.

Includes 60 annotated books by Indian authors.

184. Materials on Indians of North America: an annotated list
for children. Madison, WI, Cooperative Childrens Book Center,
1970. 15p. ED 039991.

References to 86 items dated 1931 to 1970 are included.
Also lists some AV materials and other bibliographies.

185. Graustein, Jean M. and Carol L. Jaglinski. An annotated
bibliography of young people's fiction on American Indians.
Washington, DC, Bureau of Indian Affairs, 1972. 61p. ED 060
699.

Each annotation lists the tribe involved in the story and
the suggested grade level. 250 works dating from 1933 to
1969 are included.

186. Fuson, Elgie M. Native Americans: a bibliography for
young people. Sacramento, CA, Sacramento State College, 1970.
27p. ED 059000.

Grade levels are indicated; includes 58 fiction, 152 nonfiction, 20 textbooks, and 45 curriculum guides. 1905-69.

187. Olsen, Diane. Indians in literature: a selected annotated bibliography for children. Minneapolis, University of Minnesota, 1964. 16p. ED 014353.

Entries categorized as biography and fictionalized biography, lore and legend, stories and novels, and general information and background materials.

188. An Annotated bibliography of books for libraries serving children of Indian ancestry. Toronto, Indian-Eskimo Association of Canada, 1968. 13p. ED 041655.

Includes reference books, novels, and poetry. Contains 79 entries most of which indicate grade levels 1 to 12.

189. Kahl, June. Non-stereotyped Indian literature: a bibliography. 1976. 9p. ED 128795.

This guide for teachers of grades four through eight includes fiction and nonfiction with brief annotations.

190. Newman, Killian. A Preliminary bibliography of selected children's books about American Indians. New York, Association of American Indian Affairs, 1969. 17p. ED 037516.

Lists 63 books that had been read and recommended by an American Indian.

191. An Annotated bibliography of young people's books on American Indians. Albuquerque, NM, Bureau of Indian Affairs, 1973. 62p. ED 070547.

Each of 367 books has been written by an Indian or reviewed from an Indian viewpoint.

192. Webb, Vincent J. Indian justice: a research bibliography. Monticello, IL, Council of Planning Librarians, 1976. 69p. ED 139580.

Cites 911 items from the period 1966 to 1975. Topics include cultural and social organization, social psychology, social problems, urban problems, and social policy and reform.

193. Martinez, Cecelia J. and James Heathman. American Indian education: a selected bibliography. ERIC Clearinghouse on Rural Education and Small Schools, 1969. 98p. ED 030780.

All the entries in this series of volumes are from RIE. This first volume contains 148 annotated items, and the annual supplements each have several hundred citations. Supplements are available as ED 044213, ED 058980, ED 075 121, ED 086378, ED 100547, ED 107427, ED 127056, ED 145974, and ED 164167.

194. Mech, Joyce. An Annotated bibliography of selected research reports, articles, and papers on Indian education in

the United States and Canada from 1968-1973. Tempe, Arizona
State University, Indian Education Center, 1974. 43p. ED
091128.

Most of the 176 citations were taken from professional
journals, papers delivered at meetings, and government
reports.

195. Mathieson, Moira. A Brief bibliography on teacher education and American Indians. ERIC Clearinghouse on Teacher
Education, 1974. 23p. ED 090146.

30 annotated references.

196. Dumont, Robert V. Information source: education for
American Indians. Washington, DC, Office of American Indian
Affairs, 1969. 17p. ED 050855.

60 annotated basic references.

197. Evans, G. Edward and Karin Abbey. Bibliography of language arts materials for native North Americans. UCLA, American Indian Studies Center, 1979. 154p. ED 180724 (MF)

Includes bilingual, English as a second language, and
native language materials dated from 1965 to 1975. Over
400 annotated references.

198. Gomez, Darva R. Bibliography: a resource on the education of American Indians. Albuquerque, NM, Bureau of Indian
Affairs, 1976. 159p. ED 135541.

Lists 1776 unannotated entries.

199. Green, Vicki. Annotated bibliography on Indian education. 1969. 35p. ED 059819.

Emphasis on Canadian Indians; about 180 books, articles,
films, and newspapers for teachers. Publication dates are
1873 to 1969.

200. Keller, Charles. A Selected bibliography of materials
related to American Indian education, economics, and deviant
behavior. Charleston, Eastern Illinois University, 1970.
42p. ED 055717.

More than 500 unannotated citations published from 1907
to 1968 are included.

201. Selby, Suzanne R. Bibliography on materials in the
field of education. Saskatoon, University of Saskatchewan,
Institute for Northern Studies, 1968. 110p. ED 026180.

105 books, articles, and pamphlets published from 1956 to
1968 are in this annotated list for teachers and students
interested in the education of children of Indian and Eskimo ancestry.

202. American Indian education: an abstract bibliography.
Urbana, IL, ERIC Clearinghouse on Early Childhood Education,
1975. 37p. ED 118246.

Includes 73 documents from RIE, and 28 articles from CIJE.

203. The Best of ERIC on library services to native Americans.
ERIC Clearinghouse on Rural Education and Small Schools, 1976.
30p. ED 118128.

An annotated bibliography taken from RIE and CIJE.

204. Durovich, Anna. Indian education: bibliography. Washington, DC, Bureau of Indian Affairs, 1967. 13p. ED 023518.

159 unannotated books and articles dated from 1928 to 1966.

205. Scoon, Annabelle. Bibliography of Indian education and
curriculum innovation. Albuquerque, NM, Indian School, 1971.
62p. ED 053614.

Bilingualism is an important aspect of this ERIC bibliography of 200 entries with abstracts.

206. Rice, Margaret. Changes in attitude toward the education of the American Indian as shown by government documents:
a selected and annotated bibliography. 1978. 47p. ED 156
150 (MF)

Listed chronologically from the 19th Century on, entries
include Congressional Hearings and reports, miscellaneous
documents, BIA manuals, and the Indian Policy Review
Commission's Task Force Five.

207. Brooks, I. R. and A. M. Marshall. Native education in
Canada and the United States: a bibliography. University of
Calgary, Office of Educational Development, 1976. 306p. ED
133127.

Cites about 3000 articles, speeches, papers, and books
which deal with the pedagogy, sociology, psychology, or
politics of native education. Items are dated 1900 to 1975.

208. McShane, Damian. Selected bibliography of Ojibwa and
other native American related research concerning psychoedu-
cational assessment and intervention. 1976. 43p. ED 128145.

Includes related historical, cultural, legal, economic,
and medical factors. 259 citations pertaining to Ojibwa
(Chipewa) and other native Americans from 1937 to 1975.
ERIC documents and PhD dissertations are included.

209. Osborn, Lynn R. A Bibliography of North American Indian
speech and spoken language. Lawrence, University of Kansas,
1968. 57p. ED 044223.

Lists about 600 references published from 1810 to 1967.

210. Evans, G. Edwards. Bibliography of language arts materials for native North Americans: bilingual, English as a second language, and native language materials, 1965-1974. UCLA,
American Indian Culture Center, 1977. 290p. ED 153763.

An annotated 1007 item list that includes Eskimo languages.

211. Troike, Rudolph C. Bibliographies of American Indian
languages. 1967. 180p. ED 016200.

Contains a bibliography in each of twelve language families. Unannotated.

212. Grimes, J. Larry. A Bibliography of the Uto-Aztecan
languages. 1966. 40p. ED 011662.

Contains mostly works in English and Spanish from as early
as 1732. Deals with aspects of the Sonoran, Shoshone, and
Aztecan families; also Hopi, Tewa, and Coca.

213. Burress, Lee A. A Selected annotated bibliography: literature of the American Indian. Wisconsin Council of Teachers
of English, 1971. 6p. ED 133768.

Includes 30 titles by or about Indians; fiction and nonfiction.

214. Blank, Ruth. What shall our children read? A selected
bibliography of native American literature for young people.
San Jose, CA, Indian Center, Inc., 1977. 20p. ED 147056 (MF)

Selected for non-biased subject presentation and literary
value; grouped by reading ability levels. 132 annotated
entries.

215. Buck, June M. Indian literature for junior and senior
high schools. Phoenix, Arizona State Department of Public
Instruction, 1968. 25p. ED 042531.

Annotated. Fiction, 52 entries; poetry and plays, 8 entries; myths and legends, 23 entries; nonfiction, 32 entries; and biography, 52 entries.

216. Neuman, Robert W. and Lanier A. Simmons. A Bibliography
relative to Indians of the State of Louisiana. Baton Rouge,
Louisiana State Department of Conservation, 1969. 78p. ED
046550.

456 entries, most of which are annotated. Publication
dates range from 1720 to 1969 and include prehistoric
through modern times.

217. Maine Indians: topical bibliography of books in Maine
State Library. 1975. 7p. ED 119900.

About 200 citations are included dating from 1623 to 1973.
All aspects of Maine Indians are represented.

218. Attneave, Carolyn L. and Dianne R. Kelso. American Indian annotated bibliography of mental health. Seattle, University of Washington, 1977. 436p. ED 151135.

This volume one presents 250 annotated entries, and an additional 250 unannotated items derived from personal collections, other bibliographies, and five computerized data banks. The earliest item is dated 1940.

219. Hewlett, Leroy. Indians of Oregon: a bibliography of materials in the Oregon State Library. 1969. 131p. ED 058 999.

Over 1300 publications are listed, including government documents, from the 19th and 20th Centuries.

220. South Dakota Indian bibliography. Pierre, South Dakota State Library Commission, 1972. 34p. ED072915.

Unannotated. Lists 310 books and pamphlets dating from 1894 to 1971 under the following headings: bibliography, culture, fiction, government relations, history, language, religion, and mythology.

221. Niatum, Duane and Linda Rickman. The History and culture of the Indians of Washington State: a curriculum guide. Revised edition. Olympia, WA, State Superintendent of Public Instruction, 1975. 248p. ED 152456.

The resources section includes articles, films, filmstrips, games, newspapers and journals, records and tapes, slides, and pictures.

222. Native American women: a selected topics bibliography of ERIC documents. ERIC Clearinghouse on Rural Education and Small Schools, 1977. 42p. ED 152472.

Fifty annotated entries from 1968 to 1976 taken from RIE. Topics are: role models, postsecondary education, employment, counseling, and cultural education.

ANIMAL SCIENCE

223. Miller, Larry E. Selected references and aids for teaching animal science to students of agricultural education. Blacksburg, Virginia Polytechnic Institute, 1973. 51p. ED 112097.

Includes beef, dairy, poultry, sheep, and swine in bulletins, circulars, textbooks, films, filmstrips, slides, and charts.

ANTHROPOLOGY

224. Dwyer-Shick, Susan. The Study and teaching of anthropology within academic institutions: an annotated bibliography.
Athens, University of Georgia, Anthropology Curriculum Project,
1976. 152p. ED 123164 (MF)

545 books and articles are arranged chronologically from
1848 to 1976. Indexed by author.

225. Slavin, Suzy M. Anthropology: a student's guide to reference sources. Montreal, McGill University Library, 1978.
20p. ED 156578 (MF)

Lists 100 sources from the reference collection.

226. Vigliani, Alice. Selective bibliography in anthropology
and world history resources. ERIC Clearinghouse for Social
Studies/Social Science Education, 1977. 34p. ED 148654.

Forty annotated items of current materials for teachers
of junior high and high school.

APPALACHIA

227. Schweri, William F. Bibliography of Appalachian Studies.
Lexington, University of Kentucky, Center for Developmental
Change, 1973. 30p. ED 082879.

396 articles, books, conference proceedings, theses, and
dissertations cover the period 1930 to 1972. Unannotated.

228. Link, A. D. A Planner's reference guide relating to
socioeconomic factors within Appalachia as applied to public
education. ERIC Clearinghouse on Rural Education and Small
Schools, 1970. 46p. ED 045279.

An ERIC bibliography of 90 annotated items categorized
as: delinquency, health services, dropouts, job opportunities, age factors, labor force, population characteristics, and disadvantagement.

229. Nelsen Hart M. and Anne K. Nelsen. Bibliography on Appalachia: a guide to studies dealing with Appalachia in general and including rural and urban working class attitudes
toward religion, education, and social change. Bowling Green,
Western Kentucky University, 1967. 76p. ED 024512.

Over 1000 unannotated references for use in developing
religious education programs for Appalachian peoples.

230. Taylor, Mary K. A Selected Appalachian bibliography.
1971. 15p. ED 057025.

Compiled to assist high school and junior college teachers
plan a classroom unit on Appalachian literature. It contains fiction and poetry as well as psychological and so-

ciological and economic aspects of Appalachian life and
culture. Annotated.

231. Kesner, Mernie. Bibliography for Appalachian studies.
Berea, KY, Berea College, 1973. 31p. ED 091120.

98 annotated books, and 87 other references to articles,
pamphlets, records, and tapes.

232. Bennett, George E. Library materials for schools in
Appalachia. Morgantown, University of West Virginia Library,
1974. 73p. ED 092127.

Lists fiction, poetry, drama, folklore, folk music, biography, history, geography, arts and crafts, and natural
history. Annotated. Also includes films.

233. Edwards, Pat. A Bibliography of Appalachian children's
and young people's books. Berea, KY, Berea College, 1973.
21p. ED 092976.

Topics include pioneer history, folksongs, folk tales,
biography, Cherokee Indians, and folk customs. Grade
levels and brief annotations are given.

APPRENTICESHIPS

234. Research on apprenticeship: an annotated and classified
listing of studies, 1930-1962. East Lansing, Michigan State
University, Educational Publications services, 1968. 48p.
ED 027425.

93 documents listed under: history and development, status
studies, manpower, curriculum, selection practices, guidance, and follow-up studies.

ARABIC

235. Le Gassick, T. Modern Arabic prose literature: an introduction. Ann Arbor, University of Michigan, 1970. 285p. ED
044689 (MF)

A 90 page bibliography by Howard Rowland is included with
this study.

236. Altoma, Salih J. Modern Arabic literature, 1800-1970:
a bibliographic survey of works in English. Washington, DC,
Institute of International Studies, 1975. 84p. ED 116497.

891 entries include both general and scholarly works in
the form of articles, books, dissertations, and translations of drama, fiction, and poetry.

237. Prochazka, Theodore. 1960-1967: selected bibliography of Arabic. Washington, DC, Center for Applied Linguistics, 1967. 81p. ED 014082.

615 books and articles written in European languages as well as Arabic on theoretical and applied linguistics.

238. Sobelman, Harvey. Arabic dialect studies: a selected bibliography. Washington, DC, Center for Applied Linguistics, 1962. 106p. ED 013373.

Includes four bibliographic review articles.

ARCHAEOLOGY

239. Desautels, Almuth. Archaeology: a student's guide to reference sources. Montreal, McGill University Library, 1975. 23p. ED 130967.

All types of reference works are included; subsections refer to countries or areas.

ARCHITECTURE   See Also   BUILDING DESIGN and EDUCATIONAL FACIL-
       ITIES.

240. Turner, George E. Architectural/building programming: an annotated bibliography. Monticello, IL, Council of Planning Librarians, 1973. 12p. ED 074629.

Includes 34 articles.

241. Seaton, Richard W. Architectural simulation: a mini-bib. Monticello, IL, Council of Planning Librarians, 1971. 8p. ED 106950.

Forty-four unannotated items.

242. Ewing, Gordon O. Working bibliography on scaling methods appropriate for analysis of space preferences. Monticello, IL, Council of Planning Librarians, 1974. 42p. ED 106906 (MF)

Unannotated. Draws together from several disciplines literature dealing with problems of scaling and measuring stimuli.

243. Mattar, Samir G. A Bibliography and review of building evaluation schemata and practices. Monticello, IL, Council of Planning Librarians, 1973. 23p. ED 106904 (MF)

244. Canter, David. People and buildings: a brief overview of research. Monticello, IL, Council of Planning Librarians, 1972. 32p. ED 106965.

Attempts to apply modern psychology to architecture.

245. Miller, William C. Architectural research centers: an
annotated directory. Monticello, IL, Council of Planning Librarians, 1971. 31p. ED 101438.

     Lists newsletters and journals that regularly contain re-
     search results and research oriented information, plus
     lists other directories.

246. Preiser, Wolfgang. Research on architecture and human
behavior. Monticello, IL, Council of Planning Librarians,
1974. 9p. ED 105626.

     Includes directories, conference proceedings, journals,
     bibliographies, and information systems.

247. Bunselmeier, Erich. Computerized location - allocation.
Monticello, IL, Council of Planning Librarians, 1973. 53p.
ED 105625.

     Books and articles related to environmental design. Also
     includes 106 journals relevant to the field. Unannotated.

248. Current materials on barrier-free design. Revised ed.
Chicago, National Easter Seal Society, 1978. 9p. ED 163584
(MF)

     Annotations are grouped under design, guides, planning
     resources, standards, legislation, and general.

ARIZONA

249. Boettcher, Pat and Eleanor Ferrall. Arizona in fact
and fiction for the junior high school student. 1972. 44p.
ED 099 855.

     A multimedia bibliography including reference, geography,
     natural history, history, Indians, biography, literature,
     art, and music.

250. Choncoff, Mary. Arizona in 16mm films, 8mm films, filmloops, filmstrips, slides, transparencies, cassettes, records,
photos, prints, posters, charts, study prints, maps, flags,
book returns, bookmarks, foods, microfilm, place mats, relief
model kits, stereo picture reels. Phoenix, Arizona State
Department of Education, 1976. 90p. ED 119938.

     Includes several hundred annotated entries on a variety
     of subjects. Most items were produced during the 1960's
     and 1970's.

251. Choncoff, Mary. Arizona in books for children. Phoenix,
Arizona State Department of Education, 1978. 83p. ED 157846.

     550 annotated entries on history and culture, Mexican lore,
     and the Navajo Indians.

ARKANSAS

252. Perry, Larry S. Arkansas geneaolgy bibliography. Fayetteville, University of Arkansas Library, 1977. 32p. ED
168482.

   Includes how-to manuals, bibliographies, dictionaries,
   encyclopedias, guides, and County publications of newsletters, bulletins, cemetary registers, census materials,
   marriage records, mortality schedules, wills, and County
   histories.

ART See FINE ARTS

ART EDUCATION

253. McIntyre, Barbara M. Source book of selected materials
for early childhood education in the arts. Washington, DC,
Central Atlantic Regional Educational Laboratory, 1969. 265p.
ED 033746.

   An annotated multimedia bibliography.

254. Arts and crafts. Arlington, VA, Council for Exceptional
Children, 1971. 21p. ED 050525.

   99 annotated references include research reports, conference papers, journal articles, texts, and program guides.

255. An Annotated bibliography for art. St. Paul, Minnesota
State Department of Education, 1976. 54p. ED 160539.

   450 references about art for elementary, secondary, and
   professioanl levels. All aspects of art are covered.

ART HISTORY

256. Tanner, Eric L. Art appreciation: a bibliography. 1976.
7p. ED 130969.

   Contains 50 annotated references to books published from
   1960 to 1974 concerned mainly with art history.

ART THERAPY

257. Gantt, Linda and Marilyn S. Schmal. Art therapy: a bibliography. Washington, DC, George Washington University, 1974.
148p. ED 108401.

   In eleven categories, 1175 citations are given, 1940-1973.

ARTIFICIAL INTELLIGENCE

258. Massachusetts Institute of Technology artificial intelligence bibliography. Cambridge, MIT, 1976. 36p. ED 122728.

Aspects are: games, programming languages, math functions,
language recognition, music theory, pattern recognition,
computer assisted instruction, tracking, time sharing,
robots, and computational linguistics. 350 reports, papers,
theses.

ASIAN AMERICANS

259. Endo, Russell. Social science and historical materials
on the Asian American experience. 1978. 44p. ED 162033.

Over 200 selected unannotated titles in addition to a list
of bibliographic sources.

260. Duphiney, Lorna. Oriental-Americans: an annotated bibliography. ERIC Clearinghouse on the Urban Disadvantaged,
1972. 29p. ED 060136.

Includes articles, books, dissertations, addresses, and
project reports on social, political, and educational development of Japanese and Chinese-Americans. Published
since 1960.

261. Li, Tze-chung. A Selective bibliography on Asian Americans. 1979. 18p. ED 181889.

Unannotated. Includes reference sources, monographs, documents, dissertations, and periodicals.

262. Moy, Peter. An Annotated list of selected resources for
promoting and developing an understanding of Asian Americans.
Madison, Wisconsin State Department of Public Instruction,
1978. 45p. ED 185182.

About 125 items on the Japanese, Chinese, Koreans, and
Filipino Americans. Includes 34 multimedia references.

263. Jayatilleke, Raja. The Education of Asian Americans: a
bibliography. ERIC Clearinghouse on the Urban Disadvantaged,
1975. 54p. ED 110594.

A partially annotated list of 396 items from the ERIC
system through 1974. Includes bilingual education, family
life, migration effects, race relations, and adjustment
problems.

264. A Bibliography of Asian and Asian American books for
elementary school youngsters. Olympia, Washington State Superintendent of Public Instruction, 1975. 58p. ED 117286.

An annotated, evaluative bibliography with indicated grade levels. Topics include fiction, folk and fairy tales, history, songs, games, and culture.

265. Ong, Paul M. and William W. Lum. Theses and dissertations on Asians in the United States with selection references to other overseas Asians. Davis, University of California, Department of Applied Behavioral Sciences, 1974. 120p. ED 109296.

800 unannotated items. Includes works on the Asian experience in Canada and Latin America, New Zealand, Australia, Africa, and Europe.

ASIAN LANGUAGES

266. Johnson, Dora E. Languages of Eastern Asia: a survey of materials for the study of the uncommonly taught languages. Arlington, VA, Center for Applied Linguistics, 1976. 49p. ED 132835.

Emphasis is on the adult learner whose native language is English. Annotated and classified by: Chinese, Japanese, Korean, Mongolian, and Tibetan.

267. A Selected bibliography of dictionaries. Revised edition. Arlington, VA, Center for Applied Linguistics, 1978. 9p. ED 163768.

For the American teacher of Indochinese refugees. The annotated list includes 16 bilingual dictionaries and glossaries in Vietnamese, Cambodian, Khmer, Lao, Hmong, Meo, and English.

268. Stuart, Don G. and J.W. Mulder. A Preliminary reconaissance of the languages of Asia. 1961. 233p. ED 012801.

269. Johnson, Dora E. Languages of South Asia: survey of materials for the study of the uncommonly taught languages. Arlington, VA, Center of Applied Linguistics, 1976. 52p. ED 132833.

Annotated. Languages are grouped as: Indo-Aryan, Dravidian, Munda, Tibeto-Burman, Mon-Khmer, and Burushaski.

ASIAN STUDIES   See Also the individual countries.

270. Education in Asia: a bibliography. Bangkok, United Nations Asian Institute for Economic Development and Planning, 1969. 34p. ED 049142.

Most items are in English and include books, articles, government reports, and conference papers. Unannotated.

271. Bhatia, Kanta. Reference sources on South Asia. Philadelphia, University of Pennsylvania, Institute of South Asia Regional Studies, 1978. 81p. ED 168521 (MF)

Most of the 671 titles are in English.

272. Southeast Asia: a selected functional and country bibliography. Washington, DC, Foreign Service Institute, 1972. 41p. ED 076487.

About 500 unannotated citations from 1952 to 1972 on history, geography, economics, international relations, art, and archaeology.

273. South Asia: a selected functional and country bibliography. Washington, DC, Foreign Service Institute, 1971. 38p. ED 076486.

Over 500 unannotated citations.

274. Asians and Asian Americans. San Francisco, Unified School District, 1972. 34p. ED 085452.

Includes only audiovisual educational materials.

275. Bell, Violet M. A Guide to films, filmstrips, maps, globes, and records on Asia, and a supplement including a new section on slides. New York, Asia Society, 1964. 155p. ED 080387.

This is an annotated third edition.

276. Wiese, M. Bernice. Asia: a guide to books for children. New York, Asia Society, 1966. 61p. ED 080389.

Over 300 fiction and nonfiction books mostly on China, India, and Japan.

277. Ehrman, Edith and Ward Morehouse. Preliminary bibliography on East Asia for undergraduate libraries. New York, SUNY, Foreign Area Materials Center, 1967. 486p. ED 031253.

A classified, unannotated bibliography.

278. Hay, Stephen N. Preliminary bibliography on South Asia for undergraduate libraries. New York, SUNY, Foreign Area Materials Center, 1967. 404p. ED 031252.

A classified, unannotated bibliography.

279. Embree, Ainslie T. Asia: a guide to basic books. New York, Asia Society, 1966. 63p. ED 080393.

316 books dating from 1915 to 1966. Annotated.

280. Lee, Pingkun and Angela Kao. Catalog of the Orientalia collection of the U.S. Military Academy Library. 1977. 143p.

Unannotated list of books and periodicals written mostly
in Chinese with a few works in English and Japanese.

281. Scott, William H. Recommended East Asian core collections for children's, high school, public, community college,
and undergraduate college libraries. 1974. 196p. ED 110021.

Over 1700 books and audiovisuals on China, Formosa, Japan,
Korea, Mongolia, and Tibet. Unannotated.

282. Hawkins, John N. Teacher's resource handbook for Asian
studies: an annotated bibliography of curriculum materials,
preschool through grade twelve. UCLA, Committee on Comparative and International Studies, 1976. 194p. ED 133241 (MF)

1586 multimedia items. Includes the Pacific Islands.

283. Probandt, Ruth. The Non-Western world: an annotated bibliography for elementary and secondary schools. University of
Massachusetts, School of Education, 1970. 69p. ED 047039.

Curriculum materials and books on Asia, Africa, and Latin
America.

ATHLETICS See PHYSICAL EDUCATION

ATOMIC ENERGY See NUCLEAR ENERGY

ATTRITION See DROPOUTS

AUDIOVISUAL INSTRUCTION See Also MEDIA SELECTION and
    INSTRUCTIONAL MATERIALS

284. Lewis, John P. A Guide to the literature of audiovisual
education. 1976. 44p. ED 132970.

Most of the annotated items are post-1970, and are primarily of interest to educational researchers.

285. Bonn, Thomas L. A Guide to audiovisual references: selection and ordering sources. SUNY, College at Cortland, 1977.
28p. ED 148371.

Annotated.

286. Harrison, J. A. European research in audiovisual aids,
Part I, bibliography. Strasbourg, Austria, Council of Europe,
1966. 115p. ED 019853.

Unannotated. Includes academic research, exploratory work,
experiments, trials with new methods, and uncontrolled
experiments.

287. Training methodology, Part 4: Audiovisual theory, aids
and equipment: an annotated bibliography. National Institute

of Mental Health, 1968.   124p.   ED 023981.

332 selected documents on television and film instruction. Also includes programmed instruction, graphic aids, videotapes, and computer assisted instruction.

AURALLY HANDICAPPED   See   DEAF

AUSTRALIAN ABORIGINES

288. Boyce, M. W. The Australian Aboriginal child: bibliography and abstracts. Part I: Physical and intellectual development. 1975. 19p. ED 115387.

Most of the 57 entries are journal articles.

AUTISM

289. Erskine, Richard G. Autism and childhood psychosis: annotated bibliography, 1969-1974. Urbana, University of Illinois, Department of Special Education, 1975. 175p. ED 121017.

400 citations from medical, psychological, social service, and educational sources.

290. Autism: a selective bibliography. Reston, VA, Council for Exceptional Children, 1976. 32p. ED 129001.

125 annotated documents and journal articles from 1966 to 1975.

291. Sullivan, R. C. Autism: an annotated bibliography of films, videotapes, and audiotapes. Revised ed. 1977. 23p. ED 144299 (MF)

A listing of over 60 films and tapes.

AUTO MECHANICS

292. Training materials sourcebook: motor vehicle mechanics and repairmen. Ottawa, Department of Manpower and Immigration, 1977. 328p. ED 147480 (MF)

Annotated presentation of about 400 training curriculums and instructional materials. Includes general theory, shop practice, engine systems, electrical systems, body repair and painting, and specific model maintenance.

AVIATION TECHNOLOGY

293. Marshall, Jane. Aviation and the environment: a selected annotated bibliography related to aviation's responses toward improving the environment. Washington, DC, FAA, Women's Advisory Committee on Aviation, 1971. 22p. ED 064168.

The entries explain how the airline industry and general aviation are meeting their responsibilities in solving environmental problems. The over 100 references are booklets, leaflets, speeches, articles, and congressional testimony. Most are non-technical.

AZTECS

294. Harkanyi, Katalin. The Aztecs bibliography. San Diego, University of California Library, 1972. 31p. ED 069462.

Some of the entries are in Spanish. Lists 355 unannotated items on the Aztecs of Mexico from their beginnings to the Spanish conquest.

BANKING

295. Westfall, Elizabeth W. and Anne R. Zimmerman. A Basic library for savings and loan associations. San Francisco, Federal Home Loan Bank, 1979. 18p. ED 180454 (MF)

Annotated. Covers management, housing, real estate lending, urban investment, operations and administration, legal and regulatory affairs, finance and accounting, and general reference.

BEHAVIOR MODIFICATION

296. Kremer, Barbara. Behavior modification in the classroom: an abstract bibliography. ERIC Clearinghouse on Early Childhood Education, 1971. 26p. ED 062005.

Covers theory and uses in the 42 entries taken from RIE and CIJE. Also includes descriptions of several programs.

297. Behavior modification in the classroom: an abstract bibliography. 1975. 40p. ED 118245.

Follows up the previous document with 76 items dated 1969 to 1975.

298. Behavior modification: exceptional child bibliography series. Arlington, VA, Council for Exceptional Children, 1971. 12p. ED 050528.

Includes 81 articles, texts, reports, and conference papers.

299. Behavior modification - emotionally disturbed and behavior problems: a selective bibliography. Reston, VA, Council for Exceptional Children, 1976. 24p. ED 129008.

80 annotated documents and articles dated from 1965 to 1975.

300. Rutherford, Robert B. Behavior modification and therapy with juvenile delinquents: a comprehensive bibliography. 1976. 16p. ED 120627.

Attempts to list every book and article on the subject. Unannotated.

301. Fitch, Judith P. and Marvin F. Daley. Annotated biliography on token reinforcement studies published 1967-1969. Minneapolis, Upper Midwest Regional Educational Laboratory, 1970. 94p. ED 038041.

Publications from Canada, Britain, and the USA; only half of the 240 items are annotated.

302. Behaviour modification: bibliographies in education. Ottawa, Canadian Teachers' Federation, 1974. 36p. ED 102316.

Includes 80 books, 337 articles, and 16 theses. Unannotated.

303. York, Robert. Selected bibliography related to parents as behavior modifiers. University of Washington, Child Development and Mental Retardation Center, 1975. 7p. ED 108418.

70 unannotated references dated 1958 to 1972.

304. L'Abate, Luciano and Daniel L. Whitaker. An Annotated bibliography of behavior modification with children and retardates. Atlanta, Georgia State College, Child Development Laboratory, 1967. 38p. ED 020025.

Includes 130 papers and studies.

BEHAVIORAL SCIENCE See Also PSYCHOLOGY

305. Annotated bibliography of books on how to state behavioral objectives. Montreal, McGill University, Center for Learning and Development, 1971. 5p. ED 059968.

Most of the 17 books refer to designing programmed materials and evaluations.

306. Fearon, Ross E. Behavioral disorders: catalog of library accessions. Farmington State College (Maine), 1966. 43p. ED 012982.

Arranged by Dewey Decimal numbers, the 468 items include books, research reports, hearings, and bibliographies published from 1921 to 1965.

307. Greenberg, Stu. Observational learning and imitative
behavior in children: a bibliography. 1976. 75p. ED 123158.

The 1500 books and articles also include psycholinguistics
and speech pathology. Most were written in the 1960's and
1970's, and are not annotated.

308. Tate, Eugene. An Annotated bibliography of studies on
counterattitudinal advocacy. Saskatoon, University of Saskatchewan, 1972. 155p. ED 072493.

309. Training methodology. Washington, DC, Public Health
Service, 1969. ED 031626 - ED 031629. (MF)

Part 1, Background theory and research annotated bibliography of 310 items. Part 2, Planning and administration
annotated bibliography of 447 items. Part 3, Instructional
methods and techniques annotated bibliography of 345 items.
Part 4, Audiovisual theory, aids, and equipment annotated
bibliography of 332 items.

310. Barth, Rodney J. A Selected annotated bibliography on
behavioral objectives in the English language arts. ERIC
Clearinghouse on Reading and Communication Skills, 1974. 9p.
ED 102580.

Describes books and articles designed to help elementary
and secondary teachers plan instructional goals, write
behavioral objectives, and evaluate student performance.
Includes documents that argue for and against the use of
these objectives.

311. Roen, Sheldon R. References to teaching children about
human behavior: pre-high school. 1970. 29p. ED 066411.

400 partially annotated references to books, articles, papers, reports, dissertations, and government publications.

312. Canfield, John T. A Guide to humanistic education.
1970. 46p. ED 067356.

Annotated. Includes books, games, articles, and curriculum
materials on the non-academic aspects of a child's growth
in school. Designed for those wanting to enhance positive
self-concepts, increase motivation, promote creative thinking and behavior, and promote better human relations.

313. Preiser, Wolfgang F. Environment and spatial behavior:
a selected bibliography. Monticello, IL, Council of Planning
Librarians, 1971. 34p. ED 070622.

500 unannotated citations dealing with human behavior in
institutions and public places.

314. Shea, M. Christine. Social development and behavior: an
abstract bibliography. ERIC Clearinghouse on Early Childhood
Education, 1974. 78p. ED 091084.

255 ERIC documents from RIE and CIJE dated 1970 to 1974.
Topics include peer relationships, interpersonal competence,
social attitudes, socialization, and sociometric techniques.

315. Behavioral objectives: an annotated bibliography. Des
Moines, Iowa State Department of Public Instruction, 1971. 67p.
ED 069606.

Includes how-to-do-it publications, issues relating to the
objectives-evaluative movement, references relating to the
classification of educational objectives and the theories
of conditions of learning, and audiovisual materials relating to behavioral objectives.

316. Elliott, Pamela and Ross J. Loomis. Studies of visitor
behavior in museums and exhibitions: an annotated bibliography
of sources primarily in the English language. Smithsonian
Institution, Office of Museum Programs, 1975. 39p. ED 134513.

204 references to books, articles, dissertations, and other
studies.

317. Casto, Glendon. Affective behavior in preschool children.
Logan, Utah State University, Exceptional Child Center, 1976.
244p. ED 135162.

The final section is an annotated bibliography related to
theories of emotion and overviews of affective development
in children, specific aspects of affective development,
affective development of handicapped children, affective
education and curriculum, and instrumentation and research
methodology in the study of affective development.

318. Miller, Juliet V. Student behavior and climate. University of Michigan, Counseling and Personnel Services, 1968. 60p.
ED 025825.

Annotated research which examines the nature of emotional
climates and environments, and the relationship of various
environments to student achievements, attitudes, and behaviors.

319. Hedstrom, Judith E. Selective bibliography in behavioral sciences resources. ERIC Clearinghouse for Social Studies/
Social Science Education, 1977. 37p. ED 150030.

Over 50 annotated curriculum materials, games, simulations,
and ERIC documents related to psychology and sociology.

320. Morse, William C. and Richard L. Munger. Helping children and youth with feelings: affective-behavioral science education resources for the developing self/schools. 1975. 65p.
ED 115565.

Annotated books and articles from the areas of psychology,
education, and mental health published from 1951 to 1975.
Also includes an outline of selected curriculum materials.

BIBLIOGRAPHIES

321. Sinnassamy, Francoise. <u>Survey on the present state of</u>
<u>bibliographic recording in freely available printed form of</u>
<u>government publications and those of intergovernmental organ-</u>
<u>izations</u>. Paris, UNESCO, 1977. 158p. ED 148350 (MF)

Surveys 87 countries and 42 intergovernmental organizations
on the state of national bibliographies, catalogs, and
lists of official publications.

322. Massil, S. <u>Resource sharing for national bibliographic</u>
<u>services</u>. Paris, UNESCO, 1977. 22p. ED 148352 (MF)

Includes a bibliography of 95 unannotated items.

323. Cheffins, Richard. <u>A Survey of the contents of existing</u>
<u>national bibliographies</u>. Paris, UNESCO, 1977. 52p. ED 148
353 (MF)

National bibliographies of 62 countries are examined, and
standardized information on each is presented together with
summary tables in this country-by-country analysis.

BIBLIOTHERAPY

324. Lack, Clara and Bruce Bettencourt. <u>Adult bibliotherapy</u>
<u>discussion group bibliography</u>. San Jose, CA, Santa Clara Coun-
ty Library, 1975. 21p. ED 119644.

Over 300 unannotated items which have been used at jails,
halfway houses, convalescent hospitals, alcoholic and drug
clinics, and psychiatric hospitals. Includes poetry, films,
biographies, essays, plays, short stories, and music.

325. Schultheis, Miriam and Robert Pavlik. <u>Classroom teachers'</u>
<u>manual for bibliotherapy</u>. Fort Wayne, IN, Institute for the
Study of Bibliotherapy, 1977. 95p. ED 163493 (MF)

Lists children's books, audiovisuals, and other bibliographies.

326. Weinstock, Donald J. <u>Poetry therapy: a bibliography</u>.
1979. 20p. ED 168043.

84 books, articles, and research studies on a variety of
topics, including its use in nursing, mental hospitals,
and self-discovery.

327. Narang, H. L. <u>Doctoral dissertations on bibliotherapy</u>:
<u>an annotated list</u>. 1975. 11p. ED 110961.

Describes fourteen completed dissertations in the area of
bibliotherapy and its effects.

328. Riggs, Corinne W. Bibliotherapy: an annotated bibliography. International Reading Association, 1971. 27p. ED 076936.

Updated from its 1967 version, this edition contains 165 citations ranging from 1936 to 1970.

329. Bibliotherapy: an annotated bibliography dealing with physical and self-image handicaps. Jericho, NY, Nassau County Board of Cooperative Educational Services, 1971. 26p. ED 061 689.

Includes fiction, and lists books dealing with various handicaps or with physical problems such as obesity and extremes of stature.

330. Steffens, Elizabeth. Four years' reading in bibliotherapy, 1968-1972. San Jose, CA, Santa Clara County Library, 1973. 33p. ED 088509.

Annotated. 270 short stories, plays, and prose excerpts which have been used successfully in the Agnews State Bibliotherapy Project. Main topics are: adolescence, alcoholism, anger, compassion, courtship, family, fear, identity, justice, life and death, loneliness, love, marriage, parent-child, reality, revenge, and self-concept.

BILINGUAL EDUCATION See Also ENGLISH (SECOND LANGUAGE) and LANGUAGE INSTRUCTION

331. Annotated bibliography of bilingual bicultural materials. Austin, TX, Dissemination Center for Bilingual Bicultural Education, 1974. 247p. ED 126730.

Subjects are arts and crafts, biographies, career education, children's literature, cooking, holidays, math, music, science, games and dances, ethnic studies, and teacher education.

332. Teacher training bibliography: an annotated listing of materials for bilingual bicultural teacher education. Austin, TX, Dissemination Center for Bilingual Bicultural Education, 1975. 68p. ED 108498.

About 200 books and programs for pre-service and in-service education.

333. Language maintenance. Washington, DC, National Institute of Education, Educational Equity Group, 1977. 21p. ED 138115.

ERIC documents which deal with bilingual education in the USA, Canada, Israel, Ireland, the Pacific Islands, and Southeast Asia. Annotated.

334. Cahir, Stephen. A Selected bibliography on Mexican American and Native American bilingual education in the Southwest.

ERIC Clearinghouse on Languages and Linguistics, 1975. 299p.
ED 103148.

263 annotated ERIC documents from RIE dated 1971 to 1974.

335. Gonzales, Joe R. Spanish/English and Native American/
English bibliography. Albuquerque, NM, Southwest Bilingual Education Training Resource Center, 1977. 105p. ED 158955 (MF)

Over 400 annotated professional resources and instructional
materials, 175 evaluation instruments, and 41 other bibliographies.

336. Bilingual education for children: an abstract bibliography. ERIC Clearinghouse on Early Childhood Education, 1975.
100p. ED 113009.

Includes 116 items from RIE, and 74 articles from CIJE on
ethnic groups, migrants, second language learning, and
other bibliographies.

337. Spencer, Mima. Bilingual education for Spanish speaking
children: an abstract bibliography. ERIC Clearinghouse on
Early Childhood Education, 1974. 45p. ED 091075.

Includes 86 references to programs, issues, materials, and
methodology involved in bilingual teaching.

338. Alvarado, Helen. Curriculum materials for bilingual programs: Spanish-English, pre K - 12. Mount Prospect, Bilingual
Education Service Center of Illinois, 1973. 353p. ED 084927.

Subjects are language arts, social studies, geography, science, and mathematics. Also includes encyclopedias, records,
music books, and games. Unannotated.

339. Bilingual audiovisual materials. Brooklyn, New York City
Board of Education, Bilingual Resource Center, 1973. 33p. ED
084919.

Annotated; also includes other bibliographies.

340. Diaz, Carmen. Bilingual - bicultural materials. Lawrence, University of Kansas, Special Education Instructional
Materials Center, 1973. 93p. ED 084915.

Also lists evaluative instruments for children of Spanish
speaking families. Unannotated.

341. Guide to resources for bilingual/bicultural education.
Hightstown, NJ, Northeast Area Learning Resource Center, 1975.
46p. ED 133920.

Provides information on bilingual resources, services, and
programs nationally, and in the Northeast region.

342. Bilingual ERIC publications. Brooklyn, New York City

Board of Education, Bilingual Resource Center, 1973.   12p.   ED
081280.

Annotated documents of general interest, English as a second language, and the Spanish speaking.

343.   Altus, David M. Bilingual education: a selected bibliography. ERIC Clearinghouse on Rural Education and Small
Schools, 1970. 228p. ED 047853.

176 items from RIE and CIJE.

344. Dissertations and data-based journal articles on bilingual education. UCLA, National Dissemination and Assessment
Center, 1977. 31p. ED 176541.

Unannotated list taken from DAI and CIJE, 1971-1976.

345. Rodriguez, Norma. Modular sequence: teaching reading to
bilingual learners: an annotated bibliography of reading materials for Spanish speaking students. West Hartford, CT, Hartford University, College of Education, no date. 110p. ED
106253.

346. Evaluation echoes: a teacher's guide for selecting bilingual education materials. Trenton, Puerto Rican Congress
of New Jersey, 1976. 183p. ED 143712 (MF)

Includes English and Spanish language arts, fine arts,
social studies, science, and mathematics. Unannotated.

347. Lopez-Valadez, E. J. Curriculum materials for bilingual
and multicultural education: an annotated bibliography. Arlington Heights, IL, Bilingual Education Service Center, 1976.
91p. ED 144341.

This is a Volume One on Spanish language arts for K-12,
and includes audiovisuals.

348. Berry, Dale W. Assessment and the status of bilingual
vocational training for adults. Albuquerque, NM, Kirschner
Associates, 1976. 35p. ED 131682.

This Volume Two of the final report is the annotated bibliography.

349. Caskey, Owen L. and Jimmy Hodges. A Resource and reference bibliography on teaching and counseling the bilingual student. Lubbock, Texas Technological College, School of Education, 1968. 48p. ED 032966 (MF)

Unannotated. 733 references published from 1914 to 1967.

350. Bilingual bicultural materials: a listing for library
resource centers. Revised ed. El Paso, TX, Public Schools,
1975. 109p. ED 127968.

Gives grade level, recommendations, and critical annota-

tions for filmstrips, games, recordings, kits, books, posters, and charts.

351. Jokovich, Nancy. A Bibliography of American doctoral
dissertations in bilingual education and English as a second
language, 1968-1974. ERIC Clearinghouse on Language and Linguistics, 1977. 24p. ED 136584.

200 entries. Not annotated.

352. A Bibliography of bilingual bicultural preschool material
for the Spanish speaking child. Washington, DC, InterAmerican
Research Associates, 1977. 97p. ED 142045.

Annotated. Includes curriculum guides, instructional materials, workbooks, audiovisuals, coloring books, storybooks,
and tests. ED 152432 is a 76 page supplement.

353. Hamilton, Don. Evaluation instruments for bilingual education: a revision of tests in use in Title VII bilingual education projects. Austin, TX, Education Service Center Region
13, 1972. 95p. ED 087818.

Annotated.

354. Ehrlich, Alan. Tests in Spanish and other languages and
non-verbal tests for children in bilingual programs: an annotated bibliography. City University of New York, Hunter College, Bilingual Education Unit, 1973. 24p. ED 074852.

Included are 21 tests of intelligence, general ability,
and language proficiency for Spanish, English, French, and
German.

355. Ibarra, Herb. Bibliography of ESL/bilingual teaching
materials. San Diego City Schools, 1969. 31p. ED 028002.

406 unannotated books and articles dated 1945 to 1968 are
listed for teachers and students of Spanish speaking and
bilingualism. The emphasis is on English as a second language.

356. Babin, Patrick. Bilingualism: a bibliography. 1968.
33p. ED 023097.

412 unannotated entries include books, articles, unpublished
papers, and other bibliographies.

357. Desrochers, Alain M. Social psychology of second language acquisition and bilinguality: an annotated bibliography.
University of Western Ontario, Department of Psychology, 1975.
149p. ED 155933.

Contains theoretical papers, statements of opinion, and
empirical studies in 333 annotated references, and 178
without annotations.

358. Bilingualism: a bibliography of 1000 references with special reference to Wales. Aberystwyth, University College of
Wales, 1971. 91p. ED 119465.

Items are mainly in English or Welsh dating from the end
of the 19th Century to 1970. Includes scholarly articles,
dissertations, books, and newspaper articles.

BIOLOGY

359. Sullivan, Marjorie and Helen Strader. The Birds and the
beasts were there: animals in their natural habitats. Emporia,
Kansas State Teachers College, Department of Librarianship,
1973. 37p. ED 079947.

Lists 247 print and non-print materials dealing with animal life, nature, and ecology to assist teachers and school
librarians in selecting media for grades 4 through 6, and
9 through 12.

360. Hurlburt, Evelyn M. Radioisotope experiments in high
school biology: an annotated selected bibliography. Oak Ridge,
TN, Atomic Energy Commission, 1966. 24p. ED 013754.

BIRTH CONTROL   See   FAMILY PLANNING

BLACK ENGLISH

361. Bobson, Sarah. Nonstandard dialects: an annotated bibliography of ERIC references. ERIC Clearinghouse on the Urban
Disadvantaged, 1974. 97p. ED 095227.

415 citations from RIE and CIJE, mostly dealing with Black
English.

362. Harber, Jean R. Black English, its relationship in reading: an annotated bibliography. 1976. 59p. ED 132865.

Lists articles, books, and papers that explore the disad-
vantage that children are experiencing with the use of
Black English.

363. Harber, Jean R. Reading and the Black English speaking
child: an annotated bibliography. International Reading Association, 1978. 48p. ED 149313.

The first half lists materials according to the factors
that influence the reading performance of Black children.
The second half lists materials that suggest strategies
for improving Black children's reading performance.

364. Key, Mary R. Black English: a selected bibliography.

1972. 24p. ED 081253.

200 books and articles for students and educators interested in its practical use, and in linguistic analysis.
References negative to Black English are not included.

365. Tarone, Elaine. A Selected annotated bibliography on
social dialects for teachers of Speech and English. Seattle,
University of Washington, 1970. 41p. ED 043853.

The emphasis here is on Black English.

366. Harrington, Judith. An Annotated bibliography of recent
work on Black English. 1971(?) 42p. ED 091931.

Limited to articles and reports published primarily during
1971. Includes other bibliographies in its listings.

367. Mack, Molly A. Black English and standard English: an
annotated bibliography. Burlington, University of Vermont,
1977. 27p. ED 154394.

Over 100 items include historical backgrounds, and the
effectiveness of teaching standard English to non-standard speakers and writers, in addition to attitudes of
students and academic implications.

BLACK LITERATURE

368. A Review of bibliographies on Black literature. University of Missouri, Ethnic Awareness Center, 1973. 99p. ED
079760.

61 annotated bibliographies are reviewed.

369. Britton, Jean E. Selected books about the Afro-American
for very young children, K–2. Boston, Massachusetts State Department of Education, 1969. 19p. ED 039029.

Both Black and white authors are represented with 44 books
of fiction, and 17 non-fiction. Also included are 15 bibliographies of children's books about Black Americans.

370. Dodds, Barbara. Negro literature for high school students. National Council of Teachers of English, 1968. 164p.
ED 022754 (MF)

Traces the history of Black writers from pre-Civil War
times to the present. Annotated entries include anthologies, novels, biographies, and indicate reading level.

371. Report of the Committee on Afro-American Literature.
Des Moines (Iowa) Public Schools, 1970. 15p. ED 041020.

148 annotated references to Black literature for high

school teaching units and for library purchase.

372. Houston, Helen R. A Selected Black reading list. 1976.
8p. ED 134995.

An annotated survey of Black literature for elementary
and secondary students, and lists of bibliographies and
critical works concerning the teaching of the subject.

373. Tirotta, Richard. No crystal stair: a bibliography of
Black literature. New York Public Library, 1971. 65p. ED
053231.

Includes books published since 1965 in the areas of the
arts, biography, history, politics, humor, sociology, religion, economics, and sports. Brief annotations.

374. Rollins, Charlemae. We build together. National Council
of Teachers of English, 1967. 95p. ED 076998.

Nonstereotype books for children and young people with
brief evaluative descriptions. Includes picture books,
fiction, history, biography, poetry, music, science, and
sports.

375. Latimer, Bettye I. Starting out right: how to choose
books about Black people for young children. Madison, WI,
Equal Opportunities Commission, 1972. 135p. ED 065656.

Critical and selective annotated list restricted to books
written for preschool through grade three.

376. Penn, Joseph E. The Negro American in paperback: a selected list of paperbound books compiled and annotated for secondary school students. Washington, DC, National Education
Association, Center for Human Relations, 1968. 49p. ED 038
467 (MF)

A revised edition that includes 330 titles.

377. Davis, David C. and Madeline Davis. A Selected list of
films related to Black literature. Wisconsin Council of Teachers of English, 1971. 5p. ED 133751.

29 unannotated films on several topics are listed, plus
titles of literary items related to film topics.

378. Karolides, Nicholas J. Black fiction and biographies:
current books for children and adolescents. Wisconsin Council
of Teachers of English, 1972. 9p. ED 133753.

An annotated list with reading level indicated.

379. Whitlow, Roger. A Bibliography of Black American poetry
1760 to the present. 1972. 13p. ED 112402.

More than 200 books containing poetry by Black Americans.
Not annotated.

380. Baronberg, Joan. Black representation in children's
books. ERIC Clearinghouse on the Urban Disadvantaged, 1971.
27p. ED 050188.

A search for fiction picture books involving Black people
located only 56 published between 1939 and 1971 with about
half of them portraying Blacks only. Just four were published before 1950, and seven during the 1950's. Annotated.

381. Glancy Barbara Joan. Children's interracial fiction: an
unselective bibliography. Washington, DC, American Federation
of Teachers, 1969. 122p. ED 037509.

328 annotated books having Black characters. Annotated
with grade levels indicated.

382. Redd, Virginia P. Selective bibliography on Afro-American literature (300 years): arranged chronologically by genre
and partially annotated. 1973. 12p. ED 094401.

The works of 75 novelists, 14 dramatists, 16 short story
writers, and 20 poets are included.

383. Whitlow, Roger. Contemporary Black American fiction: a
checklist of writing since the Second World War. 1974. 17p.
ED 099854.

400 titles listed by author. Unannotated.

384. Daniel. Jack L. and Linda F. Wharton. Black American
rhetoric: a selected bibliography. 1976. 9p. ED 127651.

Books, articles, and theses are annotated that define aspects of the traditional African world view and its modes
of expression, demonstrate African cultural continuity in
the New World, and show the impact of American existential
circumstances.

385. Whitlow, Roger. A Bibliography of plays written by
Black Americans 1855 to present. 1974. 14p. ED 096676.

Some of the plays are unpublished. 342 titles.

386. Doyle, Ruby Nell. Black literature for young readers:
an annotated bibliography of literature by and about Black
Americans for seventh and eighth grade students. Louisville,
KY, Board of Education, 1970. 34p. ED 046952.

Includes Black pioneers, sports, humor, poetry, songs,
and Christmas in 52 annotated and 49 unannotated items.

387. Willis, Cecilia A. Current bibliography on literature
by and about Blacks. Manhattan, Kansas State University, 1972.
121p. ED 061383.

Unannotated. Includes reference sources, biographies, civil rights, cultural life, economics, politics, and history.

BLACK MUSIC

388. Dain, Bernice and David Nevin. The Black record: a selective discography of Afro-Americana on audio discs held by
the Audiovisual Department, John M. Olin Library. Seattle,
University of Washington Library, 1973. 26p. ED 094081.

BLACK RELIGION

389. Wheelbarger, Johnny J. Black religion: a bibliography
of Fisk University Library materials relating to various aspects of Black religious life. Nashville, TN, Fisk University,
1974. 22p. ED 107309.

    Topics: Black religion, the church and race relations,
    church and state in relation to Black religion, church
    work, and the ministry. Includes oral history and taped
    interviews.

390. Davis, Lenwood G. A History of Black religion in northern areas: a preliminary survey. Monticello, IL, Council of
Planning Librarians, 1975. 13p. ED 105053.

    Unannotated reference works and selected Black periodicals
    are included. There is a focus on cults.

BLACK STUDENTS

391. Minority group performance under various conditions of
school ethnic and economic integration. ERIC Clearinghouse
for Urban Disadvantaged, 1968. 8p. ED 021947.

    Contains 151 items from research on the relation of school
    ethnic and social class composition to the academic perfor-
    mance of Black children.

BLACK STUDIES

392. Davis, Lenwood G. Poverty and the Black community: a
preliminary survey. Monticello, IL, Council of Planning Librarians, 1975. 23p. ED 131129.

    Topics are the economics of poverty, marriage and family
    life, politics of poverty, racial prejudice, civil rights,
    mental health of the poor, social structure, and housing
    problems.

393. Teaching Black: an evaluation of methods and resources.
Stanford University, Multi-Ethnic Education Resources Center,
1971. 105p. ED 058717.

Of 236 packages evaluated, 40 are recommended and described here. An annotated list of books, periodicals, and films as resources is also included.

394. The Negro in the United States: a list of significant books. Ninth ed. New York Public Library, 1965. 25p. ED 031520.

The annotations are grouped into sections on history and culture, the freedom movement, civil rights, intergroup relations, biography, literature, music, and art.

395. Bigala, John. An Annotated bibliography for teaching Afro-American studies at secondary and college levels. New York, Columbia University, National Center for Research and Information on Equal Educational Opportunity, 1971. 47p. ED 055148.

Includes books in history and literature which show the Black contribution to US history.

396. Afro-American instructional curriculum laboratory. Detroit, Michigan-Ohio Regional Educational Laboratory, 1969. 44p. ED 035991.

Includes materials for grades K-12 in its annotated bibliography of 282 citations published since 1960.

397. Paden, John N. and Edward W. Soja. The African experience. Evanston, IL, Northwestern University, 1969. 1352p. in three volumes. ED 036281.

Volume two of this set contains the bibliography of over 2500 references to books, articles, dissertations, case studies, proceedings, and others.

398. The Negro freedom movement past and present: an annotated bibliography. Detroit, Wayne County Intermediate School District, 1967. 107p. ED 030681.

Includes books for adults, youth, and children, plus some audiovisuals, and other bibliographies.

399. A Brief listing of bibliographies, periodicals, and curriculum guides on Negro literature and history. Ann Arbor, MI, Public Schools, 1969. 10p. ED 030655.

36 bibliographies, 22 periodicals, and five curriculum guides are included. Unannotated.

400. Negro history and literature: a selected annotated bibliography. New York, American Jewish Committee, 1968. 30p. ED 027332.

Classified by reading level, the list includes autobiography, poetry, fiction, and social and historical documents. There are 175 titles by Black and white authors.

401. Hussey, Edith. The Negro American: a reading list. 1957.
40p. ED 019355.

Fiction and non-fiction are included in this unannotated
list of 260 items, preschool through adult.

402. The Negro in the United States: a list of significant
books selected from a compilation by the New York Public Library. 1965. 5p. ED 019339.

116 entries include poetry, fiction, biography, and history in addition to items on the civil rights movement.
Unannotated.

403. Koblitz, Minnie W. The Negro in schoolroom literature:
resource materials for the teacher of kindergarten through the
sixth grade. Second ed. New York, Center for Urban Education,
1967. 74p. ED 019318.

Arranged by reading level, it includes over 250 annotated
books on the Black heritage.

404. Penn, Joseph E. The Negro American in paperback: a selected list of paperbound books. Washington, DC, National Education Association, 1967. 33p. ED 018506 (MF)

For secondary school level, this annotated list includes
fiction, social histories, biography, and autobiography.
ED 038467 is a revised edition that updates this list.

405. Jackson, Miles M. A Bibliography of materials by and
about Negro Americans for young readers. 1967. 92p. ED 015
091.

An annotated list of books and audiovisuals.

406. Rosenfeld, Harriet. Books to enhance the self-image of
Negro children. 1966. 18p. ED 011904.

Annotated.

407. Schlachter, Gail and Donna Belli. Blacks in an urban
environment: a selected annotated bibliography of reference
sources. Monticello, IL, Council of Planning Librarians, 1975.
47p. ED 135908.

Deals with the social, educational, psychological, political, economic, and historical aspects of Black life in
the city.

408. Herman, Henrietta. The American Negro: his history and
his contributions to our culture: a bibliography prepared for
the elementary schools as a part of the ESEA Title III project.
New York, Yonkers City School District, 1969. 45p. ED 041086.

Annotations and reading levels are provided.

409. Zimmermann, Matilde J. Teacher's guide for Afro-Ameri-

<u>can history</u>. Albany, New York State Department of Social Ser-
vices, 1969. 124p. ED 040908.

Contains a 40 page topical bibliography to aid teachers
and librarians in selecting bibliographies, guides, biographies, histories, art, children's books, films, filmstrips, and recordings.

410. Davis, Lenwood G. <u>A Working bibliography on published
materials on Black studies programs in the United States</u>. Monticello, IL, Council of Planning Librarians, 1977. 33p. ED
145002.

Unannotated. Includes books, articles, pamphlets, dissertations, reference works, and Black periodicals, plus a
list of US libraries with large Black history collections.

411. Davis, Lenwood G. <u>Blacks in the cities, 1900-1974: a
bibliography</u>. Second ed. Monticello, IL, Council of Planning
Librarians, 1975. 84p. ED 145039 (MF)

Includes bibliographies, Black newspapers inurban areas,
reports, pamphlets, and speeches, government documents,
books, and articles. Unannotated.

412. Dean, Frances C. <u>Being Black in America, K-12: a multimedia listing of the '70's</u>. Rockville, MD, Montgomery County
Public Schools, 1975. 354p. ED 152935 (MF)

Partially annotated, this catalog lists over 600 sources,
including books, records, kits, and filmstrips covering
both Black American and African history, folklore, literature, and present day life.

413. Blazek, Ron. <u>The Black experience: a bibliography of
bibliographies, 1970-1975</u>. Chicago, American Library Association, 1978. 69p. ED 157519 (MF).

An annotated listing of separately published bibliographies
comprises the major segment of the text.

414. Hume, Mildred and Gayle Marko. <u>Orodha ya vitabu: a bibliography of Afro-American life</u>. Minneapolis Public Schools,
1969. 54p. ED 038355.

251 fiction and nonfiction books are included in this annotated bibliography divided according to reading level
from kindergarten to adult. Most were published between
1938 and 1968. Also included are 19 films and 13 records.

415. Hawkins, John N. and Jon Maksik. <u>Teacher's resource
handbook for African studies: an annotated bibliography of curriculum materials, preschool through grade twelve</u>. UCLA, African Studies Center, 1976. 75p. ED 137213 (MF)

Divided by geographic regions of Africa and by grade level,
this bibliography contains 662 items.

416. Afro-American Resource Center audiovisual bibliography
and supplement, 1973. Toledo, OH, Public Schools, 1972.   186p.
ED 090076.

Over 500 annotated AV items are included emphasizing Black
history and culture. Transparencies, maps, games are listed
in addition to the films, records, and slides.

417. Clark, Vernon L. A Bibliographical guide to the study
of Black history. Chapel Hill, University of North Carolina,
Frank Porter Graham Center, 1974. 23p. ED 094880.

Stresses history from a psychological perspective, and
socio-history. Annotated.

418. Jones, Valarie A. and John Stalker. Interpreting the
Black experience in America to foreign students: a guide to
materials. Atlanta University Library, 1976. 76p. ED 125
977.

Partially annotated college level books and audiovisuals.

419. Davis, Lenwood G. The Black family in urban areas in the
United States. Second ed. Monticello, IL, Council of Planning
Librarians, 1975. 86p. ED 126184.

Includes periodicals, reference works, government documents, dissertations, reports, and pamphlets.

420. Black America. San Francisco, Unified School District,
1972. 33p. ED 085453.

This is an AV bibliography that includes African heritage.

421. Annotated bibliography of materials for the teaching of
Black history. Philadelphia, National Association of Independent Schools, 1973. 25p. ED 099256.

194 books, teacher's guides, films, and filmstrips dating
1932 to 1967 are listed. Some poetry, fiction, and biography are included.

422. The Afro-American in books for children including books
about Africa and the West Indies. Revised ed. Washington, DC,
Public Library, 1974. 73p. ED 097885.

500 briefly annotated entries. The list includes picture
books and easy reading, folklore, poetry, art, music, geography, biography, and history.

423. Kerri, James N. and Anthony Layng. A Bibliography of
Afro-American (Black) studies. Monticello, IL, Council of
Planning Librarians, 1974. 83p. ED 103565.

Unannotated.

424. A Bibliography of books and educational media related

<u>to Negro culture</u>. Miami, FL, Dade County Board of Public In-
struction, 1969. 27p. ED 046829.

A multimedia bibliography of adult, juvenile, and professional level materials. Not annotated.

425. Waffen, Leslie. <u>Audiovisual records in the National Ar-</u>
<u>chives relating to Black history</u>. Washington, DC, National
Archives and Records Service, 1972. 16p. ED 082485.

This annotated preliminary draft is a representative selection only. It dates back to the Civil War.

426. <u>Minority groups: a bibliography and supplement</u>. Salt
Lake City, Utah State Board of Education, 1968. 93p. ED 042
767.

Most of the sources are about the history and culture of
the American Black. Includes annotated books, song books,
films, and recordings.

BLACKS - EDUCATION

427. Sheppard, N. Alan. <u>The Participation of minorities in</u>
<u>vocational education, manpower, and career oriented programs</u>:
<u>special focus on Black Americans: an annotated bibliography</u>.
Blacksburg, Virginia Polytechnic Institute, 1977. 29p. ED
141641.

90 entries dating from 1963 to 1976.

428. De'Ath, Colin. <u>Black education in the United States and</u>
<u>its relevance to international development education: Black ed-</u>
<u>ucation and Black society in the United States: a bibliography</u>
<u>for development educators</u>. University of Pittsburgh, School
of Education, 1969. 56p. ED 048047.

429. Jablonsky, Adelaide. <u>Research on the education of Black</u>
<u>and Black-white populations: an annotated bibliography of doc-</u>
<u>toral dissertations</u>. ERIC Clearinghouse on the Urban Disadvan-
taged, 1974. 56p. ED 094053.

The focus is on reading and language arts, self-concept,
attitudes, aspirations, and behavior, parental and cultural influences, and vocation.

430. Davis, Lenwood G. <u>A History of Blacks in higher educa-</u>
<u>tion, 1875-1975: a working bibliography</u>. Monticello, IL, Coun-
cil of Planning Librarians, 1975. 27p. ED 104235.

Contents include reference works, periodicals, books, and
articles. Unannotated.

BLIND See BRAILLE and DEAF-BLIND and VISUALLY HANDICAPPED

BOARDS OF EDUCATION   See Also   EDUCATIONAL ADMINISTRATION and
        TRUSTEES

431. Charters, W. W. A Bibliography of empirical studies of
school boards, 1900-1951. Eugene, University of Oregon, Center for Advanced Study of Educational Administration, 1968.
15p. ED 024135.

     Unannotated list of 101 articles, books, and theses on the
     attributes behavior, attitudes, and interactions of board
     members. ED 024136 is a 24 page supplement for the years
     1952-1968. It has 223 items.

432. James, H. Thomas. School Board bibliography. Stanford
University, School of Education, 1967. 132p. ED 017068.

     Annotated bibliography of 204 books, articles, chapters,
     reports, and theses classified in 14 categories.

BOSTON, MASSACHUSETTS

433. Hollister, Robert M. and others. Boston: an urban community. Boston Public Library, 1977. ED 181928 through ED
181932.

     These five separate annotated reading lists encompass all
     aspects of Boston history and life to date. Several hun-
     dred citations are represented in this group.

BRAILLE

434. Nolan, C. Y. Bibliography of research on braille.
Louisville, KY, American Printing House for the Blind, 1971.
12p. ED 064849.

     From 1907 to 1971, 130 entries include books, articles,
     conference reports, and theses. Some German and Japanese
     publications are included.

BRAIN DAMAGE

435. A Selective bibliography on brain damaged children. The
Woods School for Exceptional Children, 1964. 69p. ED 014181

     317 classified and annotated references to behavioral char-
     acteristics of children with cerebral dysfunction.

BRAZIL

436. Hope, Henry W. A Selective bibliography of contemporary Brazilian authors. Milwaukee, University of Wisconsin, 1966. 59p. ED 012813.

   Ranging from 1934 to 1966, the list includes fiction and nonfiction in the humanities and social sciences.

BRITISH COLUMBIA

437. Goard, Dean S. and Gary Dickinson. Rural British Columbia: a bibliography of social and economic research. Vancouver, BC, University of British Columbia, 1970. 33p. ED 040 779.

   Unannotated. 286 entries cover research from about 1940 to 1969.

BUDGETING SYSTEMS

438. Tudor, Dean. Planning-Programming-Budgeting systems. Revised ed. Monticello, IL, Council of Planning Librarians, 1972. 30p. ED 106964.

439. Raider, Melvyn C. Bibliography: Program-planning-budgeting system and decision-making: budgeting and planning within the context of higher education. 1972. 11p. ED 091996.

   Unannotated. 143 books, articles, reports, and other sources.

440. Piele, Philip K. and David G. Bunting. Program budgeting and the school administrator: a review of dissertations and annotated bibliography. ERIC Clearinghouse on Educational Administration, 1969. 50p. ED 035065.

   22 dissertations are included dating from 1964 to 1969.

441. Terrey, John N. Program budgeting and other newer management tools in higher education: a descriptive and annotated bibliography. Seattle, Center for Development of Community College Education at the University of Washington, 1968. 62p. ED 024144.

   Includes 73 books, articles, bibliographies, government documents, and other reports published from 1963 to 1968.

442. Eidell, Terry L. and Philip Piele. A Bibliography of selected documents on planning, programming, budgeting systems. Eugene, University of Oregon, 1968. 6p. ED 018876.

   Contains 48 unannotated references.

443. ERIC abstracts: a collection of ERIC document resumes

on program budgeting and cost analysis. Washington, DC, American Association of School Administrators, 1970. 34p. ED 036 892.

51 citations are listed that were collected from RIE through October 1969.

444. McGivney, Joseph H. and William C. Nelson. Program, planning, budgeting systems for educators: an annotated bibliography. Columbus, Ohio State University, Center for Vocational and Technical Education, 1969. 57p. ED 035756.

This volume three of a set contains 70 references dating from 1962 to 1969.

445. Nelson, William C. Program, planning, budgeting systems for educators: a research bibliography. Columbus, Ohio State University, Center for Vocational and Technical Education, 1970. 117p. ED 038512.

This volume four of a set contains 1051 citations ranging from 1936 to 1969, but emphasizes the 1960's.

BUILDING DESIGN   See Also   ARCHITECTURE and EDUCATIONAL
        FACILITIES

446. Sinnamon, Ian T. Natural disasters and educational building design: introductory review and annotated bibliography for the Asian region. Bangkok, UNESCO, 1976. 39p. ED 130410 (MF)

Also includes the role of the school building in the event of a crisis.

447. Schellenberg, Ben. Noise and sound control in open plan schools. 1975. 26p. ED 109801 (MF)

Nineteen annotated articles and reports dealing with acoustical design.

448. Bartholomew, Robert. Indoor-outdoor space: the transitional areas and their effect on human behavior. Monticello, IL, Council of Planning Librarians, 1974. 7p. ED 106907.

Unannotated. Mostly deals with public spaces leading into or out of buildings.

449. Gust, Tim and Elaine Shaheen. References concerning architectural barriers in higher education. University of Pittsburgh, Research and Training Center in Vocational Rehabilitation, 1968(?). 5p. ED 021303.

Concern is on making buildings usable by the physically handicapped.

450. Science facilities: a classified list of literature re-

lated to design, construction, and other architectural matters. Washington, DC, National Science Foundation, 1965. 18p. ED 015635.

A list of articles papers, and catalogs in the NSF collection. Unannotated.

BURMA

451. Ba, U. Education abstracts - Burma. Washington, DC, National Science Foundation, 1968. 56p. ED 025987.

114 summaries of Burmese newspaper and periodical accounts published January through April, 1968.

452. Ba, U. Education Abstracts - Burma. Washington, DC, National Science Teachers Association, 1968. 58p. ED 027807.

129 more summaries taken from the Burmese press.

BUS DRIVING

453. Bibliography of training films for school bus driver training. 1962. 24p. ED 011799.

A list of 113 unannotated films.

BUSINESS AND BUSINESS EDUCATION See Also COOPERATIVE EDUCA-
      TION and DISTRIBUTIVE EDUCATION

454. Walker, Loretta and David Gerhan. Multinational business enterprise and its implications for library research. Schenectady, NY, Union College Library, 1973. 54p. ED 085 603.

A 38 page bibliography in various formats concludes this study. Unannotated.

455. Bibliography: college and university business administration. Washington, DC, National Association of College and University Business Officers, 1977. 20p. ED 148283 (MF)

275 unannotated references are listed.

456. Career information: business and office occupations. Revised ed. Washington, DC, American Vocational Association, 1975. 31p. ED 118771.

Organized under communications, materials support, personnel, and supervisory and administrative management. The entries were published from 1969 to 1974; unannotated.

457. Cook, Fred S. Office machines used in business today:
an annotated and classified bibliography for the years 1938
through 1964. Detroit, Wayne State University, 1965. 42p.
ED 017653.

Includes 218 books, articles, theses, and dissertations.

458. Business education: RCU research summary. California
Coordination Unit for Occupational Research & Development,
1967. 23p. ED 014565

Abstracts of 28 dissertations in business education.

459. Lanham, Frank W. and J. M. Trytten. Review and synthesis of research in business and office education. Columbus,
Ohio State University, Center for Vocational and Technical Education, 1966. 144p. ED 011566.

An unannotated compilation from 1960 to 1966.

460. Everard, Kenneth E. A Selected, annotated bibliography
for researchers in business and distributive education. Trenton, NJ, Trenton State College, Department of Business Education, 1969. 14p. ED 039350.

Includes 142 references dated from 1872 to 1967.

461. Schreier, James W. and John L. Komives. The Entrepre-
neur and new enterprise formation: a resource guide. Milwaukee, Center for Venture Management, 1973. 119p. ED 084455
(MF)

Contains over 900 items dealing with new business formation and the enterprising person. Included are books, articles, films, tapes, games, and research reports published
since 1960.

462. Fields, owen. Simulation in business and office education. Richmond, Virginia State Department of Education, 1978.
82p. ED 164802.

An annotated guide to learning experiences in all levels
of business education.

463. Hern, Ann. Annotated bibliography for business English
for secretarial programs in the junior college. 1975(?). 177p.
ED 118929(MF)

A 1970's bibliography.

464. Bidgood, Diane. Methods and materials for teachers of
integrated business programs. 1976. 86p. ED 127463.

Section III contains an annotated bibliography of 100 selected articles (1970-1976) which describe methods successfully used by teachers of integrated subjects.

465. Instructional materials for adult business and distrib-

utive education. Albany, New York State Education Department, 1969. 81p. ED 037566.

  Arranged by subject areas, with films, filmstrips, charts, transparencies, tapes, and records listed for each area. Annotated.

466. Lambert, Roger H. A Bibliography of free loan materials for business education. Third ed. Madison, Wisconsin Vocational Studies Center, 1976. 28p. ED 132274.

  Annotated.

467. Walsh, Ruth M. Business communications: a selected annotated bibliography. Urbana, IL, American Business Communication Association, 1973. 50p. ED 098583.

  Limited to practical business writing. The fields of communication theory and management information systems are not included.

468. Nasrallah, Wahib. A Selected and annotated guide to business reference sources in the University of Cincinnati libraries. 1978. 38p. ED 168526.

BUSING

469. Moll, Marita. Pupil transportation and school bus safety in Canada. Ottawa, Canadian Teachers Federation, 1977. 33p. ED 149472.

  Includes books, articles, and manuals in addition to legislation of the provinces relevant to the topic. The annotated references were produced 1973 or later.

470. Hamilton, Malcolm C. Desegregation and busing: an annotated bibliography with special reference to the case in Boston. 1976. 29p. ED 137435.

  Includes the legal, political, social, and economic background of the issue.

471. Busing for desegregation: the best of ERIC. ERIC Clearinghouse on Educational Management, 1976. 5p. ED 117784.

  Annotates 13 documents from the ERIC system.

472. Christiansen, Dorothy. Busing. Third ed. New York, Center for Urban Education, 1971. 24p. ED 061378.

  Largely comprised of journal articles in the Center's library, plus documents from the ERIC system.

CABLE TELEVISION See Also EDUCATIONAL TELEVISION and
    TELEVISION

473. <u>Legal bibliography: synopses of cases on cable television</u>.
Washington, DC, Cable Television Information Center, 1974.   25p.
ED 165782 (MF)

These cases relate to broadcast decisions, common carrier
decisions involving microwave and telephone companies, and
cable decisions involving the FCC and local government regulatory authority, pay cablecasting, copyright liability,
and regulatory fees.

474. <u>Bibliocable</u>. Revised ed. Washington, DC, Cable Television Information Center, 1974. 35p. ED 095893 (MF)

Includes 104 books, articles, and reports dealing with
access, applications, franchising, regulation, technology,
and other aspects of cable TV.

475. Molenda, Michael. <u>Annotated bibliography on the educational implications of cable television</u>. Greensboro, University of North Carolina, School of Education, 1972. 29p. ED
059607.

Consists of 156 articles, position papers, conference proceedings, government statements, and legal documents published between 1967 and 1971.

476. Newren, Edward F. <u>Cable television: a bibliographic up-
date</u>. 1976. 38p. ED 157543.

Summarizes earlier bibliographies, and provides comprehensive coverage from 1973 to 1976 in 461 unannotated citations.

477. Holmberg, N. <u>A Selected bibliography: survey of technical requirements for broadband cable teleservices</u>. Washington,
DC, Office of Telecommunications (DOC), 1973. 142p. ED 082
525.

Unannotated. Some entries date back thirty years.

478. Schoenung, James. <u>Cable television: a bibliographic re-
view</u>. Philadelphia, Drexel University, School of Library Science, 1973. 25p. ED 094781.

Areas include cable TV primers and history, bibliographies,
indexes, directories, periodicals and newsletters, government materials, and regulations. Annotated.

CALCULATORS See COMPUTERS

CANADA

479. Bruchet, Susan J. and Gwynneth Evans. <u>Theses in Canada:
a guide to sources of information about theses completed or in</u>

<u>preparation</u>. Ottawa, National Library of Canada, 1978. 32p.
ED 175485.

The sources are presented in three categories; general
bibliographies, specialized bibliographies, and theses
lists by university.

480. Rider, Lillian. <u>Canadian history: a student's guide to
reference sources</u>. Montreal, McGill University Library, 1978.
55p. ED 156577 (MF)

Contains over 250 annotated entries of materials in the
reference library at McGill University.

481. Phillips, Donna. <u>In search of Canadian materials</u>. Winnipeg, Manitoba Department of Education, 1976. 213p. ED 126
351.

Annotated bibliography of the Canadian Studies Project
Committee for school libraries. Over 1000 entries on a
broad range of subjects with an emphasis on Manitoba.
Includes audiovisuals.

482. Rider, Lillian. <u>Canadian manuscripts and archives: a
student's guide to reference sources</u>. Montreal, McGill University Library, 1975. 13p. ED 130966.

Part I lists bibliographies of manuscript and archival
collections, annual reports of government archives, and
union lists of manuscripts with annotations. Part II is
a directory.

483. Silvester, Elizabeth. <u>Canadiana: a student's guide to
bibliographic resources</u>. Montreal, McGill University Library,
1974. 26p. ED 130965.

Annotated. Part I is a national bibliography, while Part
II focuses on the provinces.

484. McAndrew, William J. and Peter J. Elliott. <u>Teaching
Canada: a bibliography</u>. Second ed. Orono, ME, University of
Maine, 1974. 98p. ED 139702.

Annotated list of over 500 entries for elementary and secondary grades, mostly published in the 1960's through 1974.
Includes films, filmstrips, slides, records, kits, and
games on history, culture, geography, and literature. Folktales, biography, and autobiography are also included.

485. Snow, Kathleen M. <u>Canadian books for schools: a centennial listing</u>. Edmonton, Alberta Teachers Association, 1968.
68p. ED 044397 (MF)

320 works written by Canadian authors about Canada. Contains fiction and nonfiction, plays, short stories, and
children's books. Annotated.

486. Silvester, Elizabeth. <u>Canadian politics and government</u>:

a student's guide to reference sources. Montreal, McGill University Library, 1978. 11p. ED 157822 (MF)

Over 50 sources in the University library are listed.

CAREER EDUCATION   See Also EMPLOYMENT   and   OCCUPATIONAL
     INFORMATION

487. Kelleher, Carol H. Second careers: a selected bibliography. Washington, DC, National Council on the Aging, 1973.
15p. ED 087851.

    50 annotated items on mid-career change, retiring military
    personnel, post-retirement careers. Guides and manuals are
    included.

488. Mathieson, Moira B. An Abstract bibliography of teacher
education programs. ERIC Clearinghouse on Teacher Education,
1972. 92p. ED 067382.

    This Part I has 150 entries from RIE dated January 1970 to
    June 1972. Part II is ED 067387 which contains 65 items
    in 47 pages.

489. A Selected bibliography of ERIC career education, career
guidance, and career development resources. ERIC Clearinghouse
on Counseling and Personnel Services, 1975. 18p. ED 108099.

    About 150 documents are included on background, issues,
    system readiness, programs, teaching and learning aids,
    and evaluations. Unannotated.

490. Brandon, George L. Research visibility: guidance and
new careers. Washington, DC, American Vocational Association,
1969. 16p. ED 034882.

    Includes 13 research reviews and a bibliography of 47
    related studies.

491. Ritvo, Phyllis T. An Annotated bibliography of selected
curriculum materials: arts and humanities occupational cluster.
Cambridge, MA, Technical Education Research Center, 1975. 220p.
ED 137606.

    A career exploration resource guide for grades 7 through
    12.

492. Lambert, Roger H. A Bibliography of free loan materials
for career education. Madison, University of Wisconsin, Vocational Studies Center, 1976. 47p. ED 132278.

    Annotated vocational education resource materials.

493. Sackrison, Robert W. and LeVene A. Olson. Annotated
bibliography of commercially produced audio, printed, and vis-

ual career education materials. Huntington, WV, Marshall University, 1975. 35p. ED 109430.

Annotations give the manufacturer, title, purpose, and brief description of the hardware or software included for kindergarten through adult.

494. Supplemental literature resource for adult career education counseling and guidance. Portland, OR, Northwest Regional Educational Laboratory, 1975. 136p. ED 109379.

Contains 103 annotated entries dated 1963 to 1974.

495. York, Edwin. Doctoral dissertations concerning career education, 1960-1971. Edison, NJ, New Jersey Occupational Resource Center, 1972. 32p. ED 109429.

781 dissertations are listed under 55 subject areas.

496. Hoffman, Fae E. Resources: recommendations for adult career resources. Silver Spring, MD, Applied Management Sciences, 1974. 433p. ED 102428.

Contains 700 annotated references to print and audiovisual materials produced in the last five years.

497. Tiederman, David V. Key resources in career education: an annotated guide. ERIC Clearinghouse in Career Education, 1976. 403p. ED 138752.

Each entry includes intended level, purpose, contents, and comments. Indexes are appended.

498. Mitchell, Anita M. The Use of media in career education. ERIC Clearinghouse on Information Resources, 1976. 63p. ED 127974.

The annotated materials are organized according to their instructional setting: classroom, small group, career center, independent study, workshop, and training institute.

499. Goyne, Grover C. Career options in the humanities: a bibliography and program guide. Los Angeles, Pepperdine University, 1976. 16p. ED 128662.

Unannotated.

500. Bibliography on career education. Washington, DC, Office of Education (DHEW), 1973. 100p. ED 086828.

Several hundred articles and documents are included such as pilot projects, curriculum guides, teaching materials, instructional programs, work experience, job training, guidance and counseling, placement and follow-up, and women in the world of work. Publication dates range from 1965 to 1972.

501. Adult career education counseling and guidance literature resource. Portland, OR, Northwest Regional Educational
Laboratory, 1974. 895p. ED 094124 (MF)

Contains 800 annotated documents in seven major groups:
counseling and guidance, adult counseling and guidance,
adult education, career education, competencies, training, and adulthood.

502. Briggs, Lloyd D. and La Nora Bloom. Career education
resources for educational personnel development: an annotated
bibliography. Washington, DC, Office of Education (DHEW),
1975. 105p. ED 126340.

503. Guide to Federal career literature. Washington, DC,
Civil Service Commission, 1976. 40p. ED 126262.

This 1976 version is a guide to Federal recruiting literature which contains descriptions of publications from
43 departments and agencies.

504. Career education: an annotated instructional materials
list K - 12. Rockville, MD, Montgomery County Public Schools,
1975. 219p. ED 118756.

Cites 80 sets of filmstrips for the elementary level, and
140 filmstrips, cassettes, pamphlets, books, kits, and
other materials for the secondary level.

505. Stakelon, Anne E. and Joel H. Magisos. Experienced based
career education: an annotated bibliography. Columbus, Ohio
State University, Center for Vocational Education, 1975. 45p.
ED 118925.

ERIC documents comprise 75 of the entries.

506. Career education resource guide. Lansing, Michigan State
Department of Education, 1975. 407p. ED 118951.

Composed of annotated instructional materials for K-10,
and a smaller section of professional readings.

507. Herr, Edwin L. The Emerging history of career education:
a summary view. Washington, DC, National Advisory Council for
Career Education, 1975. 305p. ED 122 011.

Includes books and articles published from 1971 to 1975.

508. York, Edwin G. 1900 doctoral dissertations on career
education. Edison, NJ, New Jersey Occupational Resource Center, 1975. 235p. ED 121933 (MF)

Includes those available from University Microfilms from
1970 to 1975.

509. Begle, Elsie. Career education: an annotated bibliography for teachers and curriculum developers. Palo Alto, CA,

American Institutes for Research in the Behavioral Sciences, 1973. 312p. ED 073297.

Contains abstracts of 160 references that provide a broad perspective of theories and activities, and descriptive summaries of 100 commonly available children's books for use as resource materials, plus summary information on 69 supplementary references.

510. High, Sidney C. and Linda Hall. Bibliography on Career education. Washington, DC. Office of Education (DHEW), 1973. 104p. ED 079554.

Over 900 references are included. Unannotated.

511. Bailey, Larry J. Facilitating career development: an annotated bibliography. Carbondale, Southern Illinois University, Department of Occupational Education, 1974. 272p.   ED 092674.

512. Tiedeman, David V. and Anna Miller-Tiedeman. Choice and decision processes and careers. Palo Alto, CA, American Institute for Research in the Behavioral Sciences, 1975. 135p.   ED 120338.

An annotated ERIC bibliography accompanies this review.

513. Kimmel, Karen S. Career guidance, counseling, placement, and follow-through program for rural schools. Columbus, Ohio State University, Center for Vocational Education, 1977. 328p. ED 142752 (MF)

This handbook of career guidance resources for grades K-14 includes abstracts of over 500 printed and audiovisual materials.

514. Rural career guidance: abstracts of current research, materials, and practices. San Francisco, Far West Laboratory for Educational Research and Development, 1978. 201p.   ED 151114.

Section I contains 158 abstracts from the ERIC document files, and section II includes 22 articles from CIJE.

515. Matching students and careers: a bibliography. ERIC Clearinghouse on Counseling and Personnel Services, 1970. 12p. ED 039375.

Annotated sources include journal articles, ERIC documents, books, and dissertations dating from 1963 to 1970.

516. Wolters, Virginia. New careers: information sources and bibliography. Madison, University of Wisconsin, 1969. 14p. ED 042009.

The New Careers concept involves helping the disadvantaged to help themselves. Annotated.

517. Snyder, Jane. Bibliography on life/career planning.
Boone, NC, Appalachian University, Center for Instructional
Development, 1976. 229p. ED 135975.

This annotated list was developed for use in a university course on the subject.

518. Anderson, Paul. Career development curriculum for English teachers. Minneapolis, University of Minnesota, College
of Education, 1974. 100p. ED 144069.

The publication describes classroom activities that English teachers can use in helping junior high school students to explore individual career goals. It includes an
unannotated bibliography.

519. Novak, Jan L. Career program resources: a media supplement. Madison, University of Wisconsin Vocational Studies
Center, 1977. 67p. ED 145243.

Over 200 career oriented materials including brochures,
catalogs, guides, and tests. Annotated.

520. Melton, Dale H. Periodical bibliographies on career
education. Bradenton, Florida Career Education Consortium,
1976. 50p. ED 145108.

About 250 entries are listed in a number of subject categories including science, language arts, social studies,
mathematics, physical education, industrial arts, agricultural education, vocational education, and teacher education.

521. Jezierski, Kathleen. Collage: a collection of career
education resources. Columbus, Ohio State University, Center
for Vocational Education, 1977. 93p. ED 145254.

The second and third sections consist of annotated bibliographies of which all entries were chosen from the ERIC
system.

522. Mills, Gladys H. ECS annual meeting bibliography. Denver, Education Commission of the States, 1976. 20p. ED 152
956.

An unannotated selected bibliography on career education
which has 180 entries books, journals, technical reports,
and government publications.

523. Collins, Charlene R. Job development and placement services for vocational education learners in postsecondary institutions: annotated and selected bibliography. Greeley, University of Northern Colorado, College of Education, 1977. 64p.
ED 151572.

Includes about 30 books, articles, reports, pamphlets, and
dissertations.

524. Elsas. Careers in film and television. Washington, DC, American Film Institute, 1977. 12p. ED 153649 (MF)

Includes an annotated bibliography.

525. Hedstrom, Judith E. and Mary Jane Turner. Career education sourcebook. Boulder, CO, Social Science Education Consortium, 1977. 197p. ED 153883.

The project staff analyzed over 750 career education and social studies curriculum programs, and chose 47 as exemplary to annotate and list in this document.

526. Walz, Garry R. Readings: the APGA/Impact workshop on career development and career guidance: selected readings and annotated bibliography from RIE. ERIC Clearinghouse on Counseling and Personnel Services, 1973. 351p. ED 078346.

This ERIC bibliography is for kindergarten through college age levels, plus has some entries for special populations.

527. Johnson, Norbert. Career development materials: an annotated bibliography. Mississippi State College, Coordinating Unit for Vocational Education, 1973. 20p. ED 091559.

Includes 49 books, guides, workbooks, and kits for junior and senior high school students.

528. Carsello, C. J. Professional information on career guidance: an annotated bibliography for counselors and teachers. 1977. 25p. ED 146385.

For ages kindergarten through college, as well as adults interested in career change. Includes 66 books, 21 articles, 13 audiovisuals, and 38 supplementary items that are not annotated.

529. Lawson, Dorothy M. and Dorothea V. McDonald. Career exploration occupational information for the junior high/middle school: a planning curriculum guide. Charleston, Easter Illinois University, 1977. 420p. ED 146350.

Includes units for grades 6 through 9. Section III provides a bibliography for developing a curriculum which includes books, AV, pamphlets, and sources of free materials.

530. York, Edwin G. and Madhu Kopadia. Voices for careers. Trenton, New Jersey State Department of Education, 1972. 72p. ED 069870.

Contains 502 annotated cassette tapes of value to career exploration for grade 7 through adult. The tapes are voices of well-known Americans meant to stimulate vocational interests. A name and topical index are included.

531. Career development resource materials K-6. St. Paul, Minnesota State Department of Education, 1972. 55p. ED 084 365.

400 annotated resources including books, films, filmstrips, records, and guidance kits are listed in three sections: personnel development, the world of work, and occupations.

532. Mamarchev, Helen L. and Beverly Pritchett. Career development: programs and practices. ERIC Clearinghouse on Counseling and Personnel Services, 1978. 122p. ED 163386.

The annotated result of an ERIC system computer search from November 1966 through May 1978.

533. Keene, Lois. The Career education resource center annotated catalog. Englewood, CO, Career Education Resource Center, 1979. 194p. ED 164957 (MF)

All types of materials are included in this 1978-79 version of the catalog. Contains items produced by classroom teachers, commercial publishers, business and industry, and state and federal agencies for levels kindergarten through college.

534. Bhaerman, Robert D. Community resources and community involvement in career education: an annotated bibliography. ERIC Clearinghouse on Adult, Career, and Vocational Education, 1978. 77p. ED 164980.

Includes 125 studies conducted since 1975.

535. Advisory list of instructional media for occupational education. Raleigh, North Carolina State Department of Public Instruction, 1977. 40p. ED 149753.

Includes books, films, and kits for primary through high school grades.

536. Career education resource bibliography. Milford, Delaware State Board for Vocational Education, 1973. 81p. ED 117548.

For levels K-12: includes professional books, curriculum materials, films, tapes, and other AV.

537. Mortier, Thomas E. An Annotated bibliography of career discovery and career development articles for the high school, 1971-1973. Olympia, Washington State Board for Vocational Education, 1973. 71p. ED 117302 (MF)

Philosophy, rationale, minorities, women, and the disadvantaged are included in this list of over 130 items.

538. Career development resources: a bibliography of audiovisual and printed materials K-12. St. Paul, Minnesota State Department of Education, 1975. 139p. ED 117292.

Annotated and arranged by manufacturers. Includes title, media, and grade level indexes.

539. Feingold, S. Norman. Resources: recommendations for

adult career education resources, supplement. Silver Spring,
MD, Applied Management Sciences, 1975. 201p. ED 110854.

A multimedia annotated bibliography.

540. Wernick, Walter. A Career education primer for educators.
ERIC Clearinghouse on Career Education, 1975. 109p. ED 113486.

Part II lists 50 pages of career education literature under
the headings of philosophy, programs, program organization,
administration, evaluation, and education for career education.

541. Sources of information on career education: an annotated
bibliography. Sacramento, California State Department of Education, 1975. 66p. ED 114542.

542. Bibliography on career education. Bridgeport, CT, Public
Schools, 1973. 24p. ED 114506 (MF)

Includes all the commercially produced multimedia used by
Connecticut's exemplary project in career education.

543. Ristau, Robert A. A Model for career education in higher education. Madison, University of Wisconsin, 1975. 29p.
ED 113484.

81 annotated entries published since 1966, including books,
articles, handbooks, reports, manuals, and guides.

544. Hall, Linda and Sidney C. High. Bibliography on career
education. Washington, DC, Office of Career Education (DHEW/
OE), 1979. 62p. ED 177368.

An ERIC bibliography of 460 items dated 1973 to 1978.

545. Babco, Eleanor. Science and engineering careers: a bibliography. Washington, DC, Scientific Manpower Commission,
1974. 53p. ED 161751 (MF)

Unannotated. For secondary students, their parents, and
guidance counselors.

546. Herzog, Doug. A Career education bibliography for guidance and counseling. Watertown, South Dakota Career Education
Project, 1974. 10p. ED 092746.

52 annotated titles for professionals and students.

CARPENTRY

547. Day, Gerald R. and Dennis R. Herschbach. Resource guide
for performance-based carpentry instruction. College Park,
University of Maryland, Bureau of Educational Research, 1974.
95p. ED 105269.

Curriculum resources include an evaluative annotated list
of curriculum guides, texts, and reports, and a title list
of carpentry related books.

CARPETING

548. Bayman, Robert. Carpet selection and rationale for its
use. 1975. 27p. ED 109797 (MF)

Annotated bibliography of eleven items pertinent to schools.

549. Kramer, Roger M. The Use of carpeting in the school: a
selected and annotated bibliography. ERIC Clearinghouse on
Educational Facilities, 1968. 18p. ED 025135.

A comprehensive list that covers selection, maintenance,
and acoustics.

CARTOGRAPHY

550. Steward, Harry. Education and training in mapping sciences: a working bibliography. New York, American Geographical Society, 1969. 72p. ED 049131.

Dated 1955 through 1969, the list includes 720 unannotated
references. Surveying and photogrammetry are included.

551. Taylor, D. R. F. Bibliography on computer mapping. Monticello, IL, Council of Planning Librarians, 1972. 38p. ED
106957.

Unannotated collection of journal articles.

CENSORSHIP   See Also   FREEDOM OF SPEECH

552. Donelson, Kenneth L. Current reading: a scholarly and
pedagogical bibliography of articles and books, recent and old,
on censorship. 1969. 4p. ED 026398.

75 unannotated items in six categories date from 1913 to
1968.

553. Donelson, Kenneth L. Court decisions and legal arguments
about censorship and the nature of obscenity. 1969. 6p. ED
026397.

This article from the Arizona English Bulletin includes
19 court decisions (1727-1967), and 21 articles dating
back to 1938. Unannotated, but the judges opinions in the
cases are quoted.

554. Nyka, James J. Censorship of Illinois high school newspapers. 1976. 55p. ED 151855.

Following an historical review of court decisions regarding students' rights, the paper concludes with a bibliography dealing with student press rights and related topics.

CEREBRAL PALSY

555. Rembolt, Raymond R. and Beth Roth. Cerebral palsy and related disorders, prevention and early care: an annotated bibliography. Two volumes. Austin, University of Texas, Department of Special Education, 1972. 211p. and 213p. ED 084746 and ED 084747.

Volume one contains 602 abstracts, and volume two has 483.

556. Rembolt, Raymond R. and Beth Roth. Cerebral palsy and related developmental disabilities: prevention and early care: an annotated bibliography. Three volumes. Columbus, OH, National Center on Educational Media and Materials for the Handicapped, 1975. 330p., 171p., and 165p. ED 111160, ED 111161, and ED 111162 (MF)

Volume one has 1085 entries; volume two has 433; volume three has 453. All date from 1964 to 1973.

557. Cerebral palsy: exceptional child bibliography. Arlington, VA, Council for Exceptional Children, 1971. 21p. ED 054572.

81 references to research reports, texts, journal articles, and other literature. Topics covered are etiology, clinical diagnosis, educational needs, medical treatment, physical and speech therapy.

CERTIFICATION See TEACHER EVALUATION

CHANGE IN EDUCATION See Also ALTERNATIVE EDUCATION and INNOVATIONS IN EDUCATION

558. Maguire, Louis M. An Annotated bibliography of the literature on change. Philadelphia, Research for Better Schools, 1970. 136p. ED 043965.

The 493 items emphasize educational change, innovation research, administrative change, organizational change, and social and political change.

559. Maguire, Louis M. An Annotated bibliography on administering for change. Philadelphia, Research for Better Schools, 1971. 339p. ED 056246.

560. Marien, Michael D. Alternative futures for learning: an
annotated bibliography of trends, forecasts, and proposals.
Syracuse University, Educational Policy Research Center, 1971.
247p. ED 051571 (MF)

Most of the 936 entries are books on the elementary, secondary, and higher education situations.

561. Runkel, Philip J. and Ann Burr. Bibliography on organizational change in schools; selected, annotated, and indexed.
Eugene, University of Oregon, Center for Educational Policy
and Management, 1977. 193p. ED 147973.

296 entries deal with schools, and 125 entries deal with
other organizations. Also covers citizen participation,
classroom environment, decision making, leadership, communication, and organizational theory.

562. Procedures for managing innovations: analysis of literature and selected bibliography. ERIC Clearinghouse on Educational Administration, 1970. 18p. ED 043116.

An unannotated 78 item list that stresses the how-to aspect of innovations.

563. Bibliography on growth and education. Boulder, CO, Western Interstate Commission for Higher Education, 1974. 42p.
ED 100249.

Unannotated reports and articles on a variety of related
topics.

564. Sacarto, Douglas. Bibliography on growth and education.
St. Paul, Science Museum of Minnesota, 1975. 50p. ED 123148.

567 books and articles published mainly in the 1970's on
topics of growth and its relation to education. Includes
population, planning, cybernetics, futuristics, ethics,
and problem solving.

565. Production plans (marketing plans): analysis of literature and selected bibliography. ERIC Clearinghouse on Educational Administration, 1970. 19p. ED 043120.

This 77 item review analyzes literature on educational
innovation dissemination and adoption. The role of school
personnel and regional education laboratories is included.

566. Alternative organizational forms: analysis of literature
and selected bibliography. ERIC Clearinghouse on Educational
Administration, 1970. 23p. ED 043111.

This 156 item review analyzes literature dealing with
attempts to modify tradional organizational features of
educational systems. Includes different approaches to instruction, alterations in time scheduling, and new organizational forms such as the middle school.

567. Kurland, Norman D. and Richard I. Miller. Selected and
annotated bibliography on the process of change. 1966. 47p.
ED 023025.

Over 170 books, articles, bibliographies, and unpublished
items are included dealing with educational change, social
change, group dynamics, and power structures.

568. Stuart, Michael and Charles Dudley. Bibliography on organization and innovation. Eugene, University of Oregon, 1967.
97p. ED 019722.

Educational change is the subject approached from several
social science perspectives. Unannotated and subdivided
in five categories.

569. Skelton, Gail J. and J. W. Hensel. The Change process
in education: a selected and annotated bibliography. Columbus,
OH, Ohio State University, Center for Vocational and Technical
Education, 1970. 97p. ED 041108.

Covers the communication process, and decision-making
process in educational organizations. 135 items are listed,
some of which are from the ERIC system.

570. Downey, Loren W. Planned change: a selected bibliography. University Council for Educational Administration, 1968.
29p. ED 020569.

Emphasis is on the school as a social organization, and
the contribution of sociological thought in affecting organizational change. 154 books and articles are listed
that were published between 1932 and 1968.

571. Nicodemus, Robert B. Annotated bibliography on change
in education in England and America with an emphasis on science
education. London, Chelsea College of Science and Technology,
1971. 38p. ED 059081.

Includes only research articles, and articles that contain
opinions which appear to have made a unique contribution
to the literature.

CHEATING

572. Wildemuth, Barbara M. Cheating: an annotated bibliography. ERIC Clearinghouse on Tests, Measurement, and Evaluation,
1976. 39p. ED 132182.

Includes 89 references taken from the ERIC system and from
Psychological Abstracts.

CHEMISTRY

573. Williams, Harry and Clyde King. Bibliographic guide for

<u>advanced placement: chemistry</u>. Albany, New York State Department of Education, 1965. 23p. ED 020100.

Unannotated references and audiovisuals for the secondary level.

574. Rushby, N. J. <u>Computers in chemistry teaching: a bibliography and index of CAL packages</u>. University of London, Imperial College Computer Centre, 1979. 33p. ED 176806.

36 books, reports, and papers describe several program packages available for teaching undergraduate, experimental laboratory, physical, nuclear, and X-ray chemistry.

575. Marquardt, D. N. <u>Guidelines and suggested title list for undergraduate chemistry libraries</u>. Stanford University, Advisory Council on Chemistry, 1069. 44p. ED 040037.

Includes policy guidelines for analytical, biological, inorganic, organic, and physical chemistry. The titles listed for these areas exclude basic textbooks.

CHEROKEE INDIANS

576. Hoyt, Anne K. <u>Bibliography of the Cherokees</u>. Little Rock, Southcentral Regional Education Laboratory, 1968. 61p. ED 023533.

Annotated list of books, articles, theses, and government publications dated 1832 to 1968 on all phases of Cherokee life with the emphasis on history.

CHICANAS

577. Portillo, Cristina. <u>Bibliography of writings on La Mujer</u>. Berkeley, University of California, Chicano Studies Library, 1976. 56p. ED 164216.

Areas covered include the arts, education, sociology, economics, history, health, and literature mostly dating from the late 1960's to 1976. There are 283 items primarily on United States Chicanas. Unannotated.

578. Gutierrez, Lewis A. <u>Bibliography on La Mujer Chicana</u>. Austin, University of Texas, Center for the Study of Human Resources, 1975. 20p. ED 125823.

Subjects include art, business, economics, education, family, feminism, health, history, immigration, literature, politics, and sociology. Contains 186 unannotated books and articles published between 1959 and 1974.

579. <u>Mexican American Woman curriculum material: a selected</u>

<u>topics bibliography of ERIC documents</u>. ERIC Clearinghouse on Rural Education and Small Schools, 1977. 80p. ED 152474 (MF)

Unannotated results of a CIJE and RIE search from 1960 to 1977.

580. Chapa, Evey. <u>La Mujer Chicana: an annotated bibliography</u>. Austin, TX, Chicana Research and Learning Center, 1976. 94p. ED 152439.

Includes their involvement in strikes & boycotts, in politics, employment, and in literature. Cites 320 items published between 1916 and 1975.

581. Duran, Pat H. and Roberto Cabello-Argendona. <u>The Chicanas: a bibliographic study</u>. UCLA, Chicano Studies Center, 1973. 51p. ED 076305.

281 partially annotated Chicana oriented books, articles, films, newspapers, dissertations, and documents published between 1923 and 1972.

582. Wheat, Valerie. <u>Hispanic women and education: annotated selected references and resources</u>. San Francisco, Women's Educational Equity Communications Network, 1978. 22p. ED 164 246.

The materials include bibliographies, overviews, statistical profiles, curricula and teaching materials, evaluations of materials, and perspectives on education. 82 items dated 1969 to 1978.

CHICANO LITERATURE

583. Scott, Frank. <u>Chicano literature: a selective bibliography</u>. El Paso, University of Texas, 1977. 17p. ED 147051.

Organized into general works, fiction, short stories, folklore, drama, poetry, history and criticism, and bibliography. Children's literature is also included in the 246 unannotated items dated 1896 to 1977.

584. <u>Chicano children's literature: annotated bibliography</u>. Rohnert Park, CA, Sonoma State College, 1972. 41p. ED 075 158.

Rated on a merit scale of 1 to 5, the list contains 249 books dated 1938 to 1972.

585. Dwyer, Carlota C. <u>Chicano literature: an introduction and annotated bibliography</u>. Austin, University of Texas, Department of English, 1974. 23p. ED 088080.

Includes novels, poetry, anthologies, criticism and bibliographies. Reading levels are indicated.

CHICANOS   See Also   SPANISH SPEAKING

586.   Birdwell, Gladys B.   Chicanos: a selected bibliography.
University of Houston Library, 1971. 62p. ED 048987.

   Concerns history, culture, attitudes, education, and socioeconomic status. About 600 books and 350 articles, plus
   70 ERIC documents, all dated 1877 to 1970.

587.   Cordova, Benito. Bibliography of unpublished materials
pertaining to Hispanic culture in the New Mexico WPA writer's
files. Santa Fe, New Mexico State Department of Education,
1972. 48p. ED 086439.

   An annotated list of 600 different items.

588.   Introduction to development of bibliographies for selection of materials. Fullerton, California State University Library, 1976. 12p. ED 160115 (MF)

   A collection of bibliographies on Chicanos, Cherokee folklore, Blacks in the Armed Forces, and Frederick Douglass.

589.   Selected bibliography pertaining to La Raza in the Midwest and Great Lake States (1924-1973). Revised ed. University of Notre Dame, 1973. 23p. ED 091141.

   Some of the 84 unannotated items are on Puerto Ricans, but
   the focus is on migrant labor. Also covers religion, culture, language, health, and education. Dates of the publications are 1924 to 1973.

590.   Trueba, Henry T. Mexican-American bibliography: bilingual bicultural education. 1973. 26p. ED 085120.

   Unannotated. 306 books and articles are listed.

591.   Spanish heritage and influence in the Western hemisphere.
San Francisco, Unified School District, 1972. 49p. ED 085455.

   This is an unannotated audiovisual bibliography.

592.   Schramko, Linda F. Chicano bibliography: selected materials on Americans of Mexican descent. Revised ed. Sacramento,
CA, Sacramento State College, 1970. 129p. ED 047829.

   1000 annotated items published between 1843 and 1969 are
   categorized under: education, health, history, literature
   and fine arts, social life and problems, and Chicano periodicals.

593.   Ortiz, Ana Maria. Bibliography on Hispano America history and culture. Springfield, Illinois State Commission on
Human Relations, 1972. 35p. ED 080270.

   Includes 50 entries on the Puerto Rican experience in ad-

dition to 145 entries on Chicanos written between 1945 and
1969. The unannotated list is designed for children and
students, teachers, librarians, and parents.

594. Gonzales, Jesus J. Bibliography of Mexican American
studies on various subjects. 1970. 22p. ED 050839.

Art, economy, history, literature, philosophy, political
science, psychology, religion, and sociology are included
in the 300 unannotated entries dated 1917 to 1967.

595. Nogales, Luis G. The Mexican American: a selected and
annotated bibliography. Washington, DC, Institute of International Studies, 1971. 168p. ED 050865 (MF)

Emphasizes scholarly publications and dissertations in
the 444 entries dating from 1919. A list of 64 Chicano
periodicals is included.

596. Barrios, Ernie. Bibliografia de Aztlan: an annotated
Chicano bibliography. San Diego State College, Chicano Studies Center, 1971. 177p. ED 050883.

Over 300 books and articles published from 1920 to 1971
are included on a variety of topics. Mexican history and
pre-Columbian history are present.

597. Trejo, Francisco. Chicano bibliography. Minneapolis
Public Schools, 1972. 13p. ED 076475.

Lists Chicano journals, newspapers, and reference materials in addition to the 150 citations to books, journals,
and a few dissertations.

598. Jablonsky, Adelaide. Mexican Americans: an annotated
bibliography of doctoral dissertations. ERIC Clearinghouse
on the Urban Disadvantaged, 1973. 88p. ED 076714.

Over 700 are listed.

599. Sifuentes, Octavio. Library guide to Chicanos studies.
Ventura, CA, Ventura College Library, 1976. 47p. ED 153778.

1036 resources on the history and culture, social and economic problems dated from 1899 to 1975.

600. Sonntag, Iliana. Guide to Chicano resources in the University of Arizona Library. Tucson, 1976. 110p. ED 153663.

Annotated and listed under 15 subjects.

601. Public libraries and Mexican Americans: a selected topics
bibliography of ERIC documents. ERIC Clearinghouse on Rural
Education and Small Schools, 1977. 16p. ED 152473.

Eleven annotated items from a search between 1970 and 1976
in RIE and CIJE.

602. Information services and Mexican Americans: a selected
topics bibliography of ERIC documents. ERIC Clearinghouse on
Rural Education and Small Schools, 1977. 22p. ED 152476.

     21 annotated items from RIE and CIJE dated 1964 to 1974.

603. Library services and materials for Mexican Americans: a
selected topics bibliography of ERIC documents. ERIC Clearinghouse on Rural Education and Small Schools, 1977. 57p. ED
152477.

     93 annotated items from RIE and CIJE dated 1964 to 1976.

604. Baird, Cynthia. La Raza in films: a list of films and
filmstrips. 1972. 77p. ED 065245.

     Includes pre-Columbian, the Spanish conquest, and modern
Latin America in over 200 entries on the Spanish speaking
in the United States.

605. Guerra, Manuel H. Listing of resource material concerned
with the Spanish speaking. Olympia, Washington State Office
of Public Instruction, 1971. 37p. ED 059830.

     Includes a 28 item migrant education list in addition to
the 190 sources on Mexican Americans.

606. Feeney, Joan V. Chicano special reading selections.
1972. 72p. ED 065255.

     350 annotated works in lists for primary, intermediate,
and advanced students on several aspects of Chicano life
and culture.

607. Harrigan, Joan. More materials tocante los Latinos: a
bibliography of materials on the Spanish-American. Denver,
Colorado State Department of Education, 1969. 34p. ED 031344.

     Over 120 annotated entries list audiovisual aids and read-
ing materials for students of all ages, and for educators.

608. Revelle, Keith. Chicano! a selected bibliography of materials by and about Mexico and Mexican Americans. 1969. 23p.
ED 036381.

     Includes books, articles, newspapers, journals, reports,
and speeches in the 80 annotated items dating from 1939.

609. Materials for those with a Spanish speaking background.
Madison, WI, Cooperative Children's Book Center, 1969. 10p.
ED 036371.

     151 annotated books and audiovisual materials are listed.

610. Harrigan, Joan. Materiales tocante los Latinos. Denver,
Colorado State Department of Education, 1967. 40p. ED 018292.

     An unannotated subject list of materials on the Chicano

611. Books on the Mexican American: a selected listing. Austin, Texas Education Agency, 1972. 15p. ED 080445.

68 annotated books for students and teachers.

612. Tash, Steven and Karin Nupoll. La Raza: a selective bibliography of library resources. Northridge, California State University Library, 1973. 364p. ED 131980.

Includes books, journals, microforms, government documents, records, and filmstrips under each subject heading. An author index is provided for the 3173 sources covering the period 1878 to 1972. ED 175615 is a 155 page supplement of 1600 unannotated entries which was published in 1978.

613. Hispanic Americans in the United States: a selective bibliography, 1963-1974. Washington, DC, Department of Housing and Urban Development, 1974. 31p. ED 096089.

Puerto Ricans and other Carribean peoples are included in this unannotated list of 328 books, reports, articles, and bibliographies.

614. Marquez, Benjamin. Chicano studies bibliography: a guide to the resources of the library at the University of Texas at El Paso. Fourth ed. 1975. 138p. ED 119923.

22 separate bibliographies are included in the 668 books and articles listed from 1925 to 1975. Includes audiovisuals, and is partially annotated.

615. Hyland, Anne. The Mexican American in library materials. Toledo, OH, Public Schools, 1974. 97p. ED 103320.

For K-12, materials are selected to dispel stereotyping. Some annotated 16mm films are also included.

616. Hyland, Anne. A Mexican American bibliography: a collection of print and non-print materials. Toledo, OH, Public Schools, 1974. 90p. ED 103331 (MF)

Annotated.

617. Scott, Frank. M.A. theses on the Mexican American in the University Archives of the University of Texas Library at El Paso. 1975. 21p. ED 116830.

Education, history, literature, political science, religion, and sociology are the subjects of the 81 theses written between 1942 and 1974.

618. Navarro, E. G. Annotated bibliography of materials on the Mexican-American. Austin, University of Texas, Graduate School of Social Work, 1969. 62p. ED 034633.

Includes literature and films in the various fields of social science. 134 citations (1928-1969) are listed.

619. *The Spanish speaking in the United States: a guide to materials.* Washington, DC, Cabinet Committee on Opportunities for Spanish Speaking People, 1971. 171p.   ED 133129 (MF)

Annotates more than 1300 books, bibliographies, and essays dealing with their role in the social, political, educational, and institutional development of the U.S. Includes Chicanos, Puerto Ricans, and Cuban refugees.

620. *A Guide to materials relating to persons of Mexican heritage in the United States: the Mexican American, a new focus on opportunity.* Washington, DC, Interagency Committee on Mexican American Affairs, 1969. 188p.   ED 034644.

Unannotated books, reports, hearings, articles, dissertations, bibliographies, and audiovisual materials.

621. Garza, Ben. *Chicano bibliography: education, the last hope of the poor Chicano.* Davis, University of California Library, 1969. 56p.   ED 034642.

Mexican history and prehistory are included with items relating to Chicano problems such as health, nutrition, employment, working conditions, education, and civil rights. 900 unannotated sources are listed from 1829 to 1969.

622. Segreto, Joan. *Bibliografia: a bibliography on the Mexican American.* Houston, TX, Independent School District, 1970. 25p.   ED 046616.

Includes fine arts, biography, history, and modern life. Over 100 items are listed dating from 1923. Unannotated.

623. *Hispanic heritage: an annotated bibliography.* University of Colorado, School of Education, 1969. 61p.   ED 048079.

Some comments on the quality and intended grade levels are given for the social studies teacher.

624. Strange, Susan and Rhea P. Priest. *Bibliography: the Mexican American in the migrant labor setting.* East Lansing, Michigan State University, 1968. 27p.   ED 032188.

Dated 1928 to 1967, the list includes 275 partially annotated books, articles, reports, proceedings, and theses.

625. *Mexican Americans: a selective guide to materials in the UCSB library.* Santa Barbara, University of California library, 1969. 49p.   ED 032150.

The post-1940 era is emphasized in the 500 entries which are largely sociological.

626. Gomez, Juan. *Selected materials on the Chicano.* UCLA, Mexican American Cultural Center, 1970. 15p.   ED 073869.

Over 200 unannotated books, articles, films, and journals.

627.   Mickey, Barbara H.   A Bibliography of studies concerning the Spanish speaking population of the American Southwest. Greeley, Colorado State College, Museum of Anthropology, 1969. 43p.   ED 042548.

544 unannotated references useful to an anthropological study of the Southwest.

628.   Charles, Edgar B.   Mexican American education: a bibliography.   Mew Mexico State University, 1968.   28p.   ED 016562.

Contains 90 annotated books, articles, and papers written between 1958 and 1967.

629.   Heathman, James E. and Cecilia J. Martinez.   Mexican American education: a selected bibliography.   ERIC Clearinghouse on Rural Education and Small Schools, 1969.   58p.   ED 031352.

This first issue has 156 documents taken from RIE published since 1965. Annual supplements each include over 200 citations. They are numbered ED 048961, 065217, 082881, 097187, 107428, 127053, 144778, and 164167. None are annotated.

630.   Sanchez, George I. and Howard Putnam.   Materials relating to the education of Spanish speaking people in the United States an annotated bibliography.   Austin, University of Texas, Institute of Latin American Studies, 1959.   40p.   ED 041680.

882 entries under 53 subject headings cite books, articles, pamphlets, bibliographies, and dissertations written from 1923 to 1954.

631.   Higher education for Mexican Americans: a selected bibliography with ERIC abstracts.   ERIC Clearinghouse on Rural Education and Small Schools, 1975.   61p.   ED 108818.

22 items from RIE, and 15 articles from CIJE, all dated 1972-1975.

632.   Leyba, Charles.   A Brief bibliography on teacher education and Chicanos.   ERIC Clearinghouse on Teacher Education, 1974.   17p.   ED 090147.

Includes 25 annotated entries from RIE.

633.   Test factors, instructional programs, and socio-cultural-economic factors related to mathematics achievement of Chicano students: a review of the literature.   Stanford University, School Mathematics Study Group, 1975.   33p.   ED 113198.

Summarizes the general results of the literature reviewed and concludes with an annotated bibliography.

CHILD ABUSE

634.   Bibliography on the battered child.   Revised ed.   Wash-

ington, DC, Children's Bureau (DHEW), 1969.   22p.   ED 039942.

Legal, social, medical, and psychiatric aspects of the
battered child syndrome are covered in 282 books, articles,
editorials, theses, and conference papers published between
1946 and 1969.

635. Polansky, N. A. Child neglect: an annotated bibliography.
Athens, University of Georgia, Regional Institute of Social
Welfare Research, 1975. 94p. ED 109841.

130 unannotated entries under the headings of prevention,
identification, etiology, treatment, and sequelae.

636. Kline, Donald F. and Mark A. Hopper. Child abuse: an
integration of the research related to education of children
handicapped as a result of child abuse. Logan, Utah State
University, Department of Special Education, 1975. 136p.   ED
107056.

An annotated bibliography of about 550 articles, plus 18
books, 6 dissertations, and 40 pamphlets.

637. Child abuse: a selective bibliography. Reston, VA, Council for Exceptional Children, 1976. 24p. ED 129002.

Includes 80 annotated documents and journal articles from
1968 to 1975.

638. Naughton, M. James. Child protective services: a biblio-
graphy with partial annotation and cross-indexing. Seattle,
University of Washington, Health Sciences Learning Resources
Center, 1976. 621p. ED 125233 (MF)

Includes 1500 publications concerned with child abuse and
neglect of which 700 have abstracts.

CHILD CARE   See   DAY CARE

CHILD DEVELOPMENT

639. Spencer, Mima. Socialization of young children: an abstract bibliography. ERIC Clearinghouse on Early Childhood
Education, 1973. 40p. ED 075104.

Documents from the ERIC system are included on social behavior, social development, social maturity, social influences, social and moral attitudes, and socioeconomic
status.

640. Dickerson, LaVerne T. Child development: an annotated
bibliography. 1975. 34p. ED 116788.

About 150 entries are taken from books, journals, and book
chapters dealing with factors that influence child growth.

641. Valenstein, Thelma and Martha Miller. Some learning resources in use by CDA programs. Ypsilanti, MI, High/Scope Educational Research Foundation, 1975. 68p. ED 142279.

   Unannotated list of books, pamphlets, and audiovisuals
   arranged by Child Development Associates (CDA) competency
   areas.

642. Hanson, Bette. Child development, assessment, and intervention: a bibliography of research. ERIC Clearinghouse on
Early Childhood Education, 1976. 106p. ED 125752.

   Pertains to any condition that might be expected to inter-
   fere with a child's normal progress in school; the age
   range being birth to five years. Over 1400 unannotated
   items are listed.

643. Mann, Ada Jo. A Review of Head Start research since
1969: working draft. Washington, DC, George Washington University, Social Research Group, 1976. 200p. ED 132805.

   Covers child health, social development of the child, cognitive development, the family, and the community. An annotated bibliography of 700 references to articles on Head
   Start children, services, or projects is included along
   with 90 other articles related to preschool disadvantaged
   children and/or compensatory education.

644. An Annotated bibliography on children. Washington, DC,
Bureau of Libraries and Educational Technology (DHEW/OE), 1970.
77p. ED 068146.

   Highly selective list of 500 items published in the previous five years on the major problems, trends, methodologies, and achievements in the field of child development.

645. Sterman, Cheryl and Carolyn Riley. Bibliography of infant research and development. 1976. 426p. ED 131916.

   Unannotated subject bibliography of books, articles, ERIC
   documents, and others that were mostly published in the
   1970's.

646. Sigel, Irving and Elinor Waters. Child development and
social science education. Part III: abstracts of relevant literature. Detroit, Merrill Palmer Institute, 1966. 91p. ED
023466.

   This part of the four part set contains over 60 annotated
   references to child development source materials for the
   construction of social studies curriculums.

647. The Influence of the cinema on children and adolescents:
an annotated international bibliography. UNESCO, 1961. 107p.
ED 018127.

   This review of research studies gives the conclusions of
   each.

648. Guthrie, P. D. and Eleanor V. Horne. Measures of infant development: an annotated bibliography. Princeton, NJ, Educational Testing Service, 1971. 24p. ED 058326.

Tests for measuring motor development, cognitive growth, intelligence, mental health, social maturity, and concept attainment in infants from birth to 24 months are listed.

649. Johnson, Claudia A. New and innovative services and programs for children: an annotated bibliography. 1971. 65p. ED 060965.

Over 300 items are listed on child development, education, and treatment in this preliminary draft of a PhD thesis.

650. Howard, Norma K. Mother-child home learning programs: an abstract bibliography. ERIC Clearinghouse on Early Childhood Education, 1972. 47p. ED 060962.

81 references in which the parent is the teacher in a structured environment for home learning.

651. Hamby, Trudy M. and Leroy Jones. A Descriptive guide to CDA training materials. Washington, DC, University Research Corporation, 1976. 277p. ED 144697.

162 annotated items for the Child Development Associate (CDA) program, and Head Start programs.

652. Hamby, Trudy M. A Descriptive guide to CDA training materials. Volume two. Washington, DC, University Research Corporation, 1977. 322p. ED 162717.

175 entries are listed in this second volume. Volume one is ED 144697.

653. An Annotated bibliography of child and family development program resources. Washington, DC, Dingle Associates, 1977. 129p. ED 153737.

Includes audiovisuals, journals, and newsletters dealing with child abuse, child care, child development, exceptional children, health and nutrition, parent education, and teenagers.

654. App, Anne. Bibliography: home-based child development program resources. Washington, DC, Office of Child Development (DHEW), 1973. 29p. ED 078925.

This annotated list emphasizes parent involvement.

655. Bolen, Jackie. The Growing years: a bibliography of affective materials for the preschool child. University of Southern California, Instructional Materials Center for Special Education, 1972. 38p. ED 078618.

90 annotations for normal and abnormal children.

656. Reardon, Beverly. Child development: early childhood
education and family life: a bibliography. 1977. 117p. ED
152395.

2500 books are listed as a resource for parents and students. Includes language, self-concept, marriage, death,
divorce, sex education, and many other subjects in the
unannotated listing.

657. Feldman, Ronald and Stanley Coopersmith. A Resource and
reference bibliography in early childhood education and developmental psychology: the affective domain. Davis, University
of California, 1971. 155p. ED 049817.

Achievement motivation, aggression, anger, frustration,
character and moral development, creativity, games, and
social behavior are included in theoretical treatments,
research findings, teacher practices, and curricular materials. Items are dated 1960-1969.

658. Holt, Carol Lou. Annotated film bibliography: child
development and early childhood education. St. Louis, MO,
Child Day Care Association, 1973. 148p. ED 093496.

Films for teacher training, parent education, and for
viewing by children.

659. Early childhood selected bibliography series, Number 5:
Social. ERIC Clearinghouse on Early Childhood Education, 1968.
66p. ED 024472.

Interpersonal relations, sex-role identification, and social reinforcement are the subject areas for the 45 annotated items.

660. Bolen, Jackie. A Bibliography of affective materials
for the adolescent years. University of Southern California,
Instructional Materials Center for Special Education, 1973.
71p. ED 078617.

146 annotated mutimedia instructional materials and books
for teachers who work with normal and abnormal behavior
in junior and senior high schools.

CHILD PSYCHOLOGY

661. Klein, Zanvel E. Research in the child psychiatric and
guidance clinics: a bibliography (1923-1970). University of
Chicago, Department of Psychiatry, 1971. 62p. ED 073849.

1131 unannotated English language references in child psychology and therapy. ED 089876 and 089877 are supplements.

662. Baskin, Linda B. Attachment and children: citations from
selected data bases. ERIC Clearinghouse on Early Childhood

Education, 1979. 40p. ED 165885.

Subject sections are general, institutional, day care, handicapped, separation, child abuse, peer attachment, and neonatal attachment. Unannotated.

CHILD WELFARE

663. Public policy and the health, education, and welfare of children: an abstract bibliography. ERIC Clearinghouse on Early Childhood Education, 1977. 79p. ED 138342.

Includes items from RIE dated 1970-1976, and items from CIJE dated 1972-1977.

664. America's children: bibliography on children's policy issues in the United States. New Haven, CT, Carnegie Council on Children, 1978. 16p. ED 162741.

Focus is on juvenile justice, minority children, handicapped, health, and child advocacy. Partially annotated with 85 entries.

CHILDHOOD EDUCATION   See Also   KINDERGARTEN   and   PRESCHOOL

665. Evaluation bibliography. Chapel Hill, University of North Carolina, Technical Assistance Development System, 1973. 41p. ED 082422.

Contains brief descriptions of 140 tests suitable for children under 6 years, and 10 tests for use with parents.

666. Brown, Doris. Early childhood teaching: an abstract bibliography. ERIC Clearinghouse on Early Childhood Education, 1972. 27p. ED 072842.

These documents from the early 1970's are concerned with teachers, parents as teachers, and paraprofessionals.

667. Cooke, Gary. Films in early childhood education. 1972. 29p. ED 075069.

The annotated list includes some for classroom use, and some intended as guides and resource materials for teachers.

668. Head Start curriculum models: a reference list. ERIC Clearinghouse on Early Childhood Education, 1970. 26p. ED 046517.

Lists references to books, articles, curriculum aids, and progress reports related to the 11 different Head Start curriculum models.

669. A Documentary report on recent research into preschool
education. Strasbourg, France, Council of Europe, Documentation Centre for Education in Europe, 1971. 78p. ED 108734(MF)

    Annotated bibliography of findings from work done in the
    United States and Western Europe since 1968.

670. Screening and assessment of children: an abstract bibliography. ERIC Clearinghouse on Early Childhood Education, 1975.
44p. ED 110160.

    Includes 50 entries from RIE, and 40 other journal articles
    on identifying children with potential learning problems,
    screening for language, reading, and math readiness, and
    identifying the gifted child.

671. Moskovitz, Sarah. Cross cultural early education and
day care: a bibliography. ERIC Clearinghouse on Early Childhood Education, 1975. 34p. ED 110155.

    An ERIC bibliography with references for each of 33 coun-
    tries.

672. Wallat, Cynthia. Early childhood education: organization of reference topics for use in undergraduate courses.
Pittsburgh University, Division of Teacher Development, 1973.
204p. ED 107371.

    The unannotated entries are selected from RIE and CIJE
    from 1967 to 1973. Topics are: programs, environments, e-
    valuations, testing, infants, legislation, parent educa-
    tion, teacher education, health, and learning.

673. Bartholomew, Robert. Indoor and outdoor space for children in nursery-kindergarten programs. Monticello, IL, Council
of Planning Librarians, 1973. 17p. ED 099977.

    Not annotated.

674. Annotated bibliography of FERIC materials for assistance
in implementing Chapter 74-238, "Laws of Florida", pertaining
to early childhood education. Tallahassee, Florida Educational
Resources Information Center, 1975. 63p. ED 122944.

    150 items include child development, diagnostic teaching,
    individualized instruction, kindergarten and scheduling,
    and parent education.

675. Bernbaum, Marcia. Curriculum guides at the kindergarten
and preschool levels: an abstract bibliography. ERIC Clearinghouse on Early Childhood Education, 1971. 40p. ED 060963.

    Includes 60 guides.

676. Preschool and early childhood: a selective bibliography.
Arlington, VA, Council for Exceptional Children, 1972. 31p.
ED 069065.

Includes 91 abstracts dated 1965 to 1971.

677. Anttonen, Judith and Charlotte G. Garman. An Annotated
bibliography of practical tests for young children. Revised ed.
1976. 48p. ED 156683 (MF)

89 tests for children two to six years of age. Types of
tests are: intellectual, oral language, personality, body
coordination, visual, auditory, diagnostic, and placement.

678. Cognition. ERIC Clearinghouse on Early Childhood Education, 1968. 116p. ED 023488.

The 72 annotated items include seven subdivisions: intelligence, mental processes, cognitive style, experimental
studies of learning, concept development, perception and
recognition, and motivation.

679. Language. ERIC Clearinghouse on Early Childhood Education, 1968. 47p. ED 022538.

The 38 annotated entries include: phonology, grammar, vocabulary, verbal learning, and functions of language.

680. Bibliography: early childhood education. ERIC Clearinghouse on Early Childhood Education, 1968. 11p. ED 022544.

Lists 124 unannotated professional level books.

681. Johnson, Harry A. Multimedia materials for teaching
young children: a bibliography of multi-cultural resources.
Storrs, University of Connecticut, National Leadership Institute - Teacher Education, 1972. 27p. ED 088578.

682. Butler, Annie L. Literature search and development of
an evaluation system in early childhood education: researched
characteristics of preschool children: bibliography. Bloomington, IN, Indiana University, 1971. 69p. ED 059781.

This is part one of a study which contains the bibliography of 1300 unannotated items.

683. Boggan, Lucille B. and Satoko Ackerman. Living and learning: an annotated bibliography for those who live and learn
with young children. Washington, DC, Central Atlantic Regional
Educational Laboratory, 1969. 38p. ED 032935.

Psychological, educational, and sociological entries deal
with issues of deprived youth and other special problems.
The 52 items include books, essays, speeches, and articles
on the education of young children.

684. Advisory list of instructional media for kindergarten/
early childhood education. Raleigh, North Carolina State Department of Public Instruction, 1977. 27p. ED 149749.

Annotated books, films, records, games, puzzles, and kits.

685. Bibliography on early childhood. Washington, DC, Office
of Child Development (DHEW), 1970. 37p. ED 078928.

Unannotated list of books, pamphlets, and reprints about
preschool children and early childhood education.

686. Selected convention and special conference papers Index.
Arlington, VA, Council for Exceptional Children, 1973. 65p.
ED 078613.

A cumulative index of authors and titles of papers given
at the Council's various annual and special conventions
from 1962 to 1972. Unannotated.

687. Yan, Rose. Early childhood education: a selected, annotated bibliography. Aurora, Ontario, York County Board of Education, 1973. 52p. ED 078942.

Descriptions of Canadian and U. S. programs are included,
in addition to historical surveys, and background publications.

688. Early childhood programs: topical bibliography. Reston,
VA, Council for Exceptional Children, 1977. 21p. ED 146732.

90 annotated programs for handicapped and disadvantaged
children are listed 1972-1976.

689. Early childhood education. Ottawa, Canadian Teachers
Federation, 1972. 48p. ED 069366.

This bibliography includes 318 books and papers, 228 articles, and 66 theses from 1966 to 1971 gathered from several Canadian, American, and British indexes. Unannotated.

690. The Development and education of children outside the
United States: an ERIC abstract bibliography. ERIC Clearinghouse on Early Childhood Education, 1979. 26p. ED 164125.

Included are research reports, program descriptions, and
government projects and policies relating to children's
health, education, and welfare. The items were gathered
from a search of RIE and CIJE from 1975 through 1978.

691. Thomas, Susan B. Research on approaches to early education: an abstract bibliography. ERIC Clearinghouse on Early
Childhood Education, 1974. 84p. ED 092262.

References were selected from the ERIC system, 1971-1974.
Includes studies of parental involvement, research on the
longterm effects of educational intervention programs, and
research on specific program models and model comparisons.

692. Head Start curriculum models: a reference list. Revised
ed. ERIC Clearinghouse on Early Childhood Education, 1971.
27p. ED 048947.

Citations are to books, articles, and progress reports.

693.   Goolsby, Thomas M. and Barbara M. Darby.   A Bibliography
of instrumentation methodology and procedures for measurement
in early childhood learning.   University of Georgia, Research
and Development Center in Educational Stimulation, 1969.   21p.
ED 046978.

    The test entries are listed by type; achievement, mental
ability, personality, etc. Reports, articles, and books
are also included dating 1960 to 1968.

CHILDREN AND YOUTH   See Also   INFANTS

694.   Jackson, Clara O.   Celebrating the International Year
of the Child: related bibliography.   Kent State University,
1979.   13p.   ED 175470.

    The annotated list includes publications on children's
rights, child advocacy, and on the United Nation's program
for this special observation.

695.   Sugarman, Jule M.   Research relating to children.   Washington, DC, Children's Bureau (DHEW), 1969.   149p.   ED 035908
(MF)

    Subjects include health, social, family, growth and devel-
opment, socioeconomics, and special groups of children.

696.   Ohlendorf, George W. and William P. Kuvlesky.   A Bibliography of literature on status projections of youth.   Texas
A & M University, 1967.   19p.   ED 020382.

    142 unannotated citations are listed in this part 3 of a
series. This part is on residence, income, and family orientation.

697.   Ohlendorf, George W.   A Bibliography of literature on
status projections of youth.   Texas A & M University, 1967.
36p.   ED 020381.

    323 unannotated citations are listed in this part 2 of a
series. This part is on educational aspirations and expectations. Books and journal articles are included from
1949 to 1967.

698.   Youth.   London, International Planned Parenthood Federation, 1976.   24p.   ED 134466 (MF)

    Annotated entries published since 1970 are on: youth work
and policy, youth and human rights, employment, family
planning, sex education, and population education.

CHILDREN'S LITERATURE   See Also   ADOLESCENT LITERATURE

699.   Meehan, Betty-Jo.   The Old Pacific Northwest as found in

children's literature: a bibliography. 1976. 11p. ED 132 062.

> 50 annotated children's books about the Northwestern United States include fiction, nonfiction, and biography published from 1963 to 1973. For grade levels 1 through 9.

700. Uhreen, David. Books for children with Oregon settings: a revision of a similar booklist compiled by the Jackson County Library System. 1976. 7p. ED 132063.

> Most of the 50 annotations are for fiction, and are on frontier life, pioneer families, geography, Indians, mining, trading, fishing, and the Oregon Trail.

701. Ladley, Winifred C. Sources of good books and magazines for children: an annotated bibliography. Newark, Delaware, International Reading Association, 1970. 17p. ED 079705.

> Of the 68 sources listed, none are published before 1950.

702. Kelly, R. Gordon. American children's literature: an historiographical review. 1973. 22p. ED 088105.

> The five bibliographic essays are from a special issue of American Literary Realism, Volume 6, No. 2, and survey the subject from 1870 to 1910.

703. Guilfoile, Elizabeth. Books for beginning readers. National Council of Teachers of English, 1962. 79p. ED 029 870.

> Annotated survey of 320 books published since 1957.

704. Pederson, Beverly. Something to chew on: Canadian fiction for young adults. Saskatoon, Saskatchewan, Public Library, 1979. 40p. ED 184132.

> Over 300 annotated titles are in this list about Canada or by Canadian authors.

705. Ott, Helen Keating. Helping children through books: a selected booklist. Revised ed. Bryn Mawr, PA, Church and Synagogue Library Association, 1979. 40p. ED 184582 (MF)

> Most of the annotated entries are fiction that deal with special concerns and contemporary problems.

706. Books for under fives in multi-racial Britain. London, Commission for Racial Equality, 1978. 12p. ED 182355.

> 40 annotated titles considered useful for ethnic minority children.

707. Stahlschmidt, Agnes. Bringing children and books together: a bibliography of methods. 1979. 19p. ED 181459.

> 49 annotations that suggest activities that vary from being

highly structured with expected outcomes to open-ended
with more flexible responses for use in teaching literature appreciation.

708. Stalker, John C. Energy conservation in tradebook selection: a bibliographic approach to children's literature.
1979. 13p. ED 179927.

An unannotated guide to the field of children's literature to help teachers discover and evaluate the available
books.

709. Reading with your child through age 5. New York, Child
Study Association of America, 1970. 41p. ED 045681 (MF)

Over 175 annotated books of all types for reading to a
child.

710. Sacco, Margaret. A Selective bibliography of government
publications on children's books and children's literature,
and bibliographies of children's books and children's literature. 1976. 17p. ED 137822.

Includes local, state, national, and international government publications with brief annotations.

711. Rollock, Barbara. The Black experience in children's
books. Revised ed. New York Public Library, Countee Cullen
Branch, 1974. 128p. ED 099440.

Annotated list of books suitable for children of all ages,
and some books intended for adults to share with children.

712. Tea and muskets: a Bicentennial booklist. Somerville,
Mass., Boston Area Women in Libraries, 1976. 21p. ED 139427
(MF)

An annotated evaluative list of historical literature for
grades K-8 including fiction set in America from the earliest settlers to 1812. Focuses on books featuring women
as the main characters.

713. Petty, Mary E. Suspense books to read to primary children: a bibliography. 1976. 8p. ED 128799.

Annotated.

714. Thumler, Debra L. Friendship values in children's books:
a bibliography. 1976. 12p. ED 128815.

The appropriate grade or reading level is indicated for
the 70 annotated titles.

715. Perisho, Priscilla. Interfaith relations in children's
books: a bibliography. 1976. 14p. ED 128808.

Annotated historical and fictional selections include the

Jewish, Quaker, Mormon, and Amish groups as well as others.

716. Odland, Norine. New books for young readers. University of Minnesota, College of Education, 1975. 101p. ED 128777
(MF)

   Part 1 is annotated for ages 3 to 13, and part 2 is for
   over 13 years. A supplementary volume is ED 147760.

717. Monson, Dianne L. and Bette J. Peltola. Research in
children's literature: an annotated bibliography. Newark, Del.
International Reading Association, 1976. 97p. ED 126489.

   332 entries include master's and PhD theses, mostly dated
   from 1960 to 1974.

718. Root, Shelton L. Adventuring with books: 2400 titles
for pre-K to grade 8. Urbana, IL, National Council of Teachers
of English, 1973. 404p. ED 071092.

   Mostly published since 1967, the annotated list includes
   books in all fields.

719. Cianciolo, Patricia. Adventuring with books: a booklist
for pre-K to grade 8. New edition. National Council of Teachers of English, 1977. 507p. ED 141829.

   Recommended age levels and annotations are given for the
   books which cover all types and subject areas.

720. Advisory list of instructional media: easy books. Raleigh, North Carolina State Department of Public Instruction,
1977. 48p. ED 149744.

   Annotated list of primary or elementary level books.

721. Hornburger, Jane M. Coping with change through literature. 1975. 13p. ED 105521 (MF)

   Presents an annotated bibliography of 18 children's books
   that deal with change.

722. Aubrey, Irene E. Notable Canadian children's books.
Ottawa, National Library of Canada, 1974. 103p. ED 136815.

   The annotated bibliography aims to show the historical
   development of the literature. Included are books from
   the 18th Century to the modern period, lists of books
   which were awarded the bronze medal from 1947 to 1975,
   and a list of fiction for the young French Canadian.

723. Baron, Bonnie and Sara Hadley. Bibliography: books for
children. Washington, DC, Association for Childhood Education
International, 1977. 103p. ED 149348 (MF)

   Classified by age and subject with an author and title
   index. Annotated fiction and nonfiction are included.

724. Hillyer, Mildred. Bibliography of Spanish and Southwestern Indian cultures library books. Grants, NM, Municipal
Schools, 1969. 24p. ED 047846.

The 239 books were published between 1926 and 1968. Some
include annotations and suggested age levels, while many
are about famous members of their ethnic groups.

725. Odland, Norine and Carmen Richardson. A Bibliography
of materials relating to children's literature. 1973. 9p.
ED 089298.

This paper has 103 partially annotated books and articles.

726. Anttonen, Judith. An Annotated bibliography of children's books to refresh and update the early childhood teacher.
1976. 77p. ED 147861 (MF)

300 titles for ages two to seven years are classified in
23 categories.

727. Books for mentally retarded children. Cincinnati, OH,
Hamilton County Public Library, 1973. 35p. ED 084749.

Annotated list of books for educable and trainable mentally retarded children six to 15 years of age. 300 titles.

728. Madden, Peter. Guide to children's magazines, newspapers, and reference books. Washington, DC, Association for
Childhood Education International, 1977. 13p. ED 158290 (MF)

Annotated. Includes sports, science, history, and hobbies.

729. Diamond, Joan. Picture books for creative thinking: a
bibliography. Cedar Falls, University of Northern Iowa Extension Service, 1974. 20p. ED 114772.

An annotated list intended for use in the primary grades.

730. Brochtrup, William A. Too good for words: an annotated
bibliography of wordless children's books. 1975. 14p. ED
112379 (MF)

Describes 119 books for children without words that were
mostly published in the 1970's.

731. Bibliography: books for children. Washington, DC, Association for Childhood Education International, 1974. 112p.
ED 092871 (MF)

Includes annotated fiction and nonfiction, picture and
picture story books, ABC's, poetry, and reference books.

CHILDREN'S PLAY

732. Quilitch, H. Robert. Bibliography of children's play

and toys. 1974. 15p. ED 101749.

Lists 237 titles from 1893 to 1970 taken from library catalogs, Psychological Abstracts, Child Development Abstracts, Education Index, and the Reader's Guide.

733. Rogers, Mary Brown and Luciano L'Abate. Bibliography on play therapy and children's play. Atlanta, Georgia State College, Child Development Laboratory, 1969. 26p. ED 035897.

Books, articles, dissertations, and reports dealing with normal and abnormal children. The unannotated citations date from 1925 to 1968.

734. Kaylan-Masih, Violet and Janis Adams. Imaginary play companion: annotated abstract bibliography. Lincoln, University of Nebraska, Agricultural Experiment Station, 1975. 52p. ED 113034.

An historical perspective is presented with 48 entries dating from 1891 to 1975 which include books and articles.

CHINA

735. Goldberg, Robert. Recent materials on China and U. S.-China relations: an annotated bibliography. Columbus, Ohio State University, Service Center for Teachers of Asian Studies, 1974. 36p. ED 109002.

This bibliographic essay includes books, articles, and audiovisuals from 1971 to 1974.

736. Williams, Jack F. China in maps, 1890-1960: a selective and annotated cartobibliography. East Lansing, Michigan State University, Asian Studies Center, 1974. 293p. ED 120042.

Includes government published maps produced by the United States, China, Japan, Great Britain, Germany, France, and the USSR.

737. Ching, Eugene and Nora C. Audiovisual materials for Chinese studies. New York, American Association of Teachers of Chinese Language and Culture, 1974. 178p. ED 139706 (MF)

300 films, 61 feature-length films, 122 filmstrips, 53 slide collections, 98 records, and 132 audiotapes are annotated in this compilation. Grade levels range from elementary to college.

738. Gregory, Peter B. and Noele Krenkel. China: education since the cultural revolution: a selected, partially annotated bibliography of English translations. San Francisco, Evaluation and Research Analysts, 1972. 29p. ED 064463.

Includes books, pamphlets, papers, and journal articles.

CHINESE

739. Lau, Chau-Mun. The Chinese in Hawaii: a checklist of
Chinese materials in the Asia and Hawaiian collections of the
University of Hawaii Library. 1975. 61p. ED 142597.

   Includes mainly works in Chinese, and relevant Chinese-
   English bilingual items published since 1897.

740. Wang, W. and Liu, Lillian. Bibliography and glossary
for Chinese grammar. Columbus, Ohio State University, Research
Foundation, 1963. 143p. ED 011645.

   An unannotated bibliography of 937 titles from American
   and foreign books, and articles. The citations are given
   in Pinyin and English.

741. Dunn, Robert. Chinese-English and English-Chinese dictionaries in the Library of Congress: an annotated bibliography. Washington, DC, Library of Congress, 1977. 145p. ED
155932.

   Includes subject dictionaries and polyglot dictionaries.

CHURCH LIBRARIES

742. White, Joyce L. Church library literature, 1950-1975:
a bibliographic essay. 1978. 50p. ED 183140.

   A review of the literature on libraries in or attached
   to church buildings.

CINEMA   See   FILMS

CITIES   See   URBAN STUDIES

CITIZENSHIP

743. Bibliography for teachers of Americanization. Albany,
New York State Education Department, 1968. 25p. ED 039440.

   Contains 13 bibliographies and 52 teaching guides of which
   27 are devoted specifically to citizenship. Annotated.

CIVIL LIBERTIES

744. Eichman, Barbara. A Selective bibliography of audiovisual materials reflecting a civil liberties theme. New York,
American Civil Liberties Union, 1976. 78p. ED 140794.

Annotated list of 167 motion pictures, films, filmstrips, records, cassettes, plus 16 games and simulations for the elementary and secondary levels.

CLASSICS   See LATIN

COLLECTIVE BARGAINING

745. Julius, Daniel J. and John C. Allen. Collective bargaining in higher education. New York, City University, Bernard Baruch College, National Center for the Study of Collective Bargaining in Higher Education, 1975. 173p. ED 115140 (MF)

An annotated bibliography of 992 items with reference to affirmative action, arbitration awards, court cases, NLRB decisions, and state and federal legislation.

746. Smith, H. Dean. Negotiations sourcebook: sources of information on collective bargaining for educators. Seattle, University of Washington, Bureau of School Service and Research, 1973. 69p. ED 096754.

Unannotated.

747. Myers, Donald A. A Bibliography on professionalism and collective bargaining. Washington, DC, American Federation of Teachers, 1974. 25p. ED 098186.

Includes 191 annotated entries.

748. Garfin, Molly. Collective bargaining in higher education: bibliography. New York, City University, Bernard Baruch College, National Center for the Study of Collective Bargaining in Higher Education, 1977. 200p. ED 139334 (MF)

This is the fifth in a series of annual bibliographies regarding faculty and non-faculty in public and private colleges and universities. The annotated list mostly includes 1976 citations, but does have earlier ones that were not included in its earlier annual volumes.

749. Garfin, Molly. Collective bargaining in higher education: bibliography. 1976. 241p. ED 125448 (MF)

This is the fourth annual bibliography of the National Center (see above). It covers academic freedom, bargaining in Canada, faculty attitudes, grievance procedures, tenure, strikes, students, and women.

750. Julius, Daniel J. and Kenneth Dressner. Higher education collective bargaining: other than faculty personnel. New York, City University, Bernard Baruch College, 1975. 142p. ED 122706 (MF)

Includes books, articles, and newsletter items.

751. Moore, Connie. Negotiation bibliography. Kansas City,
University of Missouri, School of Education, 1975. 56p. ED
122404 (MF)

  Includes 271 annotated entries since 1968 pertinent to
  teacher strikes and negotiations. Books, articles, theses,
  pamphlets, papers, and addresses are included.

752. Ubben, Gerald C. Collective negotiation and the educational administrator: annotated bibliography. Knoxville, University of Tennessee, University Council for Educational Administration, 1967. 30p. ED 019759

  Lists 274 books, pamphlets, and articles on the subject
  published between 1956 and 1967.

753. Markus, Frank W. Negotiations bibliography. Kansas City,
University of Missouri, School of Education, 1968. 46p. ED
023178.

  Over 500 items published between 1964 and 1967 are listed
  without annotation. Audiovisuals and dissertations are
  also included.

754. Piele, Philip. Selected bibliography on collective negotiations. ERIC Clearinghouse on Educational Administration,
1968. 12p. ED 024133.

  About 150 entries are in this unannotated bibliography
  for the years 1966 and 1967.

755. ERIC abstracts: a collection of ERIC document resumes
on collective negotiations in education. Washington, DC, A-
merican Association of School Administrators, 1969. 35p. ED
035978.

  62 entries are listed from all issues of RIE through June
  1969.

756. Piele, Philip and John S. Hall. Administrator techniques
in collective negotiations: a guide to recent literature. ERIC
Clearinghouse on Educational Administration, 1969. 23p. ED
027643.

  Covers examples of negotiable items, organizing data, the
  ground rules, the team, the environment, the proposals,
  impasse situations, and writing and implementing the final
  outcome. 44 annotated entries are included.

757. Hudson, Bennett and James L. Wattenbarger. Collective
bargaining in higher education: a selected, annotated bibliography. Gainesville, University of Florida, Institute of Higher Education, 1972. 17p. ED 060849.

  Entries cover the role of the administrator, unions and
  professional associations, and strikes and sanctions. Recent books and articles are predominant.

758. Allen, John C. Collective bargaining in higher education, 1971-1973. New York, City University, National Center
for the Study of Collective Bargaining in Higher Education,
1973. 58p. ED 077416.

    Unannotated.

759. Resource manual for basic skills in collective bargaining in the public schools. Rutgers University, Institute of
Management and Labor Relations, 1977. 245p. ED 140407.

    Includes books, articles, films, and instructional games
    for educators.

760. Weinberg, William. Training resources manual for impasse procedures in public school negotiations. Rutgers University, Institute of Management and Labor Relations, 1977.
167p. ED 140408.

    Designed as an instructional aid and as a ready reference
    for more complex problems of bargaining. Includes films.

761. Tener, Barbara. Training resource manual on arbitration
in the public schools. Rutgers University, Institute of Management and Labor Relations, 1976. 164p. ED 140409.

    Lists a number of other relevant bibliographies. Not an-
    notated.

762. Tice, Terrence N. Resources on academic bargaining and
governance. Washington, DC, Academic Collective Bargaining
Information Service, 1974. 49p. ED 093198.

    Brief annotations are included.

COLLEGE See HIGHER EDUCATION and COMMUNITY COLLEGES

COLONIAL HISTORY See Also REVOLUTIONARY WAR

763. Glosser, Mary Sue and Marcia B. Goldstein. Teachers'
Bicentennial resources manual. Boston, Massachusetts Bicentennial Commission, 1976. 146p. ED 123151.

    Contains ideas and resources to help K-12 teachers plan
    Bicentennial projects and teach about U. S. colonial his-
    tory.

764. Job, Amy G. America's revolutionary period, 1760-1785:
a bibliography of the holdings of the Sarah Byrd Askew Library
and the AV center of the William Paterson College of New Jersey. 1975. 126p. ED 117748 (MF)

    A subject list of 850 book and non-book items; includes
    songs and music. Annotated.

765.   Parker, Marion and Stella Denton.   1776: a guide to Bicentennial books, 1763-1790.   New York, Newburgh Free Library,
1975.   89p.   ED 117746.

This annotated bibliography lists over 300 fiction and
non-fiction books that are contained in the children's
department of the library.

766.   Wiley, Karen B. and Roxy Pestello.   Materials for teaching about the Bicentennial: an annotated bibliography.   ERIC
Clearinghouse for Social Studies/Social Science Education,
1975.   99p.   ED 113218.

Over 100 entries are included for the elementary and
secondary teacher.

COLORADO

767. Kolesar, A.   A Bibliography of Colorado State University
imprints in the Colorado State University Library.   1978. 28p.
ED 157533.

170 unannotated items. This is the first supplement to
the first edition, ED 143376.

COMMUNICATION   See Also   NONVERBAL COMMUNICATION

768.   Yang, Shou-Jung.   Mass communications in Taiwan: an annotated bibliography.   Singapore, Asian Mass Communications
Research and Information Centre, 1977.   76p.   ED 149370 (MF)

Most of the entries are in Chinese, and include published
and unpublished materials dated 1945 to 1973.

769.   Mass Communication in India: an annotated bibliography.
Singapore, Asian Mass Communication Research and Information
Centre, 1976.   230p.   ED 149369 (MF)

Describes published and unpublished material written in
English from 1945 to 1973. The entries are grouped into
21 sections, and an author- title index is provided.

770.   Yu, Timothy.   Mass Communication in Hong Kong and Macao:
an annotated bibliography.   Singapore, Asian Mass Communication
Research and Information Centre, 1976.   43p.   ED 149368 (MF)

Most of the 122 items are written in Chinese, and a few
are in English. All are dated 1945 to 1973.

771.   Panday, Narendra R.   Mass Communication in Nepal: an annotated bibliography.   Singapore, Asian Mass Communication Research and Information Centre, 1977.   44p.   ED 158305 (MF)

772.   Espejo, Cristina and Guy de Fontgalland.   Mass Communi-

cation in Singapore: an annotated bibliography. Singapore,
Asian Mass Communication Research and Information Centre, 1977.
70p.   ED 149367 (MF)

Most of the entries are written in English, and a few are
in Chinese. All are dated 1945 to 1973.

773.   Hachten, William A. Mass communication in Africa: an
annotated bibliography. Madison, University of Wisconsin,
1971.   130p.   ED 136285.

Includes over 500 works by American, European, and African
scholars and writers which concern the African press, film,
broadcasting, periodicals, and other aspects of mass communications.

774.   Falcione, Raymond L. Organizational communication abstracts, 1975. Urbana, IL, American Business Communication
Association, 1976.   127p.   ED 144160 (MF)

Includes about 700 books, articles, papers, dissertations,
and government documents that were published in 1975 that
are relevant to organizational communications. Interpersonal, intragroup, and intergroup aspects are covered.

775.   Rahim, Syed A. Communication policy and planning for
development: a selected annotated bibliography. University
of Hawaii, East-West Center, 1976.   282p.   ED 150670.

Lists 395 English language publications that pertain to
53 countries. Indexed by subject and country.

776.   A Bibliography of literature used in communication theory courses. Austin, University of Texas, Center for Communication Research, 1973.   127p.   ED 078478.

Unannotated list of readings used in several major universities in the United States.

777.   Weber, Dianne. Teleconferencing: a bibliography. Madison, University of Wisconsin, EDSAT Center, 1971. 42p.   ED
066053.

Includes 168 unannotated references to books, parts of
books, articles, conference papers, and news items.

778.   Lanigan, Richard L. Communication theories and models:
a bibliography of contemporary monographs. 1977. 12p.   ED
145494.

Unannotated list of books, papers, essays, and articles
from special encyclopedias.

779.   Casmir, Fred L. Sources in international and intercultural communication. ERIC Clearinghouse on Reading and Communication Skills, 1977.   17p.   ED 141845.

Annotated bibliography of books, articles, and ERIC items.

780.   Morris, Clyde.   Communication and conflict resolution.
East Lansing, Michigan State University, Department of Communication, 1969.   84p.   ED 061214.

The focus of the 46 annotated entries is on ways to com-
municate as an alternative to destructive behavior.

781.   Norberg, Kenneth D.   Iconic signs and symbols in audiovisual communication: an analytical survey of selected writings
and research findings.   Sacramento State College, 1966.   129p.
ED 013371.

The field of analogic, or iconic, signs was explored to
develop an annotated, comprehensive, and current bibliography, and prepare an analysis of the subject.

782.   Seelye, H. Ned and V. Lynn Tyler.   Intercultural commun-
icator resources.   Provo, Brigham Young University, Language
Research Center, 1977.   106p.   ED 140622.

An annotated compilation of books, audiovisuals, and other
bibliographies.

783.   Littlejohn, Stephen W.   A Bibliography in small group
communication.   1969.   78p.   ED 067712.

500 annotated citations from sources in various subject
areas published since 1950. Includes expository articles,
theoretical writings, and experimental studies.

784.   Balachandran, Sarojini.   Employee communication: a bibliography.   Urbana, IL, American Business Communication Association, 1976.   55p.   ED 130331.

On communication in management, reports to employees, attitude surveys, employee publications, bulletin boards, and
employee evaluation, ratings, motivation, and training.
Includes partially annotated items published since 1965.

785.   Givens, Randal J.   Review of the literature of the feedback concept.   1974.   63p.   ED 099913.

An extensive unannotated bibliography accompanies this
paper that was presented at the annual meeting of the
Texas Speech Communication Association. Theoretical and
experimental literature is reviewed.

786.   Litvin, Joel.   Value orientations in teaching interpersonal communication.   1976.   46p.   ED 147883.

Lists representative readings for a humanistic approach,
a skills-oriented approach, and a business-oriented approach. The bibliography is an unannotated part of a
conference paper.

787.   Wellman, Barry and Marilyn Whitaker.   Community, network,
communication: an annotated bibliography.   Monticello, IL,

Council of Planning Librarians, 1972.   140p.   ED 106963.

Annotated entries concerned with the impact of communications on networks of primary relationships and their organization into communities.

788.   Weaver, Richard L.   Bibliography of sources for verbal
and nonverbal communications activities.   1976.   15p.   ED 137
869.

57 entries with annotations and evaluations for elementary,
secondary, and college classrooms are given.

789.   Gruner, Charles R.   An Annotated bibliography of empirical studies of laughter-provoking stimuli as communication.
1973.   11p.   ED 074533.

Most of the studies are experimental in design and report
original research on humor as communication. Includes 54
items from 1939 to 1972.

790.   White, Anthony G.   Towards a scientific study of information and communication theory relative to groups and organizations: a bibliographic essay.   Monticello, IL, Council of
Planning Librarians, 1974.   19p.   ED 108291 (MF)

Discusses the application of mathematical ordering and
analysis to the study of organizations, and examines the
relationship between organizational structure and interpersonal communication.

COMMUNICATION DISORDERS

791.   Lunin, Lois F.   Information sources in hearing, speech,
and communication disorders.   Baltimore, Information Center
for Hearing, Speech, and Disorders of Human Communication,
1968.   311p.   ED 028576.

759 annotated books, articles, and films are included.

COMMUNICATION SATELLITES

792.   Gray, E. M.   Information products resulting from satel-
lite studies at the Institute of Telecommunication Sciences.
Washington, DC, Office of Telecommunications (DOC), 1977.   95p.
ED 163982.

The annotated bibliography covers 1958 through 1976.
Topics are propagation, antennas, modulation or signal
design, electromagnetic interference and frequency sharing, system design and assessment, and noise.

793.   Morgan, Robert P. and Jai P. Singh.   A Guide to the lit-

erature on applications of communications satellites to educational development. ERIC Clearinghouse on Educational Media
and Technology, 1972. 23p. ED 060661.

An introductory and non-technical survey. Annotated.

794. An Annotated bibliography of UNESCO publications and
documents dealing with space communication, 1953-1977. Paris,
UNESCO, 1977. 102p. ED 175465 (MF)

Contains its papers, reports, and articles.

COMMUNICATION SKILLS

795. Salsbury, Marilyn L. Occupational communication competencies: a list of audiovisual aids for helping pupils acquire
occupationally useful oral communication capabilities. Olympia,
WA, Washington Research Coordinating Unit for Vocational Education, 1968. 23p. ED 029951.

Includes 83 annotated films, filmstrips, and tapes for use
by teachers.

796. Daly, John A. Communication apprehension: a preliminary
bibliography of research. 1974. 18p. ED 101406.

Works concerning reticence, stage fright, speech anxiety,
and similar constructs in public speaking and interpersonal communication are included. Writing apprehension is
also listed in the 243 unannotated entries.

COMMUNITY COLLEGES See Also HIGHER EDUCATION

797. Dennison, John D. and Alex Tunner. The Impact of Community colleges: bibliography. Revised ed. Vancouver, BC,
BC Research, 1972. 153p. ED 116737.

With a special emphasis on Canadian material, the list includes over 1800 items from 1965 to 1971. The history and
philosophy are covered along with faculty and teaching,
students and curriculum, systems analysis, administration
and finance. Unannotated.

798. Wallace, Terry H. The Division/department chairperson
in the community college: an annotated bibliography. Pennsylvania State University, Center for the Study of Higher Education, 1975. 27p. ED 111458.

Focuses on the role of the chairperson, but includes
selection and appointment procedures. Entries were selected from the previous 11 years of Education Index and
Dissertation Abstracts in addition to CIJE. Some entries
are pertinent to the secondary school.

799. Riess, Louis C. Faculty participation in the governance
of higher education: a bibliography. 1970. 14p. ED 043330.

Includes 161 entries with particular emphasis on the community college. Unannotated.

800. Davis, Harold E. Bibliography of innovation and new
curriculum in American two-year colleges, 1966-1969. 1970.
17p. ED 044107.

Includes 165 articles, books, and reports for the period
1966-1969, and covers nursing, community services, disadvantaged, remedial, inner city, and foreign students
among other topics.

801. Rinnander, Elizabeth. About administration and governance. ERIC Clearinghouse for Junior College Information,
1977. 26p. ED 144631.

Presents an overview of community college governance within the categories of administrative organization, cluster
colleges, multicampus districts, the board of trustees,
collective bargaining, management by objectives, and management information systems.

802. Booth, Barbara. State reports on two-year colleges: a
selected bibliography of ERIC documents. ERIC Clearinghouse
for Junior College Information, 1977. 90p. ED 144632 (MF)

Includes abstracts of 531 state reports for the period
1968 through 1977. 46 of the fifty states are represented.

803. Giles, Louise. Aspects of the junior college field: a
bibliography, 1950-1968. Washington, DC, American Association
of Junior Colleges, 1969. 81p. ED 031193.

This is an unannotated subject bibliography from the association's Project for New Institutions.

804. Reusch, Natalie R. The Junior and community college
faculty: a bibliography. Revised ed. ERIC Clearinghouse for
Junior College Information, 1969. 41p. ED 031251.

292 unannotated entries.

805. Warren, Alex M. An Annotated bibliography of the American two-year college: its role and function. 1968. 59p.
ED 026991.

Technical colleges, vocational colleges, municipal colleges,
and community colleges are represented in this list of articles and books primarily published between 1965 and 1968.

806. Roueche, John E. and Natalie Rumanzeff. The Junior and
community college faculty: a bibliography. UCLA, National
Faculty Association of Community and Junior Colleges, 1968.
20p. ED 016490 (MF)

807. Roueche, John E. The Junior and community college: a bibliography of doctoral dissertations, 1964-1966. Washington, DC, American Association of Junior Colleges, 1967. 22p. ED 013656 (MF)

214 are listed with a subject index. Unannotated.

808. Ogilvie, William K. Abstracts of graduate studies on the community college, 1961-1966. Northern Illinois University, 1966. 83p. ED 013607.

Lists 21 masters degree theses.

809. Giles, Frederic T. and Omar L. Olson. Community college boards of trustees: an annotated bibliography. Seattle, University of Washington, 1967. 39p. ED 014974.

Includes published and unpublished material of particular relevance to the new trustee, and concerning the role of the trustee.

810. Parker, Franklin. The Junior and community college: a bibliography of doctoral dissertations, 1918-1963. Washington, DC, American Association of Junior Colleges, 1965. 48p. ED 011194.

More than 600 dissertations are listed under several subject headings. Not annotated.

811. Burnett, Collins W. The Community junior college: an annotated bibliography with introductions for school counselors. Columbus, Ohio State University, School of Education, 1968. 129p. ED 024382.

Includes books and articles, but excludes dissertations and unpublished material. Covers the history, philosophy, objectives, functions, organization, student personnel, and research and evaluation.

812. Boss, Richard D. and Roberta Anderson. Community junior college: a bibliography. Corvallis, Oregon State System of Higher Education, 1967. 179p. ED 020724.

A classified list of materials mostly published since 1956. Unannotated.

813. The Community college: the public junior college movement. Fifth ed. Gainesville, University of Florida, College of Education, 1968. 14p. ED 022467.

Over 200 entries date from 1924 to 1967, and include books, articles, and documents. Not annotated.

814. Sanchez, Bonnie. About community college community education and community services. ERIC Clearinghouse for Junior College Information, 1977. 23p. ED 140927.

Contains 40 annotated references since 1965.

815. Alvarado, Andrew. About community college finance. ERIC
Clearinghouse for Junior College Information, 1977. 17p. ED
140928.

Contains 27 annotated references since 1973 including books,
articles, and ERIC documents.

816. Owen, Harold James. Self-study manual for state governing and coordinating boards for community/junior colleges. Second ed. National Council of State Directors of Community/jun-
ior Colleges, 1977. 41p. ED 151035 (MF)

This manual includes an unannotated bibliography of 171
references concerning community college governing boards.

817. Berry, James J. Instructional methods at the community
college, 1970–1977. 1978. 32p. ED 151038.

An unannotated bibliography is included in this paper
which discusses individualized instruction, programmed
instruction, student-faculty interactions, and peer tutoring.

818. Rader, Hannelore B. The Newest dimension of the community college - community services: a selected and annotated bibliography. 1978. 21p. ED 156301.

Includes 77 items on the problems of community program
development. ERIC materials since 1970 are listed in addition to selected books, articles, and dissertations.

819. Myles, Leslie and Thomas W. MacClure. An Annotated bibliography on establishing an office of institutional research.
1974. 21p. ED 095960.

68 citations cover the need, organization, objectives, and
subject matter for any proposed community college research
institute.

820. Kapraun, E. Daniel. Community services in the community
college: a bibliography. University of Virginia, Center for
Higher Education, 1973. 26p. ED 101768.

Over 250 references on both the theoretical and practical
aspects of the subject. The unannotated items are drawn
from CIJE, RIE, and the Reader's Guide.

821. Sanchez, Bonnie. About community college remedial and
developmental education. ERIC Clearinghouse for Junior College
Information, 1977. 26p. ED 142264.

This annotated brief highlights important literature since
1968. 49 references.

COMMUNITY DEVELOPMENT See Also URBAN STUDIES

822. Mezirow, Jack D. The Literature of community development: a bibliographic guide. Washington, DC, Agency for International Development, 1963. 184p. ED 048565.

1585 items in twenty subject fields designed for use in training Peace Corps personnel. Unannotated.

823. Reaves, John S. Educational materials for community resource development: an annotated bibliography for extension professionals. Ithaca, NY, Northeast Center for Rural Development, 1978. 116p. ED 164217.

Most of the citations were published in the 1970's, but some of the 400 date back to 1948. Community services, housing, land use, natural resources, and development processes and strategies are included.

824. Survey of literature prior to 1967 on the community with selected annotations, reading lists, and periodicals. Ottawa, Canadian Department of Forestry and Rural Development, 1968. 45p. ED 033314.

Provides 41 items on community planning, services, and participation. Some entries refer to social change, human services, and the dimensions of poverty.

825. Stanley, T. Brock. Community facilities planning: a selected interdisciplinary bibliography. Monticello, IL, Council of Planning Librarians, 1971. 28p. ED 101435.

Includes items on history, principles, goals, forecasting, administration, and financing.

826. Brown, Ruth E. Community action programs: an annotated bibliography. Monticello, IL, Council of Planning Librarians, 1972. 39p. ED 106961.

Items discuss the formation and operation of community action agencies, and their impact on the community.

COMMUNITY EDUCATION

827. Hiemstra, Roger P. Community education: a bibliography. Lincoln, University of Nebraska, Department of Adult and Continuing Education, 1971. 11p. ED 056284.

Cites 82 unannotated books and articles.

828. Mackey, Greg. Community education multimedia bibliography. 1977. 235p. ED 143355.

The purpose of this annotated bibliography in chart form is to acquaint community educators with what media materials are available where, based on a survey of community education centers and state department offices.

829. <u>Illinois Consortium of Institutions of Higher Learning</u> <u>for Community Education interim report</u>. 1976. 52p. ED 148 193.

The report includes a 21 page unannotated bibliography on community education.

830. Christensen, Ardis. <u>Bibliography on community education</u>. ERIC Clearinghouse on Rural Education and Small Schools, 1974. 74p. ED 091092.

39 annotated documents from RIE, and 47 journal articles from CIJE are included, some dating from 1956.

COMMUNITY SCHOOLS

831. <u>A Resource book on community school centers</u>. New York, Educational Facilities Laboratory, 1979. 27p. ED 168191 (MF)

An annotated compendium of general background information, and for planning community schools.

832. Thornton, James E. and Joseph Gubbels. <u>The Community</u> <u>school: a working bibliography</u>. Burnaby, BC, Pacific Association for Continuing Education, 1974(?). 23p. ED 109465.

Includes 90 books and reports, 52 articles and conference proceedings, and 24 dissertations. Most entries were published in the 1960's and 1970's, and are unannotated.

833. <u>Community schools: the best of ERIC</u>. ERIC Clearinghouse on Educational Management, 1974. 4p. ED 095609.

Contains 22 annotated entries on the development, role, financing, curriculum, and research.

834. Higham, Charlene E. <u>Joint occupancy</u>. 1975. 25p. ED 109800 (MF)

Fifteen annotated articles and reports dealing with the joint use of buildings and facilities by schools and other public or private organizations.

835. <u>Community schools: the best of ERIC</u>. ERIC Clearinghouse on Educational Management, 1976. 5p. ED 130374.

Twelve more annotated documents from the ERIC system on shared facilities, including legal matters, and the philosophical assumptions and attitudes on the community education movement.

836. <u>Bibliographies in education: community schools</u>. Ottawa, Canadian Teachers Federation, 1972. 33p. ED 090355.

Unannotated books, articles, theses, and ERIC documents.

837. <u>Community schools</u>. Ottawa, Canadian Teachers Federation, 1972. 33p. ED 086695.

Contains 99 books, 367 articles, and 26 theses written from 1967 to 1972. Unannotated.

COMMUNITY STUDY

838. Quinn, Bernard. <u>Understanding the small community: some informational resources for the town and country apostolate</u>. Washington, DC, Center for Applied Research in the Apostolate, 1967. 64p. ED 026154.

This annotated bibliography focuses upon understanding life in the small community. Includes case studies, community theory, and rural sociology.

COMMUTING STUDENTS

839. Kazlo, Martha P. and Mark W. Hardwick. References on <u>commuting students</u>. University of Maryland, Office of Commuter Services, 1973. 6p. ED 087367.

Includes 64 unannotated references.

COMPENSATORY EDUCATION

840. Watt, Lois B. <u>Books related to compensatory education</u>. Washington, DC, Office of Education, Bureau of Research, 1969. 52p. ED 034840 (MF)

The annotated bibliography relates to the needs of disadvantaged children, and lists the recent textbooks and trade books for young people, plus professional resources for teachers.

841. Jayatilleke, Raja. <u>Collegiate compensatory programs</u>. ERIC Clearinghouse on the Urban Disadvantaged, 1976. 71p. ED 128498.

This annotated bibliography covers materials from the ERIC system from 1970 through 1976. Some topics are college bound students, college admission, entrance examinations, open enrollment, placement, college preparation, and Black colleges.

842. <u>Project Follow Through: an ERIC abstract bibliography</u>. ERIC Clearinghouse on Early Childhood Education, 1977. 111p. ED 140978.

Cites ERIC documents and journal articles from 1975 to 1977.

843. Select bibliography on high risk education for Appalachian youth: programs and practices. Washington, DC, Appalachian Regional Council, 1969. 3p. ED 039076.

Unannotated list of 47 books, articles, and reports published between 1960 and 1969.

COMPETENCY BASED EDUCATION   See   PERFORMANCE BASED EDUCATION

COMPETENCY TESTS   See also   TESTS AND MEASUREMENTS

844. Annotated bibliography on minimum competency testing.
Portland, OR, Northwest Regional Education Laboratory, 1978.
28p. ED 156186 (MF)

The 52 citations were compiled to assist educators in designing and implementing minimum competency testing programs.

845. Wildemuth, Barbara M. Minimal competency testing: issues
and procedures: an annotated bibliography. ERIC Clearinghouse
on Tests, Measurements, Evaluation, 1977. 20p. ED 150188.

Includes 28 items.

COMPUTER ASSISTED INSTRUCTION

846. Suydam, Marilyn N. The Use of computers in mathematics
education: bibliography. ERIC Information Analysis Center for
Science, Mathematics, and Environmental Education, 1973. 100p.
ED 077733.

Topical annotated list of books and articles on general
uses, and tutorial, practice, and problem-solving modes.

847. Clark, Richard E. The Best of ERIC: recent trends in
computer assisted instruction. ERIC Clearinghouse on Educational Media and Technology, 1973. 15p. ED 076025.

Categories are: planning and utilization, case studies,
attitudes toward CAI, cost effectiveness, research trends,
and future prospects. 40 annotated articles make up the
bibliography.

848. Barnes, O. Dennis and Deborah B. Schrieber. Computer
assisted instruction: a selected bibliography. Washington,
DC, Association for Educational Communications and Technology,
1972. 240p. ED 063769 (MF)

835 articles, books, parts of books, technical reports,
and memos comprise this list. An author index is provided
to these entries compiled from many different sources.

849. Rushby, N. J. <u>Computer based learning in the Soviet Union</u>. University of London, Imperial College Computer Centre, 1978. 16p. ED 176805 (MF)

Topics include: problem solving models, decision strategies, programmed instruction, simulation, educational games, databases, and testing. The 86 references are to papers and journal articles.

850. Rushby, N. J. <u>Computer based learning in Europe: a bibliography</u>. University of London, Imperial College Computer Centre, 1978. 18p. ED 176804.

Topics include: teacher training, simulation, rural education, model construction, program evaluation, instructional sequencing, and computer graphics. 172 references.

851. Twelker, Paul A. and Carl J. Wallen. <u>Instructional uses of simulation: a selected bibliography</u>. Portland, OR, Northwest Regional Educational Laboratory, 1967. 242p. ED 019755.

Recent annotated references also include the design of instructional systems.

852. Fletcher, J. D. <u>A Note on the effectiveness of computer assisted instruction</u>. Stanford University, Institute for Mathematical Studies in Social Science, 1972. 11p. ED 071450.

Annotated list of 16 studies that discuss programs that have been effectively used in math, science, nursing, and language.

853. Beard, Marian. <u>Computer assisted instruction: the best of ERIC</u>. ERIC Clearinghouse on Information Resources, 1976. 42p. ED 125608.

Includes documents from 1973 through mid-1976. Annotated.

854. <u>Computer uses in instructional programs: bibliographies in education</u>. Ottawa, Canadian Teachers Federation, 1969. 19p. ED 034728.

From the previous five years 60 general references are listed. 144 other annotated items are on specific subjects such as guidance and counseling, simulation and games, testing, and problem solving.

855. Lyman, Elisabeth R. <u>PLATO highlights</u>. Third revision. Urbana, University of Illinois, Computer-based Education Laboratory, 1975. 37p. ED 124143.

Describes the development of PLATO (programmed logic for automatic teaching operations), and lists chronologically PLATO publications written between 1961 and 1975.

COMPUTERS See also DATA PROCESSING

856. Suydam, Marilyn N. Calculators: a categorized compilation of references. Columbus, OH, Calculator Information Center, 1979. 188p. ED 171572.

Most references are annotated and some are non-American
resources.

857. Computer science and technology publications. Washington, DC, National Bureau of Standards, Institute for Computer
Sciences and Technology, 1977. 20p. ED 145834.

Most items are dated for the three previous years, and include computer security, networking, and automation technology.

858. Computer simulation: a bibliography of selected Rand
publications. Santa Monica, CA, Rand Corporation, 1971. 40p.
ED 057620.

Annotates over 150 of their publications on theory, design,
and use of simulation.

859. Computing technology: a bibliography of selected Rand
publications. Santa Monica, CA, Rand Corporation, 1972. 118p.
ED 057619.

Includes over 300 abstracts of unclassified studies dealing with various aspects of the subject dating from 1963
to 1971.

860. Bibliography: computers in the mathematics and science
classroom. Sunnyvale, CA, Fremont Union High School District,
1975. 29p. ED 107296.

The annotated list includes print and AV materials for
students and teachers.

861. Gibson, E. Dana. Audiovisual aids for automation. San
Diego State College, 1965. 92p. ED 012306.

Includes 100 films, 84 filmstrips, and 31 slide sets on
data processing, numerical control, and computer systems.
Most entries are annotated and were produced in the early
1960's.

862. Computer science: a dissertation bibliography. Ann Arbor, MI, University Microfilms International, 1978. 96p. ED
161668 (MF)

Lists over 6300 doctoral dissertations, and includes a
title list of masters theses from 1962 to 1974. ED 161669
is an 80 page supplement that has 916 more doctoral theses
and 49 selected masters theses from 1975 to 1977.

863. Dirr, Peter J. Computers in education: a bibliography.
1974. 8p. ED 105677.

Contains 78 unannotated references dated 1968 to 1974.

CONFLICT

864. Bolton, Charles K. and Mark E. Lindberg. Conflict: the conditions and processes in community, organizations, and interpersonal relationships. Monticello, IL, Council of Planning Librarians, 1971. 22p. ED 101434.

  Unannotated.

865. Curriculum materials on war, peace, conflict, and change: an annotated bibliography with a listing of organizational resources. New York, Center for War/Peace Studies, 1972. 37p. ED 081712.

  Compiled from a survey of teachers and other professionals, the document describes 13 projects, two of which are the Amherst Project and the Harvard Social Studies Project.

CONFLICT RESOLUTION

866. Edney, C. W. and Randolph T. Barker. Conflict and conflict resolution: a bibliography. 1975. 45p. ED 111033.

  The role of communication is the focus in sections on intrapersonal and interpersonal conflict, group and societal conflict, organizational and political conflict, and theoretical bases of conflict. Unannotated.

867. Bjerstedt, Ake and Evy Gustafsson. Towards peace education: abstracts on some reports related to conflict resolution and peace education. Malmo, Sweden, School of Education, Department of Educational and Psychological research, 1977. 92p. ED 151252.

  Describes 90 ERIC documents published from 1966 to 1976 on all educational levels.

868. Conflict resolution: the best of ERIC. ERIC Clearinghouse on Educational Management, 1975. 5p. ED 108273.

  Eleven annotated items on theory and practice as it relates to education. Entries are drawn from fields of psychology, sociology, political science, and management science.

CONSERVATION See ENVIRONMENTAL EDUCATION

CONSUMER EDUCATION See also HOME ECONOMICS

869. Johnston, William L. Selected audiovisual materials for consumer education. New version. Trenton, New Jersey State

Department of Education, 1974. 42p. ED 099271.

Listed in this annotated bibliography are 92 films, kits, slide sets, and audio cassettes produced between 1964 and 1974 for the elementary and secondary levels. Topics include purchasing, advertising, money management, credit, fraud, and consumer laws.

870. Walstad, William B. Annotated bibliography of micro-economic analysis for consumer economics workshops. 1975. 92p. ED 121657.

258 books, pamphlets, articles, games, films, and kits designed for secondary level students are listed, all produced between 1960 and 1970.

871. Forgue, Raymond E. Audiovisual materials in adult consumer education: an annotated bibliography. Blacksburg, Virginia Polytechnic Institute, 1978. 37p. ED 159379.

Includes 85 titles on fraud and deception, food and nutrition, credit, energy, housing, and money management.

872. Spitze, Hazel T. Teaching aids for consumer and home-making programs. Urbana, University of Illinois, Division of Home Economics Education, 1972. 153p. ED 117541.

191 annotated items for high school classes with teaching techniques.

873. Johnston, William L. and Nancy B. Greenspan. A Guide to instructional resources for consumers' education. Washington, DC, Office of Consumers' Education (DHEW), 1977. 67p. ED 163 203.

For professional and general use with all ages, 295 print and non-print resources and teaching aids are described.

874. Nyheim, Charlotte and Sharon Smith-Hangsen. Consumer resource guide: a selected bibliography. Sacramento, California State Department of Consumer Affairs, 1977. 64p. ED 147 255 (MF)

Over 1000 unannotated multimedia resources are listed for educators and/or individual consumers. Most were published since 1970.

875. Bailey, Lena C. Review and synthesis of research on consumer and homemaking education. Columbus, Ohio State University, Center for Vocational and Technical Education, 1971. 78p. ED 048482.

Entries include the disadvantaged and teacher education also. The 110 reports and papers were written between 1966 and 1969.

876. Gorman, Anna M. and Joel Magisos. Bibliography of re-

search on consumer and homemaking education. Columbus, Ohio
State University, Center for Vocational and Technical Education, 1970. 69p. ED 039336.

877. Consumer education resources. Ypsilanti, Eastern Michigan University, Consumer Education Center, 1976. 85p. ED
135972.

Annotated entries include guides, newsletters, magazines,
textbooks, kits, filmstrips, cassettes, and 16mm films
for elementary grades through adult.

878. USDA consumer education materials for wise food shopping
and nutritious meal planning. New York, Consumer and Marketing Service (USDA), 1971. 34p. ED 060461.

Topics include food stamps, donated foods, food inspection
and grading, and child nutrition. Unannotated.

879. Consumer education bibliography. New York Public Library, 1971. 199p. ED 056962 (MF)

This annotated second edition contains over 4000 books,
pamphlets, AV aids, and teacher materials. It has a subject index.

880. Garman, E. Thomas. Developing a resource center in consumer education: an annotated bibliography. DeKalb, Northern
Illinois University, 1971. 146p. ED 058137.

Contains 1300 entries arranged under 18 content areas,
such as food, clothing, automobiles, credit, savings, in-
vestments, life insurance, taxes, and careers.

881. Garman, E. Thomas. Bibliography of books on consumer
affairs. 1978. 9p. ED 184531.

Unannotated list of books published from 1963 to 1978.
115 entries.

882. An Annotated bibliography for consumer and homemaking
education. Springfield, Illinois State Board of Vocational
Education and Rehabilitation, 1974. 97p. ED 099612.

Designed for secondary school level through adult.

883. Blucker, Gwen. An Annotated bibliography of games and
simulations in consumer education. Springfield, Illinois
State Office of the Superintendent of Public Instruction, 1974.
102p. ED 103332 (MF)

Evaluations of 32 simulations are given under topics of
money management, insurance, credit, credit unions, consumer law, consumer frauds, economics, ecology, clothing,
housing, and automobiles.

884. Vickers, Carole A. A Guide to free and inexpensive con-

sumer education resources. Huntington, WV, Marshall University, Department of Home Economics, 1976. 330p. ED 130949.

The annotated multimedia bibliography of 149 lists falls
under 20 subject headings, and were mostly published in
the 1970's.

CONTINUING EDUCATION

885. Kleis, Russell J. Bibliography on continuing education.
East Lansing, Michigan State University, Office of Studies in
Continuing Education, 1972. 113p. ED 078242.

Unannotated. Principally books divided into 12 sections.

886. Continuing education in the professions. ERIC Clearinghouse on Adult Education, 1969. 100p. ED 033250.

225 annotated items that include other bibliographies,
surveys, and general works in the whole spectrum of professional occupations.

887. Continuing education in the professions. ERIC Clearinghouse on Adult Education, 1967. 12p. ED 014026.

An earlier version of the above which contains 21 items.

888. Continuing education for teachers: bibliographies in education. Ottawa, Canadian Teachers Federation, 1975. 71p.
ED 115652.

A partially annotated bibliography arranged under 12 subject headings. Most of the entries are from 1970 to 1975,
and some are available through ERIC.

889. Selected bibliographic survey of resources for community services and continuing education. University of Maryland,
Division of Conferences and Institutes, 1975. 33p. ED 118831

Within 14 subject categories, 114 books and 32 professional journals are listed.

890. Pezullo, Diane. About staff development: a brief highlighting important literature since 1970 on community college
staff development. ERIC Clearinghouse for Junior College Information, 1978. 26p. ED 158794.

Annotated entries also include rural and small colleges,
and national cooperative and consortium arrangements.

COOPERATIVE EDUCATION

891. Haines, Peter G. and David Hyslop. A Reference bibliography for general work experience and cooperative occupation-

al plans of instruction. East Lansing, Michigan State University, Department of Secondary Education and Curriculum, 1971(?) 43p. ED 065732.

The unannotated references include unpublished state bulletins, research reports, and items in the ERIC system.

892. Brownlee, Roland H. A Selected bibliography of references to cooperative education in two-year and four-year colleges and universities. 1974. 20p. ED 095952.

Includes books and articles, some with brief annotations, with the emphasis on business and liberal arts programs.

893. Reference lists for HECE occupational areas. Austin, Texas Education Agency, 1975. 76p. ED 118858.

Includes annotated citations for reference books, pamphlets, and AV material in the following areas: art and craft aide, bridal consultant, child care aide, clothing assistant, consumer aide, dietetic aide, fabric coordinator, floral designer, food service employee, food tester, and textiles.

894. Cohen, Arthur M. and Lewis C. Solmon. Cooperative education - a national assessment: an annotated bibliography. Silver Spring, MD, Applied Management Sciences, 1976. 326p. ED 129860.

134 items that concern program description, evaluation, and impact, feasibility studies, across-program assessments, methodological concerns, and bibliographies and guidelines.

895. An Annotated bibliography of instructional materials in cooperative occupational education. Springfield, Illinois State Board of Vocational Education and Rehabilitation, 1974. 157p. ED 099615.

Fields covered include applied biology and agriculture, business, marketing, management, health, industry, and personal and public services.

896. Work experience and cooperative education programs: bibliographies in education. Ottawa, Canadian Teachers Federation, 1974. 29p. ED 102315.

Lists 126 books, 217 articles, and six theses. Not annotated.

897. Cooperative education planning study: annotated bibliography. Pittsburgh, PA, CONSAD Research Corporation, 1975. 59p. ED 109510.

106 entries cover its history, philosophy, and present status.

898. Stakelon, Anne E. and Joel H. Magisos. Evaluation of

work experience, cooperative education, and youth manpower programs: an annotated bibliography. Columbus, Ohio State University, Center for Vocational and Technical Education, 1975. 67p.
ED 117184.

Includes over 110 items from CIJE, RIE, and the National
Technical Information Service.

899. Leventhal, Jerome I. Readings in cooperative education.
Philadelphia, Temple University, Department of Distributive
Education, 1976. 51p. ED 123474.

Selected for review were 23 journal articles on theory and
planning, implementation, special programs, and the post-
secondary level.

900. Peart, Edna F. Characteristics of cooperative agreements
between post-secondary institutions and business, industry,
and labor: annotated and selected bibliography. Greeley, University of Northern Colorado, College of Education, 1977. 98p.
ED 151570.

Lists readings which offer guidelines or criteria for initiating or writing post-secondary cooperative educational
agreements, and reviews agreements selected that represent
a variety currently being utilized or advocated for use in
the adult cooperative education field.

COOPERATIVE EXTENSION SERVICE

901. Cooperative extension. ERIC Clearinghouse on Adult Education, 1968. 64p. ED 024002.

This annotated bibliography contains 109 indexed entries
arranged under several headings.

CORRECTIONAL EDUCATION   See also   REHABILITATION

902. Nuttall, John H. A Bibliography for tutors in correctional facilities. 1975. 8p. ED 114804.

19 annotated books and articles related to remedial reading for institutionalized adults.

903. Semberger, Franklin M. A Bibliography for correctional
education. Tallahassee, Florida State University, Department
of Adult Education, 1970(?) 71p. ED 052446.

Unannotated list concerning rehabilitation of prison in-
mates through high school completion, literacy training,
and trade skills such as carpentry and electronics.

904. Correctional education: a bibliography. Washington, DC,

Bureau of Prisons, 1972. 16p. ED 061438.

Over 100 unannotated entries under the headings of: history and philosophy, organization and administration, program content, evaluation of programs, methods, and current trends.

905. Plotz, Robert L. Probation education programs: an annotated bibliography. New York, City University, Center for Advanced Study in Education, 1977. 36p. ED 154164.

Includes 75 books, articles, dissertations, papers, and speeches on prison education and probation published between 1960 and 1976.

906. Nichols, Jack D. A Selected bibliography on training in correctional institutions. Fayetteville, Arkansas Vocational Education Research Coordinating Unit, 1969. 34p. ED 034 041.

Contains 78 partially annotated citations from 1958 to 1968. The books and articles are supplemented by a list of 44 publications of the Rehabilitation Research Foundation.

907. Willis, Michael J. Resources for educators of adults: annotated bibliography for the education of public offenders. Albany, New York State Education Department, Division of Continuing Education, 1978. 265p. ED 159428 (MF)

908. Boston, Guy D. Techniques for project evaluation: a selected bibliography. Washington, DC, National Institute of Law Enforcement and Criminal Justice, 1977. 71p. ED 147337.

Annotated compilation to assist federal, state, and local agencies.

CORRESPONDENCE STUDY

909. Macken, E. Study of needs and technological opportunities in home-based education. Stanford University, Institute for Mathematical Studies in Social Sciences, 1975. 185p. ED 115895.

Contains a literature review on correspondence study in the United States, and an extensive annotated bibliography surveying the instructional uses of computers, television, and other media as they relate to the subject.

910. Macken, E. Home-based education: needs and technological opportunities. Stanford University, 1976. 133p. ED 126 331.

Literature review on correspondence study, and an annotated bibliography on computer assisted instruction.

911. Lambert, Michael P. A Bibliography on education for home study educators. Washington, DC, National Home Study Council, 1974. 9p. ED 094202.

Unannotated current and classic titles are included.

COUNSELING See also GUIDANCE

912. Sanchez, Bonnie M. About community college counseling: a brief highlighting important literature since 1972 on counseling in the community college. ERIC Clearinghouse for Junior College Information, 1978. 27p. ED 160141.

48 annotated items from the ERIC system.

913. Stern, Lewis R. Applications of video in counseling and counselor training: an annotated reference source. 1975. 26p. ED 117636.

Over 300 articles and texts dated 1947 through 1975 on the subject as it relates to psychotherapy and therapist training.

914. Counseling and psychotherapy: a selective bibliography. Arlington, VA, Council for Exceptional Children, 1972. 32p. ED 074683.

Over 100 abstracts from the holdings of the Exceptional Child Information Center. The documents are dated 1968 to 1972.

915. Galant, Richard and Nancy J. Moncrieff. Outreach counseling: relevant resources in high interest areas. ERIC Clearinghouse on Counseling and Personnel Services, 1974. 16p. ED 105370.

64 annotated dissertations, articles, and ERIC documents on creative approaches in counseling that go beyond the traditional office oriented concept.

916. Dosa, Marta L. Information counseling: the best of ERIC. ERIC Clearinghouse on Information Resources, 1977. 44p. ED 152336.

A review essay that includes articles from CIJE and ERIC documents.

917. Glick, Barry. Counseling and personnel services in adult education. ERIC Clearinghouse on Adult Education, 1969. 51p. ED 029234.

Headings are: student personnel services, counseling services, admissions and selection, retention and dropouts, and financial assitance. Includes 94 annotated entries dating from the late 1960's.

918. An Elementary guidance bibliography of books and journal articles. St. Paul, Minnesota State Department of Education, 1968. 75p. ED 029312.

Unannotated subject bibliography.

919. Kopita, Ronald R. Searchlight: relevant resources in high interest areas: outreach counseling. ERIC Clearinghouse on Counseling and Personnel Services, 1973. 12p. ED 082116.

36 annotated articles and ERIC documents.

920. Roueche, John E. and Natalie Rumanzeff. Counseling and guidance in the junior college. ERIC Clearinghouse for Junior College Information, 1968. 16p. ED 022452.

Lists 163 annotated entries dating from 1955 to 1968.

921. Counseling and psychotherapy. Arlington, VA, Council for Exceptional Children, 1971. 25p. ED 052573.

Includes 88 annotated items from the holdings of the Exceptional Child Information Center. Covers group therapy particularly in reference to emotionally disturbed children.

COUNSELORS

922. Ruby, Marc E. and Richard W. Pratt. New roles for counselors: a search of the ERIC data base for material relevant to the changing position of the counselor as he works within the school and community. ERIC Clearinghouse on Counseling and Personnel Services, 1975. 38p. ED 116078.

923. Pratt, Richard W. Counselor licensure and certification: an ERIC search. ERIC Clearinghouse on Counseling and Personnel Services, 1975. 83p. ED 116077 (MF)

Describes what has been done in the counseling field, and what related professional areas have done. Some of the annotated entries provide information to be used in drafting legislation.

COURTS

924. Sheridan, William H. and Alice B. Freer. Legal bibliography for juvenile and family courts. Washington, DC, Children's Bureau (DHEW), 1968. 42p. ED 033401 (MF)
Unannotated.

CREATIVITY

925. Hlavsa, Jaroslav. The Psychology of creativity: a bibliography up to 1970. Prague, Czechoslovakia, Research Institute for Machinery Technology and Economics, 1972. 359p. ED
073842.

   The 2419 references are in seven languages, but most are
   in English. The introduction and notes are in Czech and
   English. Unannotated.

926. Bibliography on creativity. Harvard University, 1966.
8p. ED 011301.

   Lists 50 unannotated references from the early 1960's.

927. Carlson, Ruth K. Literature and creative expression.
1969. 15p. ED 036519.

   This annotated bibliography contains 96 entries for films,
   records, and books under several subject headings. A 21
   item bibliography is appended entitled, "Educating the im-
   agination through children's literature".

928. Research on creativity: an annotated list of relevant
ETS reports, 1953-1970. Princeton, NJ, Educational Testing
Service, 1970. 35p. ED 050133.

   On the characteristics of creative persons, and the prediction of creativity.

CREDIT SYSTEM (EDUCATION)

929. Rolfe, Brenda. The Credit system: an annotated bibliography. Toronto, Ontario Institute for Studies in Education,
1974. 30p. ED 085894.

   The literature search emphasizes Canadian material with
   experiential reports from the provinces. The books, theses,
   research reports, pamphlets, articles, and videotapes are
   dated 1967 to 1974.

CRIMINOLOGY

Dowling, Anne. Reference materials in criminal justice: a
selective, annotated bibliography. Albany, State University
of New York Library, 1979. 21p. ED 183166.

   The list of over 100 entries does not contain criminal law
   and procedure.

CUBA

931. Cuban Studies Newsletter. University of Pittsburgh,

Center for International Studies, 1970. 20p. ED 049107.

This first issue of the newsletter is devoted to an extensive bibliography of books, parts of books, articles, and
pamphlets. Subjects include agriculture, art, biography,
economics, education, foreign relations, guerilla warfare,
history, literature, politics, public health, religion,
and sociology. Titles are in English or Spanish.

CULTURAL EDUCATION

932. Resources for schools: multicultural education. Canberra,
Australian Schools Commission, 1977. 49p. ED 161445.

Includes fiction, folktales, myths, legends, customs, cook-
ery, costumes, festivals, folk dances, folk songs, and
descriptive history and travel. Annotated.

933. Grove, Cornelius L. The Intensively annotated bibliography on cross-cultural problems in education. New York, Columbia University, Institute of International Studies, 1975.
50p. ED 111912.

Among the topics dealt with are language and linguistics,
bilingual education, preservice and inservice education,
nonverbal education, visual perception, cultural patterns,
testing, and international exchange programs. 125 items.

934. Grove, Cornelius L. The Annotated bibliography on cross
cultural education problems: fugitive literature. ERIC Clearinghouse on the Urban Disadvantaged, 1978. 41p. ED 164707.

Cites conference papers, research reports, speeches, term
papers, and dissertations that deal with those problems
in human interaction that stem from differences in cultural
background.

935. Mathieson, Moira B. and Rita M. Tatis. Multicultural education: a selected annotated bibliography. ERIC Clearinghouse
on Teacher Education, 1970. 18p. ED 043572.

Lists 70 documents dealing with cultural differences and
cross-cultural educational problems in the elementary,
secondary, and collegiate situations.

936. Cardenas, Jose A. Multicultural education: an annotated
bibliography. San Antonio, TX, Intercultural Development Research Association, 1976. 35p. ED 151430.

This classified bibliography was compiled from an ERIC
computer search, and from manual searches at various university libraries. Includes models, program strategies,
teacher training, and community involvement.

937. Advisory list of instructional media for cultural arts.

Raleigh, North Carolina State Department of Public Instruction, 1977. 38p. ED 149743.

An annotated list of books, films, filmstrips, recordings, and slides for primary through senior high school levels.

938. DeCrow, Roger. Cross cultural interaction skills: a digest of recent training literature. ERIC Clearinghouse on Adult Education, 1969. 78p. ED 029159.

A bibliography with 48 abstracts of new methods and innovative programs, mostly written during the late 1960's.

939. Altman, H. and E. A. Frechette. Culture and civilization: a bibliography for teachers of foreign languages. 1972. 43p. ED 070333.

400 unannotated references for teachers in American schools and colleges.

940. Howard, Norma K. Cultural and cross-cultural studies: an abstract bibliography. ERIC Clearinghouse on Early Childhood Education, 1974. 57p. ED 099115.

Cites documents describing cultural differences and their influence on children's cognitive, social, emotional, and language development. The unannotated entries also concern pre-school and day care environments.

CURRICULUM GUIDES AND CURRICULUM DEVELOPMENT

941. Tyler, Louise L. A Selected guide to curriculum literature: an annotated bibliography. Washington, DC, National Education Association, Center for the Study of Instruction, 1970. 138p. ED 037405 (MF)

Includes 68 references.

942. Curriculum planning and evaluation: the best of ERIC. ERIC Clearinghouse on Educational Management, 1975. 5p. ED 114952.

The 14 items attempt to define what the topic is, and discuss the role of various groups in it.

943. Schubert, William H. The Literature of curriculum development: toward centralization and analysis. 1976. 92p. ED 163617.

Includes an historical discussion of curriculum literature, and a chronological bibliography. The unannotated list is from a paper presented at the annual meeting of the American Educational Research Association.

944. Knight, Merle M. An Annotated bibliography for curric-

ulum materials analysis. Boulder, CO, Social Science Education Consortium, 1969. 22p. ED 040094 (MF)

   A guide for teachers and others who seek a better understanding of the many facets of curriculum theory, concepts,
   and terminology.

945. Rinnander, Elizabeth. About the curriculum. ERIC Clearinghouse for Junior College Information, 1977. 26p. ED 143
394.

   This annotated bibliography includes important literature
   since 1967 on community college curriculum and instruction.
   Contains books, articles, and ERIC documents.

946. Richardson, Leroy P. Undergraduate curriculum improvement: a conceptual and bibliographic study. Durham, NC, National Laboratory for Higher Education, 1971. 52p. ED 052
765.

   This review contains a summary, findings, and recommendations in addition to an extensive unannotated bibliography.

947. Designing and evaluating college courses: an annotated
bibliography. Montreal, McGill University, Center for Learning and Development, 1971. 7p. ED 059967.

   22 books on objectives, innovative teaching methods, evaluation, design, and educational experimentation.

948. OISE materials for schools. Toronto, Ontario Institute
for Studies in Education, 1978. 42p. ED 182196.

   This annotated bibliography lists published and unpublished
   elementary and secondary school materials developed in connection with OISE projects from 1970 to 1978.

949. Christensen, Donald J. Curriculum leaders: improving
their influence. Washington, DC, Association for Supervision
and Curriculum Development, 1976. 95p. ED 128934 (MF)

   The last chapter is an annotated bibliography in this report from the ASCD working group on the role, function,
   and preparation of the curriculum worker.

950. Curriculum guides. Arlington, VA, Council for Exceptional Children, 1971. 24p. ED 051592.

   Annotated citations to curriculum guides primarily applicable to the education of the mentally handicapped, aurally
   handicapped, learning disabled, and gifted.

951. Winkeljohann, Rosemary. Recommended English language
arts curriculum guides for K-12 and criteria for planning and
evaluation. ERIC Clearinghouse on Reading and Communication
Skills, 1977. 34p. ED 144104.

   An annotated collection to publicize good curriculum planning and guide writing, and to serve as a model for schools revising their programs and seeking a variety of sample frameworks, units, and lesson plans.

CZECH-AMERICANS

952. Psencik, Leroy F. Czech contributions in American culture. Austin, Texas Education Agency, 1970. 17p. ED 053023.

This bibliographic essay includes books and periodicals covering the historical, cultural, literary, musical, religious, culinary, and educational aspects of the Czech experience. The 46 annotated items focus on their role in Texas.

CZECH LANGUAGE

953. Henzl, Vera M. A Bibliography of Czech teaching materials. 1975. 39p. ED 134029.

Compiled to meet the need of linguists and teachers who intend to teach courses in Czech to foreigners and are in need of materials to develop practical and linguistically sound curriculum.

DANCE

954. Hanna, Judith L. The Anthropology of dance: a selected bibliography. 1978. 19p. ED 166111.

Over 250 books, articles, and papers are cited that were mostly published in the 1960's and 1970's. Includes communication and semiotics, symbolism and ritual, aesthetics, creativity, cognition, perception, emotion, movement notation, and the structural analysis of dance.

955. Pease, Edward J. Researching the music of dance: a guide to the methodology, a bibliography, a discography, and other basic information. Bowling Green, Western Kentucky University, 1980. 90p. ED 184546.

Intended for dance historians and teachers of the art who need access to information about dance music, scores, and recordings, this manual includes a discussion of information resources, an annotated bibliography, a guide to recordings, and a selected discography of the music of dance.

DATA PROCESSING See Also COMPUTERS

956. Piele, Philip. Selected bibliography of journal articles

on educational data processing. Eugene, University of Oregon, 1967.   10p.   ED 017060.

145 unannotated items published between 1960 and 1967.

DAY CARE

957.   Howard, Norma K.   Day care: an annotated bibliography. ERIC Clearinghouse on Early Childhood Education, 1971.   19p. ED 052823.

Contains annotations of items dealing with program, staff, building, equipment, licensing, standards, financing, governmental involvement, and community support. ED 069402 is the first supplement with 44 articles covering 1969-1971. ED 089884 is the second supplement which is an ERIC bibliography with 97 entries. It brings the list up to 1974.

958.   Infant day care: an abstract bibliography.   ERIC Clearinghouse on Early Childhood Education, 1976.   45p.   ED 129469.

Selectively cites ERIC items from 1972 through 1975.

959.   Younger, Carolyn T.   Family day care: an annotated bibliography.   Toronto, Community Day Care Coalition, 1975.   44p. ED 119875.

Some critical comments are offered on the 70 articles, conference papers, progress reports, book chapters, and pamphlets that are cited.

960.   A Feasibility study for a comprehensive competency based training and certification system for child care personnel in the Commonwealth of Pennsylvania: annotated bibliography. Washington, DC, Educational Projects Incorporated, 1972.   43p.   ED 072014.

This final report appendix includes 196 references.

961.   Wells, Alberta.   Day care: an annotated bibliography. Minneapolis, Institute for Interdisciplinary Studies, 1971. 367p.   ED 068199.

Categories for the 1500 entries are: general, child development, specific programs, personnel, economic issues, licensing standards, legislation and regulation, evaluation, facilities, and supplies. The books, articles, research papers, manuals, program reports, and Congressional acts and hearings were published from 1961 to 1970. ED 068200 is the first supplement with 220 items published between 1964 and 1971, and ED 068201 is the second supplement with 90 entries.

962.   Reif, Nadine.   An Annotated bibliography of day care reference materials.   Pennsylvania State University, Institute for the Study of Human Development, 1972.   42p.   ED 088609.

A topical ERIC bibliography covering 27 aspects of the subject.

963. <u>Good references on day care</u>. Washington, DC, Children's Bureau (DHEW), 1968. 27p. ED 027969.

The 70 annotated entries include guides, standards, staff training, parent involvement, health, and social services.

964. Frost, Judith and Miriam Meyers. <u>Day care reference sources: an annotated bibliography</u>. Minneapolis, Kenny Rehabilitation Institute, 1970. 35p. ED 039700.

Lists Minnesota State and some federal publications in addition to books, catalogs, and bibliographies.

965. Webb, Jeanne and Marnee Pennington. <u>Child care resource materials</u>. Lincoln, Nebraska State Department of Economic Development, 1976. 103p. ED 134345.

An annotated bibliography of books, films, and filmstrips on various topics related to child care.

DEAF See also SIGN LANGUAGE

966. <u>Aurally handicapped – programs: a selective bibliography</u>. Reston, VA, Council for Exceptional Children, 1973. 23p. ED 090710.

85 abstracts on programs for aurally handicapped children were selected from the Council's computer file. Items were published from 1964 to 1973.

967. <u>Aurally handicapped – research: a selective bibliography</u>. Reston, VA, Council for Exceptional Children, 1973. 26p. ED 090711.

100 abstracts of publications from 1965 to 1973 treat aspects such as testing, identification, speech, visual learning, and school performance.

968. McIntyre, Keren H. <u>Bibliography on the deaf and hard of hearing</u>. University of Southern California, 1968. 47p. ED 040524.

Includes over 400 research reports, manuals, journal articles, curriculum guides, instructional materials, and AV aids. Unannotated.

969. Parlato, Salvatore J. <u>Films on deafness</u>. New York, Rochester School for the Deaf, 1979. 71p. ED 175425.

Contains summaries of 192 16mm films on communication, the nature of deafness, education and training, multi-handicaps, and noise pollution.

970. Trboyevich, Goldie. A Bibliography: easy reading for
deaf children. Knoxville, University of Tennessee, Southern
Regional Media Center for the Deaf, 1967. 86p. ED 029425.

An annotated bibliography of 312 fiction and nonfiction
books published between 1960 and 1966.

971. Geoffrion, Leo D. and Karen E. Schuster. Auditory handicaps and reading: an annotated bibliography. Newark, Delaware,
International Reading Association, 1980. 64p. ED 182708.

201 items on the reading achievement of the deaf is designed
to aid those who wish to learn more about how children with
severe auditory handicaps read, and some of the instructional approaches currently being advocated.

972. Annotated bibliography of instructional media: vocational
education for the deaf. 1967. 196p. ED 025593.

This training manual of over 700 resources is from the
report of a workshop for improving instruction of the deaf
held at Ball State University, Muncie, Indiana.

973. Services for the deaf: check this out. Merrillville, IN,
Lake County Public Library, 1976. 31p. ED 125600.

Includes materials on the deaf child, books on manual communication, resource books, poetry, lipreading materials,
biographies, pamphlets, and films without words. The fiction portion of the guide is annotated.

974. Relationship between auditory abilities and academic
skills: bibliography. Baltimore, Johns Hopkins Medical Institutions, 1969. 7p. ED 046632.

21 studies on reading ability, school achievement, intelligence, personality, conceptual thinking ability, and English morphological abilities.

975. A Bibliography of reading for deaf children. 1972. 113p.
ED 065970.

Annotated list of 630 selections for K-12 published from
1961 to 1971.

976. Instructional materials appropriate for use in deaf education. University of Southern California, Instructional materials Center for Special Education, 1973. 26p. ED 085929.

Includes 125 reading series or programs. Annotated.

977. Frank, Steven A. List of available periodicals related
to deafness. Washington, DC, Gallaudet College, 1978. 60p.
ED 165375.

A title list of 400 foreign and United States periodicals
with addresses and subscription rates.

DEAF-BLIND

978. Stoddard, Denis W. and Jamie Glazer. Selected annotated
bibliography of deaf-blind prevocational training literature.
Raleigh, North Carolina State Department of Public Instruction,
1976. 20p. ED 123817.

    The 47 entries include books, journal articles, conference
    proceedings, and regional center reports.

979. Blea, William A. and Robert Hobron. Literature on the
deaf-blind: an annotated bibliography. Sacramento, CA, Southwestern Region Deaf-Blind Center, 1970. 193p. ED 072579.

    Includes books, conference proceedings, and articles that
    date back to the 1800's.

980. Blea, William A. Literature on the deaf-blind: an annotated bibliography. Sacramento, CA, Southwestern Region Deaf-
Blind Center, 1976. 48p. ED 135194.

    This collection includes 350 entries relating to the edu-
    cation and training of deaf-blind individuals.

981. Hammer, Edwin K. Deaf-blind children: a list of references. Dallas, TX, Callier Hearing and Speech Center, 1969.
63p. ED 040520.

    Unannotated journal articles, newspaper accounts, and
    professional reports dealing with various aspects of the
    subject.

982. Stuckey, Ken. Education of deaf-blind: bibliography.
Watertown, Mass., Perkins School for the Blind, 1972. 84p.
ED 087145.

    550 unannotated print materials including conference pro-
    ceedings, and 26 film and video tapes related to the ed-
    ucation and training of deaf-blind children and adults.
    Two supplements bring the bibliography up to 1976; they
    are ED 098766 and ED 137992.

DEANS (COLLEGE)

983. Winandy, Donald H. The Academic deanship: an annotated
bibliography. 1967(?) 11p. ED 013657.

    Lists 43 books and other documents about the work of the
    dean in undergraduate collegiate education.

DEATH

984. Bernstein, Joanne. Helping children cope with death and

separation: resources for teachers. ERIC Clearinghouse on
Early Childhood Education, 1976. 37p. ED 125753.

Includes an annotated list of children's books, books about
bibliotherapy, and a selection of films, filmstrips, and
cassettes on the subject.

985. Marshall, Ruben. The Concept of death in children's literature. 1975. 26p. ED 111431.

This paper gives evaluative annotations for 65 fiction and
nonfiction books. Appended is an unannotated bibliography
which includes books for adults, children's books, films,
videotapes, audiotapes, and records.

DEBATE

986. Walsh, Grace. Forensics bibliography. Speech Communication Association, 1973. 5p. ED 089383.

An annotated list of 28 books on debate, forensics, argu-
mentation, discussion, and public speaking.

DECISION-MAKING

987. Pierce, Milo C. Participation in decision-making: a
selected bibliography. Monticello, IL, Council of Planning
Librarians, 1972. 17p. ED 106956.

The focus is on employee, faculty, and student participation in this unannotated list from the areas of business,
education, psychology, and sociology.

988. Participative decision making: the best of ERIC. ERIC
Clearinghouse on Educational Management, 1975. 5p. ED 101415.

21 annotated sources represent a wide range of thought on
the pros, cons, and methods of involving various groups
of people in the school's decision making process.

989. Hall, John S. Models for rational decision making: analysis of literature and selected bibliography. ERIC Clearinghouse on Educational Management, 1970. 15p. ED 043115.

This review analyzes the trend to replace hierarchical authority structures with more rational models for decision
making drawn from management science. Includes 54 unannotated references.

990. Urbick, Thelma. Decision-making: CAPS current resources
index. Ann Arbor, University of Michigan, Counseling and Personnel Services Information Center, 1968. 59p. ED 021305.

Roles are emphasized in this unannotated bibliography.

DELINQUENTS   See   JUVENILE DELINQUENTS

DEMOGRAPHY   See   POPULATION EDUCATION

DENTISTRY

991. Boquist, Constance and Jeanette V. Haase. An Historical
review of women in dentistry: an annotated bibliography. Cambridge, Mass., Radcliffe College, 1977. 112p. ED 148223.

  The majority of the 263 citations are to professional and
  scientific books and journals. The period covered is 1865
  to 1977.

DESEGREGATION   See   SCHOOL INTEGRATION

DIAL ACCESS

992. Ingle, Henry T. Dial access in education. ERIC Clearinghouse on Educational Media and Technology, 1970. 9p. ED
038875.

  Ten annotated ERIC documents published between 1962 and
  1968 are included.

DISADVANTAGED   See also   MINORITY GROUPS   and   POVERTY

993. Morgan, Carolyn A. and Virlyn A. Boyd. Annotated bibliography of publications and reports resulting from Southern Regional Cooperative Research Project S-44: factors in the adjustment of families and individuals in low income rural areas
of the South. Clemson University, Department of Agricultural
Economics and Rural Sociology, 1966. 34p. ED 023875.

  Includes 83 publications dated 1960 to 1965.

994. Urbick, Thelma. Helping procedures for use with the disadvantaged. Ann Arbor, University of Michigan, Counseling and
Personnel Services Information Center, 1968. 157p. ED 025815.

  Annotated citations include articles, theses, and ERIC documents focusing on sociological and psychological characteristics of disadvantaged populations.

995. Gordon, Edmund W. Disadvantaged populations. New York,
Yeshiva University, 1967. 8p. ED 014521.

  The unannotated bibliography includes book-length treatments
  of the subject, demographic and status studies, and literature on cultural and social patterns.

996. Flaxman, Erwin and Victor Zinn. The Education of teachers of the disadvantaged: a selected bibliography. New York,

Yeshiva University, 1965(?)   13p.   ED 011907.

Includes 110 unannotated books, articles, speeches, dissertations, conference proceedings, and selected reports of
teacher education programs produced in the 1960's.

997. Bibliography on the problems of southwestern minority
groups and for teachers of adult students from different cultural backgrounds. 1968. 21p. ED 041682.

Cites 169 books and articles published between 1928 and
1967, plus a selected list of 69 professional books for
teachers. Both lists are unannotated.

998. Jablonsky, Adelaide. Doctoral research on the disadvantaged. ERIC Clearinghouse on the Urban Disadvantaged, 1974.
26p. ED 106418.

This annotated list covers 1965 to 1972.

999. Millman, Linda I. and Catherine S. Chilman. Poor people
at work: an annotated bibliography on semi-professionals in education, health, and welfare services. Washington, DC, Social
and Rehabilitation Service (DHEW), 1969. 47p. ED 038510.

150 articles are included that were written since 1964.

1000. Research on the disadvantaged: an annotated list of relevant ETS studies, 1951-1969. Princeton, NJ, Educational Testing Service, 1969. 54p. ED 037392.

Eleven testing categories include 98 references.

1001. An Annotated bibliography: public employment and the
disadvantaged. Washington, DC, National Civil Service League,
1970. 50p. ED 042866.

On the selection, testing, training, and employment of
public servants on all levels.

DISADVANTAGED - EDUCATION

1002. Educating the disadvantaged child: annotated bibliography. Albany, New York State Education Department, 1968. 95p.
ED 030682.

ED 045754 is a 93 page supplement dated October 1969.

1003. Brandon, George L. Research visibility: Manpower development, vo-ed for the disadvantaged. Washington, DC, American
Vocational Association, 1970. 16p. ED 042916.

Sixteen research reviews are included in addition to 18
other studies that are listed. One section is on disadvantaged youth and the Neighborhood Youth Corps project.

1004. Holcomb, Beverly J. Training the socio-economically disadvantaged: a selected, annotated bibliography. Little Rock, Arkansas State Department of Education, 1969. 221p. ED 042918.

Concerns planning, counseling, and socialization for the disadvantaged including the hard-core unemployed, and drop-outs. One section is on school desegregation.

1005. Regan, Lynda. Annotated bibliography: educational op-portunity programs. Albany, New York State Education Depart-ment, 1974. 116p. ED 101027.

Concentrates on reading, math, and bilingual education for the disadvantaged. Urban education, health education, and nonstandard English are other areas dealt with in rela-tion to migrants, native Americans, and the Spanish speak-ing.

1006. Jablonsky, Adelaide. Special secondary school programs for the disadvantaged: an annotated bibliography of doctoral dissertations. ERIC Clearinghouse on the Urban Disadvantaged, 1974. 71p. ED 102223.

Covers college preparatory programs, Upward Bound, Outward Bound, follow-up studies, and evaluation. The dissertations are from 1965 to 1973.

1007. Theiss, Frances C. Science and mathematics for disad-vantaged children: an annotated bibliography. ERIC Informa-tion and Analysis Center for Science, Mathematics, and Environ-mental Education, 1972. 21p. ED 066313.

1008. Poliakoff, Lorraine. The Disadvantaged. ERIC Clear-inghouse on Teacher Education, 1970. 36p. ED 044382.

165 ERIC documents from the late 1960's on individualized instuction, and teacher education.

1009. Gordon, Edmund W. An Annotated bibliography on higher education of the disadvantaged. ERIC Clearinghouse on the Urban Disadvantaged, 1970. 69p. ED 038478.

The 125 citations focus on programs and practices, civil rights and access to higher education, student character-istics, admissions and guidance, and the Black college.

1010. Brandon, George L. Research visibility: the disadvan-taged and the handicapped. Washington, DC, American Vocational Association, 1970. 16p. ED 038540.

Fifteen reviews and 36 additional citations focus on the need for vocational education for youths and adults in these categories.

1011. Watt, Lois B. The Education of disadvantaged children: a bibliography. Washington, DC, Office of Education, 1967.

37p. ED 011898.

Contains professional resources, elementary and secondary
level textbooks, and children's literature. Includes 350
partially annotated items dating from 1963.

1012. Thompson, Wenda. A Selective bibliography on new media
and the education of the culturally disadvantaged. Washington,
DC, Educational Media Council, 1966. 23p. ED 015961.

Unannotated books, articles, and papers.

1013. Lewis, Gertrude M. and Esther Murow. Educating disadvantaged children in the elementary school: an annotated bibliography. Washington, DC, Office of Education, 1966. 37p.
ED 064415.

Includes books and articles from 1960 to 1965, primarily
from a search of Education Index.

1014. Dimitroff, Lillian. An Annotated bibliography of audiovisual materials related to understanding and teaching the culturally disadvantaged. Washington, DC, National Education
Association, 1969. 44p. ED 034440 (MF)

Major emphasis is on the inner city population, while
most of the selections were chosen to sensitize adults
rather than to instruct children.

1015. Teaching the rural disadvantaged: preliminary bibliography. Washington, DC, National Education Association, 1968.
5p. ED 020062.

Deals with characteristics and learning problems in the
75 books, articles, and bibliographies.

1016. Jablonsky, Adelaide. Early childhood education for the
disadvantaged: an annotated bibliography of doctoral dissertations. ERIC Clearinghouse on the Urban Disadvantaged, 1973.
203p. ED 079438.

Covers such issues as reading, parent involvement, paraprofessionals, summer programs, Black dialects, Head Start
programs, and Follow Through programs.

1017. Rosen, Pamela. Tests for educationally disadvantaged
adults. Princeton, NJ, Educational Testing Service, 1973.
12p. ED 083318.

This annotated bibliography describes 65 instruments that
date back to 1925; includes aptitude and achievement tests.

DISADVANTAGED YOUTH

1018. Bynum, Effie M. A Selected ERIC bibliography on pre-

college preparation of students from disadvantaged backgrounds.
ERIC Clearinghouse on the Urban Disadvantaged, 1969. 30p. ED
029069.

Includes educational planning, description of programs and
practices, and research and evaluation. The annotated entries date from 1965 to 1969.

1019. Disadvantaged youth: exceptional child bibliography
series. Arlington, VA, Council for Exceptional Children, 1971.
26p. ED 054577.

101 annotated references on socioeconomic influences, environmental influences, teaching methods, learning disabilities, cognitive development, and language development.

1020. Law, Gordon F. Research visibility: disadvantaged
youth, rural poverty, and the urban crisis. Washington, DC,
American Vocational Association, 1968. 16p. ED 030749.

Includes fifteen reviews and lists 29 related studies.

1021. Aurbach, Herbert A. A Selected bibliography on socio-
culturally disadvantaged children and youth and related topics.
University of Pittsburgh, Learning Research and Development
Center, 1966. 34p. ED 010523.

The unannotated bibliography covers poverty, schools,
integration, delinquency, sociology, and psychology.

1022. Disadvantaged children in Canada. Ottawa, Canadian
Teachers Federation, 1970. 16p. ED 041965.

191 unannotated items from the 1960's are listed.

1023. Watt, Lois B. Literature for disadvantaged children:
a bibliography. Washington, DC, Office of Education, 1968.
18p. ED 052270.

Categories include: fantasy, folklore, poetry, rhymes,
biography, history, intercultural understanding, rural
and urban life, arts, hobbies, and beginning science.
Each book is annotated and rated for grade level.

1024. Mathieson, Moira B. and Rita M. Tatis. Understanding
disadvantaged youth: their problems and potentials: an annotated bibliography. ERIC Clearinghouse on Teacher Education,
1970. 22p. ED 044380.

This resource guide for teachers contains 102 entries from
the late 1960's.

1025. Love, Ruth B. References on counseling minority youth.
Sacramento, California State Department of Education, 1964.
21p. ED 034232.

Concerns vocational education and financial aid for the
disadvantaged in addition to guidance and counseling.

1026.   Rubin, Leonard. An Annotated bibliography on the employment of disadvantaged youth, 1960-1966. Washington, DC,
Bureau of Social Science Research, Inc., 1969. 76p. ED 035
732.

    150 articles deal with the social and psychological aspects
of youth employment. Government documents and books are excluded.

1027.   Jablonsky, Adelaide. The Jobs Corps: a review of the
ERIC literature. ERIC Clearinghouse on the Urban Disadvantaged,
1970. 33p. ED 036662.

    Annotates 46 items on the history and need, planning and
program descriptions, administration, instruction, guidance,
evaluations, and recommendations.

1028.   Jablonsky, Adelaide. The Neighborhood Youth Corps: a
review of the ERIC literature. ERIC Clearinghouse on the Urban
Disadvantaged, 1970. 23p. ED 036661.

    Annotates 21 items on program descriptions, evaluation
reports, and reaction papers.

1029.   Kopita, Ronald R. Searchlight: relevant resources in
high interest areas: vocational counseling of disadvantaged
students. ERIC Clearinghouse on Counseling and Personnel Services, 1973. 23p. ED 082113.

    Includes 69 ERIC documents for use with minority and dis-
advantaged youth in elementary and secondary schools.

DISCIPLINE

1030.   School discipline: bibliographies in education. Ottawa,
Canadian Teachers Federation, 1972. 24p. ED 064771.

    An unannotated list of 56 books, 254 articles, and 20 the-
ses written between 1961 and 1971.

1031.   Mikulsky, Daniel. Discipline in the schools: an annotated bibliography. New York, City University, Center for Advanced Study in Education, 1976. 39p. ED 139077.

    The 63 articles, books, and papers cover corporal punish-
ment, the role of the disciplinarian, attitudes toward and
solutions to behavior problems.

1032.   Classroom discipline: the best of ERIC. ERIC Clearinghouse on Educational Management, 1978. 5p. ED 147921.

    Includes classroom discipline without punishment, the prin-
cipal's role, faculty training, and student-teacher relationships. The twelve annotated items also cover behavior
extinction and contingency management.

1033. School discipline: bibliographies in education. Ottawa,
Canadian Teachers Federation, 1975. 19p. ED 105608.

An unannotated list of recent books, articles, theses, and
doctoral dissertations.

DISCUSSION GROUPS

1034. Petty, Robert M. The Optimal size for discussion groups.
Monticello, IL, Council of Planning Librarians, 1973. 21p. ED
106967.

Annotated entries from the field of social psychology regarding the feelings of clinicians and counselors.

1035. Ellison, John W. An Annotated bibliography of materials
designed and organized for adult use in discussion groups. Dayton, OH, Wright State University, 1970. 135p. ED 044603.

A wide variety of materials in the social sciences are
included in this list of print and non-print publications.

DISTRIBUTIVE EDUCATION

1036. Ertel, Kenneth A. and Gary R. Smith. Distributive education library list. Boise, Idaho State Board of Vocational
Education, 1964. 42p. ED 012778.

Unannotated list developed for institutions preparing
teacher-coordinators who will teach distributive education.

1037. A Selected and annotated bibliography related to coop-
erative and project methods in distributive education. East
Lansing, Michigan State University, Department of Secondary
Education and Curriculum, 1972. 148p. ED 066600.

Includes 495 journal articles, books, theses, and dissertations dating back to 1896.

1038. Levendowski, J. C. Selected instructional materials
for distributive education. Sacramento, California State Department of Education, Council for Distributive Teacher Education, 1966. 39p. ED 017651.

An unannotated topical bibliography.

1039. Hirshfield, Marvin and Jerome I. Leventhal. A National
state of the art study of curriculum instructional materials
for distributive education. Philadelphia, Temple University,
Division of Vocational Education, 1973. 366p. ED 105195.

An annotated multimedia compilation for advertising services, apparel and accessories, automotive, finance and

credit, floristry, food distribution, food services, and
general merchandise. ED 105196 is the second volume of the
set and includes marketing, retailing, salesmanship, hardware, building materials, farm and garden supplies, home
furnishings, hotels, insurance, international trade, real
estate, transportation, recreation, and tourism. Volume 2
has 399 pages.

1040. Leventhal, Jerome I. Teacher resource bibliography for
marketing and distribution and distributive education, 1968-
1971. Trenton, NJ, Epsilon Delta Epsilon, 1971. 129p. ED
079474.

   Contains books, articles, and AV aids for advertising,
   salesmanship, sensitivity, grooming, display, marketing,
   and attitudes and motivation. Unannotated.

1041. The Evaluation of distributive education programs. ERIC
Clearinghouse on Tests, Measurement, and Evaluation, 1975. 22p.
ED 107717.

   An annotated bibliography taken from RIE and CIJE.

1042. Lambert, Roger H. A Bibliography of free loan materials
for distributive education. Third ed. Madison, University of
Wisconsin Vocational Studies Center, 1976. 25p. ED 132277.

   An annotated listing.

DIVORCE

1043. Kessler, Sheila. Divorce bibliography. 1975. 27p.
ED 119095.

   This partially annotated listing was prepared for a workshop at Georgia State University. Its two bibliographies
   are for the marriage and divorce counselor.

DORMITORIES

1044. Ebbers, Larry H. and Kenneth L. Stoner. Assessing student development in the residential environment: a bibliography
of related research. 1973. 31p. ED 109960.

   Covers organization and administration, programming, and
   counseling in residence halls. This annotated bibliography
   is part of a paper presented to the American College Personnel Association Conference.

1045. Ebbers, Larry H. Residence halls in U.S. higher education: a selective bibliography. Ames, Iowa State University
Library, 1973. 627p. ED 086097.

   The writings from the past 75 years cover historical development, financing, planning, construction, organization, administration, programming, personnel, counseling, food service, legal issues, fire prevention, and married, graduate, and foreign student housing. Some annotations and an author index are included. ED 165625 is a 143 page annotated supplement issued in 1978 which is available in microfiche only.

1046. Student housing: a selected bibliography. ERIC Clearinghouse on Educational Facilities, 1970. 26p. ED 041375.

This unannotated list covers design and the environment of the residence hall and its effect on student performance and behavior. Also includes case studies in addition to items on planning, financing, and operations.

1047. Kramer, Roger M. Student housing: a selected and annotated bibliography. ERIC Clearinghouse on Educational Facilities, 1968. 28p. ED 025136.

Architecture and other aspects of student housing are the focus of this bibliography.

DRAMA See THEATRE ARTS

DROPOUTS

1048. Isaacson, Arlene. College student attrition: an annotated bibliography. New York, City University, Brooklyn College, 1974. 213p. ED 101633.

Includes research studies published from 1965 to 1973, but excludes dissertations.

1049. Jablonsky, Adelaide. Dropouts: an annotated bibliography of doctoral dissertations. ERIC Clearinghouse on the Urban Disadvantaged, 1974. 126p. ED 096362.

Categories are prediction, prevention, and characteristics of dropouts, plus school climate and teacher influence on school holding power. The dissertations were announced from 1965 to 1973.

1050. Noel, Lee and Lois Renter. College student retention: an annotated bibliography of recent dissertations. Iowa City, American College Testing Program, 1975. 34p. ED 121233.

Concerns community colleges and public and private colleges and universities. Years of the dissertations are 1970–1975.

1051. Pezullo, Diane. About student attrition/retention in the community college. ERIC Clearinghouse on Junior College Information, 1978. 27p. ED 160179.

An annotated list of ERIC documents since 1973.

1052. Jablonsky, Adelaide. ERIC-IRCD resources on the school dropout. ERIC Clearinghouse on the Urban Disadvantaged, 1970. 27p. ED 037589.

Includes books, federal and state agency publications, foundation publications, NEA reports, and other bibliographies, but no journal articles.

1053. Jablonsky, Adelaide. The School dropout and the world of work: a review of the ERIC literature. ERIC Clearinghouse on the Urban Disadvantaged, 1970. 27p. ED 035780.

Extensively annotated, this bibliography relates to the employment problems, programs, and prospects of the school dropout.

DRUGS, DRUG ABUSE, AND DRUG EDUCATION

1054. Phillips, Joel L. A Cocaine bibliography. Rockville, MD, National Institute on Drug Abuse, 1974. 137p. ED 109114.

Includes over 1800 unannotated references from the scientific and popular literature on the socio-psychological, biomedical, political, and economic aspects of cocaine and coca from 1585 to the present.

1055. Drug therapy: a selective bibliography. Arlington, VA, Council for Exceptional Children, 1972. 16p. ED 069064.

Includes 46 abstracts ranging from 1965 to 1971.

1056. Selected readings for the professional working with drug related problems. Madison, University of Wisconsin, 1970. 27p. ED 058579.

An unannotated bibliography on alcohol and numerous other drugs and stimulants.

1057. A Bibliography on drug abuse and drug education. Wiesbaden, West Germany, United States Air Forces in Europe, 1973. 279p. ED 088891.

A multimedia annotated list of books, dissertations, pamphlets, documents, articles, and AV materials which includes fiction and has a subject index.

1058. Drug abuse research instrument inventory. Cambridge, Mass., Social Systems Analysis, 1973. 30p. ED 076611.

Annotated and in six sections: attitudes, measurement of effects of drugs, differentiation and characteristics of a user, access and extent, education and knowledge, and programs and evaluations.

1059. Bowden, R. Renee. Annotated bibliography of literature on narcotic addiction. Albany, New York State Narcotic Addiction Control Commission, 1968. 80p. ED 078312.

150 abstracts summarize the present state of knowledge and the methods of treatment.

1060. The Drug problem and the schools: ERIC abstract series. Washington, DC, American Association of School Administrators, 1971. 24p. ED 047430.

Includes relevant ERIC documents that have been announced in RIE through 1970.

1061. National Clearinghouse for Drug Abuse Information selected reference series, series 6, number 1. Rockville, MD, National Institute of Mental Health, 1973. 20p. ED 081603.

Fifty annotated citations provide an overview of the problem in the field of industry, and discuss industry's role in employing ex-addicts in addition to covering areas of concern such as safety, security, and legal matters.

1062. Drug dependence and abuse: a selected bibliography. National Institute of Mental Health, 1971. 57p. ED 049476.

Both the popular and scientific literature are covered for socio-cultural aspects, etiology, treatment, prevention, law and public policy.

1063. Brooks, Gary D. and Bonnie S. The Literature on drug abuse. El Paso, University of Texas, 1970. 25p. ED 043041.

Over 350 books, articles, and pamphlets produced since 1960 are listed.

1064. Kopita, Ronald R. Searchlight: relevant resources in high interest areas: counseling for drug abuse. ERIC Clearinghouse on Counseling and Personnel Services, 1973. 19p. ED 082107.

70 reviews cover the techniques and school programs for education and prevention of drug abuse.

1065. Bibliography for drug abuse and narcotics. Stony Brook, NY, SCOPE, 1968. 47p. ED 031728.

Short annotations are included for some of the items which date back to 1926. Includes alcohol and glue sniffing.

1066. Polydrug use: an annotated bibliography. Biloit, WI, Student Association for the Study of Hallucinogens, 1975. 40p. ED 120655.

The focus is on the use of combinations of drugs, the concomitant use of separate drugs, and the consecutive or sequential use of two or more substances in an alternating fashion.

1067. Drugs and drug abuse: a bibliography. Stony Brook, NY,
State University, 1974. 24p. ED 116079.

Includes street drug use, and prescribed use for psychiatric patients. Annotated.

1068. Guthrie, P. D. Measures pertaining to health education:
drugs: an annotated bibliography. ERIC Clearinghouse on Tests,
Measurement, and Evaluation, 1972. 46p. ED 068569.

The instruments described are designed to assess attitudes,
behaviors, practices, knowledge, and correlations in the
area of drugs and drug abuse. Nicotine and alcohol are excluded.

1069. Dealing with the drug problem: the best of ERIC. ERIC
Clearinghouse on Educational Management, 1978. 5p. ED 162396.

Annotates 12 ERIC documents which describe established
drug education programs, recommend characteristics of such
programs, and suggest alternative techniques for drug education programs.

1070. Drug abuse education: a selected bibliography of books,
pamphlets, recordings, transparencies, and slides for school
libraries. Albany, New York State Education Department, 1972.
28p. ED 068858.

An unannotated list for the professional and student.

1071. Pearlman, Samuel. Recommended book and pamphlet publications on drugs and drug use for a college or university library. New York, City University, Brooklyn College, 1970. 6p.
ED 043904.

A paper presented at the American Psychological Association convention. The unannotated list includes British,
Canadian, and U.S. publications.

1072. Laing, James M. Drug education - use and abuse: a resource bulletin. Pleasant Hill, CA, Contra Costa County Department of Education, 1970. 326p. ED 037766.

A multimedia annotated guide that includes federal and
state publications, plus curriculum resource guides and
instructional units.

1073. Galant, Richard and Nancy J. Moncrieff. Counseling for
drug abuse. ERIC Clearinghouse on Counseling and Personnel
Services, 1974. 23p. ED 105361.

Reviews 81 documents and articles that cover techniques
and school programs for education and prevention of drug
abuse. Some dissertations are included.

EARLY CHILDHOOD EDUCATION See CHILDHOOD EDUCATION and PRE-
    SCHOOL EDUCATION

EARTH SCIENCE

1074. Graham, Mildred W. Selected bibliography for earth
science education. Columbus, Ohio State University, 1970. 12p.
ED 050941.

   Partially annotated collection of 100 articles, plus some
   relevant dissertations dating from 1960.

1075. Berg, J. Robert. Annotated bibliography of geological
education. Washington, DC, American Geological Institute,
1963. 29p. ED 012248.

   A chronological listing of professional articles from 1919
   to 1962.

1076. Mayer, Victor J. and Charles Wall. Research in earth
science education: an annotated bibliography. ERIC Information
Analysis Center for Science, Mathematics, and Environmental
Education, 1972. 47p. ED 068317.

   ERIC documents, articles, and dissertations are included
   for elementary, secondary, and college levels.

ECOLOGY See also ENVIRONMENTAL EDUCATION

1077. Gemmecke, Barbara J. Ecology, pollution, conservation:
a bibliography of instructional materials for elementary school
teachers. Terre Haute, Indiana State University, Curriculum
Research and Development Center, 1971. 52p. ED 072009.

   Annotated with grade levels indicated. Includes articles,
   films, charts, pictures, and other resources.

1078. Lussenhop, Martha. Children's ecology books. 1971.
27p. ED 061054.

   100 annotated entries with grade levels indicated. Picture
   books and fiction are included.

1079. Ecology and the environment: a dissertation bibliography.
Ann Arbor, MI, University Microfilms International, 1978. 96p.
ED 161665 (MF)

   5500 dissertations from 1970 to 1976 are in this unannotated list. Also included is a related title list of masters theses.

ECONOMICS, ECONOMIC EDUCATION, AND ECONOMIC DEVELOPMENT See
     also MARKETING

1080. Nappi, Andrew T. Learning economics through children's

stories: a bibliographic reference. Third ed. New York, Joint
Council on Economic Education, 1978. 98p. ED 162946 (MF)

This is a resource for teaching ideas for K-6. It includes
100 descriptive summaries of appropriate children's books,
and 70 summaries of articles and research on the teaching
of economics at the elementary level.

1081. Dawson, George G. Research in economic education: a
bibliography. New York University, Center for Economic Education, 1069. 48p. ED 043534.

660 unannotated reports of research mostly done in the
1960's, but some dating back to the 1920's. ED 043535 is
a 20 page supplement of 246 studies began since 1969.

1082. Some basic readings and references in world-of-work
economic education: annotated bibliography. New York, Joint
Council on Economic Education, 1973. 16p. ED 092462.

Selected for educators, but much can be useful to mature
students.

1083. Hedstrom, Judith E. Selective bibliography in economics
resources. ERIC Clearinghouse for Social Studies/Social Science Education, 1977. 38p. ED 148655.

Annotates 43 current references for high school teachers.
Includes consumer economics.

1084. Crum, Norman J. Cost-benefit and cost-effectiveness
analyses: a bibliography of applications in the civilian economy. Santa Barbara, CA, General Electric Company, 1969. 28p.
ED 047715.

The annotated list applies to such areas as transportation,
communication, and health.

1085. Kronish, Sidney J. Audiovisual materials for teaching
economics. New York, Joint Council on Economic Education,
1972. 61p. ED 102062 (MF)

Over 100 items for the elementary and secondary school
teacher. Annotated.

1086. Deitch, Kenneth M. and Eugene McLoone. The Economics
of American education: a bibliography including selected major
references for other nations. Bloomington, IN, Phi Delta
Kappa, 1966. 69p. ED 024108.

Unannotated list of 724 books and articles mostly written
in the 1960's.

1087. Alexander-Frutschi, Marian C. Human resources and economic growth: an international annotated bibliography on the
role of education and training in economic and social development. Menlo Park, CA, Stanford Research Institute, 1963. 413p.

Primarily devoted to developing nations, especially India, Mexico, Japan, and the African states.

EDUCATIONAL FACILITIES   See also   ARCHITECTURE and   BUILDING
   DESIGN

1088. Piele, Philip. and Darrell Wright. Life-cycle costing.
Columbus, OH, Council of Educational Facility Planners, 1976.
7p. ED 120896.

An overview of recent literature is presented along with
15 ERIC abstracts.

1089. Facilities for special education. Columbus, OH, Council
of Educational Facility Planners, 1977. 7p. ED 133809.

Includes 18 annotated documents from the ERIC system.

1090. Higher education facilities: comprehensive planning
grants program bibliography. Washington, DC, Office of Education, Bureau of Higher Education, 1970. 76p. ED 047426.

Consists of state by state bibliographies of planning
source documents.

1091. Isler, Norman P. Temporary school facilities: an annotated bibliography. ERIC Clearinghouse on Educational Facilities, 1969. 16p. ED 033568.

Contains ERIC documents concerned with temporary, mobile,
and portable structures.

1092. Wakefield, Howard E. Flexible educational facilities:
an annotated reference list. ERIC Clearinghouse on Educational
Facilities, 1968. 32p. ED 025143.

Includes documents on learning centers, libraries, health
centers, fine arts centers, and domes for the school and
college situation.

1093. Wakefield, Howard E. Safety factors in educational
facilities. ERIC Clearinghouse on Educational Facilities,
1968. 31p. ED 025142.

The annotated bibliography covers stairways, site planning,
air structures, handicapped, laboratory design, fallout
protection, fire protection, and mobile classrooms.

1094. Wakefield, Howard E. Standards for educational facilities: an annotated reference list. ERIC Clearinghouse on
Educational Facilities, 1968. 28p. ED 025141.

1095. Conrad, M. J. School plant planning: an annotated bibliography. Columbus, Ohio State University, School of Education, 1968. 70p. ED 025138.

Includes books and articles on district surveys, enrollments, evaluations, room needs, and room specifications.

1096. McGuffey, C. W. A Review of selected references relating to the planning of higher education facilities. Tallahassee,
Florida State University, Associated Consultants in Education,
1967. 100p. ED 018961.

1097. Clasen, Robert E. Forty years of school plant dissertations: a review with suggestions for future research. Madison, University of Wisconsin, 1964. 27p. ED 018927.

A bibliographic review beginning with the year 1921.

1098. Bibliography of facilities information. Washington, DC,
American Association of Junior Colleges, 1967. 15p. ED 014
293.

Unannotated subject list of junior college planning, design, and construction.

1099. Wakefield, Howard E. Educational specifications: an
annotated reference list. ERIC Clearinghouse on Educational
Facilities, 1968. 54p. ED 024257.

Concerned with the preparation and use of on the college,
elementary, and secondary level.

1100. Wakefield, Howard E. Evaluating educational facilities:
an annotated reference list. ERIC Clearinghouse on Educational
Facilities, 1968. 33p. ED 024256.

A compilation of ERIC documents for all levels of education.

1101. Wakefield, Howard E. Locating educational facilities:
an annotated reference list. ERIC Clearinghouse on Educational
Facilities, 1968. 54p. ED 024255.

Concerns site selection for all levels of education.

1102. Wakefield, Howard E. The Maintenance of educational
facilities: an annotated reference list. ERIC Clearinghouse
on Educational Facilities, 1968. 30p. ED 024253.

Concerns the physical plant and equipment.

1103. Hartman, Robert R. Thermal environment in school facilities: a selected and annotated bibliography. ERIC Clearinghouse on Educational Facilities, 1968. 28p. ED 024252.

Compiled for the school planner, architect, and school
administrator.

1104. Phelon, Philip S. Campus and facilities planning in
higher education: the process and personnel: an annotated bibliography. Albany, New York State Education Department, 1968.
21p. ED 021410.

1105. Building renovation and modernization. Columbus, OH, Council of Educational Facility Planners, 1976. 9p. ED 131 522.

Fifty documents from the ERIC system discuss why, when, and how to remodel schools.

1106. Facilities for early childhood education: a selected bibliography. ERIC Clearinghouse on Educational Facilities, 1970. 18p. ED 041376.

The unannotated list concerns planning for nursery and kindergarten facilities, playgrounds, and classrooms.

1107. Coursen, David. Playground facilities and equipment. ERIC Clearinghouse on Educational Management, 1977. 33p. ED 146662.

44 documents and articles discuss theory, planning, and finance. The handicapped are also given consideration.

1108. Analysis and programming educational facilities. ERIC Clearinghouse on Educational Facilities. 1970. 21p. ED 041 378.

Includes 80 articles, books, and ERIC documents. This selective bibliography is not annotated.

1109. Effects of facilities on educational achievement: a selected bibliography. ERIC Clearinghouse on Educational Facilities, 1970. 57p. ED 041379.

1110. Physical facilities. Arlington, VA, Council for Exceptional Children, 1971. 22p. ED 053516.

91 annotated entries concern all aspects of facilities environments for the handicapped child.

1111. Deaton, Francesca A. A Bibliography of higher education facilities publications. Raleigh, NC, Higher Education Facilities Services, Inc., 1973. 54p. ED 077395.

Unannotated papers, articles, and books on all facets of planning and utilization.

1112. Piele, Philip and Darrell Wright. Evaluating the existing school plant. Columbus, OH, Council of Educational Facility Planners, 1976. 5p. ED 117783.

An analysis and 18 annotated items are presented, ten of which are available through the ERIC system.

1113. Science facilities: an interpretive bibliography. ERIC Clearinghouse on Educational Facilities, 1970. 82p. ED 037 994.

All science disciplines are included for schools and colleges. Annotated.

1114. Martin, W. Edgar. Selected references on facilities
and equipment for elementary schools. Washington, DC, Office
of Education, 1962. 11p. ED 037889 (MF)

1115. Piele, Philip and Darrell Wright. Computerized planning
methods. Columbus, OH, Council of Educational Facility Planners, 1976. 7p. ED 119283.

   Includes annotations of 15 ERIC documents that involve
   the use of computers in school planning.

1116. Facilities for community services. Columbus, OH, Council of Educational Facility Planners, 1976. 9p. ED 128872.

   Annotations of 29 ERIC documents that discuss the community use of school buildings.

1117. D'Amico, Louis A. and William D. Brooks. The Spatial
campus: a planning scheme with selected and annotated bibliography. Bloomington, Indiana University, School of Education,
1968. 117p. ED 031881.

   The directions of the development and relationship of the
   urban college campus with its community are examined in
   289 annotated articles. Includes a separate section of
   482 items on building descriptions with and without floor
   plans.

1118. Wakefield, Howard E. Construction costs of educational
facilities: an annotated reference list. ERIC Clearinghouse
on Educational Facilities, 1968. 58p. ED 024258.

   For all levels of education.

1119. Isler, Norman P. Cost factors in the planning, design,
financing, and construction of elementary and secondary educational facilities: an interpretive bibliography. ERIC Clearinghouse on Educational Facilities, 1970. 70p. ED 035268.

   The 57 entries include school bond elections, federal and
   state aid, renovation and remodeling, and design methodologies in addition to other topics.

1120. Systematic methods in school planning, programming, and
design: a selected bibliography. ERIC Clearinghouse on Educational Facilities, 1970. 46p. ED 035267.

   Lists 94 publications, primarily for architects.

1121. Conrad, M. H. Educational facilities planning: a selected, annotated bibliography. Columbus, Ohio State University, College of Education, 1975. 79p. ED 108395.

EDUCATIONAL FINANCE

1122. Dulac, Claude. Educational finance bibliography. Ottawa, Statistics Canada: Education, Science, and Culture Division, 1978. 141p. ED 168149.

An unannotated list of documents in English and French for primary and secondary level. Most items were published in the United States or Canada.

1123. The Politics and economics of school finance. Washington, DC, American Association of School Administrators, 1971. 26p. ED 047429.

Includes ERIC documents on the subject through 1970.

1124. Trulove, William T. Annotated bibliography on private financing of higher education. ERIC Clearinghouse on Educational Administration, 1968. 13p. ED 024157.

Contains books, articles, pamphlets, and dissertations dealing with voluntary private support by foundations, business firms, alumni, and others since 1960.

1125. Beard, Fred M. Public school finance annotated bibliography with particular emphasis on New Mexico. Denver, CO, Designing Education for the Future, 1967. 19p. ED 018327.

Includes 83 entries dating from 1922.

1126. Gould, Elaine S. Selected and annotated bibliography on financing education. Washington, DC, Agency for International Development, 1973. 49p. ED 119382.

Deals with acquisition and distribution of funds in the United States and developing countries. A historical perspective is included in the 200 items, none published prior to 1960.

1127. Issue category bibliographies. Eugene, University of Oregon, Center for Educational Policy and Management, 1977. 13p. ED 142219.

This annotated bibliography is concerned with school finance, in addition to governance, organization, personnel, and community involvement. Most entries are taken from a search of RIE and CIJE.

1128. School financial elections: the best of ERIC. ERIC Clearinghouse on Educational Management, 1977. 5p. ED 145504.

The eleven annotated entries deal with voter behavior, the "taxpayers' revolt", campaign strategies, and citizens' attitudes.

1129. Piele, Philip and Darrell Wright. Fiscal planning for school construction. Columbus, OH, Council of Educational Facility Planners, 1976. 7p. ED 120895.

The 17 ERIC documents also include renovations and wings.

1130. Rogers, Daniel C. _Summary of studies of cost analysis_
in educational planning and management. Washington, DC, Agency
for International Development, 1971. 9p. ED 125072.

  Contains 27 case studies by the International Institute
  for Educational Planning.

1131. _Financing lifelong learning: annotated bibliography_.
Albany, New York State Education Department, 1977. 22p. ED
150270 (MF)

  Cites 79 books, reports, articles, papers, and hearings
  on financing postsecondary education.

1132. Beslin, Ralph. _Education finance in Canada_. Ottawa,
Canadian Teachers Federation, 1978. 18p. ED 154538.

  A partially annotated bibliography with 68 books, 69 articles, and six theses.

1133. Isler, Norman P. _Operating costs of educational facil-_
ities. ERIC Clearinghouse on Educational Facilities, 1970.
58p. ED 037964.

  The annotated ERIC documents include property accounting,
  insurance programs, purchasing, food service, and maintenance.

1134. Janeway, Sally. _School finance reform: a bibliography_.
Washington, DC, Lawyers Committee for Civil Rights Under Law,
1972. 33p. ED 070147.

  Topics are: aid to private schools, alternative state funding schemes, legal aspects of school finance, politics of
  school finance, property taxes, and finance in urban school
  districts. Court decisions are included along with the
  books and articles.

1135. Shulman, Carol H. _Financing higher education_. ERIC
Clearinghouse on Higher Education, 1971. 25p. ED 048519.

  The bibliography includes 80 annotated entries.

1136. Tompkins, Dorothy C. _Local public schools: how to pay_
for them? Berkeley, University of California, Institute of
Governmental Studies, 1972. 108p. ED 077070.

  This 756 item unannotated bibliography was prompted by the
  Serrano decision of the California Supreme Court in August
  1971. The items are drawn from the literature on public
  administration, law, education, and state and local government.

1137. _Educational finance: an ERIC bibliography_. Washington,
DC, President's Commission on School Finance, 1972. 444p. ED
064792 (MF)

  Includes all CIJE and RIE entries on the subject to 1971.

EDUCATIONAL HISTORY

1138. Nakosteen, Mehdi. Conflicting educational ideals in
America, 1775-1831: documentary source book. Boulder, University of Colorado, School of Education, 1971. 480p. ED 049958.

  The annotated bibliography includes 4500 entries with some
  surveying the cultural setting of educational thinking in
  this time period. Other issues covered are public vs. private education, coed vs. separate, academic freedom, teacher education, teaching and learning theory, and equality
  of educational opportunity.

EDUCATIONAL OBJECTIVES

1139. Cox, Richard C. and Carol E. Wildemann. Taxonomy of
educational objectives, cognitive domain: an annotated bibliography. University of Pittsburgh, Learning Research and Development Center, 1970. 54p. ED 043089.

1140. Kuhn, G. Michael and Lorraine R. Gay. Instructional
objectives: a national compendium. Tallahassee, Florida State
Department of Education, 1972. 144p. ED 062743.

  The annotated bibliography contains instructional objectives and objectives-based materials collected from state
  departments of education, school systems, and commercial
  producers.

EDUCATIONAL PLANNING

1141. Models for planning: analysis of literature and selected
bibliography. ERIC Clearinghouse on Educational Administration,
1970. 17p. ED 043114.

  The list reviews 77 items of current research trends and
  applications.

1142. Marien, Michael. Essential reading for the future of
education: a selected and critically annotated bibliography.
Revised ed. Syracuse University, Research Corporation, 1971.
74p. ED 063649.

  Includes 200 references on educational and social planning,
  general trends, and future descriptions.

1143. Systems analysis for educational planning: selected,
annotated bibliography. Washington, DC, Organization for Economic Cooperation and Development, 1969. 196p. ED 057471.

  In English and French. Concerns the uses of applied to
  specific educational problems, and quantitative methods.

1144. Educational planning: a bibliography. Paris, France,
International Institute for Educational Planning, 1964. 141p.
ED 035982.

A listing of 11 annotated bibliographies is followed by
four sections with brief descriptions of over 500 items
related to educational planning in both the developed and
developing nations.

1145. Hinds, Richard H. Educational program planning and related techniques: annotated bibliography. Miami, Dade County
Florida Public Schools, 1969. 15p. ED 029375.

97 entries for educators in large school systems. Includes
system analysis, mathematical models, and cost-benefit
studies.

1146. Planning for a change: a resource catalog. Chicago,
Center for New Schools, Inc., 1973. 106p. ED 083668.

The 293 annotated entries are a search for alternatives
in planning for new school programs. Includes films and
videotapes.

1147. Wattenbarger, James L. Coordination of higher education: an annotated bibliography. Gainesville, University of
Florida, Institute of Higher Education, 1970. 30p. ED 040684.

The 120 items deal primarily with statewide planning, governing boards, and coordination and control of higher education.

1148. Hudson, Barclay M. Educational planning: notes on the
state of the art. 1977. 93p. ED 151936 (MF)

This paper addresses planning at the national level, and
concludes with an extensive bibliography.

1149. Temkin, Sanford. An Evaluation of comprehensive planning literature with an annotated bibliography. Philadelphia,
Research for Better Schools, Inc., 1970. 90p. ED 048332.

Covers system-wide planning, and politics, communication,
implementation, and community relations.

1150. Cook, Desmond L. References on network planning in education, research management, project selection, and program
management. Columbus, Ohio State University, Educational Research Management Center, 1966. 9p. ED 020580.

Includes over 100 entries on the topics in the forms of
addresses, articles, books, reports, and microforms published between 1959 and 1968.

1151. Marien, Michael D. Alternative futures for learning:
an annotated bibliography of trends, forecasts, and proposals.
Syracuse University, Research Corporation, 1971. 242p. ED
071998.

This planning document covers elementary through college levels with publications dating back to 1950.

1152. Webster, Maureen. Educational planning and policy: an international bibliography. Syracuse University, Research Corporation, 1969. 661p. ED 042238.

Most of the 4900 sources listed are in English in this unannotated bibliography on worldwide educational planning techniques and experiences. Also includes evaluations and futures planning.

1153. Choi, Susan and Richard Cornish. Selected references in educational planning: bibliography and selection criteria. San Jose, CA, Santa Clara County Office of Education, 1975. 91p. ED 100050.

A current bibliography organized by subjects.

1154. Barr, Charles W. The School in the urban comprehensive plan: a partial bibliography. Monticello, IL, Council of Planning Librarians, 1972. 40p. ED 106958.

Stresses urban and school planning concepts that influence community physical development and its financing, and the necessary school-community relationships. Annotated.

1155. Piele, Philip and Darrell Wright. Community participation in planning. Columbus, OH, Council of Educational Facility Planners, 1976. 7p. ED 123698.

Annotations of 17 ERIC system documents on the techniques and circumstances of involving the community in school planning.

1156. Piele, Philip and Darrell Wright. Educational specifications. Columbus, OH, Council of Educational Facility Planners, 1976. 5p. ED 123697.

Annotations of 13 ERIC system documents on the planning and construction of new school facilities.

1157. Murtha, D. Michael. Systematic methods in school planning and design: a selected and annotated bibliography. ERIC Clearinghouse on Educational Facilities, 1968. 43p. ED 024 251.

The books, articles, and reports cover the process in terms of practice, theory, methods, decisions, and computer applications.

1158. Pundiak, Jean. Planning bibliography for education: a planning handbook for districts. Trenton, New Jersey State Department of Education, 1975. 143p. ED 113828.

The annotations are categorized as theory and models, community participation, goal development, needs assessment, problem analysis, selection of alternatives, implementation, and evaluation.

EDUCATIONAL RESEARCH

1159. Trew, Karen. Register of research in education: Northern Ireland. Belfast, Northern Ireland Council for Educational Research, 1971. ED 127212 and ED 127213 (MF)

Volume one (78p) contains over 250 research theses and 57 selected articles on all facets of educational research in the country from 1949 to 1970. Volume two (114p) is a supplementary compilation bringing the literature up to 1972.

1160. Wolcott, Harry F. Ethnographic approaches to research in education: a bibliography on method. University of Georgia, Anthropology Curriculum Project, 1975. 33p. ED 111714 (MF)

Over 100 annotated items, mostly by anthropologists, deal with the problems of educational research and how to overcome them.

EDUCATIONAL TECHNOLOGY

1161. Berthold, Jeanne S. Educational technology and the teaching-learning process: a selected bibliography. Cleveland, Case Western Reserve University, 1969. 59p. ED 043231 (MF)

1162. Johnson, Charles E. and Glenn E. Duncan. Bibliography of selected references concerned with the applications of systems technology in education. Athens, University of Georgia, College of Education, 1969. 17p. ED 040932.

Includes 69 books and 182 articles published since 1960. Unannotated.

1163. Anderton, Ray L. and Joseph L. Mapes. Doctoral research in library media completed and underway. Boulder, University of Colorado, School of Education, 1970. 82p. ED 047495.

On computers in education, audiovisual techniques, media training, programmed instruction, simulation and games, and visual literacy.

1164. Dodge, Bernard J. Audiovisual resources for teaching instructional technology: an annotated listing. ERIC Clearinghouse on Information Resources, 1978. 77p. ED 152337.

For college and adult levels. Topics include media production, communications, development and innovation, evaluation, and the psychology of learning.

1165. Huang, Che-tsao. Monograph of studies in educational technology, 1960-1970. 1979. 98p. ED 184555.

    468 dissertations are listed.

1166. New technology in education: selected references. Washington, DC, Library of Congress, Congressional Research Service, 1971. 146p. ED 056486.

    Includes books, articles, and reports published in the
    1960's.

1167. Scanlon, Robert G. and JoAnn Weinberger. Compiled bibliography on improving productivity of school systems through
educational technology. Philadelphia, Research for Better
Schools, Inc., 1973. 65p. ED 086241.

    Includes 800 unannotated books, articles, reports, and
    papers mostly written in the previous six years.

EDUCATIONAL TELEVISION   See Also CABLE TELEVISION   and   TELE-
        VISION

1168. Bernbaum, Marcia. Educational television for preschool
and kindergarten children: an abstract bibliography. ERIC
Clearinghouse on Early Childhood Education, 1971. 26p. ED
056755.

    Articles and documents from the ERIC system evaluate
    "Sesame Street", and describe various aspects of the
    Appalachia Preschool Television Program.

1169. Television and education: a bibliography. New York,
Television Information Office, 1960. 9p. ED 014872.

    Partially annotated. Lists publications related to educa-
    tional and instructional television.

1170. Bierschenk, Bernhard. Television as a technical aid in
education and in educational and psychological research: a bibliographical account of German literature. Malmo, Sweden,
School of Education, 1971. 60p. ED 053616.

    All entries are in German and were written between 1960
    and 1970. Not annotated.

1171. An Annotated bibliography on the use of videotapes in
schools. South Paris, ME, Oxford Hills High School, 1970.
9p. ED 041447.

    Includes 26 articles and papers.

1172. Educational television bibliography. Pleasantville, NY,
General Precision, Inc., 1964(?) 13p. ED 017126.

    Contains present uses, theory, and recommendations with
    brief annotations.

1173. Seibert, Warren F. Instructional television: the best
of ERIC. ERIC Clearinghouse on Educational Media and Technology, 1973. 27p. ED 082535.

Annotated entries cover overviews, children and TV, cable
TV, continuing education, public television, international
developments, and other bibliographies and guides.

1174. A Bibliography of educational television and related
communication systems. National Association of Educational
Broadcasters, 1967. 49p. ED 020652.

1175. Carpenter, C. R. The Conditions, requirements, and variables affecting the quality of complex learning mediated by
instructional television systems. Pennsylvania State University, Department of Psychology, 1968. 7p. ED 037100.

48 reports published between 1962 and 1969 are presented
in this unannotated bibliography.

1176. Purdy, Leslie. Telecourse students: how well do they
learn? 1978. 16p. ED 154851.

This paper presented at the annual meeting of the American
Association of Community and Junior Colleges includes 28
references in its unannotated bibliography.

1177. Elsas, Diana. Guide to classroom use of film and television. Washington, DC, American Film Institute, 1977. 16p.
ED 153651 (MF)

Annotated.

1178. Seibert, Warren F. Instructional television: the best
of ERIC, 1974-1975. ERIC Clearinghouse on Information Resources, 1976. 35p. ED 126858.

An annotated bibliography which updates ED 082535.

1179. Carlson, Robert A. Educational television in its cultural and public affairs dimension: a selected literature review of public television as an issue in adult education. ERIC
Clearinghouse on Adult Education, 1973. 50p. ED 086890.

More than half of this booklet is devoted to an annotated
bibliography which is in two parts on "the conflicting
hopes, and the reality".

1180. DiBella, Cecilia M. Resources for schools. Boston,
Massachusetts State Department of Education, 1977. ED 152270
and ED 152271.

Part one is a catalog of their publications in 45 pages
which includes educational TV, and part two is a 25 page
annotated list of videotapes for teaching in a variety of
subject areas. Grade levels and showing times are indicated for each entry.

ELECTRICITY

1181. Krewatch, A. V. Electrification programs and materials for vocational agriculture, technical occupations, and trade and industry teaching programs and for 4-H electric clubs. Oakbrook, IL, Farm Electrification Council, 1967. 99p. ED 018622

An unannotated multimedia bibliography of 613 items.

ELECTRONICS

1182. Losee, Robert M. A Selective bibliography of commercial radio and television engineering. Shorewood, WI, EBR Press, 1975. 36p. ED 107263.

Includes reference books, case studies, filmstrips, and motion pictures in the field, and including lighting, management, and microwave transmission theory.

ELEMENTARY EDUCATION

1183. Bibliographies in education: elementary education. Ottawa, Canadian Teachers Federation, 1974. 40p. ED 099144.

An unannotated list of books, articles, papers, and theses produced from 1968 to 1973.

ELEMENTARY AND SECONDARY EDUCATION ACT (ESEA)

1184. Osman, David S. The Elementary and Secondary Education Act of 1965 as amended: selected annotated bibliography. Washington, DC, House Committee on Education and Labor, 1973. 74p. ED 096370.

This committee print provides a brief description of the aims, findings, and recommendations of the major books, articles, and government reports which have appeared on the subject.

1185. Finley, Mary M. A Selective annotated bibliography on the Elementary and Secondary Education Act. 1975. 22p. ED 156746.

The entries give an overview, purposes, descriptions, and and evaluations of ESEA.

EMOTIONALLY DISTURBED See Also MENTAL HEALTH

1186. Activities for emotional development. Jacksonville,

Florida Learning Resources System, 1975. 34p. ED 133957.

Unannotated list of 183 children's books categorized by
such needs as patience, responsibility, adoption, embarr-
assment, and physical handicaps.

1187. Emotionally disturbed research: a selective bibliography. Reston, VA, Council for Exceptional Children, 1973. 26p.
ED 085942.

Includes 95 abstracts from the Council's information center
holdings. Publication dates are 1960 to 1973.

1188. Emotionally disturbed programs: a selective bibliography. Reston, VA, Council for Exceptional Children, 1973. 28p.
ED 085919.

Abstracts of 90 programs are given which were published
from 1964 to 1973.

1189. Emotionally disturbed - counseling and therapy: a selective bibliography. Reston, VA, Council for Exceptional Children, 1976. 33p. ED 129011.

145 abstracts are included from the Council's information
center holdings. Publication dates are 1950 to 1975.

1190. Emotionally disturbed - educational programs: a selective bibliography. Reston, VA, Council for Exceptional Children, 1976. 22p. ED 129010.

Includes 75 abstracts from the Council's holdings published
since 1950.

1191. Emotionally disturbed - teaching methods and programs.
Reston, VA, Council for Exceptional Children, 1977. 22p. ED
146733.

100 annotated entries since 1972 are included.

1192. Klein, Zanvel E. Background and treatment of the emotional behavior disorders of children: a bibliography of research, 1925-1970. Chicago, Michael Reese Hospital and Medical Center, 1970. 96p. ED 107027

Lists about 1000 unannotated citations from the literature
of psychology, psychiatry, education, social work, and
public health on children under 12 years of age.

1193. Research relating to emotionally disturbed children.
Washington, DC, Children's Bureau (DHEW), 1968. 190p. ED
025879.

Unannotated citations to 842 research projects which have
been reported to the Bureau since 1956.

EMPLOYMENT See also UNEMPLOYMENT

1194. Manpower planning and utilization. Washington, DC, Civil Service Commission, 1971. 62p. ED 068694.

An annotated subject bibliography that includes forecasting, policies, planning, shortages, changes, jobs, and skills.

1195. Bibliography of employment and training literature. Corvallis, Oregon State University, Institute for Manpower Studies, 1978. 369p. ED 162118 (MF)

This first volume contains 5600 annotations. ED 162119 through ED 162121 conclude the set, the last volume being an index volume.

1196. McCracken, David. Intensive training for job entry skills: a selected bibliography for use in program development. Columbus, Ohio State University, Center for Vocational and Technical Education, 1969. 15p. ED 034061.

43 unannotated entries on needs, descriptions, development, and evaluations.

1197. Equal opportunity in employment. Washington, DC, Civil Service Commission, 1971. 139p. ED 069916.

The annotated bibliography covers minority groups, older workers, women, and the handicapped.

1198. Delap, Owen E. Manpower and employment statistics publications of the Bureau of Labor Statistics: a selected bibliography. 1969. 35p. ED 033219.

Includes 338 partially annotated entries dating from 1963 to 1969.

1199. Williams, C. Brian. Manpower management in Canada: a selected bibliography. Kingston, Ontario, Queen's University, Industrial Relations Centre, 1968. 127p. ED 034043.

A subject arrangement of 1125 unannotated citations dating from 1960. Includes U.S. and Canadian studies.

1200. Garbin, A. P. Worker adjustment - youth in transition from school to work: an annotated bibliography of recent literature. Columbus, Ohio State University, Center for Vocational Education, 1968. 143p. ED 021070.

165 entries dating from 1960 are included; most are journal articles, many of which are empirical studies.

1201. Manpower and operations research studies of the U.S. Employment Service and state employment services, 1958-1967: a selected bibliography. Washington, DC, Bureau of Employment Security (DOL), 1968. 153p. ED 026516.

The unannotated list is categorized by states.

1202. Klausner, Samuel Z. The Work Incentive Program: making

adults economically independent: bibliography and appendices.
University of Pennsylvania, 1972. 215p. ED 078168.

This volume two of the study contains the unannotated bibliography for the project sponsored by the Manpower Administration of the Department of Labor.

1203. Selected bibliography on fair employment. Washington,
DC, Equal Employment Opportunity Commission, 1976. 13p. ED
128737.

Lists books, articles, legal citations, and government
documents published since 1969.

1204. Stockard, Jean and Joan Kalvelage. A Selected annotated
bibliography on job sharing. Eugene, University of Oregon,
Center for Educational Policy and Management, 1977. 10p. ED
139125.

29 entries including research reports and other bibliographies concern working patterns of less than full-time employment.

ENERGY

1205. Thomas, Gerald and Irving McKane. Energy: systems for
control, maintenance, and storage: a bibliography. Keene, NH,
Keene State College, Vocational Teacher Education, 1978. 23p.
ED 162854 (MF)

Lists 249 journal articles on energy and aspects of its
technology, all published since 1972.

1206. Technical books and monographs. Oak Ridge, TN, Energy
Research and Development Administration, 1977. 146p. ED 144
795 (MF)

An annotated bibliography of commercial publications, and
some by nonprofit institutions, and the Federal government.

1207. Energy/environment/economy: an annotated bibliography
of selected U.S. Government publications concerning United
State energy policy. Green Bay, WI, ENVIRO/INFO, 1973. 24p.
ED 077704.

Includes 109 publications that deal with policy issues
and statistical reportage.

1208. Sweeney, Betsy. The Energy handbook. Victoria, BC,
Greater Victoria Environmental Center, 1974. 33p. ED 127731.

Intent focuses on the energy shortage, and doing something
about the energy crisis. Entries cover conservation and
alternative energy sources, in addition to energy education
with a Canadian perspective.

ENERGY CONSERVATION   See also   ENVIRONMENTAL EDUCATION

1209. ERIC document resumes on energy conservation and the
schools. Washington, DC, American Association of School Administrators, 1976. 18p. ED 120894.

Contains 24 annotations that offer practical suggestions
for reducing consumption, and examines the efficiency of
various systems.

1210. Berman, Richard M. and Irmgard Hunt. Energy directory
and bibliography. New York State Alliance to Save Energy,
1977. 33p. ED 159052.

Provides annotations to consumer oriented books and articles.

1211. Gil, Efraim. Energy efficient planning: an annotated
bibliography. Chicago, American Society of Planning Officials,
1976. 25p.   ED 164308.

Includes 114 citations for planners.

1212. Lengyel, Dorothy L. Selected resource materials for
developing energy conservation programs in the small business
and commercial sector. Pennsylvania State University, College
of Agriculture, 1978. 20p. ED 157784.

The annotated list is for building operators, planners,
and architects.

1213. Lengyel, Dorothy L. Selected resource materials for
developing energy conservation programs in the government sector. Pennsylvania State University, College of Agriculture,
1978. 24p. ED 157783.

This annotated list is aimed at local government officials,
and includes solar heating, building design, planning, and
legal considerations.

1214. McDaniel, Margaret. The Energy crisis: aids to study.
Lincoln, Massachusetts Audubon Society, 1974. 25p. ED 093765.

Over 100 current annotations are given for books, articles,
curriculum materials, and audiovisual aids.

ENERGY EDUCATION

1215. Energy: an annotated bibliography of selected energy
education materials. Lincoln, Massachusetts Audubon Society,
1977. 64p. ED 162912.

Includes books, articles, pamphlets, bibliographies, simulations, and audiovisual materials.

1216. Rinehart, Milton. Energy education: a bibliography of abstracts from "Resources in Education" from 1966-1978. Columbus, Ohio State University, Information Reference Center for Science Education, 1979. 159p. ED 166067 (MF)

Over 500 ERIC documents are listed which include instructional materials and teaching activity guides.

1217. Rinehart, Milton. Energy education: a bibliography of citations from "Current Index to Journals in Education" from 1966-1978. Columbus, Ohio State University, Information Reference Center for Science Education, 1979. 143p. ED 168874 (MF)

Over 500 annotated journal articles from CIJE are included in this bibliography.

1218. Scherner, Sharon. The Energy education bibliography: an annotated bibliography of key resources for energy and conservation education. Portland, OR, Energy and Man's Environment, Inc., 1978. 32p. ED 167453 (MF)

References include story books, teaching guides, multimedia kits, catalogs, bibliographies, posters, and photograph collections. The 180 items are for K-12 classroom teachers and curriculum developers.

1219. Energy education materials inventory: an annotated bibliography of currently available materials, K-12, published prior to May 1976. University of Houston, Texas Energy Institute, 1978. 301p. ED 160439 (MF)

About 800 items are included that are referenced by type of media, subject, and grade level. ED 183360 is a 444 page Volume Two of this set.

1220. Coon, Herbert L. and John F. Disinger. Energy education programs: elementary school programs and resources. ERIC Information Analysis Center for Science, Mathematics, and Environmental Education, 1979. 43p. ED 183386.

Includes descriptions of 14 programs in use, and an annotated bibliography of their listed resources.

1221. Energy conservation in the school curriculum. Boston, Massachusetts State Department of Education, 1975. 25p. ED 150755 (MF)

The first part is an address by S. David Freeman, and the second is the descriptive bibliography of instructional materials produced by state education agencies.

1222. Wert, Jonathan M. and Barry K. Worthington. Energy: selected resource materials for developing energy education and conservation programs. Revised ed. Pennsylvania State University, College of Agriculture, 1978. 34p. ED 157782(MF)

Includes teaching materials and consumer awareness items.

1223. Fowler, J.M. and K.W. Mervine. Energy and the environment. University of Maryland, Department of Physics and Astronomy, 1973. 53p. ED 075230.

Considers not only the natural sciences, but also ethics, economics, and politics. The annotated bibliography covers general references, energy policy, electric power, nuclear power, fossil fuels, and future sources of energy.

1224. Energy education materials bibliography. St. Paul, Minnesota State Energy Agency, 1978. 65p. ED 162900.

The 100 annotated entries provide background materials and classroom activities for teachers and students. ED 184856 is a 35 page update issued in October 1979.

ENGINEERING

1225. A Selected, annotated bibliography on employment of minority engineers. Washington, DC, National Academy of Sciences, National Research Council, 1975. 22p. ED 149881.

Designed for guidance, recruiting, and hiring personnel in industry, research, education and government. Puerto Rican, Chicano, and American Indian engineering graduates are the central concern of this bibliography.

1226. Rushby, N.J. Computers in engineering teaching. University of London, Imperial College Computer Centre, 1978. 29p. ED 176807.

Cites 26 books, papers, and programs for use in teaching aeronautical, chemical, civil, electronic, mechanical, and nuclear engineering.

ENGLISH INSTRUCTION See also BILINGUAL EDUCATION and LANGUAGE INSTRUCTION

1227. Annotated index to the "English Journal", 1944-1963. Champaign, IL, National Council of Teachers of English, 1964. 185p. ED 071097.

The first supplement to this is ED 067664 which includes 1100 articles from 1964 to 1970.

1228. Moore, Walter J. Annotated index to "Elementary English" 1924-1967. Champaign, IL, National Council of Teachers of English, 1968. 273p. ED 071094.

Citations for all the articles in this journal are listed.

1229. Bailey, Dorothy D. Teaching English to the culturally different. Westchester State College (Pa.), 1967. 42p. ED 017503.

This annotated bibliography includes prose, poetry, and textbooks.

1230. Butler, Donna and Robert V. Denby. ERIC documents on the teaching of English, 1956-1968. Champaign, IL, National Council of Teachers of English, 1969. 75p. ED 029045.

A comprehensive list of 942 items available from the ERIC system.

1231. Scannell, William J. Annotated list of recommended Elementary and secondary curriculum guides in English. Champaign, IL, National Council of Teachers of English, 1969. 41p. ED 033950.

Provides 50 guides that were reviewed and recommended as good models.

1232. Neidlinger, Susan and James H. Mason. Bibliography: the teaching of English in college, 1954-1968. Champaign, IL, National Council of Teachers of English, 1968. 61p. ED 023704.

Includes 1100 books and journal articles on composition, rhetoric, grammar, and linguistics.

1233. Rowland, J. Carter. An Annotated bibliography on the college teaching of English. Champaign, IL, National Council of Teachers of English, 1966. 61p. ED 038432 (MF)

Includes 481 journal articles on freshman English, drama and television, speech, journalism, and the preparation of English teachers.

1234. Winkeljohann, Rosemary. Recommended English language arts curriculum guides K-12, and criteria for planning and evaluation. ERIC Clearinghouse on Reading and Communication Skills, 1978. 33p. ED 158315.

Annotated list of guides recommended for 1976-1978.

1235. Aids to English language teaching. London, British Council, English Teaching Information Centre, 1975. 73p. ED 111220.

The annotated bibliography is useful for both native and non-native speakers of English at the primary and secondary levels.

1236. Basic bibliographies on the teaching of English. ERIC Clearinghouse on the Teaching of English, 1970. 85p. ED 049 247.

Includes 20 other annotated bibliographies.

1237. Brown, James L. A Selected and annotated bibliography on the teaching of freshman English composition in two and four year colleges. 1974. 11p. ED 100414.

Contains 41 journal articles, some of which are on team teaching and individualized instruction.

1238. Feldman, Marjorie. Easy reading materials for adults learning English. Revised ed. Chicago, Central YMCA Community College, 1976. 13p. ED 128063.

Vocabulary level is indicated in these items for adults who are beginning to read.

ENGLISH (SECOND LANGUAGE)   See also   BILINGUAL EDUCATION   and LANGUAGE INSTRUCTION

1239. Pedtke, Dorothy A. Reference list of materials for English as a second language. Washington, DC, Center for Applied Linguistics, 1969. 207p. ED 025773 (MF)

This annotated supplement to ED 014723 and ED 014724 covers the years 1964 to 1968.

1240. Aitken, Kenneth G. TESL applications to the cloze procedure: an annotated bibliography. 1975 16p. ED 109922.

38 theses and articles relate the cloze procedure to teaching English as a second language (TESL).

1241. Fox, Robert P. A Selected list of instructional materials for English as a second language: college level. ERIC Clearinghouse on Language and Linguistics, 1975. 25p. ED 107 158.

The 130 annotated entries include textbooks, reading, composition, vocabulary workbooks, conversation guidebooks, audiolingual manuals, idiom workbooks, and pattern drills.

1242. Greis, Naguib. TESL bibliography. 1975. 18p. ED 125 316.

195 unannotated items for prospective teachers of English to speakers of other languages.

1243. Greis, Naguib. ESL bibliography. 1975. 19p. ED 126 732.

117 unannotated items for English as a second language. Includes library skills, oral skills, reading, writing, and tests.

1244. Robson, Barbara and Kenton Sutherland. A Selected annotated bibliography for teaching English to speakers of Vietnamese. Washington, DC, Center for Applied Linguistics, 1975. 68p. ED 108519.

For children, adults, and the teachers. Includes audiovisuals, reference materials, and tests.

1245. A Bibliography of reading materials for adult students
of English as a second language. Arlington, VA, Center for
Applied Linguistics, 1976. 21p. ED 129062.

A wide variety of topics are provided for students at all
levels of reading ability. Annotated.

1246. A Selected annotated bibliography of materials for teaching English to Indochinese refugee adults. Arlington, VA, Center for Applied Linguistics, 1978. 46p. ED 165457 (MF)

The focus is on the adult refugee who is planning employment or vocational training.

1247. Pfannkuche, Anthony. Teaching English as a second language to adults: textbooks for basic courses. Arlington, VA,
Center for Applied Linguistics, 1976. 12p. ED 122632 (MF)

This annotated list is designed for teaching English to
Vietnamese and Cambodian refugees.

1248. Macha, Dyne and Paul Angelis. An Annotated bibliography
of materials for teaching advanced written skills in English
as a second language. 1976. 20p. ED 132823.

Primarily a bibliography of textbooks.

1249. Fifield, Ruth. English as a second language bibliography. El Centro, CA, Imperial County Schools, 1968. 19p. ED
024513.

Contains sections on professional materials, instructional
materials, audiovisual items, and Spanish language curriculum materials. 250 resources dating from 1946 are included.
Unannotated.

1250. Bibliography of materials available for use in English
as a second language classes. San Diego, CA, City Schools,
1967. 23p. ED 026153.

About 250 books, articles, and resource materials are cited
in this annotated bibliography.

1251. Escobar, Joanna S. and John Daugherty. An Annotated
bibliography of adult ESL instructional materials. Arlington
Heights, IL, Bilingual Education Service Center, 1976. 331p.
ED 132389.

Includes basic texts, composition, spelling, conversation,
pronunciation, grammar, reading, listening, vocabulary,
literacy, and games and simulations.

1252. English as a second language bibliography: adults. Arlington, VA, National Clearinghouse for Bilingual Education,
1978. 34p. ED 165472.

Includes vocational education, employment, and survival
skills, plus ESL tests and teacher aids.

1253._English for speakers of other languages: a bibliography_.
London, British Council, English Teaching Information Centre,
1974. 59p. ED 111219.

   Most of the books listed were published in England since
   1959. Annotated.

1254. Farnan, John. _A Selected bibliography on English language learning and teaching in Thailand_. 1979. 19p. ED 176
593.

   Includes unannotated books, articles, and microforms. Reference materials include studies on Thai language and culture, anthropological and sociological references, various
   bibliographies, contrastive studies, and works in phonetics
   and phonology.

1255. Garcia-Zamor, Marie and David Birdsong. _Testing in Eng-
lish as a second language: a selected, annotated bibliography_.
ERIC Clearinghouse on Languages and Linguistics, 1977. 32p.
ED 135206.

   Most of the items listed were published since 1969, and
   include texts and articles that treat the general aspects
   of second language testing, testing theory, design, and
   assessments.

1256. Marckwardt, Maybelle. _A Selected list of instructional
materials for English as a second language: elementary level_.
ERIC Clearinghouse on Language and Linguistics, 1975. 11p.
ED 105753.

   An annotated list of 42 textbooks, AV aids, puzzles,
   games, readers, and workbooks.

1257. Joseph, Grace. _A Selected ERIC bibliography on teaching
English as a second language to the illiterate_. ERIC Clearinghouse on Languages and Linguistics, 1975. 28p. ED 105779.

   The 44 annotated entries include teacher training, programs, instructional and resource materials, and theory
   and methodology.

1258. _English for special purposes_. London, British Council,
English Teaching Information Centre, 1973. 68p. ED 111170.

   The teaching and learning of English as a foreign language
   for special purposes is the focus of this bibliography.
   Annotated.

1259. Rowe, Pauline. _Textbooks for English as a second language: an annotated bibliography_. Los Angeles City Schools,
1971. 29p. ED 051688.

1260. Flaherty, Jane F. _Resources for the ESL teacher_. Union,
NJ, Newark State College, Adult Education Resource Center,
1970. 22p. ED 053590.

Includes textbooks, readings, audiovisual aids, and professional materials. A section on ESL test preparation
and references on testing is also contained in this unannotated bibliography.

1261. Brilliant, Nancy. Teaching English to speakers of other
languages: a selected bibliography. 1971. 15p. ED 106480.

Lists 200 annotated entries on general linguistics, contrastive studies, learning theory, bibliographies, periodicals, and testing.

ENROLLMENT PROJECTIONS

1262. Declining enrollments: the best of ERIC. ERIC Clearinghouse on Educational Management, 1976. 5p. ED 131523.

Eleven annotations from the ERIC system concern the school
districts experiences and present forecasting models.

1263. Piele, Philip and Darrell Wright. Enrollment forecasting. ERIC Clearinghouse on Educational Management, 1976. 9p.
ED 117782.

Includes 29 annotated entries from the ERIC system on the
topic from the perspective of administrators, planners,
mathematicians, and demographers.

1264. Lins, L. J. Methodology of enrollment projections for
colleges and universities. American Association of Collegiate
Registrars and Admissions Officers, 1960. 78p. ED 025919.

Contains an unannotated bibliography of books, articles,
and reports on the subject.

ENVIRONMENTAL EDUCATION

1265. Conservation: selected bibliography. Australian Conservation Foundation, 1971. 12p. ED 064077.

The unannotated list covers the history, ethics, methods,
and politics of the subject.

1266. McDaniel, Margaret. Aids to environmental education.
Lincoln, Massachusetts Audubon Society, 1974. 69p. ED 093763.

This annotated list for preschool through grade six contains bibliographies, books for students, books and activity guides for teachers, filmstrips, graphics, magazines,
and curriculum materials.

1267. McDaniel, Margaret. Aids to environmental education:
grades 7 through 14. Lincoln, Massachusetts Audubon Society,
1974. 115p. ED 093764.

1268. Lamb, William G. A Sourcebook for secondary environmental education. Austin, University of Texas, Science Education Center, 1973. 117p. ED 093682.

Includes annotated bibliographies of print and AV items.

1269. Stitt, Thomas R. An Annotated bibliography for environmental educators. Springfield, Illinois State Board of Vocational Education and Rehabilitation, 1973. 38p. ED 086511.

Over 130 items arranged by occupation: biology, agriculture, business, marketing, management, health, industrial
and public service.

1270. Davies, James N. A Bibliography of environmental education for elementary and secondary teachers. 1978. 31p.
ED 161689.

Unannotated books and journal articles from the 1970's.

1271. Saveland, Robert N. and Patricia L. Tolbert. A Bibliography of environmental education articles from the "Journal
of Geography". Athens, University of Georgia, Geography Curriculum Project, 1979. 20p. ED 173193 (MF)

Includes over 100 articles, 1973-1978, for use by environmental educators for grades K-12, and at the university
level.

1272. Rivkin, G. W. and S. L. Brecher. Environmental information resources for state and local elected officials: general
reference guide. Washington, DC, Environmental Protection
Agency, and Rivkin Associates, Inc., 1977. 147p. ED 159041.

Contains primary and secondary sources.

1273. An Annotated catalog of environmental learning resources. Columbus, Ohio State Department of Education, 1973. 56p.
ED 092387.

Includes classroom aids and reference materials for the
teacher. Covers environmental awareness, ecological concepts, current problems, nature study, outdoor and conservation education techniques.

1274. Eckman, Tom. Environmental games and simulations. 1974.
9p. ED 091161.

Describes 135 products currently on the market.

1275. Steinwachs, Barbara. A Selected list of urban, environmental, and social problem gaming/simulations. Ann Arbor, University of Michigan, Extension Service, 1977. 31p. ED 148605
(MF)

Descriptive information is given on each of the games,
some of which are commercially produced, and some which
were developed at the University. Many are computerized,

and all are for the elementary through high school level.

1276. Resource guide to environmental education. Trenton,
New Jersey State Department of Education, 1971. 78p. ED 081
591.

   Lists curriculum materials for kindergarten through adult
   levels, and includes books, articles, and multimedia resources.

1277. Stegner, Robert W. A Sourcebook for population-environ-
mental studies. Newark, University of Delaware, 1972. 230p.
ED 065432.

   This annotated guide lists books, periodicals and 16mm
   films dating from 1955.

1278. Pepe, Thomas F. Environmental education: a bibliography
pertaining to the environment, environmental education, and
environmental education programs and materials. Conshohocken,
PA, Research and Information Services for Education, 1971.
90p. ED 053988.

   An unannotated list for K-12 with emphasis on ecology and
   pollution. It includes RIE citations from 1967 in addition
   to books, films, filmstrips, kits and charts. Some tests
   are included, too.

1279. Man and environment: a bibliography. Miami, Florida,
National Association for Environmental Education, 1970. 113p.
ED 056931.

   Annotated list of books, articles, and reports.

1280. Lockard, J. David. World trends in environmental education. Paris, UNESCO, 1976. 79p. ED 141179 (MF)

   An annotated bibliography compiled for a UNESCO program.

1281. Swan, Fred C. Environmental awareness bibliography.
Philadelphia, Friends Council on Education, 1971. 35p. ED
063145.

   This annotated bibliography has sections on outdoor education, conservation education, nature education, and environmental education; it includes programs, courses of study
   and lesson plans.

1282. Horn, B. Ray. A Basic reading list on state environmental education planning processes and problems. 1973. 6p.
ED 077699.

   This conference paper contains 26 references in its bibliography.

1283. Selected bibliography and audiovisual materials for
environmental education. St. Paul, Minnesota State Department

of Education, 1971. 46p. ED 051069.

99 books are annotated with grade level indicated in addition to the films and filmstrips.

1284. Audiovisual materials for environmental education. St. Paul, Minnesota State Department of Education, 1971. 31p. ED 066327.

For primary through senior high school levels.

1285. Healy, Mary K. and Phyllis Root. A Beginning. 1972. 46p. ED 071866.

This annotated bibliography was prepared for the Sierra Club Conference on Education for Environmental Awareness. Print and non-print items are included for K-12 levels.

1286. Cummings, Alice and Dorothy Byars. Environmental education: an annotated bibliography of selected materials and services available. Washington, DC, National Education Association, 1975. 25p. ED 125864 (MF)

1287. Voelker, Alan M. Environmental education related research, 1969-1972: an annotated bibliography. Madison, University of Wisconsin, Center for Environmental Communications and Education Studies, 1973. 61p. ED 103280.

Includes curriculum organization, instruction strategies, program development and evaluation, and resources and facilities.

ENVIRONMENTAL STUDIES

1288. Grenfell, Adrienne. Public concern with environmental problems: a bibliography. Washington, DC, Library of Congress, Congressional Research Service, 1978. 37p. ED 162889 (MF)

Contains attitude surveys, opinion polls, recent histories, philosophical discussions of environmental ethics, and narrative descriptions of public reaction to specific environmental matters.

1289. Science policy, technology assessment, and the environment: an annotated bibliography. Green Bay, WI, ENVIRO/INFO, 1973. 20p. ED 089947.

Includes 69 government publications concerning relationships of science advancement and environmental quality.

1290. Environment and the community: an annotated bibliography. Washington, DC, Department of Housing and Urban Development, 1971. 70p. ED 065438.

309 books, reports, and articles dating from 1964 intended for concerned citizens, architects, and planners.

1291. Dunlap, Riley E. Sociological and social-psychological
perspectives on environmental issues: a bibliography. Monticello, IL, Council of Planning Librarians, 1975. 39p. ED 141189.

   Unannotated list of books, articles, and papers on beliefs,
   attitudes, opinions, and perceptions related to environmental issues.

1292. Dinsmore, John. International environmental policy: an
annotated bibliography. Green Bay, University of Wisconsin,
1972. 22p. ED 062167.

   113 entries which present discussions or viewpoints on the
   formulation of international policy.

1293. Hagevik, George. Planning for environmental quality.
Monticello, IL, Council of Planning Librarians, 1969. 14p.
ED 101422.

   Unannotated bibliography on specific environmental problems, and the nature of related decision making.

ESKIMOS

1294. Hippler, Arthur E. Eskimo acculturation: a selected,
annotated bibliography of Alaskan and other Eskimo acculturation studies. Fairbanks, University of Alaska, ISEGR, 1970.
214p. ED 048983.

   Includes about 200 items dating back to 1831.

1295. Hippler, Arthur E. and John R. Wood. The Alaska Eskimos: a selected, annotated bibliography. Fairbanks, University
of Alaska, ISEGR, 1977. 335p. ED 165963.

   Includes 732 entries in English dating back to 1843, but
   the majority were published since 1900.

1296. Reed, E. Irene. List of materials developed by the
Eskimo language workshop. Fairbanks, University of Alaska,
Center for Northern Educational Research, 1974. 10p. ED 093
184.

   An unannotated list of materials in Yupik and English prepared for levels K-3. Most of the items are fiction, but
   there are listed teacher's handbooks and other aids, in
   addition to video and audio tapes in Yupik.

1297. Multimedia resource list: Eskimos and Indians. Toronto,
Ontario Department of Education, 1969. 41p. ED 040916.

   Culture, myths, legends, biography and fiction are represented in film, tape, maps, slides, records, and picture
   sets. Not annotated.

1298. Carney, R. J. and W. O. Ferguson. A Selected and anno-

tated bibliography on the sociology of Eskimo education. Edmonton, University of Alberta, Boreal Institute, 1965. 64p.
ED 037280.

A partially annotated list of books, papers, and articles
(300 items) published since 1877.

1299. Luccock, John. An Annotated bibliography of literature
by and about Canadian Eskimos for ages 5 to 14. 1972. 9p.
ED 072412.

Includes incidents, stories, myths, legends, and poetry.

ESPERANTO

1300. Tonkin, Humphrey R. Esperanto and international language problems: a research bibliography. Washington, DC, Esper-
antic Studies Foundation, 1977. 50p. ED 174029 (MF)

Basic texts, bibliographies, and brief abstracts of literature in the field are included.

ETHICS   See   VALUES EDUCATION

ETHNIC LITERATURE   See also   BLACK LITERATURE, ET AL

1301. Prichard, Nancy S. A Selected bibliography of American
ethnic writing, and supplement. Champaign, IL, National Council of Teachers of English, 1969. 49p. ED 041921.

Includes items by or about Blacks, Chicanos, American Indians, and Asian Americans in the form of poetry, fiction,
biography, autobiography, drama, art, and music.

1302. Mangione, Anthony R. The Story that has not been told.
1973. 31p. ED 088088.

An annotated bibliography designed to help teachers improve
the self-image of immigrant pupils and their parents. Literature of eleven ethnic groups is represented in this paper presented to the National Council of Teachers of English conference.

1303. Fitzgerald, Bonnie. Bibliography of literature and
cross-culture values. Urbana, IL, National Council of Teachers
of English, 1973. 17p. ED 082220.

Age level is provided for 103 annotated citations that include fiction, poetry, folktales, biography, legends, and
music of Blacks, Chicanos, and American Indians.

1304. Portraits, the literature of minorities: an annotated
bibliography of literature by and about four ethnic groups in
the United States for grades 7-12. Los Angeles County Superintendent of Schools, 1970. 79p. ED 042771.

Organized by literary types representing Blacks, Chicanos, American Indians, and Asian Americans. ED 065887 is an annotated 71 page supplement issued in June 1972.

ETHNIC STUDIES   See also MINORITY GROUPS   and specific groups

1305. Annotated bibliography of multi-ethnic curriculum materials. Columbia, MO, Midwest Center for Equal Educational Opportunities, 1974. 165p. ED 114378.

Includes 16mm films, filmstrips, sound recordings, photo aids, learning kits, simulations, games, booklets, and books. The first through the sixth supplements are ED 114 379-381, 129703, 150076, 144862. and the index to the set is available as ED 160475.

1306. A Selected annotated bibliography of material relating to racism, Blacks, Chicanos, native Americans, and multi-ethnicity. East Lansing, Michigan Education Association, 1971. 75p. ED 069445.

294 entries that date from 1945 include fiction, biography, periodicals, records, films, and filmstrips. Three annotated supplements are ED 117230 (105p), ED 117231 (77p), and ED 117290 (87p).

1307. Nance, Elizabeth. A Community of people: a multi-ethnic bibliography. Portland, OR, Public Schools, 1974. 135p. ED 121872 (MF)

An annotated multimedia list that focuses on eight minority groups.

1308. Bibliography of multi-ethnic and sex-fair resources materials. Boston, Massachusetts State Department of Education, 1976. 34p. ED 162007 (MF)

This annotated multimedia bibliography aims to promote nondiscriminatory education, and present research studies examining bias in school texts and environments.

1309. Abraham, Pauline. Bibliography: Indians of North America, Mexican American, Negroes - civil rights. 1974. 50p. ED 092301.

Includes 70 annotated entries of fiction and nonfiction for junior and senior high schools.

1310. Paquette, Dan. A Model program in multi-ethnic heritage studies: annotated bibliographies of ethnic studies materials. Mankato State College (Minnesota), Minority Group Study Center, 1974(?) 30p. ED 114397.

Concentrates on the history, immigration, experiences, attitudes, and aspirations of European immigrants, including the Italians, Polish, Slavic, Germans, Swedish, and Norwegians.

1311. Kolm, Richard. Bibliography on ethnicity and ethnic groups. Rockville, MD, National Institute of Mental Health, 1973. 255p. ED 090340.

Explores the theory and the social, cultural, and psychological consequences of membership in a minority or ethnic group. Annotated.

1312. Onouye, Wendy. A Guide to materials for ethnic studies. Revised ed. Seattle, WA, Shoreline Community College, Learning Resources Center, 1972. 178p. ED 090111.

References on Blacks comprise about one-half of the guide; the other groups included are Chicanos, American Indians, and Asian Americans. Both print and nonprint materials are included.

1313. Kotler, Greta. Bibliography of ethnic heritage studies program materials. Washington, DC, National Center for Urban Ethnic Affairs, 1976. 41p. ED 148983.

The unannotated bibliography is organized by state and indexed by ethnic groups, audience, subject and form.

1314. Jakle, John A. Ethnic and racial minorities in North America: a selected bibliography of the geographical literature. Monticello, IL, Council of Planning Librarians, 1973. 73p. ED 134670.

Arranged by 46 ethnic groups. Unannotated.

1315. Inglehart, Babette and Anthony R. Mangione. Multi-ethnic literature: an annotated bibliography on European ethnic group life in America. New York, American Jewish Committee, 1974. 62p. ED 091701.

Includes anthologies, fiction, drama, poetry, biography, history, and criticism.

1316. Poliakoff, Lorraine. Ethnic groups: Negroes, Spanish speaking, American Indians, and Eskimos. ERIC Clearinghouse on Teacher Education, 1970. 29p. ED 044384.

Cites 117 documents in the ERIC system for 1968 and 1969.

1317. Thompson, Bryan and Mary Vance. Ethnic groups in urban areas; community formation and growth: a selected bibliography. Monticello, IL, Council of Planning Librarians, 1971. 18p. ED 060148.

Deals with ethnic settlement patterns and their determining factors, and subsequent migrations.

1318. Haberbosch, John F. Annotated bibliography: Afro-Amer-

ican, Hispano, and Amerind. Denver, Colorado State Department
of Education, 1969. 48p. ED 033635 (MF)

    A multimedia list dating back to 1861. One section deals
    with school segregation, politics, voting, discrimination,
    and civil rights in Colorado.

1319. Local library resources for a multi-ethnic curriculum;
a model program in multi-ethnic heritage studies. Mankato
State College (Minnesota), 1975(?) 240p. ED 115633.

    Includes a multimedia listing for the seven different
    American ethnic groups.

1320. Jackson, Anne. Ethnic groups: their cultures and contributions. Little Rock, Arkansas State Department of Education, 1970. 162p. ED 063062.

    Includes 701 annotated items dating back to 1929 on Blacks,
    Chicanos, American Indians, and Asian Americans.

1321. Ethnic and cultural studies: a bibliography. Baltimore,
Maryland State Department of Education, 1978. 25p. ED 156580
(MF)

    This resource list of bibliographies is designed to help
    teachers and librarians select curriculum materials about
    ethnic groups.

1322. Haller, Elizabeth S. New perspectives: a bibliography
of racial, ethnic, and feminist resources. Harrisburg, Pennsylvania State Department of Education, 1977. 299p. ED 146284.

    Annotated and compiled to help high school personnel locate
    resources to develop effective school programs which sup-
    port sex equality and ethnic/racial pluralism.

1323. Gold, Milton J. and Carl A. Grant. Multicultural education: a functional bibliography for teachers. Omaha, University of Nebraska, Center for Urban Education, 1977. 46p. ED
143563.

    An annotated list of 200 citations for teaching ethnic
    studies in grades K-12 with special emphasis on group
    values.

1324. Hylton, V. Wendell. Media resource center bibliography:
multiethnic, multicultural, multimedia materials. Richmond,
Virginia State Department of Education, 1975. 40p. ED 150959.

    Short descriptions and recommended audience levels are
    given.

1325. Nichols, Margaret S. and Peggy O'Neill. Multicultural
resources for children: a bibliography of materials for preschool through elementary school. Stanford, CA, Multicultural
Resources, 1977. 217p. ED 152394.

4000 unannotated items concern Blacks, Spanish speaking, Asian Americans, American Indians, and Pacific Island cultures. All types of resources are included, and grade levels are indicated.

1326. Caselli, Ron. The Minority experience: a basic bibliography of American ethnic studies. Revised ed. Santa Rosa, CA, Sonoma County Superintendent of Schools, 1975. 106p. ED 111902.

Includes about 1500 books published since 1940 which provide a historical approach to current problems. Civil rights, racial issues, immigration, socialization, bilingualism, and religion are some of the topics.

1327. Bengelsdorf, Winnie. Ethnic studies in higher education: state of the art and bibliography. Washington, DC, American Association of State Colleges and Universities, 1972. 261p. ED 069204.

1328. Weed, Perry L. Ethnicity and American group life: a bibliography. New York, American Jewish Committee, 1972. 26p. ED 073208.

Material is included on the immigrant experience, social and political development, and the contemporary rediscovery and resurgence.

1329. Gollnick, Donna M. Multicultural education and ethnic studies in the United States: an analysis and annotated bibliography of selected ERIC documents. ERIC Clearinghouse on Teacher Education, 1976. 179p. ED 120103.

The main categories are concept materials, classroom materials, curriculum materials, and program materials.

1330. Bibliography of the sources for the evaluation and selection of instructional materials which will insure proper recognition of ethnic and cultural minorities. Baltimore, Maryland State Department of Education, 1973. 14p. ED 095885.

An annotated multimedia bibliography of 50 bibliographies.

1331. Bronaugh, Juanita and George E. Ayers. Multiethnic materials: a selected bibliography. Racine, WI, Unified School District, 1976. 78p. ED 129957.

Some subjects are discrimination, segregation, Blacks, Chicanos, American Indians, and the culture of these and other groups. Includes professional books and articles, pamphlets, films, filmstrips, audiotapes, and ethnic cookbooks. Unannotated.

1332. Gilmore, Dolores D. and Kenneth Petrie. People: annotated multiethnic bibliography, K-12. Rockville, MD, Montgomery County Public Schools, 1973. 345p. ED 099864.

Designed as a materials selection tool for schools.

1333. <u>Amebook: a multi-ethnic bibliography</u>. Bel Air, MD, Harford County Public Schools, 1976. 40p. ED 139382.

Annotated bibliography of culture patterns and contemporary problems.

1334. <u>New York State Education Department materials, programs, services for multicultural education</u>. Albany, 1977. 85p. ED 142465.

A multimedia annotated list concerning Blacks, Puerto Ricans, and American Indians. It contains descriptions of elementary and secondary curriculum materials for ethnic studies, bilingual education, and art education.

1335. Spicer, Harold O. <u>Focus on ethnic literature in the in the classroom</u>. Terre Haute, Indiana Council of Teachers of English, 1977. 34p. ED 139037.

An annotated multimedia bibliography for first through sixth grade for the study of three ethnic groups: Blacks, Chicanos, and American Indians.

1336. <u>Annotated bibliography of multi-ethnic curriculum materials</u>. Lincoln, Nebraska State Department of Education, 1975. 81p. ED 103513.

1337. <u>Materials and human resources for teaching ethnic studies: an annotated bibliography</u>. Boulder, CO, Social Science Education Consortium, Inc., 1975. 284p. ED 128233.

Includes 1000 entries on ethnic peoples in the United States published since 1965. For K-12.

1338. <u>Multi-ethnic reading and audiovisual materials for young children: annotated bibliography</u>. Washington, DC, Day Care and Child Development Council of America, Inc., 1972. 11p. ED 073202.

Arranged in four sections: Blacks, Chicanos, American Indians, and reference sources.

1339. Griffin, Louise. <u>Multi-ethnic books for young children: annotated bibliography for parents and teachers</u>. ERIC Clearinghouse on Early Childhood Education, 1970. 77p. ED 046519 (MF)

Age levels are given for books on American Indians, Eskimos, Appalachians, Blacks, Hawaiians, Filipinos, Chicanos, Jews, and others of European descent.

1340. <u>Ethnic studies resource manual</u>. Boston, Massachusetts Bicentennial Commission, 1976. 34p. ED 123179.

Lists 387 publications issued since 1935 most of which are intended to be readings for students on 41 different ethnic groups. About 30 AV items are included, too.

EUROPE

1341. Western Europe: a selected functional and country bibliography. Washington, DC, Foreign Service Institute, 1972.
23p. ED 076491

    Includes about 300 unannotated references on the histori-
    cal perspective, European unity, and the Atlantic Alliance.

1342. Eastern Europe and the USSR: a selected functional and
country bibliography. Washington, DC, Foreign Service Institute, 1972. 38p. ED 076492.

    Includes about 500 unannotated references on the ideology
    and nature of communism, international communication, the
    evolution of the USSR, historical background on communist
    East Europe, and a section on post World War II.

1343. Apanasewicz, Nellie and Seymour M. Rosen. Eastern Europe education: a bibliography of English language materials.
Washington, DC, Office of Education (DHEW), 1966. 41p. ED
045545.

    An annotated list of 233 items published since the late
    1950's on the arts, education, goals, graduate studies,
    and the Ministries of Education.

EVALUATION See also PROGRAM EVALUATION and TEACHER EVAL-
        UATION

1344. Eidell, Terry L. Annotated bibliography on the evaluation of educational programs. ERIC Clearinghouse on Educational Administration, 1968. 19p. ED 025857.

    Includes 64 books, pamphlets, and articles published since
    1964.

1345. Pettman, Philip J. Student evaluation of faculty, 1965-
1970: an annotated bibliography. University of Minnesota,
Measurement Services Center, 1971(?) 16p. ED 054735.

    The 107 articles include surveys, reviews, and experiments.

1346. Strang, Ernest W. Building state capacity in dissemination: literature review. Durham, NC, National Testing Service, Inc., 1977. 130p. ED 142191.

    Designed for educational researchers and evaluators.

1347. ERIC document resumes on staff evaluation. Washington,
DC, American Association of School Administrators, 1976. 27p.
ED 131518.

    47 items consider the measurement of staff effectiveness.

1348. Evaluation of teacher performance: an annotated bibliography. Washington, DC, National Education Association, 1978.
9p. ED 152755 (MF)

Includes 43 entries.

1349. Sanchez, Bonnie M. About staff evaluation: a brief
highlighting important literature since 1966 on community college staff evaluation. ERIC Clearinghouse for Junior College
Information, 1978. 23p. ED 158799.

An annotated bibliography of published and unpublished
material from the ERIC system.

1350. Bunda, Mary Anne. Evaluation bibliography. Kalamazoo,
Western Michigan University, School of Education, 1976. 67p.
ED 166244 (MF)

Lists 603 books and articles including case studies, evaluation reports, theory, measurement textbooks, educational
objectives and accountability, evaluation methods, teacher
evaluation, and tests and testing. Not annotated.

1351. Earles, James A. and William R. Winn. Assessment centers: an evaluation bibliography. Lackland AFB, TX, Air Force
Human Resources Laboratory, 1977. 27p. ED 141408.

Includes articles on personnel evaluation and testing programs.

1352. Poli, Rosario. Student evaluation. Columbus, Ohio Education Association, 1970. 32p. ED 076892.

An annotated bibliography for primary through college
levels. Includes self-evaluation.

1353. Wildemuth, Barbara M. Research and evaluation studies
from large school systems. ERIC Clearinghouse on Tests, Measurement, and Evaluation, 1977. 82p. ED 142584.

Contains 149 ERIC documents from forty school districts.

EXCEPTIONAL CHILDREN See GIFTED and HANDICAPPED

EXCHANGE PROGRAMS

1354. Cotner, Thomas E. International educational exchange:
a selected bibliography. Washington, DC, Office of Education
(DHEW), 1961. 120p. ED 025976.

Emphasis is on international fellowships, scholarships,
and exchange of persons programs. Lists books, articles,
pamphlets, public laws and regulations.

1355. Spencer, Richard E. and Ruth Awe. International educa-

tional exchange: a bibliography. New York, Institute of International Education, 1970. 158p. ED 054708.

 The unannotated list includes the exchange of teachers,
 students, and specialists, and covers selection, orientation, advisors, grants, adjustment, community relations,
 follow-up evaluations, and immigration policies.

EXPERIENTIAL LEARNING

1356. Emerson, George. The Development of an experiential
approach to learning in the community college. Ed. D. Dissertation, Nova University, 1976. 226p. ED 146955.

 This thesis is a literature review on the philosophy and
 theory, the role of the student and teacher, student characteristics, methods, styles, and behavioral objectives.

1357. Stutz, Jane P. and Joan Knapp. Experiential learning:
an annotated literature guide. Princeton, NJ, Cooperative
Assessment of Experiential Learning Project, 1977. 157p. ED
148859 (MF)

 Includes the rationale and history, program planning and
 types of programs, implementation, evaluation, and financing.

EXTENDED SCHOOL YEAR See YEAR ROUND SCHOOLS and SCHOOL
     CALENDARS

FAMILY LIFE

1358. Family life literature and films: an annotated bibliography. Fourth ed. Minneapolis, Minnesota Council on Family
Relations, 1971. 204p. ED 060464.

 Includes human sexuality, adolescence, marriage, parent-
 child relationships, middle and later years, and social
 problems. A 244 page annotated supplement is available
 as ED 118235.

1359. Figley, Charles R. Transition into parenthood: the social psychological effects of the first child on marital and
parent behavior: a general bibliography. 1974. 37p. ED 106
680.

 Unannotated references from the medical and social sciences.

1360. Bibliography of research in children, youth, and family
life. Ann Arbor, University of Michigan, Research Center for
Group Dynamics, 1970. 22p. ED 044473 (MF)
 Current research which has no annotations.

1361. Bodine, George E. Family crisis: a broad spectrum bibliography. 1979. 16p. ED 183148.

Over 400 entries are grouped under 15 categories that include theoretical and clinical material, and research devoted to specific crisis areas.

1362. Billings, Mary D. Coping: books about young people surviving special problems. Washington, DC, Office of Education (DHEW), 1977. 14p. ED 150981.

The annotated entries are organized by grade level and deal with family life, mental health, and physical handicaps.

FAMILY PLANNING   See also   POPULATION EDUCATION

1363. Library bulletin. London, International Planned Parenthood Federation, 1975. 43p. ED 125880 (MF)

This issue of their bulletin combines an acquisitions list with special annotated bibliographies.

1364. Rosario, Florangel Z. A Researcher's guide to social-psychological communication variables in family planning research. University of Hawaii, East-West Center, 1973. 35p. ED 165809.

Most of the 274 annotated references are empirical studies in family planning communication.

1365. A Selected bibliography. New York, Planned Parenthood, 1972. 17p. ED 068296.

Annotated list for specialists and professionals in the fields of population studies and family planning.

FANTASY LITERATURE   See also   FOLKLORE

1366. Fantasy for young adults. Sacramento, California Library Association, 1975. 41p. ED 112388.

An annotated author list with a title index.

1367. Werner, Nancy E. Flights of fancy: a bibliography of fanciful literature. Washington, DC, Office of Education (DHEW), 1968. 35p. ED 025401.

Includes poetry, folktales, tall tales, myths and legends, fairy tales, and fables. The individual titles and anthologies are annotated.

FARM LABOR

1368. Fujimoto, Isao and Jo Clare Schieffer. Guide to sources on agricultural labor. Davis, University of California, Department of Applied Behavioral Sciences, 1969. 43p. ED 032 177 (MF)

  Includes bibliographies by federal and state agencies, and an annotated list of 98 items which provide a social and historical overview with special emphasis on California.

FATHERS See also PARENT EDUCATION

1369. Honig, Alice S. Fathering: a bibliography. ERIC Clearinghouse on Early Childhood Education, 1977. 78p. ED 142293.

  Contains over 1000 entries dating back to 1941. Some of the references are annotated.

FILIPINO-AMERICANS

1370. Rockman, Ilene F. Understanding the Filipino-American, 1900-1976: a selective bibliography. Monticello, IL, Council of Planning Librarians, 1976. 25p. ED 151429 (MF)

  Books, articles, theses, dissertations, government documents, and other bibliographies are included. Unannotated.

FILMS AND FILM MAKING

1371. Hooker, Charlotte S. The Feature films of Milos Forman: a bibliography of the literature. 1973. 8p. ED 087053.

  Includes 104 entries on four films. Not annotated.

1372. Ladevich, Laurel. A Selected annotated bibliography for use in teaching an introductory film course. ERIC Clearinghouse on Reading and Communication Skills, 1974. 5p. ED 091797.

  Evaluates books by type: basic texts, history, criticism, theory, and general reference.

1373. Anderson, Barbara E. The Art and literature of motion pictures: a study in bibliographic and filmographic control. 1978. 73p. ED 163955 (MF)

  Surveys major filmographies and includes a bibliography.

1374. Perry, Larry S. Bibliography on film. Fayetteville, University of Arkansas Library, 1979. 13p. ED 168607.

  This is a multimedia guide to the literature of film.

1375. Elsas, Diana. Third world cinema. Washington, DC,
American Film Institute, 1977. 28p. ED 153615.

Annotated bibliography of books and journals on film in
Africa, Latin America, and Southeast Asia.

1376. Elsas, Diana. Animation. Washington, DC, American Film
Institute, 1977. 27p. ED 153614.

The annotated bibliography deals with making and teaching
animation, and the history of studios, animation, and ani-
mators.

1377. Elsas, Diana. Movie and TV nostalgia. Washington, DC,
American Film Institute, 1977. 27p. ED 153612.

An annotated list of books and journals on movies and television. Includes general reference books.

1378. Elsas, Diana. Film music. Washington, DC, American
Film Institute, 1977. 25p. ED 153613.

Includes annotated books and journals on history, biography, genre surveys, theory, technical aspects, and special
reprint series.

1379. Zaslavsky, Gerald. Lights! cameras! action! - filmmak-
ing for the junior high school, grades 7-9: an annotated bibliography and filmography. New York University, Bobst Library,
1973. 39p. ED 088472.

Topics include animation, cinematography, documentaries,
editing, scripting, special effects, television, and film
careers. Some few of the entries date back to 1920.

FINANCE See EDUCATIONAL FINANCE

FINE ARTS

1380. Hauck, Alice and Karen Markey. Fine arts reference
books. Baltimore, Johns Hopkins Library, 1976. 74p. ED 136
814 (MF)

Includes 166 annotated titles from their collection.

1381. Wildemuth, Barbara M. and Debra S. Eichinger. Program
evaluation in the arts: an annotated bibliography. ERIC Clearinghouse on Tests, Measurement, and Evaluation, 1977. 42p. ED
151424.

Contains 56 items on the evaluation of school fine arts
programs. These ERIC documents include project reports,
journal articles, and dissertations published from 1963
to 1976. Dance, drama, and music are included.

1382. Lueders, Edward. The College and adult reading list of books in literature and the fine arts. Champaign, IL, National Council of Teachers of English, 1967. 466p. ED 083597.

Includes 760 annotated recommended books in literature, art, and music.

1383. Nakamoto, Kent and Kathi Levin. Marketing the arts: a selected and annotated bibliography. Madison, WI, Association of College and University and Community Arts Administrators, 1978. 19p. ED 180430 (MF)

Contains theoretical articles, reports of studies, and guides for marketing techniques.

FIRE PROTECTION   See also   SAFETY EDUCATION

1384. Cohn, Bert M. Fire safety educational material. Chicago, Gage-Babcock and Associates, Inc., 1974. 42p. ED 114 553.

Mainly written for adults and directed to occupants of one and two family dwellings. An annotated bibliography makes up 34 pages of the document and lists 156 articles and books, and 31 films.

FLANNEL BOARDS

1385. Robertson, Ina. Flannel boards: back to the basics in audiovisual materials, too. 1977. 13p. ED 159667.

Describes 29 journal articles and book chapters that provide information on using flannel boards. Construction of the boards and ideas for stories are also included along with three relevant films.

FLOURIDATION

1386. Mitchell, Bruce. Flouridation bibliography: referendums, public participation in decision-making, and methodologies for attitude perception studies. Monticello, IL, Council of Planning Librarians, 1972. 28p. ED 106960.

Primarily about Canadian experiences with flouridation of public water supplies.

FOLKLORE   See also   FANTASY LITERATURE

1387. Rosen, Joan G. A Bibliography of folklore for the social studies curriculum, grades 3-6. 1976. 26p. ED 129638.

An annotated multimedia list that has one section dealing
with folklore of Pennsylvania, and another on Eskimos.

1388. Crammer, Marjorie. Bibliography of American folklore:
index to materials in books on select American folklore characters. Hyattsville, MD, Prince George's County Memorial Library System, 1975. 22p. ED 117727.

About 200 real and imaginary persons are indexed in the
list of books presented.

1389. Advisory list of instructional media: fairy tales and
folklore. Raleigh, North Carolina State Department of Public
Instruction, 1977. 20p. ED 149745.

An annotated booklist for primary through high school level.

1390. Coughlan, Margaret N. Folklore from Africa to the United States: an annotated bibliography. Washington, DC, Library
of Congress, 1976. 162p. ED 136289.

The works cited attempt to trace folktales from their or-
igins.

1391. Slavin, Suzy. Folklore: a guide to reference sources.
Montreal, McGill University Library, 1979. 8p. ED 176326.

Deals principally with traditional oral folk literature
and the folk tale narrative with references to arts, customs, crafts, legends, and riddles.

FOOD SERVICE

1392. Rifenbark, Ray. Food service facilities. 1975. 22p.
ED 109804 (MF)

Includes 14 annotated articles on school and college food
service programs.

1393. Nejelski, Leo. Selected research abstracts of published
and unpublished reports pertaining to the food service industry, including recommendations for research needs. New York,
Food Research Center for Catholic Institutions, 1969. 142p.
ED 039347.

Contains 251 research abstracts dating back to 1956.

1394. Food service programs for children: an annotated bibliography. Washington, DC, National Agricultural Library, 1975.
79p. ED 140479 (MF)

578 citations on the National School Lunch Program, the
School Breakfast Program, and the special Milk Program.

1395. Miller, William O. 20 million for lunch. 1968. 63p.
ED 031062.

A bibliography is included with this comprehensive treatment of school lunch programs and facilities.

1396. Energy conservation in the food system: a publications
list. Washington, DC, Federal Energy Administration, 1976. 81p.
ED 140510.

An annotated list of government publications.

FOOD STAMPS

1397. Cameron, Colin. Food stamps: a bibliography. Madison,
University of Wisconsin, Institute for Research on Poverty,
1977. 57p. ED 147413.

Annotated entries date from the 1930's giving the history
of these programs. Advocacy of the program, and debate on
its abuses are found in other items listed.

FOOTBALL

1398. Clemence, William J. Annotated football bibliography:
an applied project in physical education. 1977. 39p. ED 150
094.

Limited to the areas of coaching techniques and philosophy,
fundamentals of offense and defense, injuries, and conditioning at the high school and college level.

FOREIGN LANGUAGE INSTRUCTION See LANGUAGE INSTRUCTION

FOREIGN STUDENTS

1399. Spencer, Richard E. and Ruth Awe. A Bibliography of
research on foreign student affairs. Urbana, University of
Illinois, Office of Instructional Resources, 1968. 370p. ED
021629.

Includes about 4000 unannotated entries.

FORESTRY

1400. Schwab, Judith L. Social sciences in forestry: a current selected bibliography. Blacksburg, Virginia Polytechnic
Institute and State University, 1979. 87p. ED 180793.

Annotated entries on the social sciences applied to forestry such as production, manufacturing, marketing, trade,
and demand for output. Earlier compilations in this series
are ED 142426, 148580, 155043, 160442, and 164251.

FOSTER CARE

1401. Foster family services: a selected reading list. Washington, DC, Children's Bureau (DHEW), 1977. 84p. ED 148483.

These annotated materials for social workers cover administration, worker and parent roles, recruiting of homes,
and helping children and parents.

FREEDOM OF SPEECH See also CENSORSHIP

1402. Tedford, Thomas L. Freedom of speech: a selected annotated basic bibliography. ERIC Clearinghouse on Reading and
Communication Skills, 1977. 7p. ED 137876.

Lists 36 general books, and some specifically on obscenity
and pornography.

1403. Annotated bibliography and index of the Freedom of Information Center reports and papers. Columbia, MO. Freedom
of Information Center, 1978. 37p. ED 158335.

Includes 389 reports and 38 summary papers on a variety
of issues in mass communications.

FRENCH

1404. Naylor, J. W. French readers for primary schools: an
annotated bibliography. Leeds, England, Nuffield Foundation,
1966. 84p. ED 043254.

Describes 39 readers, some suitable for secondary levels.

1405. Savignon, Sandra J. Films for French: a teacher's guide.
Urbana, University of Illinois, Visual Aids Service, 1973. 67p.
ED 081268.

Evaluates over 100 films for college level use.

1406. Bibliography of instructional materials for the teaching of French. Sacramento, California State Department of Education, 1977. 175p. ED 145714 (MF)

An annotated list to aid language fluency and cultural a-
wareness. The entries cover humanities, social sciences,
and science and math in textbooks, filmstrips, and tapes.

1407. Dunlap. Connie R. French language and literature: a
selected annotated bibliography. Ann Arbor, University of
Michigan Libraries, 1974. 55p. ED 154815.

A guide to the literature for graduate students.

1408. Selective critical bibliography of interest to students
of French and Spanish. Norman, University of Oklahoma Library,
1966(?) 21p. ED 010939.

Evaluates 92 widely used scholarly journals in the field.

1409. Klaar, R. M. French dictionaries. London, Centre for
Information on Language Teaching, 1976. 73p. ED 182976.

Includes current dictionaries by type: French monolingual,
French-English, English-French, etymology, phonetics, proper names, place names, slang, and children's dictionaries.
Some Belgian, Canadian, and Swiss French dictionaries are
also included.

FUTURES AND FUTURISM

1410. A Brief annotated bibliography on societal futures, educational futures, educational alternatives and change, and
resources: societal and educational. Sacramento, California
State Department of Education, 1979. 20p. ED 181165 (MF)

Includes 73 publications for educators.

1411. Marien, Michael. The Hot list Delphi: an exploratory
survey of essential reading for the future. Syracuse University, Research Corporation. 1972. 99p. ED 071192.

Lists 236 books and articles rated by a panel of 14 experts.
The readings are for policymakers, professionals, students,
and concerned citizens.

1412. Futures: the best of ERIC. ERIC Clearinghouse on Educational Management, 1974. 5p. ED 098651.

Includes 21 annotated documents from the ERIC system.

1413. Padbury, Peter and Diane Wilkins. The Future: a bibliography of issues and forecasting techniques. Monticello, IL,
Council of Planning Librarians, 1972. 104p. ED 106962.

An unannotated list prepared for a series of courses at
the University of Waterloo.

1414. Ehler, Charles N. Integrative forecasting: literature
survey. Monticello, IL, Council of Planning Librarians, 1972.
67p. ED 106955.

Covers alternative futures, planning, and forecasting.

GAMES   See also   SIMULATION

1415. Annotated list of locally developed educational games.
Revised ed. Danville. PA, Project SESAME, 1969. 194p. ED
092066.

Subject areas are business education, foreign languages,
geography, health, language arts, math, science, and social
studies for K-12.

1416. Shubik, Martin and Garry D. Brewer. Reviews of selected
books and articles on gaming and simulation. Santa Monica, CA,
Rand Corporation, 1972. 55p. ED 077221.

Includes 48 items dating back to 1898 on theory, psychological aspects, and applications to political and social
policy-making. Covers several types of table games, war
games, and instructional games.

1417. Jensen, Ida-Marie. Simulation/games: a selected bibliography for the use of educators/administrators. Logan, Utah
State University Library, 1971. 82p. ED 077823.

Contains over 1000 partially annotated citations to books,
articles, dissertations, and ERIC documents.

GENETICS See also HEREDITY

1418. Sorenson, James R. Social and psychological aspects of
applied human genetics: a bibliography. Bethesda, MD, Fogarty
International Center (DHEW), 1973. 105p. ED 081883.

Includes books and articles centered in particular around
problems, issues, and discussions of genetic counseling.

GEOGRAPHY

1419. Lewthwaite, Gordon R. A Geographical bibliography for
American college libraries. Revised ed. Washington, DC, Association of American Geographers, 1970. 225p. ED 052108 (MF)

Over 1700 annotated entries recommended as a core collection for undergraduate libraries. Nearly all are in English and are recent publications.

1420. Wise, John H. Geography in education: a bibliography.
Montreal, Canadian Association of Geographers, 1974. 18p.
ED 121664.

About 200 books and articles on the teaching of geography
in secondary schools are included. Principles and practice
are reflected in the Canadian, British, Australian, and
American literature.

1421. Saveland, Robert N. and Clifton W. Pannell. Inventory of recent U.S. research in geographic education. Athens, University of Georgia, Geography Curriculum Project, 1975. 64p. ED 113282.

    Chapters include history and philosophy, curriculum, materials, method, evaluation, and teacher training. Articles, dissertations, and ERIC documents dating from 1965 are in this unannotated bibliography.

1422. Ball, John M. A Bibliography of geographic education. Athens, University of Georgia, Geography Curriculum Project, 1969. 120p. ED 092436.

    An annotated list of books, articles, theses, and pamphlets published since 1950 for all educational levels.

1423. Young, Bruce. Bibliography and review of geography department discussion papers. Waterloo, Ontario, Wilfred Laurier University, Department of Geography, 1976. 100p. ED 125 966.

    Contains partially annotated fugitive publications of over 70 university departments of geography in Australia, New Zealand, Canada, the United States, and the United Kingdom.

1424. Wheeler, James O. Bibliography on geographic thought, philosophy, and methodology, 1950-1974. Athens, University of Georgia, Geography Curriculum Project, 1975. 47p. ED 107 561 (MF)

    Cites books and articles since 1950 on the several aspects of geography education. Not annotated.

1425. Church, Martha. A Basic geographical library: a selected and annotated book list for American colleges. Washington, DC, Association of American Geographers, 1966. 164p. ED 107 591.

    Includes general works, aids, thematic geography, and regional geography.

1426. Holtgrieve, Donald G. and Carol Mathiason. Field trips in geographic education: an annotated bibliography. Oak Park, IL, National Council for Geographic Education, 1975. 15p. ED 138527 (MF)

    125 references for planning, conducting, and evaluating field trips for elementary and secondary teachers.

GEOLOGY   See   EARTH SCIENCE

GERMAN

1427. Schneider, Gerd K. Topical bibliography in theoretical and applied German linguistics. ERIC Clearinghouse on Language and Linguistics, 1972. 182p. ED 061787.

Includes 1860 books, some dating from the turn of the century. Not annotated.

1428. Dusel, John P. Bibliography of instructional materials for the teaching of German, kindergarten through grade twelve. Sacramento, California State Department of Education, 1975. 85p. ED 112661.

Reading materials, films, songbooks, and records are grouped into subjects of art, language arts, literature, music, science and math, social sciences, and others. Unannotated.

1429. Teaching materials for German: course materials for adult beginners and self-instruction in German. London, Centre for Information on Language Teaching, 1976. 34p. ED 163789.

A multimedia annotated bibliography.

1430. Teaching materials for German: G1, course materials. London, Centre for Information on Language Teaching, 1977. 57p. ED 162534.

A multimedia annotated bibliography.

1431. Teaching materials for German: G3, readers. London, Centre for Information on Language Teaching, 1978. 64p. ED 163791.

An annotated list of 91 readers.

1432. Buck, Kathryn and Arthur Haase. Textbooks in German, 1942-1973: a descriptive bibliography. New York, Modern Language Association of America, 1974. 173p. ED 098821.

Lists 645 entries published in the United States for junior high through college.

1433. A Bibliography of texts and reference works for the teacher of German. Munich, Germany, Goethe Institute 1969. 10p. ED 034456.

120 items dating from 1960 are annotated in this compilation sponsored by the American Association of Teachers of German.

1434. Feder, Helga. Reference resources in German literature: an annotated guide. New York, City University Graduate School, 1975. 37p. ED 122638 (MF)

Limited to German language resources that were published in Germany.

GERONTOLOGY

1435. Jones, Dorothy M. <u>Words on aging: a bibliography of</u>
<u>selected annotated references.</u> Washington, DC, Administration
on Aging (DHEW), 1970. 186p. ED 052417 (MF)

This seventh edition lists articles published from 1963
through 1967, and selected books dating back to 1900. ED
062613 is a 101 page supplement published in May 1971.
Both documents include materials on the process of aging,
economic aspects, health and medical care, and social and
environmental services.

1436. <u>Comprehensive bibliography on educational gerontology.</u>
Ann Arbor, MI, Institute of Gerontology, 1971. 155p. ED 059
483.

Subjects include programs, senior centers, recreation,
consumer education, nutrition, volunteers, and other bibliographies. Unannotated.

1437. Bodine, George E. and William Sobotor. <u>The Hospice: an</u>
<u>integrated bibliography</u>. Syracuse University, 1979. 33p. ED
176784.

The annotated list of books and articles provides an interdisciplinary overview of present day terminal care and
the hospice alternative.

1438. Bowman, Robyn. <u>Aging in the modern world</u>. 1978. 30p.
ED 156145.

This annotated list is intended as a core collection for
for public libraries.

1439. Conrad, James H. <u>An Annotated bibliography of the his-</u>
<u>tory of old age in America</u>. 1977. 41p. ED 156184.

Includes 152 citations for books, articles, government
publications, pamphlets, and dissertations. Some items
date back to 1846.

1440. Galant, Richard and Nancy J. Moncrieff. <u>Counseling the</u>
<u>aging</u>. ERIC Clearinghouse on Counseling and Personnel Ser-
vices, 1974. 25p. ED 105366.

The 100 annotated entries include articles, dissertations,
and ERIC documents.

1441. Goodman, Sara. <u>Selected resources on aging</u>. 1978.
86p. ED 162923.

An annotated bibliography that contains 30 films, filmstrips, and other AV items in addition to the 150 books.

1442. Meagher, Christine M. <u>Information resources for social</u>
<u>services training</u>. New York State Department of Social Ser-
vices, 1978. 55p. ED 160491 (MF)

Most of the 31 reference resources emphasize gerontology.

1443. Arnold, Willim E. Communication and aging. Tempe, Arizona State University, Department of Communication and Theatre, 1977. 120p. ED 165203.

The bibliography is on a wide variety of topics and includes over 1800 entries.

1444. Jacobs, H. Lee. Education for aging: a review of recent literature. Washington, DC, Adult Education Association
of USA, 1970. 118p. ED 038552.

237 annotated items cover studies and reports on wide range
of behavior patterns relative to the aging process.

1445. Education for aging: current information sources. ERIC
Clearinghouse on Adult Education, 1968. 20p. ED 019564.

This annotated bibliography relates to the characteristics
and learning abilities of older adults. Includes training
programs and retirement education.

1446. Ward, Betty A. Education on the aging: a selected annotated bibliography. Washington, DC, Department of Health,
Education, and Welfare, 1960. 155p. ED 048560.

Includes titles on educational programs and activities
for developing skills, knowledge, habits, and attitudes
necessary for purposeful living during the years of later
maturity.

1447. Boggs, David L. and Loretta C. Buffer. Continuing education and aging: annotated bibliography. 1976. 19p. ED
128588.

Contains 35 references.

1448. Molina, Alexis. Minority aged: a bibliography. New
York Columbia University, Institute for Urban and Minority
Education, 1977. 44p. ED 142659.

The 368 references include anthropological and cross cultural studies on urban areas, low income groups, ethnicity,
and race. Not annotated.

1449. Suzuki, Peter T. Minority group aged in America: a
comprehensive bibliography of recent publications on Blacks,
Mexican-Americans, Native Americans, Chinese, and Japanese.
Monticello, IL, Council of Planning Librarians, 1975. 27p.
ED 133 384.

1450. Retirement and preparation for retirement: a selected
bibliography and sourcebook. Toronto, Ontario Ministry of
Community and Social Services, 1972. 37p. ED 072355.

An unannotated bibliography of 218 books, articles, and
other documents.

1451. DeCrow, Roger. New learning for older Americans: an

overview of national effort. Washington, DC, Adult Education
Association of U.S.A., 1974. 162p. ED 107928.

Contains data on 3500 programs reported on in a 20 item
questionnaire survey. Also includes an annotated bibliography of 176 entries.

GIFTED

1452. The Gifted. Arlington, VA, Council for Exceptional
Children, 1969. 26p. ED 036037.

Includes 89 abstracts dealing with counseling, creativity,
achievement, characteristics, education, and other topics
related to the gifted child.

1453. Nolte, Jane. Nearly everything you've always wanted to
know about the gifted and talented. Wauwatosa, Wisconsin Council for the Gifted and Talented, Inc., 1976. 56p. ED 140553.

Includes bibliographies of suggested readings.

1454. Gifted talented: a general reading list: a selective
bibliography. Arlington, VA, Council for Exceptional Children,
1973. 31p. ED 078614.

Presents 100 abstracts from the Council's complete holdings. Some documents date back to 1926.

1455. McMurray, J. G. The Exceptional student of secondary
school age: a bibliography for psychology and education, 1960-
1970. 1971. 149p. ED 051613.

The journal articles listed cover gifted children, handicapped, behavior problems, and learning problems.

1456. Thomas, Susan B. Concerns about gifted children: a
paper and abstract bibliography. ERIC Clearinghouse on Early
Childhood Education, 1974. 44p. ED 091083.

The annotated bibliography contains 70 documents from RIE
and CIJE which examine special education and the gifted
related to programs, curriculum guides, and other resources.

1457. Curriculum guides: a selective bibliography. Arlington,
VA, Council for Exceptional Children, 1972. 31p. ED 065959.

Includes abstracts of 100 guides for gifted and handicapped
children dated 1965 to 1971.

1458. Gifted and talented programs: a selective bibliography.
Reston, VA, Council for Exceptional Children, 1973. 22p. ED
090704.

Eighty annotated entries are on elementary and secondary

curriculums, the disadvantaged gifted, creativity, and the teaching of literature.

1459. Gifted and talented research: a selective bibliography. Reston, VA, Council for Exceptional Children, 1973. 28p. ED 090723.

Includes abstracts of 100 research documents on educational motivation, creativity, acceleration, identification, and psychological adjustment.

1460. Gifted and talented curriculum: a selective bibliography. Reston, VA, Council for Exceptional Children, 1974. 23p. ED 091914.

59 abstracts dating from 1961 are listed to aid curriculum development of primary through senior high levels.

1461. Gifted and creativity research: a selective bibliography. Arlington, VA, Council for Exceptional Children, 1972. 31p. ED 069073.

Includes 79 abstracts of research that date back to 1926.

1462. Gifted and creativity programs: a selective bibliography. Arlington, VA, Council for Exceptional Children, 1972. 23p. ED 065958.

Contains abstracts of 80 programs dating from 1955.

1463. Gifted, handicapped, disadvantaged, underachievers: a selective bibliography. Reston, VA, Council for Exceptional Children, 1976. 20p. ED 129024.

Contains abstracts of 65 documents dating from 1957.

1464. Gifted - teaching methods, curriculum, teacher training: a selective bibliography. Reston, VA, Council for Exceptional Children, 1976. 21p. ED 129025.

Includes 75 abstracts that date from 1955 to 1975.

1465. Gifted - programs, teaching methods and curriculum. Reston, VA, Council for Exceptional Children, 1977. 16p. ED 146735.

Includes annotations of 60 documents dated 1973 to 1976.

1466. Programming for the gifted: general, arts and humanities, math and science: a selective bibliography. Reston, VA, Council for Exceptional Children, 1976. 27p. ED 129026.

Includes annotations of 125 documents dated 1965 to 1975.

1467. Gifted: parenting, legislation, and public policy: a selective bibliography. Reston, VA, Council for Exceptional Children, 1976. 18p. ED 129012.

Includes annotations of 72 documents dated 1958 to 1975.

1468. Creativity: research, tests and measurements, intelligence: a selective bibliography. Reston, VA, Council for Exceptional Children, 1976. 19p. ED 129013.

Contains abstracts of 60 documents dated 1964 to 1975.

1469. Creativity: general, classroom, problem solving: a selective bibliography. Reston, VA, Council for Exceptional Children, 1976. 23p. ED 129014.

85 annotated documents are included dating from 1962.

1470. Identification of the gifted: a selective bibliography. Reston, VA, Council for Exceptional Children, 1976. 17p. ED 129015.

Includes 60 abstracts of documents and journal articles dated 1959 to 1975.

1471. Gifted: identification and assessment. Reston, VA, Council for Exceptional Children, 1977. 14p. ED 146734.

Includes 50 abstracts dated 1973 to 1976.

1472. Broome, Elizabeth and Mary H. Fisher. A Selective bibliography and recommended materials for teachers of gifted and talented students. Raleigh, North Carolina Department of Public Instruction, 1973. 13p. ED 102774.

An unannotated list of over 100 theory and practice books, including activity books.

1473. Verbeke, Maurice G. and Karen. The Education of the gifted child, 1965-1971: an annotated bibliography. Glassboro, NJ, Glassboro State College, Department of Educational Administration, 1973. 127p. ED 116361 (MF)

Includes 400 books, articles, theses, and other monographs.

1474. Reading materials for exceptionally talented children as suggested by their teachers. Raleigh, North Carolina Department of Public Instruction, 1968. 19p. ED 036915.

An unannotated list of books in language, social studies, science, and mathematics for elementary through senior high school.

GOAL ATTAINMENT See also ACHIEVEMENT

1475. Garwick, Geoffrey. Bibliography on goal attainment scaling. Third ed. Minneapolis, Program Evaluation Resource Center, 1976. 23p. ED 128379.

Unannotated. Includes implementation and research findings.

GOVERNMENT   See also   POLITICAL SCIENCE

1476. Burg, Nan C. Local government: form and reform: a selected bibliography. Monticello, IL, Council of Planning Librarians, 1974. 73p. ED 106909 (MF)

Deals with administration, structure, and training in county and metropolitan government. The unannotated bibliography lists various state reports with an emphasis on Pennsylvania.

GOVERNMENT PUBLICATIONS

1477. Draft syllabus of resources for teaching government publications. Chicago, American Library Association, 1976. 108p.
ED 125668.

Covers municipal, local, state documents, and international
documents in addition to U.S., Canadian, and British government publications.

1478. Palic, Vladimir M. Government publications: a guide to
bibliographic tools. Fourth ed. Washington, DC, Library of
Congress, 1975. 444p. ED 126954.

Brief annotations are arranged by geographic area. Includes
current and retrospective aids for official publications
issued by the United States, foreign countries, and international organizations.

1479. Bernier, Bernard A. Popular names of U.S. government
reports: a catalog. Washington, DC, Library of Congress, 1976.
274p. ED 152307 (MF)

This unannotated list is the third edition and has references to the Checklist of US Public Documents, the Document Catalog, and the Monthly Catalog. SuDoc class numbers
are included.

GRADING SYSTEMS

1480. Wallace, Terry H. Innovative grading practices: an annotated bibliography. 1976. 17p. ED 132996.

51 reports, documents, and dissertations focus on undergraduate education including community colleges.

1481. Caldwell, J. H. Current research on grading systems of
possible significance to junior colleges: an annotated bibliography. ERIC Clearinghouse for Junior College Information,
1973. 16p. ED 071650.

Lists articles in addition to describing nine systems.

GRADUATE STUDY   See also   HIGHER EDUCATION

1482. Powel, John H. and Robert D. Lamson. An Annotated bibliography of literature relating to the costs and benefits of
graduate education. Washington, DC, Council of Graduate
Schools in the U.S., 1972. 66p. ED 069200 (MF)

1483. Rose, Judith C. Graduate education in English: a selected annotated bibliography. Philadelphia, Temple University,
1967. 20p. ED 038431.

    Includes 90 books and articles dating from 1959 that deal
    with course requirements and teacher preparation.

1484. Heiss, Ann M. Graduate and professional education: an
annotated bibliography. Berkeley, University of California,
Center for R & D in Education, 1967. 131p. ED 016293.

    Covers general education and some professional areas:
    architecture, business, clinical psychology, dentistry,
    engineering, law, library science, medicine, nursing,
    social work, teaching, and theology.

GRANTS

1485. Elnor, Nancy. While you're up, get me a grant: a basic
bibliography on grants. Revised ed. San Francisco, Bay Area
Social Responsibilities Round Table, 1976. 12p. ED 122727
(MF)

    The annotated list covers foundations, proposal writing,
    fund raising, grant administration, revenue sharing, and
    charitable giving.

GRAPHIC ARTS

1486. Macdonald-Ross, Michael and Eleanor B. Smith. Bibliography for textual communication: publications relevant to research on the design of texts for the adult learner. Walton,
England, Open University, Institute of Educational Technology,
1974. 80p. ED 092146.

GREAT LAKES REGION

1487. Johnson, Pam. Educators' guide to Great Lakes materials: books, films, maps, and pamphlets for classroom use. Madison, University of Wisconsin, Sea Grant Program, 1978. 42p.
ED 164293 (MF)

    This annotated list is for grades six through nine and

emphasizes Lakes Michigan and Superior. It includes both
fiction and nonfiction, but has no scientific publications
listed with a copyright date prior to 1970.

GREECE

1488. Witzel, Anne and Rosemary Chapman. A Critical bibliography of materials on Greece. Toronto, Ontario, Board of Education Research Department, 1969. 25p. ED 080442.

   Annotates 35 books from a visitor's point of view dating
   back to 1951. Also lists some films and filmstrips.

GREEK See LATIN

GRIEVANCE PROCEDURES

1489. Grievance procedures: the best of ERIC. ERIC Clearinghouse on Educational Management, 1974. 4p. ED 096730.

   Includes 15 annotated documents and articles related to
   public schools.

GUIDANCE See also COUNSELING

1490. Glovinsky, Sanford J. Bibliography of guidance and
guidance-related materials. Detroit, Wayne County Intermediate
School District, 1969. 63p. ED 032587.

   Annotates books and audiovisual items, and covers mental
   health, sociological grouping, testing materials, and vo-
   cational-occupational information.

1491. Sloan, Nancy. Orientation approaches to increase student awareness of occupational options. ERIC Clearinghouse on
Counseling and Personnel Services, 1969. 16p. ED 033255.

   This annotated bibliography includes research and innovative programs for all levels on vocational orientation.

1492. Films on guidance. Hartford, Connecticut State Department of Education, 1965. 55p. ED 018587.

   Over 400 16mm sound films are annotated for use in helping
   students relate their interests and abilities to educational and vocational planning.

1493. Advisory list of instructional media for guidance. Raleigh, North Carolina State Department of Public Instruction,
1977. 39p. ED 149747.

An annotated list of books, films, filmstrips, kits, recordings, and slide sets for primary through senior high
school.

1494. Galant, Richard and Nancy J. Moncrieff. Group guidance:
relevant resources in high interest areas. ERIC Clearinghouse
on Counseling and Personnel Services, 1974. 22p. ED 105371.

Contains 91 articles, dissertations, and ERIC documents
on group counseling, group dynamics, and training needed
for working with groups. Annotated.

1495. Biasco, Frank. Elementary school guidance bibliography.
Tallahassee, Florida State University, Department of Counselor
Education, 1970. 15p. ED 037742.

Unannotated list of 70 books and articles.

1496. Friesen, J. D. Computer based systems in guidance and
counseling: an annotated bibliography. Vancouver, University
of British Columbia, Faculty of Education, 1970. 24p. ED 046
006.

36 project reports are included along with books, articles,
government publications, and unpublished works.

1497. Kopita, Ronald R. Searchlight: relevant reources in
high interest areas: group guidance. ERIC Clearinghouse on
Counseling and Personnel Services, 1973. 24p. ED 082117.

Includes 58 annotated books, articles, dissertations, and
ERIC documents.

HANDICAPPED

1498. Aubert, Halldis. Handicap - sport: a preliminary bibliography on sport for the disabled and the ill, 1960-1973.
Second ed. 1973. 186p. ED 080532.

Includes about 2000 unannotated entries in this comprehensive world bibliography. Some are in foreign languages.

1499. Fearon, Ross E. Sensory disorders, speech defects, and
physical handicaps. Farmington State College (Maine), 1966.
75p. ED 012538.

Lists 877 items in the Mantor Library by Dewey decimal
number.

1500. Materials from the National Arts and the Handicapped
Information Service: annotated bibliography. New York, 1978.
32p. ED 183158.

Describes media and materials on the subject of arts and
handicapped persons produced since 1970.

1501. Guide to resources for severely/profoundly handicapped.
Hightstown, NJ, Northeast Area Learning Resource Center, 1975.
88p. ED 131654.

The bulk of the document is devoted to descriptions of
various model programs, and includes an annotated bibliography of bibliographies.

1502. Trammell, Georgia R. The Multihandicapped: a selective
bibliography of nonprint and print materials. Olympia, Washington State Library, 1976. 67p. ED 140835.

This annotated revision includes Braille magazines and
other media for the blind, deaf, mentally disturbed, retarded, and offenders.

1503. Design needs of the physically handicapped: a selected
bibliography. ERIC Clearinghouse on Educational Facilities,
1970. 38p. ED 037992.

The annotated list includes criteria, guidelines, and
standards for planning, designing, and constructing environments for the handicapped.

1504. Cohen, Shirley and Nancy Koehler. A Selected bibliography on attitudes toward the handicapped. New York, City
University Graduate School, 1975. 12p. ED 140517.

Includes 85 references for professionals and children,
1962-1975.

1505. Cohen, Shirley and Nancy Koehler. Fostering positive
attitudes toward the handicapped: a selected bibliography of
multimedia materials. New York, City University Graduate
School, 1975. 9p. ED 140515.

Lists 34 items including video and audiotapes, 16mm films,
filmstrips, and records.

1506. Attitudes toward the handicapped. Reston, VA, Council
for Exceptional Children, 1977. 17p. ED 146730.

Contains 70 annotated citations published since 1972.

1507. Dudek, R. A. Human rehabilitation techniques. Washington, DC, National Science Foundation, 1977. 244p. ED 149
570.

Presented is the unannotated bibliography to volume one
of a six volume final report which describes the activities and findings of a research project to identify the
policy-related aspects and technology involved in the efforts to aid disabled individuals in the United States.

1508. Materials on creative arts for persons with handicapping conditions. Revised ed. Washington, DC, American Alliance for Health, Physical Education, and Recreation, 1977.

103p. ED 159857 (MF)

Includes over 1000 printed items for arts and crafts, dance and movement therapy, drama, puppetry, music therapy, poetry, bibliotherapy, creative writing, and photography.

1509. Facilities for mainstreaming the handicapped. Columbus, OH, Council of Educational Facilities Planners, 1977. 9p. ED 132643.

Nineteen annotated documents from the ERIC system are included for planning or improving school facilities to meet the needs of the handicapped.

1510. Perkins, Dorothy C. Workshops for the handicapped: an annotated bibliography. Los Angeles, California State College, Rehabilitation Counseling Program, 1969. 57p. ED 036955.

Includes 154 publications on planning, administration, and management of programs.

1511. Stubbins, Joseph. Workshops for the handicapped: an annotated bibliography. Los Angeles, California State College, 1965. 74p. ED 013005.

This annotated bibliography lists 146 articles, books, and conference reports since 1961.

1512. Perkins, Dorothy C. Workshops for the handicapped: an annotated bibliography. Los Angeles, California State College, 1965. 54p. ED 012543.

This version of the above two entries lists 126 books, articles and conference reports.

HANDICAPPED - EDUCATION

1513. Hinrichs, Roy S. and Gary A. Stone. Sources of information: vocational programs for the handicapped. State College, Mississippi Research and Curriculum Unit for Vocational and Technical Education, 1976. 82p. ED 131194 (MF)

Includes over 100 annotated citations reporting views of vocational training for the mentally and physically handicapped since 1970.

1514. Herschbach, Dennis R. Teaching special needs students: selected resources for vocational teachers and teacher educators. University of Maryland, Department of Industrial Education, 1977. 36p. ED 146428.

Lists books and articles related to the handicapped and disadvantaged on program design, student behavior, individualized instruction, and evaluation.

1515. <u>Curricula for the severely/profoundly handicapped and</u>
<u>multiply handicapped.</u> Austin, Texas Education Agency, 1978.
133p. ED 163673.

   An annotated directory of 84 curriculum materials available.

1516. Magisos, Joel H. and Paul E. Schroeder. <u>Educational</u>
<u>personnel for the disadvantaged, handicapped, and minorities</u>:
<u>information sources.</u> Columbus, Ohio State University, Center
for vocational and Technical Education, 1974. 30p. ED 106521

   Includes 31 annotated items since 1963 from RIE and CIJE.

1517. Christensen, Nancy A. <u>A Selected bibliography for vo-</u>
<u>cational training and placement of the severely handicapped.</u>
Palo Alto, CA, American Institutes for Research in the Behavioral Sciences, 1975. 114p. ED 116436 (MF)

   A partially annotated article bibliography on features of
   rehabilitation, employment opportunities, progress and
   recommendations, sheltered workshops, and job and skills
   training. Contains 250 items dated 1965 to 1975.

1518. Gaines, Debby. <u>Educational technology for the severely</u>
<u>handicapped: a comprehensive bibliography.</u> Topeka, Kansas
Neurological Institute, 1975. 65p. ED 108416.

   Includes 650 unannotated references on educational programs for the handicapped dating from 1955. Covers behavioral management, motor development, parent training, physical education, academic skills, vocational training,
   recreation, self-help, sex education, social skills, language and speech problems.

1519. Friedle, Mike and Lucy Fox. <u>A Selected bibliography</u>
<u>related to the vocational training of severely handicapped</u>
<u>persons.</u> Seattle, University of Washington, Child Development
and Mental Retardation Center, 1974. 16p. ED 108419.

   Lists 100 references, 1927-1975; some are annotated.

1520. Lambert, Roger H. <u>A Bibliography of materials for hand-</u>
<u>icapped and special education.</u> Second ed. Madison, University
of Wisconsin, Center for Studies in Vocational and Technical
Education, 1975. 81p. ED 123839.

   A multimedia list of 1621 items coded by specific skill
   area or handicap. ED 134679 is a 38 page supplement published in 1976 containing over 300 more citations.

HANDICAPPED - PHYSICAL EDUCATION

1521. <u>Aquatics for the impaired, disabled, and handicapped.</u>
Washington, DC, American Association for Health, Physical Education, and Recreation, 1972. 31p. ED 080515.

Includes 107 annotated books and articles mostly from the later 1960's.

1522. <u>Annotated listing of films for physical education and recreation for impaired, disabled, and handicapped persons</u>. Washington, DC, American Association for Health, Physical Education, and Recreation, 1973. 50p. ED 080477.

The 16mm films listed also cover camping, outdoor education, perceptual motor activities, and other related areas.

1523. Klappholz, Lowell. <u>Annotated research bibliography in physical education, recreation, and psychomotor function of mentally retarded persons</u>. Washington, DC, American Alliance for Health, Physical Education, and Recreation, 1975. 293p. ED 113907 (MF)

Includes 860 studies and references dating back to 1888.

1524. <u>Recreation for the handicapped: a selection of recent books and pamphlets</u>. Chicago, National Easter Seal Society, 1975. 12p. ED 113905.

Lists 96 items concerned with planning and modifying recreational activities for physically handicapped children. Camping, crafts, and hobbies are some of the subjects covered in this unannotated list.

1525. Geddes, Dolores M. and Liane Summerfield. <u>Physical education and recreation for individuals with multiple handicapping conditions: references and resources</u>. Revised ed. Washington, DC, American Alliance for Health, Physical Education, and Recreation, 1978. 43p. ED 159855 (MF)

Sections cover cerebral palsied, deaf-blind, and other handicapping conditions. Contains 161 references and descriptions of 35 audiovisual aids.

1526. Geddes, Dolores M. and Liane Summerfield. <u>Integrating persons with handicapping conditions into regular physical education and recreation programs</u>. Revised ed. Washington, DC, American Alliance for Health, Physical Education, and Recreation, 1977. 80p. ED 159856 (MF)

Part four contains an annotated bibliography of 261 items.

1527. <u>Listing of materials</u>. Washington, DC, American Alliance for Health, Physical Education, and Recreation, 1975. 7p. ED 117608 (MF)

An unannotated list of publications on various aspects of physical education for the handicapped produced since 1972.

1528. <u>A Bibliography of surveys in physical education and recreation programs for impaired, disabled, and handicapped persons</u>. Washington, DC, American Alliance for Health, Physical Education, and Recreation, 1973. 18p. ED 092557.

The 114 items are limited to program status, surveys of
opportunities, populations served, participation, needs,
and problems.

HANDICAPPED CHILDREN

1529. Counseling and psychotherapy with the handicapped. Arlington, VA, Council for Exceptional Children, 1969. 13p. ED
036035.

Presents 41 abstracts on various methods of working with
handicapped and emotionally disturbed children.

1530. Klig, Sally and Joseph Perlman. The Assessment of children with sensory impairments: a selected bibliography. New
York, City University Graduate School, 1976. 46p. ED 141969.

Lists 113 items on screening and assessment instruments
and techniques appropriate for use with visually handicapped, aurally handicapped, or deaf-blind children.

1531. Assessment of selected resources for severely handicapped children and youth: a selected, annotated bibliography.
Cambridge, MA, Abt Associates, Inc., 1974. 258p. ED 134615.

The references are listed under four handicapping conditions: mentally retarded, emotionally disturbed, deaf-
blind, and multiply handicapped. Annotated.

1532. Multiply handicapped: a selective bibliography. Arlington, VA, Council for Exceptional Children, 1972. 31p. ED
072589.

Contains 100 abstracts dating from 1947.

1533. Multiply handicapped: a selective bibliography. Reston,
VA, Council for Exceptional Children, 1973. 24p. ED 090706.

Includes 90 abstracts published since 1962 on evaluations,
programs, and research on the retarded, deaf-blind, and
multiply handicapped.

1534. Exceptional children: a general reading list: a selective bibliography. Reston, VA, Council for Exceptional Children, 1973. 20p. ED 090713.

75 abstracts dating back to 1960 treat identification, behavior modification, parents, learning disabilities, mental retardation, language development, and the gifted.

1535. Severely handicapped: a selective bibliography. Reston,
VA, Council for Exceptional Children, 1973. 25p. ED 090714.

100 abstracts dating back to 1958 treat evaluation, institutions, training techniques, and behavior modification.

1536. Identification and intervention of handicaps in early childhood: a selective bibliography. Reston, VA, Council for Exceptional Children, 1973. 22p. ED 090722.

85 abstracts dating back to 1958 treat preschool curriculum, prevention of learning disabilities, screening programs, and intervention programs. ED 146731 is a 22 page supplement containing 85 entries for the years 1974-1976.

1537. Homebound or hospitalized: a selective bibliography. Reston, VA, Council for Exceptional Children, 1973. 23p. ED 085917.

Contains abstracts of 60 documents published between 1965 and 1972.

1538. Miller, Susan. Tests used with exceptional children: annotated bibliography. Des Moines, Iowa, Drake University, 1975. 98p. ED 132773.

Includes 86 instruments which are used in screening and formulating diagnoses for vision, hearing, intelligence, social, emotional, speech, reading, arithmetic, and general achievement.

1539. Smith, Frank T. and Jill. The Exceptional child and the law: annotated bibliography. Arlington, TX, National Association for Retarded Citizens Library, 1975. 20p. ED 132791.

Contains 150 print and nonprint materials on legislation and advocacy concerning the rights and privileges of the handicapped.

1540. Krantz, Murray and Vilia Sauerberg. Roundtable in research on the psychomotor development of young handicapped children: annotated bibliography. Milwaukee, WI, Vasquez Associates, Ltd, 1975. 114p. ED 119442.

Includes 75 empirical studies dated 1958 to 1974.

1541. Severely and multiply handicapped: program descriptions, operant conditioning: a selective bibliography. Reston, VA, Council for Exceptional Children, 1976. 30p. ED 129020.

Lists 140 abstracts dating back to 1967.

1542. Speech handicapped: general, research, programs: a selective bibliography. Reston, VA, Council for Exceptional Children, 1976. 38p. ED 129022.

Includes 190 abstracts of documents and articles dated from 1968 to 1975.

1543. Down's syndrome: a selective bibliography. Reston, VA, Council for Exceptional Children, 1976. 23p. ED 129023.

Includes 100 abstracts of documents and articles (1966-75)

1544. <u>Normalization: general, aurally handicapped, visually</u>
<u>handicapped, physically handicapped, emotionally disturbed</u>:
<u>a selective bibliography</u>. Reston, VA, Council for Exceptional
Children, 1976. 27p. ED 129027.

   Includes 100 abstracts for documents and journal articles
   dating from 1966 to 1975. ED 146743 is a 16 page supplement with 65 entries issued in 1977.

1545. Bartholomew, Robert. <u>Indoor and outdoor space for men-</u>
<u>tally and physically handicapped children</u>. Monticello, IL,
Council of Planning Librarians, 1973. 11p. ED 106905.

   Intended to present users' requirements to designers. Not
   annotated.

1546. <u>Parent attitudes and parent counseling</u>. Reston, VA,
Council for Exceptional Children, 1977. 16p. ED 146744.

   This annotated bibliography contains 50 citations on attitudes of and counseling for parents of handicapped children.

1547. <u>Guide to resources for parents of the handicapped child</u>.
Hightstown, NJ, Northeast Area Learning Resource Center, 1975.
49p. ED 131653.

   Lists 80 unannotated references for parents plus a bibliography of books for handicapped children.

1548. Cohen, Shirley. <u>A Selected bibliography for and about</u>
<u>parents of the handicapped</u>. New York, City University Gradu-
ate School, 1975. 15p. ED 116369.

   Includes writings by parents, and some articles for the
   professional. The 90 unannotated items date from 1950 to
   1973.

1549. Klafter, Marcia B. <u>Working with parents of the handi-</u>
<u>capped: a resource guide</u>. King of Prussia, PA, Eastern Penn-
sylvania Regional Resources Center for Special Education, 1979.
114p. ED 182888.

   Designed to support training efforts for parents of handicapped children, this bibliography lists about 700 multimedia items dating from 1970.

1550. Moore, Coralie B. and Kathryn G. Morton. <u>A Reader's</u>
<u>guide for parents of children with mental, physical or emo-</u>
<u>tional disabilities</u>. Silver Spring, MD, Montgomery County
Association for Retarded Citizens, 1976. 148p. ED 143179.

   Includes 600 references with brief annotations on eleven
   specific handicaps. Also lists books for children about
   children with handicaps.

1551. <u>Physically handicapped, special health problems, and</u>

cerebral palsy research: a selective bibliography. Reston, VA, Council for Exceptional Children, 1973. 29p. ED 085920.

Contains 100 abstracts dating back to 1963.

1552. Physically handicapped, special health problems, and cerebral palsy programs: a selective bibliobraphy. Reston, VA, Council for Exceptional Children, 1973. 22p. ED 085943.

Contains 85 abstracts dating from 1963.

1553. Physically handicapped, special health problems, and cerebral palsy: a selective bibliography. Arlington, VA, Council for Exceptional Children, 1972. 31p. ED 074682.

Contains 100 abstracts dating from 1964.

1554. Physically handicapped and special health problems. Arlington, VA, Council for Exceptional Children, 1971. 21p. ED 052572.

Includes 77 annotated references to texts, articles, program guides, research and medical reports on handicapped children.

1555. O'Connell, Dorothy. Multiply handicapped children: a bibliography. ERIC Clearinghouse on Early Childhood Education, 1973. 43p. ED 075098.

Unannotated documents and articles from RIE and CIJE.

1556. Physical facilities: a selective bibliography. Arlington, VA, Council for Exceptional Children, 1972. 32p. ED 072 591.

Includes 100 abstracts dating from 1952.

HANDICAPPED CHILDREN - EDUCATION See also MAINSTREAMING

1557. Cook, Iva Dean. Annotated bibliography of special education instructional materials. Charleston, West Virginia State Commission on Mental Retardation, 1975. 212p. ED 143 196.

Categories include art, health, safety, homemaking, language arts, math, music, phonics, physical education, science, social studies, tests, and vocational education.

1558. Tringo, John L. Films for special education. Boston, New England Special Education Instructional Materials Center, 1972. 102p. ED 079887.

Annotates 500 films in a variety of areas for special education.

1559. Cohen, Shirley and Nancy Koehler. Educating severely

handicapped children and youth: a selected bibliography. New
York, City University Graduate School, 1976. 16p. ED 140514.

Lists 170 entries dating from 1970 with emphasis on deaf-
blind, behavior modification, and teacher training.

1560. Mycue, Elena De Los Santos. Young children with handicaps. ERIC Clearinghouse on Early Childhood Education, 1973.
ED 076262 and ED 076265.

Part one is a 49 page abstract bibliography on emotional
disturbances and specific learning disabilities, and part
three is a 47 page abstract bibliography on educable and
trainable mentally handicapped. All entries are taken from
RIE and CIJE.

1561. Van Etten, Carlene. Directory of Head Start instructional materials. Reston, VA, Council for Exceptional Children, 1974. 25p. ED 091882.

The annotated bibliography contains 71 listings for teachers of handicapped children.

1562. Home instruction programs for exceptional students ages
0-5. Tallahassee, Florida State Department of Education, 1974.
28p. ED 089528.

Includes annotated bibliographies and programs for trainable mentally retarded, hearing impaired, visually handicapped, language and speech handicapped, and physically
or multiply handicapped children from birth to age 5.

1563. Florida developed products listing: education for exceptional students. Fifth ed. Tallahassee, Florida State Department of Education, 1975. 154p. ED 113920.

Annotates 200 instructional materials primarily for handicapped children.

1564. Smith, Anne P. Mainstreaming: idea and actuality. Albany, New York State Department of Education, Division for
Handicapped Children, 1973. 24p. ED 111157.

Includes an annotated bibliography of 14 references.

1565. Draper, Ingrid L. A Selected special education bibliography and resource guide. Detroit Public Schools, 1975. 102p.
ED 121038.

Compiled to assist Head Start personnel who are not experienced in special education for a variety of handicapping
conditions.

1566. McMurray, J. G. The Exceptional adolescent: a bibliography for psychology and education. Toronto, Ontario Educational Research Council, 1975. 285p. ED 121007.

Includes journal articles in English published since 1970.

Entries cover intellectual, sensory, physical, behavioral, social, and learning problems.

1567. Regular class placement/special classes: a selective bibliography. Arlington, VA, Council for Exceptional Children, 1972. 24p. ED 065967.

Includes 70 abstracts on handicapped and gifted students dating from 1957. ED 146739 is a 24 page supplement with 95 entries dated 1973–1976.

1568. Adams, Anne H. Early childhood education for handicapped children: a bibliography of selected books. Austin, University of Texas, Department of Special Education, 1971. 24p. ED 071207.

Lists 167 books on child development, preschool education, child behavior, cognitive development and stimulation, and educational methods and techniques for variously handicapped or disadvantaged children.

1569. Harbin, Gloria and Lee Cross. Early childhood curriculum materials: an annotated bibliography. Chapel Hill, University of North Carolina, Technical Assistance Development System, 1975. 109p. ED 119409.

Presents 60 commercially distributed instructional materials or programs for use with handicapped preschool children.

1570. Severely and multiply handicapped: teaching methods/ assessment: a selective bibliography. Reston, VA, Council for Exceptional Children, 1976. 30p. ED 129021.

Contains 120 abstracts dating from 1966.

1571. Severely and multiply handicapped: programs, teaching methods, and curriculum: 1977 topical bibliography. Reston, VA, Council for Exceptional Children, 1977. 22p. ED 146745.

Includes 85 annotated citations dated 1972 to 1976.

1572. Wynne, Suzan. Mainstreaming and early childhood education for handicapped children: review and implications of research. Washington, DC, Wynne Associates, 1975. 296p. ED 108426.

The 291 books, reports, and articles focus on the preschool child. Most entries are annotated.

1573. Edgar, Eugene. Bibliography: early childhood education for the handicapped. Seattle, University of Washington, Child Development and Mental Retardation Center, 1975. 12p. ED 108 415.

The 50 annotated citations dating from 1961 present an overview and cover integration, social factors, parents, paraprofessionals, Head Start, communication development, curricula, and child development.

1574. Haring, Norris G. <u>Annotated bibliography</u>. Seattle, University of Washington, Child Development and Mental Retardation Center, 1975. 74p. ED 108414.

Includes 300 references on the education of severely and profoundly handicapped children dated from 1951 to 1973. Physical therapy, behavior shaping, cognitive and communication development, and self-care development are among the topics.

1575. <u>Audiovisual instruction: a selective bibliography</u>. Arlington, VA, Council for Exceptional Children, 1972. 32p. ED 074686.

Contains 100 abstracts dating from 1965.

1576. <u>Instructional materials: a selective bibliography</u>. Arlington VA, Council for Exceptional Children, 1972. 32p. ED 072593.

Contains 100 abstracts for handicapped and gifted children dating from 1960.

1577. Greene, Frederick L. <u>Resources for professionals involved with the education or treatment of multi-impaired and visually handicapped children</u>. Greeley, CO, Rocky Mountain Special Education Instructional Materials Center, 1969. 64p. ED 042285.

Sources cover concomitant handicaps including hearing impairment, mental retardation, speech impairment, emotional disturbances, educational handicaps, and vocational rehabilitation.

1578. <u>Union Catalog 1973 supplement: special education instructional materials center network</u>. Raleigh, North Carolina State Department of Public Instruction, 1973. 187p. ED 081151.

Annotates 650 professional books under 24 handicapping conditions.

HAWAII

1579. <u>Hawaiiana books for boys and girls</u>. Honolulu, Hawaii State Department of Education, 1967. 12p. ED 031492.

This annotated bibliography lists over 200 books for elementary and secondary students.

HEALTH EDUCATION See also MENTAL HEALTH

1580. Leyasmeyer, Edith and Laurie A. Whitmarsh. Continuing
education in the health professions: an annotated bibliography.
St. Paul, Northlands Regional Medical Program, Inc., 1969. 69p.
ED 052456.

148 items are selected primarily for the physician on
theory, practice, and evaluation of continuing education
for the busy practioner or instructor.

1581. Flagle, Charles D. Systems analysis in health manpower
education: a bibliography. Bethesda, MD, Health Resources Administration, (DHEW), 1973. 19p. ED 091576.

Includes the annotated results of an extensive literature
search.

1582. Beyrer, Mary E. and Rose L. Daniels. A Topical list of
theses and dissertations in health education. Washington, DC,
American Alliance for Health, Physical Education, and Recreation, 1978. 146p. ED 166181 (MF)

820 entries include masters and doctoral theses through
1972.

1583. Current awareness in health education. Atlanta, GA,
Center for Disease Control (DHEW), 1978. 20p. ED 164488.

The annotated list of journal articles, monographs, and
government reports covers patient education, community
health education, sex education, lifestyles, smoking, and
self-care.

1584. Dykstra, Ralph R. and Peter J. Dirr. Drug and health
mediagraphy: personal health. Buffalo, State University of
New York, Educational Research and Development Complex, 1974.
87p. ED 106992 (MF)

Lists 400 books, pamphlets, films, and filmstrips on dental health, first aid and survival, nutrition, and safety
education.

1585. Solleder, Marian K. Evaluation instruments in health
education: a bibliography of tests of knowledge, attitudes,
and behavior for elementary, secondary, and college levels.
Washington, DC, American Association for Health, Physical Education, and Recreation, 1965. 32p. ED 034314 (MF)

Annotates 73 tests, half of which were produced in the
1960's.

1586. Ferrante, Jeanne and Walter Brandt. Health education:
a bibliography for K-12. New York, Burnt Hills-Ballston Lake
Central Schools, 1969. 29p. ED 046791.

The health topics included are: physical, mental, sociological, environmental, and community. Briefly annotated.

1587. Singer, Robert W. and Raymond A. Weiss. Completed re-

search in health, physical education, and recreation including
international sources. Washington, DC, American Association
for Higher Education, 1970. 296p. ED 045603 (MF)

One section lists 801 articles from 127 journal sources,
and another section lists 877 master's theses and doctoral
dissertations.

1588. Isquith, Robert N. and Charles T. Webb. Spanish language health communication teaching aids: a list of printed materials and their sources. Bethesda, MD, Health Services and
Mental Health Administration (DHEW), 1972. 61p. ED 073868.

Includes 450 items, some bilingual. Subjects covered are:
alcoholism, allergies, cancer, dental health, drugs, infant
care, tuberculosis, nutrition, diabetes, consumer education, environmental health, family planning, and VD.

HEALTH OCCUPATIONS

1589. Equivalency and proficiency testing: a descriptive compilation of existing testing programs in allied health and
other health occupations, with an annotated bibliography.
Bethesda, MD, National Institutes of Health, 1971. 87p. ED
054335.

The bibliography section contains 108 items.

1590. A Bibliography for continuing educators of health manpower. Syracuse University, 1973. 175p. ED 083443.

A topical annotated bibliography of 440 items, 59 of which
are other bibliographies or literature reviews.

1591. A Technology of health manpower utilization: uniform
measurement and evaluation. Bethesda, MD, National Institutes
of Health, 1973. 67p. ED 080698.

An annotated bibliography of recent studies on the use of
personnel in the health industry.

1592. Health manpower: an annotated bibliography. Chicago,
American Hospital Association, 1972. 44p. ED 070862.

Covers minority group employment, career counseling, medical corpsmen, nursing education, and some case histories.

1593. Fabriele, Peter and Carrie R. Losi. Health careers bibliography for guidance counselors. Second ed. Trenton, New
Jersey Health Careers Service, 1970. 130p. ED 092759.

Lists 1500 selected items published since 1964. Not annotated.

1594. Solon, Lindy. An Annotated bibliography for health

occupations: a guide for teachers and students. Springfield,
Illinois Professional and Curriculum Development Unit for Vocational and Technical Education, 1975. 236p. ED 113509.

This health career bibliography lists 115 items for the
secondary level.

1595. An Annotated bibliography of basic documents related to
health manpower programs. Rockville, MD, Health Resources Administration (DHEW), 1974. 78p. ED 105122.

Includes documents and studies considered to be landmarks
in that they appear to have influenced legislation or policy of the federal government. The emphasis is on the 1956
to 1974 period.

1596. National assessment of clinical education of allied
health manpower: bibliography. Washington, DC, Booz Allen and
Hamilton, Inc., 1974. 559p. ED 122014.

This is the last volume of a four part report. It contains
434 annotated entries dating from 1965 in sections on content, credentialing, standards, continuing education, students, management, resources, and financing.

1597. Lambert, Roger H. A Bibliography of free loan materials
for health occupations education: vocational education resource
materials. Third edition. Madison, University of Wisconsin,
Vocational Studies Center, 1976. 25p. ED 132275.

Annotated.

1598. Brown, Monica V. and Carol J. Harten. Health manpower
planning. Monticello, IL, Council of Planning Librarians,
1970. 18p. ED 045804.

Presents 208 citations dating from 1952. Not annotated.

1599. Kintgen, Jean. Interpretation of literature on career
ladders and lattices in health occupations education. Columbus,
Ohio State University, Center for Vocational and Technical Education, 1970. 29p. ED 042919.

Includes 56 ERIC documents issued since 1966. These are
conference reports, curriculum development studies, papers
and speeches, program descriptions and evaluations, and
program guides.

HEALTH SCIENCES   See also   HOSPITALS

1600. Health economics studies information exchange: reports
of current research in health economics and medical care administration. Arlington, VA, Public Health Service (DHEW), 1966.
385p. ED 024773.

Includes 355 annotated reports.

1601. Jumba-Masagazi, A. The Sociology of family health: a bibliography. Nairobi, Kenya, East African Academy, 1971. 124p. ED 058131.

Centers on the East African environment and includes citations from the fields of anthropology, medicine, religion, economics, labor, and nutrition.

1602. Health sciences: a dissertation bibliography. Ann Arbor, MI, University Microfilms International, 1978.   156p. ED 161664 (MF)

Includes masters and doctoral theses, but excludes those in the field of psychology.

1603. Selected bibliographies and state-of-the-art review: international health planning reference series. Rockville, MD, Office of International Health (DHEW), 1979. ED 183764 through ED 183769.

These six separate documents present annotated bibliographies on health sciences in developing countries. Volume one is on communicable diseases and has 112 entries in 79 pages. Volume two is on environmental health and has 462 references in 192 pages. Volume three is on health manpower planning and has 223 references in 82 pages. Volume 4 is on socio-cultural factors and has 193 references in 88 pages. Volume five is on pharmaceutical supply systems and has 110 references in 29 pages. Volume six is on health facility planning and has 131 references in 51 pages.

HEALTH SERVICES

1604. Carmody, James. Ethical issues in health services: a report and annotated bibliography. Bethesda, MD, Public Health Service (DHEW), 1970. 42p. ED 058128.

A bibliography follows the discussion of each of these issues: the right to health care, death and euthanasia, human experimentation, genetic engineering, and abortion.

1605. Cordes, Sam. Social science research on rural health care delivery: a compilation of recent and ongoing studies. Pennsylvania State University, Department of Agricultural Economics and Rural Sociology, 1977. 60p. ED 153777.

Includes summaries of 89 studies in the United States.

1606. Aday, Lu Ann. The Utilization of health services: indices and correlates: a research bibliography. Bethesda, MD, Public Health Service (DHEW), 1972. 112p. ED 076873.

An annotated and comprehensive critical review of empirical literature.

1607. Bibliography on the comprehensive health service pro-

<u>gram</u>. Washington, DC, Office of Economic Opportunity, 1970.
37p. ED 044488.

This annotated bibliography contains 40 speeches, papers,
and articles describing projects in eight states, and an
additional 27 annotations which provide background information on the purposes and nature of the program.

1608. Bikshapathi, Adepu. <u>Health and the urban poor: a bib-
liography</u>. ERIC Clearinghouse on the Urban Disadvantaged,
1975. 62p. ED 114445.

Lists 526 unannotated articles, books, and reports dating
from 1970 on issues relating to health problems of urban
minority youth.

1609. Erbstoeszer, Marie. <u>Health services organizational and
administrative techniques: a selected annotated bibliography</u>.
Monticello, IL, Council of Planning Librarians, 1974. 31p.
ED 105058.

Includes books, pamphlets, and articles focusing on fund-
raising, assessment of community facts and issues, agency
management, network analysis, public budgeting, and public
relations.

HEREDITY   See also   GENETICS

1610. Rosenfield, Geraldine and Howard Yagerman. <u>The New en-
vironment-heredity controversy: a selected annotated bibliogra-
phy</u>. New York, American Jewish Committee, 1973. 53p. ED 087
825.

Presents as many points of view from various scientific
disciplines as have been published since the appearance
of Arthur Jensen's 1969 article on intelligence being
based on heredity.

HIGH SCHOOL GRADUATES

1611. Peng, Samuel S. <u>National longitudinal study of the
high school class of 1972: review and annotations of study
reports</u>. Durham, NC, Research Triangle Institute, 1977. 86p.
ED 151370.

Includes over 150 articles, papers, dissertations, government publications, contract reports, and studies in progress.

HIGHER EDUCATION   See also   COMMUNITY COLLEGES

1612. Kelsey, Roger R. <u>A Bibliography on higher education</u>.

Baltimore, Maryland State Teachers Association, 1969.   178p.
ED 033672.

Includes over 5800 books pertaining to all aspects of
higher education. The unannotated entries are divided into
16 subject groups, and were all published since 1955.

1613.   Piele, Philip. Number and subject index of selected
documents on higher education.   Eugene, University of Oregon,
1966(?)   81p.   ED 012110.

Includes 1000 entries; not annotated.

1614.   Higher education as a field of study.   Chicago, Association of Professors of Higher Education, 1972.   59p.   ED 076
110.

Presented is a literature review with a 53 item bibliography as a conclusion.

1615.   Shrier, Irene and David E. Lavin.   Open admissions: a
bibliography for research and application.   New York, City
University, Office of Program and Policy Research, 1974.   79p.
ED 090840.

Covers minorities, dropouts, aspirations, career patterns,
and social mobility of college graduates among other topics. Not annotated.

1616.   Patterson, Lewis D.   Consortia in American higher education.   ERIC Clearinghouse on Higher Education, 1970.   23p.
ED 043800.

Discusses the practical problems of interinstitutional
cooperation, and provides an annotated bibliography of
52 references.

1617.   Lepchenske, George L.   Higher educational consortia organization: functional structures of administration and management.   1976.   25p.   ED 176619.

The bibliography includes 52 items. Not annotated.

1618.   Kelsey, Roger R.   AAHE bibliography on higher education.
Washington, DC, American Association for Higher Education,
1970.   57p.   ED 038907.

Lists 1473 books on all aspects of higher education. Not
annotated.

1619.   Chambers, M.M.   Current bibliography of higher education in other nations.   Illinois State University, Department
of Educational Administration, 1976.   67p.   ED 130587.

Includes 400 entries on 40 different countries. Most of
the citations are in English, a few in French or German.
Seventy percent were written after 1974.

1620. Parsons, Kermit C. and Jon T. Lang. An Annotated bibliography on university planning and development. New York,
Society for College and University Planning, 1968. 163p. ED
083889.

A topical bibliography that includes all aspects of the
subject.

1621. McKnight, Philip C. and Mark A. Paskal. On the improve-
of instruction in higher education: a bibliography. Lawrence,
University of Kansas, 1973. 29p. ED 074898.

An unannotated list of publications dealing with theory and
research, particularly in psychology and sociology. Includes student evaluation of teaching, and the use of innovative curricula and media.

1622. Mills, Gladys H. Accountability vs. autonomy in post-
secondary education. Denver, Education Commission of the
States, 1972. 7p. ED 096903.

Lists 80 citations, some from the ERIC system.

1623. Beeler, Kent D. Source bibliographies on higher education, 1968-1972. 1972. 98p. ED 102895.

The bibliographies included cover all aspects of higher
education.

1624. Barak, Robert J. The State and higher education: a bibliography of the literature up to 1972. 1974. 87p. ED 104
318.

Annotated.

1625. Fink, Ira S. The Economic impact of institutions of
higher education on local communities: an annotated bibliography. Berkeley, University of California, Board of Regents,
1976. 112p. ED 138128 (MF)

Contains 74 items dating from 1958.

1626. Songe, Alice H. The Land grant movement in American
higher education: an historical bibliography of the land grant
movement and the individual land grant institutions. Washington, DC, National Association of State Universities and Land
Grant Colleges, 1962. 70p. ED 116523.

The first part deals with the history of the Morrill Act
of 1862. Entries in the bibliography date back to 1858.

1627. Caldwell, John. Histories of American colleges and universities: a bibliography. 1976. 80p. ED 129138.

The list includes 700 unannotated entries limited to historical studies. Memoirs and ephemeral materials are excluded.

1628. Isler, Norman P. Planning in higher education: an interpretive bibliography. ERIC Clearinghouse on Educational
Facilities, 1969. ED 032743 through ED 032748.

In six parts: Part one is on facilities and space utilization and has 46 pages; Part two is on campus planning and
has 42 pages; Part three is on special facilities in higher
education planning and has 40 pages; Part four is on case
histories in campus planning and has 44 pages; Part five
is on financial aspects of higher education planning and
has 19 pages; Part six is on the community and junior college and has 64 pages. These six separate documents are
all unannotated.

HIGHER EDUCATION - ADMINISTRATION AND GOVERNANCE   See also
       TRUSTEES

1629. Nash, George and Stefan Uhse. A Review of the literature on college administrators and administrations. New York,
Columbia University, Bureau of Applied Social Research, 1966.
42p. ED 030385.

Reviews 79 books and articles.

1630. Robinson, Lora H. and Janet D. Shoenfeld. Student participation in academic governance. ERIC Clearinghouse on Higher Education, 1970. 28p. ED 035786.

The annotated bibliography includes surveys of current
practice, arguments for and against, hypothetical models,
and methods for increasing student involvement.

1631. Command, Edward M. Governance in higher education: a
bibliography. Olympia, Washington State Board for Community
College Education, 1970. 56p. ED 099018.

An annotated list of books and ERIC documents on the many
aspects of the topic.

1632. Sceiford, Chester L. and Ray E. Wheeler. University
governance: current changes and an annotated bibliography.
Bloomington, University of Indiana, Bureau of Institutional
Research, 1970. 38p. ED 048825.

Focuses on student participation on the board of trustees
and on various advisory committees.

1633. Harris, Evelyn J. Governance of the university: a selected bibliography. 1971. 37p. ED 050691.

Includes books, articles, and ERIC documents on the historical aspects, objectives, roles, and structure.

1634. Wren, Scott C. Student participation in the governance
of institutions of higher education: an annotated bibliography.

Berkeley, University of California, 1975. 70p. ED 111242.

Includes 137 items published since 1968.

1635. Retzlaff, Bernice R. Higher education administration: an annotated bibliography of research reports funded by the Cooperative Research Act, 1956-1970. Washington, DC, National Center for Educational Research and Development (DHEW), 1971. 19p. ED 051760.

Categories are: communication, faculties, financing, institutional management, instructional programs, and students.

1636. Fougeres, Viviane. Programme on institutional management in higher education: list of documents. Paris, Organisation for Economic Cooperation and Development, 1970. 60p. ED 046339.

An unannotated bibliography, international in scope.

1637. Bibliography on institutional governance. Washington, DC, Association of Governing Boards of Universities and Colleges, 1969. 9p. ED 032003.

Includes 96 references focusing on trustees, but also notes student participation. The publications date from 1933, and some are specific to church-related schools.

HINDUISM

1638. Dell, David. Focus on Hinduism: audiovisual resources for teaching religion. New York, SUNY, Foreign Area Materials Center, 1977. 123p. ED 157832 (MF)

An annotated list of materials produced in the 1960's and 1970's.

HISTORY BOOKS

1639. Wagar, W. Warren. Books in world history: a guide for teachers and students. Bloomington, Indiana University Press, 1973. 191p. ED 133270 (MF)

Over 380 books are annotated in popular and scholarly categories. Those most appropriate for high schools are indicated accordingly.

HMONGS

1640. An Annotated bibliography of materials on the Hmongs

of Laos. Arlington, VA, Center for Applied Linguistics, 1978.
31p. ED 159902.

    Fiction is included in this list on Hmong language and cul-
ture. Items date from 1945.

HOLOCAUST See also JEWISH STUDIES

1641. Friedlander, Henry. On the holocaust: a critique of
the treatment of the holocaust in history textbooks accompanied
by an annotated bibliography. New York, B'nai B'rith Anti-
Defamation League, 1973. 32p. ED 157857 (MF)

    Includes 150 resources including eyewitness accounts.

1642. A Selected and annotated resource list of materials on
the holocaust. New York, B'nai B'rith Anti-Defamation League,
1977. 65p. ED 157858 (MF)

    Contains over 200 books and films in twenty categories.

HOME ECONOMICS See also CONSUMER EDUCATION

1643. Home economics library resource materials: a multimedia
listing. Winnipeg, Manitoba Department of Education, 1974.
159p. ED 118903.

    The annotated entries are arranged by the Dewey Decimal
system, and the grade level information is provided.

1644. Harding, Margaret. Helping low-income homemakers: programs and evaluations: a selected annotated bibliography. Ithaca, NY, SUNY, College of Human Ecology, 1969. 159p. ED 036
695.

    Includes intervention strategies and the role of social
service agencies in the 208 entries.

1645. Manning, Sarah L. and Marilyn Dunsing. Selected bibliography of theses and research in family economics and home
management. Washington, DC, American Home Economics Association, 1965. 56p. ED 028290.

    A classified list of unannotated journal articles pub-
lished since 1961.

1646. Rotz, Patricia H. and Ruth Whitmarsh. The Employment
aspect of home economics education: a selective bibliography
with annotations. Urbana, University of Illinois, Division
of Home Economics Education, 1965. 71p. ED 017631.

    A topical bibliography dating from 1950.

1647. Chadderdon, Hester and Alyce M. Fanslow. Review and

synthesis of research in home economics education. Columbus,
Ohio State University, Center for Vocational and Technical Education, 1966. 118p. ED 011563.

159 studies on teacher education are included dating from
1959.

1648. Nelson, Helen Y. Review and synthesis of research on
home economics education. Columbus, Ohio State University,
Center for Vocational and Technical Education, 1970. 67p.
ED 038519.

This update of the previous document includes 102 reports
for the period 1965-1969.

1649. Judson, Julia. Home economics research abstracts, 1963-
1968: rehabilitation. Washington, DC, American Home Economics
Association, 1969. 25p. ED 033217.

Includes 35 dissertation abstracts and 26 journal articles
which relate to aspects of rehabilitation and indicate
the extent to which home economists are contributing to
the field. Annotated.

1650. Mather, Mary E. Home economics research abstracts.
Washington, DC, American Home Economics Association, 1968.
66p. ED 043728.

Includes 96 master's theses and 11 doctoral dissertations
completed in 1967.

1651. Horn, Fern M. Annotated bibliography of instructional
materials for use by home economics teachers with educable
mentally retarded students. Stevens Point, University of Wisconsin, 1974. 50p. ED 093106.

Lists 143 items, some of which are for student use.

1652. Lambert, Roger H. A Bibliography of free loan materials for home economics education. Third ed. Madison, University of Wisconsin, Vocational Studies Center, 1976. 39p.
ED 132273.

Annotated.

1653. Gorman, Anna M. and Doris E. Manning. A Listing of
data collection instruments for use in research in home economics education, 1962-1969. Columbus, Ohio State University,
Center for Vocational and Technical Education, 1971. 104p.
ED 050275.

Includes 168 research studies and ERIC documents.

HORTICULTURE

1654. Moore, Eddie A. Student performance objectives and

<u>selected references for teaching ornamental horticulture</u>.
East Lansing, Michigan State University, College of Agriculture,
1976. 201p. ED 159358 (MF)

HOSPITALS

1655. Altshuler, Anne. <u>Books that help children deal with a
hospital experience</u>. Rockville, MD, Health Services Administration (DHEW), 1974. 28p. ED 115375.

    The books are for preschool and elementary levels, and are
    evaluated and rated in the annotations.

1656. <u>Annotated references on engineering maintenance, sanitation public health, sanitation health care facility, house-
keeping, and purchasing</u>. Los Angeles, UCLA, Division of Vocational Education, 1970. 22p. ED 054355.

    These five annotated hospital-related bibliographies con-
    tain 130 entries.

HOTEL AND RESTAURANT MANAGEMENT

1657. Malkames, James P. <u>Hotel and restaurant management: a
bibliography of books and audiovisual materials</u>. Nanticoke,
PA, Luzerne County Community College, 1975. 138p. ED 118179.

    Includes 1300 items. Not annotated.

HOUSING   See also   DORMITORIES

1658. <u>Annotated bibliography on housing and settlements for
low income people</u>. Honolulu, University of Hawaii, East-West
Center, 1976. 47p. ED 142232.

1659. Newbacher, Gary D. <u>Low income housing mixing: an annotated bibliography</u>. Monticello, IL, Council of Planning Librarians, 1975. 21p. ED 103568.

1660. <u>Equal opportunity in housing: a bibliography of research</u>.
Washington, DC, Department of Housing and Urban Development,
1974. 38p. ED 106384.

    This annotated list in eight sections includes materials
    published since 1969. Covers new communities, demographic
    patterns, fair housing laws, real estate practice, and
    government policy.

HUMAN DEVELOPMENT

1661. Griggs, Mildred B. and Nancy Carlson. The Psychomotor
domain: a selective bibliography with annotations. Urbana,
University of Illinois, Division of Home Economic Education,
1966. 20p. ED 020318.

   Includes 75 citations dating from 1923 for those concerned
   with developing physical abilities and skills.

1662. Mills, Gladys H. Education to make a life: bibliography. Denver, Education Commission of the States, 1974. 34p.
ED 102440.

   This wide ranging bibliography covers alcohol and drug
   education, lifestyles, leisure activities, marriage and
   family relations, race relations, sex education, social
   indicators, and value concepts. Not annotated.

HUMAN RELATIONS

1663. Durham, Lewis E. A Bibliography of research: explora-
tions, human relations training and research. Washington, DC,
National Training Laboratories, 1967. 36p. ED 014016.

   Includes 175 studies dating from 1947. Annotated.

1664. Human relations: training and research. ERIC Clearinghouse on Adult Education, 1968. 22p. ED 016159.

   Contains 36 annotated entries.

1665. Martin, William R. An Annotated bibliography on human
relations and humanistic education. ERIC Clearinghouse on
Teacher Education, 1980. 62p. ED 180981.

   Lists instructional and resource materials including films
   and other AV items.

1666. Harvey, Robert and Robert V. Denby. Human relations in
the schools, sensitivity training, and self-image enhancement:
abstracts of ERIC documents. Champaign, IL, National Council
of Teachers of English, 1970. 53p. ED 044400.

   The 115 ERIC items include books, articles, reports, and
   speeches, plus classroom activities.

1667. Jayatilleke, Raja. Human relations in the classroom.
ERIC Clearinghouse on the Urban Disadvantaged, 1976. 49p.
ED 128496.

   Categories include group relations, interpersonal relations, self concept, environment, student and teacher attitudes, activism, violence, and teacher education. Annotated. ED 107732 is a 58 page supplement.

1668. Rose, Peter I. Research bulletin on intergroup rela-

tions. New York, B'nai B'rith, Anti-Defamation League, 1963.
49p. ED 017571.

Annotations cover prejudice, racial and ethnic minorities,
community patterns, and cross-cultural studies.

1669. Guthrie, P.D. Measures of social skills: an annotated
bibliography. Princeton, NJ, Educational Testing Service,
1971. 28p. ED 056085.

Annotates various instruments for use with preschool
through third grade.

HUMAN RESOURCES

1670. HumRRO bibliography of publications as of 30 June 1971.
Alexandria, VA, Human Resources Research Organization, 1971.
355p. ED 061727.

An annotated list for improving human performance through
behavioral and social science research.

1671. Manpower research projects sponsored by the US Department of Labor through 30 June 1968. Washington, DC, Manpower
Administration (DOL), 1968. 223p. ED 026507.

The annotated bibliography dates from 1963.

1672. A Limited index to the manpower literature. Corvallis,
Oregon State University, Institute for Manpower Studies, 1976.
704p. ED 131222.

Annotated.

1673. Manpower information: an annotated bibliography. Phoenix, Arizona State Employment Security Commission, 1970. 38p.
ED 041124.

Includes 196 books and articles dating from 1960 on local
and national situations.

1674. Index to publications of the Manpower Administration.
Washington, DC, Manpower Administration (DOL), 1972. 44p.
ED 076793.

A cumulative index of 800 entries under 55 subjects covers the period January 1969 through December 1972. Not
annotated.

1675. Ryerson, William R. Manpower management studies: selected abstracts. Springfield, VA, National Technical Information Service, 1972. 63p. ED 078205.

Contains 58 studies on model simulations, job analysis,
projection methods, and program development.

1676. A Bibliography of manpower projections for the North
Central Region. Washington, DC, Bureau of Labor Statistics,
1968. 66p. ED 039316.

The annotated studies are listed by state: Illinois, Indiana, Kentucky, Michigan, Minnesota, Ohio, and Wisconsin.

1677. Moore, Larry F. Guidelines for manpower managers: a
selected annotated bibliography. Vancouver, University of
British Columbia, 1969. 81p. ED 040289.

Includes 323 journal articles and some monographs dating
from 1962 on changes and developments in management
thought.

1678. Goldstaub, Jesse. Manpower and educational planning:
an annotated bibliography. University of Pittsburgh, School
of Education, 1968. 62p. ED 030195.

Lists 110 documents mostly published in the 1960's. The
topics relate to demographics, economics, rural education,
administration, and planning.

1679. Mather, William G. Man, his job, and the environment:
a review and annotated bibliography of selected recent research
on human performance. Washington, DC, National Bureau of Standards, 1970. 109p. ED 048511.

Contains studies of human reactions to work and environmental stress. Simulations, clinical studies, and on-the-job
performance are included.

1680. Darcy, Robert L. Economics of human resources: a bibliography. Athens, University of Ohio, College of Business
Administration, 1968. 14p. ED 048478.

Lists over 150 articles and government documents selected
as representative works. Not annotated.

1681. Barlow, Esther M. and Maria S. Christensen. Annotated
bibliography of the Air Force Human Resources Laboratory technical reports, 1968-1975. Brooks AFB, TX, 1976. 223p. ED
132439.

Deals with personnel and training research conducted by
the laboratory in a variety of disciplines, including psychology, operations research, mathematics and computers,
economists, and engineers.

1682. Magness, P. J. Annotated bibliography of the Personnel
Research Division reports, 1973-1975. Lackland AFB, TX, Air
Force Human Resources Laboratory, 1976. 26p. ED 130036.

Includes 60 technical reports on individual aptitude, motivation, morale, attitude, and environmental factors.

1683. Index to publications of the Manpower Administration,

January 1969 through June 1973. 1973. 43p. ED 086813.

Includes 850 publications under 54 subject headings.

1684. Wood, W. D. and H. F. Campbell. Cost-benefit analysis and the economics of investment in human resources: an annotated bibliography. Kingston, Ontario, Queen's University, Industrial Relations Center, 1970. 217p. ED 045848 (MF)

Cites 389 books and articles representing a survey of the literature of theory and application.

1685. Hill, Nancy V. and E. Evan Brown. Impact of governmental transfer payments on human resource development: a bibliography. State College, Miss., Southern Rural Development Center, 1978. 169p. ED 161570.

Includes 764 entries, mostly annotated, dating from 1969.

HUMAN SERVICES

1686. Approaches to human services planning. Revised ed. Germantown, MD, Aspen Systems Corporation, 1978. 59p. ED 154252

An annotated bibliography of 43 books and reports.

HUMANISTIC EDUCATION

1687. Linder, Steven. ERIC and the now humanistic education: an unofficial bibliographic index of ERIC humanistic education documents. 1975. 18p. ED 110063.

Includes 148 documents in 34 categories. Not annotated.

HUTTERITES

1688. Riley, Marvin P. The Hutterite brethren: an annotated bibliography with special reference to South Dakota Hutterite colonies. Brookings, South Dakota State University, Agricultural Experiment Station, 1965. 189p. ED 046574.

332 items are included that were published since 1875.

HYPERACTIVITY

1689. Hyperactivity: drug therapy, food additives, allergies: a selective bibliography. Reston, VA, Council for Exceptional Children, 1976. 19p. ED 129029.
Annotates 65 items published since 1968.

1690. Hyperactivity – general: a selective bibliography. Reston, VA, Council for Exceptional Children, 1976. 21p. ED 129 028.

Annotates 84 documents and articles published since 1967.

IMMIGRANTS

1691. A Bibliography for teachers: education for a multi-cultural society. Third ed. London, Community Relations Commission, 1974. 39p. ED 093182.

The annotated materials are for all age groups and are concerned primarily with the problems and interests of immigrants in Britain.

INDIA

1692. Narang, H. L. Children's literature of India – legends, folklore, fiction: an annotated bibliography. 1970. 5p. ED 108184.

Includes 61 books for kindergarten through ninth grade.

1693. Pattanayak, D. P. Indian languages bibliography of grammars, dictionaries, and teaching materials. New Delhi, India, Educational Resources Center, 1973. 90p. ED 126674 (MF)

The books and articles on fourteen languages are subdivided by type of material.

INDIANA

1694. Popovich, Mark. Indiana newspaper history: an annotated bibliography. Muncie, IN, Sigma Delta Chi, 1974. 57p. ED 117713.

Contains 415 entries.

INDIANS See AMERICAN INDIANS

INDIVIDUALIZED INSTRUCTION See also CORRESPONDENCE STUDY
     and PROGRAMMED INSTRUCTION

1695. Weisgerber, Robert A. Individualized learning. ERIC Clearinghouse on Educational Media and Technology, 1972. 32p. ED 057610.

Over 100 annotated ERIC documents are included representing some of the best submitted on the subject from 1969
to 1972.

1696. A Progress report: individually prescribed instruction.
Philadelphia, Research for Better Schools, Inc., 1969. 63p.
ED 036147.

An annotated bibliography concludes the report.

1697. Wade, Serena E. Individualized instruction: an annotated bibliography. ERIC Clearinghouse on Educational Media
and Technology, 1968. 22p. ED 029519.

Includes 31 books, articles, and ERIC documents, and 32
ESEA Title III innovative projects. The entries were produced from 1964 to 1968.

1698. Individualizing instruction: a selected bibliography.
Dayton, OH, Institute for Development of Educational Activities, 1968. 23p. ED 030619.

Lists 206 books, articles, films, and pamphlets. Tactics
and strategies in subject areas are included. Partially
annotated.

1699. Bibliography on individualized instruction. Harvard
University, 1966. 9p. ED 011308.

85 unannotated references are provided dating from 1958.
Computer assisted instruction and teaching machines are
included in the books and articles listed.

1700. Dudgeon, Paul J. A Bibliography on the implementation
and management of individualized and personalized education
programs. 1975. 15p. ED 117364.

Presents 150 books, articles, dissertations, reports, and
ERIC documents. Most were produced since 1971.

1701. Dirr, Peter J. Individual instruction: a bibliography.
1974. 8p. ED 105678.

Computer assisted instruction, diagnostic teaching, and
instructional materials are included for the handicapped
and non-handicapped child. The 58 references dating from
1969 are not annotated.

1702. Poliakoff, Lorraine. Individualized instruction. ERIC
Clearinghouse on Teacher Education, 1970. 23p. ED 044381.

Cites 88 ERIC documents processed in 1968 and 1969.

1703. Ruskin, Robert S. Individualized instruction in higher
education: a bibliography. Washington, DC, Georgetown University, Center for Personalized Instruction, 1974. 37p. ED 091
967 (MF)

Programmed instruction and the audiotutorial method are
included in the unannotated list of books, articles, and
conference papers.

1704. Thompson, Glenn J. <u>Individualized instruction and the
role of the media specialist</u>. 1975. 13p. ED 114109.

This conference paper lists 60 entries in its bibliography. Not annotated.

1705. Davis, Harold S. <u>Independent study: an annotated bib-
liography</u>. Cleveland, OH, Educational Research Council, 1966.
30p. ED 022256 (MF)

Team teaching, nongraded schools, instructional materials
centers, flexible scheduling, and curriculum needs are
considered in this list of 150 books, articles, and pamphlets. Most entries are from the 1960's.

1706. <u>Independent study: bibliographies in education</u>. Ottawa,
Canadian Teachers Federation, 1970. 19p. ED 045585.

Includes 29 books and 218 articles from the previous five
year period. Not annotated.

1707. <u>Individualized instruction: bibliographies in education</u>.
Ottawa, Canadian Teachers Federation, 1970. 49p. ED 046881.

Includes 244 books, papers, and pamphlets, and 333 articles
from the previous five year period. Not annotated.

1708. <u>Bibliography of publications of the Wisconsin Research
and Development Center for Cognitive Learning</u>. Madison, University of Wisconsin, 1977. 274p. ED 148658.

The annotated entries focus on individualized education,
learning characteristics, and learning motivation. Over
500 books, reports, and technical papers are included. ED
163944 is a 92 page supplement containing about 100 items.

INDONESIA

1709. Prakoso, M. H. <u>Mass communication in Indonesia: an
annotated bibliography</u>. Singapore, Asian Mass Communication
Research and Information Centre, 1978. 70p. ED 165174 (MF)

Contains 281 entries on a variety of aspects of the subject.

INDUSTRIAL ARTS EDUCATION   See also   VOCATIONAL EDUCATION

1710. Jelden, David L. <u>Summaries of studies in industrial
arts, trade and industrial, and technical education from 1930</u>.
Washington, DC, American Council on Industrial Arts Teacher

Education, 1970. 969p. ED 037583.

962 abstracts of dissertations and staff studies are included. ED 062560 is a 514 page supplement with more than
400 abstracts, and ED 076846 is a 463 page supplement with
366 additional abstracts.

1711. Stunard, E. Arthur. Books annotated by American Council for Elementary School Industrial Arts. Washington, DC.
The Council, 1971. 208p. ED 057236.

Subjects include automation, communication, electricity,
glass, magnets, plastics, sound, clocks, wheels, and transportation.

1712. Titles for technology: an annotated bibliography. Trenton, New Jersey State Department of Education, 1967. 107p.
ED 027371.

Includes about 400 books suitable for use in elementary
industrial arts.

1713. Blankenbaker, Keith and W. R. Miller. Annotated bibliography of periodical articles related to the interpretation
of industry, 1960-1970. Washington, DC, American Industrial
Arts Association, 1970. 19p. ED 038542.

The 100 entries relate to the operational aspects of technology in industrial arts.

1714. Industrial arts technology bibliography: an annotated
reference for librarians. Albany, New York State Education
Department, 1970. 64p. ED 043771.

Designed as a selection tool for librarians for all aspects
of industrial arts education.

1715. Hinrichs, Roy S. and Gary A. Stone. Resource information for industrial arts. State College, Mississippi Research
and Curriculum Unit for Vocational and Technical Education,
1976. 42p. ED 127435.

Includes 350 books, journals, films, and catalogs recommended for starting an industrial arts library.

INDUSTRIAL DEVELOPMENT

1716. Development and structure of industry: instructional
aids list and bibliography. Platteville, Wisconsin State University, College of Industry, 1969. 53p. ED 037557.

INFANTS See also CHILDREN and DAY CARE

1717. Thomas, Sharon E. Current infant research: an abstract bibliography. ERIC Clearinghouse on Early Childhood Education, 1974. 42p. ED 099142.

An unannotated list extracted from RIE and CIJE, 1972-1974.

1718. Van de Kamp, Jacqueline. Sudden unexpected death in infants. Bethesda, MD, National Library of Medicine, 1973. 7p. ED 086364.

Includes 108 citations. Not annotated.

1719. Cross, Lee. Planning programs and activities for infants and toddlers: a bibliography. Chapel Hill, University of North Carolina, Technical Assistance Development System, 1975. 34p. ED 112545.

The 100 references are applicable to handicapped and non-handicapped children. Items date from 1961.

1720. Honig, Alice S. Infant education and stimulation: a bibliography. ERIC Clearinghouse on Early Childhood Education, 1973. 60p. ED 081499.

For birth to 3 years of age, 475 references to programs are cited. Includes curricula, materials, testing, and evaluation.

INFORMAL EDUCATION   See   NONFORMAL EDUCATION and OPEN EDUCATION

INFORMATION DISSEMINATION

1721. Havelock, Ronald G. Bibliography on knowledge utilization and dissemination. Ann Arbor, University of Michigan, Institute for Social Research, 1972. 250p. ED 061466.

This is an annotated revised edition covering all fields of knowledge.

1722. Selected readings on information for industry. The Hague, Netherlands, International Federation for Documentation, 1974. 50p. ED 104347 (MF)

Includes 68 annotated references on the problems of getting information to industry, and establishing information services within industrial firms.

1723. A Bibliography of Project Intrex publications, 1966-1973. Cambridge, Massachusetts Institute of Technology, Electronic Systems Laboratory, 1973. 16p. ED 094797.

Lists articles, book chapters, conference papers, theses, and instructional aids written by the staff at MIT. Not annotated.

INNOVATION IN EDUCATION   See also   CHANGE IN EDUCATION

1724.   Chorness, M. H.   Use of resource material and decision processes associated with educational innovation: a literature survey.   Berkeley, CA, Far West Laboratory for Educational Research and Development, 1969.   158p.   ED 026747.

This annotated bibliography covers innovation, change, decision making, and the role of various agents in the field of education.

1725.   Bibliography on new forms of post-secondary education. Washington, DC, InterAmerican Development Bank, 1977.   291p. ED 157412.

Includes 658 annotated entries on educational innovations. In English.

1726.   Leonard, Ann.   Installation of educational programs and procedures: an annotated bibliography.   Los Alamitos, CA, Southwest Regional Laboratory for Educational Research and Development, 1971.   20p.   ED 108373.

Lists 70 books and articles.

1727.   Paulston, Rolland G.   Evaluating educational reform: an international casebook.   1976.   449p.   ED 133243.

Sponsored by the World Bank, this publication includes 400 annotated references relating to theory and practice of educational reform and innovation. The second part cites case studies in 57 developing nations, and 26 developed nations.

1728.   Factors involved in the transfer of innovations: a summary and organization of the literature.   San Francisco, Public Affairs Counseling, 1976.   158p.   ED 139075.

Reviewed is literature relating to innovation, diffusion, organizational behavior, and public administration.

1729.   Ohliger, John.   Bibliography of comments on the Illich-Reimer deschooling theses.   ERIC Clearinghouse on Teacher Education, 1974.   65p.   ED 090145.

Includes a partial listing of the writings of Ivan Illich and Everett Reimer which are commented on in the books and articles in the main bibliography. The two authors are cited 570 times; most are in English, but 145 are in German, and 52 are in French.

1730.   Meaders, O. Donald and Sue Sutton.   A Bibliography for shared time (dual enrollment): a concept for providing educational programs.   East Lansing, Michigan State University, 1966.   19p.   ED 017682.

Includes 85 books and articles. Partially annotated.

INSERVICE EDUCATION   See   TEACHER EDUCATION

INSTRUCTIONAL MATERIALS

1731. Perkins, Flossie L. Book and non-book media: annotated
guide to selection aids for educational materials. Urbana, IL,
National Council of Teachers of English, 1972. 299p. ED 081
008.

    This is a revised and expanded version of Ralph Perkin's
    1967 title "Book Selection Media".

1732. Klein, M. Frances. About learning materials. Washington, DC, Association for Supervision and Curriculum Development, 1978. 55p. ED 154801 (MF)

    This handbook is intended for persons having responsibil-
    ity for selecting learning materials for student use. It
    annotates 40 resource publications that identify and eval-
    uate instructional materials.

1733. Advisory list of instructional media: fiction books.
Raleigh, North Carolina State Department of Public Instruction,
1977. 69p. ED 149746.

    An annotated list for elementary and secondary levels.

1734. Mirwis, Allan. Guides to educational media software.
Brooklyn, Educational Media Information Service, 1977. 164p.
ED 144531 (MF)

    This catalog includes 372 annotated entries.

1735. Cohen, Shirley and Nancy Koehler. Instructional materials: a bibliography for their selection, evaluation, and use.
New York, City University Graduate School, 1975. 6p. ED 140
516.

    Includes 60 entries dating from 1956. Not annotated.

1736. Advisory list of instructional media for media education.
Raleigh, North Carolina State Department of Public Instruction,
1977. 17p. ED 149752.

    An annotated list for elementary and secondary levels.

1737. Schumacher, Sanford P. A Comprehensive keyword index
and bibliography on instructional system development. Wright-
Patterson AFB, OH, Air Force Human Resources Laboratory, 1974.
246p. ED 089718.

    Lists 2692 items dating from 1953. Not annotated.

1738. Lewis, Richard B. The Effective use of media in innovative schools. ERIC Clearinghouse on Educational Media and

Technology, 1973. 18p. ED 082534.

Includes 37 recent ERIC documents.

1739. Naegle, V. J. The Evaluation of instructional materials: bibliography. Washington, DC, Mid-Atlantic Region Special Education Instructional Materials Center, 1970. 5p. ED 044447.

The unannotated entries are extracted from RIE and CIJE.

INSTRUCTIONAL MATERIALS CENTERS See also LIBRARIES

1740. Poli, Rosario. Instructional materials centers: annotated bibliography. Columbus, Ohio Education Association, 1970. 28p. ED 057564.

Covers guidelines and staffing for the elementary and secondary levels in 74 articles and reports.

1741. Davis, Harold S. Instructional materials center: an annotated bibliography. Cleveland, OH, Educational Research Council, 1967. 39p. ED 022257 (MF)

Includes 211 books and articles on planning, staffing, and operating the facility for the primary grades through the college level. Topics include team teaching, independent study, libraries, and curriculum laboratories.

1742. Davis, Harold S. Instructional media center: an annotated bibliography. Cleveland, OH, Educational Research Council of America, 1971. 36p. ED 069151.

This edition has 185 books, pamphlets, and articles all published since 1960.

1743. Newman, Mayrelee. The Best of ERIC: learning resource centers. ERIC Clearinghouse on Educational Media and Technology, 1973. 14p. ED 071431.

Contains 50 annotated entries for public school/early childhood, community college, college and university, and adult education.

1744. Ducote, Richard L. Learning resource centers: best of ERIC: a selected, annotated bibliography. ERIC Clearinghouse on Information Resources, 1977. 72p. ED 154824.

Contains 200 documents added to the ERIC system since 1972 on the adaptation of learning resource center concepts to specific situations for elementary through college levels.

1745. Alderman, Belle Y. School library media centres: an annotated bibliography. Canberra, Australian Schools Commission, 1976. 49p. ED 125526.

Includes 150 books, articles, and AV materials for elementary and secondary school librarians.

1746. Strand, Shelby E. So this is how you run a media center: organizing, administering, and developing a school instructional media center: an annotated bibliography. Grand Forks, University of North Dakota, 1970. 93p. ED 045112.

Lists 114 references.

1747. Webster, Donald F. and Elizabeth Bronner. Bibliography for a professional reference shelf in educational communications. 1972. 28p. ED 142239.

284 items are annotated that date back to 1949.

INTEGRATION See SCHOOL INTEGRATION

INTELLECTUAL FREEDOM See also CENSORSHIP

1748. Hill, Robert. Intellectual freedom: a bibliography. 1972. 12p. ED 088098.

Includes books and articles dating from 1966 on current problems and past events.

INTELLIGENCE

1749. Bibliography on mental ability. Harvard University, 1966. 8p. ED 011302.

Fifty unannotated references are provided to books, reports, and articles dating from 1955. Includes the gifted and the retarded.

INTERNATIONAL EDUCATION

1750. Newman, Arthur J. Select bibliography: international education. 1973. 25p. ED 076473.

This topical bibliography in 18 sections lists 350 books and articles dating from 1930. Unannotated.

1751. Graham, Robert H. Comparative and international education: a selective bibliography. 1971. 55p. ED 053611.

The unannotated entries date from 1965 and are organized by topic and country primarily for the university level.

INTERVIEWING

1752. Crouch, Wayne W. The Information interview: a comprehensive bibliography and an analysis of the literature. ERIC
Clearinghouse on Information Resources, 1979. 49p. ED 180
501.

    Annotates the literature since 1960, especially as it in-
volves library personnel.

IOWA

1753. Buckingham, Betty Jo and Mary Lou McGrew. Iowa and some
Iowans: a bibliography of Iowa history and Iowa authors for
elementary and secondary school students, teachers, and library media specialists. Second ed. Des Moines, Iowa State Department of Public Instruction, 1974. 206p. ED 101755.

    An annotated multimedia bibliography. ED 163940 is a 78
page supplement issued in 1978.

IROQUOIS

1754. Weinman, Paul L. A Bibliography of the Iroquoian literature. Albany, New York State Education Department, 1969.
261p. ED 055724.

    This partially annotated list cites over 2500 items which
date back to 1609.

ISRAEL

1755. Gotliffe, Harvey. Mass communication in Israel: a bibliography of articles, pamphlets, and books written in English.
1974. 23p. ED 101409.

    The unannotated list covers advertising, broadcast author-
ity, censorship, film, press, propaganda, radio, television
and the theatre.

JAPAN AND THE JAPANESE

1756. Kublin, Hyman. What shall I read on Japan: an introductory guide. Tenth ed. New York, Japan Society, Inc., 1971.
20p. ED 063182.

    111 books are annotated and classified in this guide for
smaller libraries. All are published since 1941.

1757. Shulman, Frank J. Doctoral dissertations on Japan and Korea, 1969-1974: a classified bibliographical listing of international research. Ann Arbor, MI, University Microfilms, 1976. 95p. ED 148910 (MF)

1758. White, Anthony G. An Urban minority: Japanese Americans. Monticello, IL, Council of Planning Librarians, 1973. 8p. ED 143719 (MF)

   72 unannotated citations cover race relations, prejudice, their role in US history, housing, acculturation, and adaption.

1759. Rockman, Ilene F. Japanese American identity in the United States, 1945 to the present: a selected annotated bibliography. 1975. 24p. ED 102091.

   Includes 100 books, articles, and dissertations, but excludes items on internment and relocation.

1760. Beauchamp, Nancy J. Modern Japanese novels in English: a selected bibliography. Columbus, Ohio State University, Service Center for Teachers of Asian Studies, 1974. 44p. ED 109045.

   This annotated list is limited to full-length novels with post-1945 translations. Excludes short stories and fugitive works.

JEWISH STUDIES See also HOLOCAUST

1761. Garber, Zev. Alternative teaching methods in teaching introduction to Judaism. 1974. 58p. ED 099077 (MF)

   This conference paper includes an unannotated bibliography of 133 items on American Jewry.

1762. Lubetski, Meir and Edith. Writings on Jewish history: a selected annotated bibliography. New York, American Jewish Committee, 1974. 31p. ED 128252.

   Includes fiction and nonfiction, biographies and autobiographies for grades 5 through 12.

1763. Herman, Edward. Jewish Americans and their backgrounds: sources of information. Chicago, American Library Association, 1976. 31p. ED 124469 (MF)

   An annotated multimedia guide to resources mostly published in the 1970's.

1764. Cantor, Aviva. Bibliography on the Jewish woman: a comprehensive and annotated listing of works published 1900-1978. Fresh Meadows, NY, Biblio Press, 1979. 68p. ED 166 112 (MF)

1765. Greenberg, Barbara. Bibliography of resources in Jewish special education. 1973. 10p. ED 075963.

An annotated multimedia list.

1766. Guide to select adult Jewish educational materials: a resource for adult Jewish education leaders. New York, American Association for Jewish Education, 1966. 60p. ED 010866.

The annotated bibliography includes materials published by the 17 member organizations affiliated with the national council on Jewish education.

1767. Goldberg, Mark. Jewish studies in the secondary school: materials and sources, 1881-1917: the great migration. Stony Brook, State University of New York, American Historical Association Project, 1972. 17p. ED 058143.

An annotated English language bibliography compiled from the holdings of the New York Public Library.

1768. Abrams, Joan. Jewish holidays. 1977. 57p. ED 150589.

An overview of the Hebrew literature on holidays is followed by an annotated bibliography.

JOB ANALYSIS See also EMPLOYMENT

1769. Fine, Sidney A. Functional job analysis: an annotated bibliography. Kalamazoo, MI, Upjohn Institute for Employment Research, 1975. 27p. ED 116037.

The entries date from 1951.

1770. Farrell, William T. Hierarchical clustering: a bibliography. Los Angeles, California State University Foundation, 1975. 28p. ED 121258.

The 184 items are on cluster analysis in classification, and research in task analysis. Not annotated.

JOB SATISFACTION

1771. Vocational choice and job satisfaction. California Coordinating Unit for Occupational Research and Development, 1967. 53p. ED 013958.

Includes 115 studies dating from 1960.

1772. Taylor, James C. The Quality of working life: an annotated bibliography, 1957-1972. Los Angeles, UCLA, Center for Organizational Studies, 1972. 579p. ED 078158.

Contains books, articles, case studies, empirical research.

JOURNALISM

1773. Eberhard, Wallace B. and Christopher E. Bickers. Georgia journalism: a selected, annotated bibliography. 1974. 18p. ED 097713.

Intended for secondary teachers, it includes biographies, autobiographies, history, communication law, and the mass media.

1774. Schacht, J. H. A Bibliography for the study of magazines. Urbana, University of Illinois, College of Communications, 1972. 55p. ED 101381.

The annotated readings were compiled for a course in magazine editing and include all aspects of the process.

1775. The Suburban press: first steps toward an annotated bibliography. DeKalb, Northern Illinois University, Suburban Press Research Center, 1974. 21p. ED 128824.

Lists journal articles from about 20 different publications.

1776. Davis, Lenwood G. A History of journalism in the Black community: a preliminary survey. Monticello, IL, Council of Planning Librarians, 1975. 37p. ED 159696 (MF)

Topics include Black authors, the role of the Black press, race relations and the Black press, Black women in journalism, and Black-controlled broadcast media.

1777. Pickett, Calder M. Recent books in journalism history: a bibliographical essay. 1977. 35p. ED 159695 (MF)

This paper was presented to the annual meeting of the Association for Education in Journalism (61st), and includes surveys, collections, oral history, memoirs, books linked to the Bicentennial, state histories, newspaper histories, and biographies.

1778. Hardt, Hanno. Shield legislation for journalists: a bibliography. Iowa City, University of Iowa, School of Journalism, 1973. 37p. ED 092981.

Lists secondary sources, and extracts of state laws plus relevant briefs outlining the decisions in recent court cases.

1779. Dowling, Ruth. Guidelines for journalism instructional programs and effective student publications. ERIC Clearinghouse on Reading and Communication Skills, 1977. 36p. ED 141 832.

An unannotated selected bibliography is included on objectives, standards, policies, and financial considerations.

JUNIOR HIGH SCHOOLS   See   MIDDLE SCHOOLS

JUVENILE DELINQUENTS

1780.   Juvenile delinquency.   Arlington, VA, Council for Exceptional Children, 1971.   13p.   ED 054571.

   The annotated bibliography contains 43 books, articles,
   and research reports dealing with causes, prevention, rehabilitation, counseling, and psychotherapy.

1781.   Daniels, Lincoln.   The Prevention of juvenile delinquency.   Washington, DC, Social and Rehabilitation Service
(DHEW), 1968.   18p.   ED 030899 (MF)

   This annotated bibliography dating from 1960 covers theory,
   identification, programs for control and prevention, and
   gangs.

1782.   Rutherford, Robert B. and Christine Ann Swist.   Behavior modification with juvenile delinquents: bibliography.   1973.
13p.   ED 094296.

   Includes programs in residential situations, intervention
   with families, basic education courses, and community
   based projects. Not annotated.

KINDERGARTEN   See   PRESCHOOL EDUCATION

KOREA AND KOREANS

1783.   Kang, Kilsoo.   A Short bibliography in the English language material on Korea and its education.   University of Pittsburgh, School of Education, 1968.   16p.   ED 051072.

   Includes 128 entries. Not annotated.

1784.   Hahn, Taeyoul.   Mass communication in the Republic of
Korea: an annotated bibliography.   Singapore, Asian Mass Communication Research and Information Centre, 1977.   78p.   ED
158304 (MF)

   The list represents theory and practice relative to many
   disciplines.

1785.   Kim, Christopher.   Working papers on Asian American
studies: annotated bibliography on Koreans in America.   Los
Angeles, UCLA, Asian American Studies Center, 1976.   28p.   ED
139898 (MF)

   Topics include immigration history, deportation cases,
   Korean students in the USA, political activities of Kor-

eans in the USA, the Asiatic Exclusion League, and Koreans
in Hawaii, Montana, and California.

LABOR

1786. Labor mobility: selected references. Washington, DC,
Department of Labor Library, 1967. 15p. ED 021998.

Includes 170 books, articles, and government publications
dating from 1953.

1787. Current references and information services for policy
decision making in state and local government labor relations:
a selected bibliography. Washington, DC, Labor Management Services Administration (DOL), 1971. 95p. ED 063498.

Contains 550 unannotated listings.

1788. Darcy, Robert L. and Philip E. Powell. A Basic manpower
economics library. Revised ed. Arkadelphia, Ark, Henderson
State College, Russell Center for Economics Education, 1970.
9p. ED 045475.

Annotates 33 publications dating from 1963.

1789. O'Leary, Charles J. and John R. Hanson. Recognition:
a source book on labor for teachers and students. Orono, University of Maine, Bureau of Labor Education, 1973. 16p. ED
097270.

This annotated multimedia bibliography for secondary teachers lists materials published from 1959 to 1973.

1790. Bureau of Labor Statistics publications, 1886-1971:
numerical listings, annotations, and subject index. 1972.
188p. ED 076823.

This is a complete catalog of all BLS publications, including 1724 bulletins, and 400 reports plus eight current
journal titles.

1791. Brooks, Thomas R. Labor and migration: an annotated
bibliography. Brooklyn, City University of New York, Center
for Migration Studies, 1970. 40p. ED 044500.

131 works focus on immigration and internal migration as
it affects organized and unorganized labor.

1792. Compton, Luvenia. The History of the labor movement in
the United States: a bibliography. 1976. 120p. ED 139732.

Most of the 1560 unannotated entries have been published
since the 1930's.

LABORATORIES

1793. Legget, R. F. and N. B. Hutcheon. The Design of research laboratories. Ottawa, National Research Council of Canada, Division of Building Research, 1966. 43p. ED 029 453.

An annotated bibliography of 95 items is appended to this report. The first part is a general assessment, and the second is on air conditioning and conditioned rooms.

1794. A Selected bibliography on microbiological laboratory design. Washington, DC, Public Health Service (DHEW), 1967. 17p. ED 029472.

An unannotated subject bibliography.

1795. Safety cabinet bibliography. Fort Detrick, MD, Army Biological Laboratories, 1969. 6p. ED 029475.

Annotates 32 sources on safety cabinets for laboratory facilities.

LAKE TAHOE

1796. Trimm, Maureen. Lake Tahoe: a bibliography: its history, natural history, and travel guides. 1977. 46p. ED 149787.

A selective list of 258 monographs and 58 maps. Not annotated.

LAND USE

1797. Clark, Robert A. Selected references on land use inventory methods. Monticello, IL, Council of Planning Librarians, 1969. 18p. ED 101421.

Includes 83 unannotated references.

1798. Kracht, James B. The Application of models to the planning process with special emphasis on land use. Monticello, IL, Council of Planning Librarians, 1971. 20p. ED 101437.

This unannotated bibliography on land use models and transportation models is designed for urban and regional planners.

LANDSCAPING

1799. Taylor, Patricia. Landscape designs for schools. 1975. 24p. ED 109796 (MF)

Annotated list of 15 books and articles.

LANGUAGE DEVELOPMENT   See also   LINGUISTICS

1800. Bibliography on language development. Harvard University, 1966(?) 9p. ED 011307.

Includes 65 unannotated references to books, articles,
and reports dating from 1958.

1801. Language development in disadvantaged children: an annotated bibliography. ERIC Clearinghouse for Urban Disadvantaged, 1968. 86p. ED 026414.

Covers bilingualism, dialectology, developmental influences, and developmental status and processes.

1802. Bernbaum, Marcia. Early language development: an abstract bibliography. ERIC Clearinghouse on Early Childhood
Education, 1971. 29p. ED 056754.

Documents from RIE and CIJE review language research and
curriculum practices to improve language skills.

1803. Valdman, Albert and Joel Walz. A Selected bibliography
on language learners' systems and error analysis. ERIC Clearinghouse on Languages and Linguistics, 1975. 75p. ED 105772.

An unannotated bibliography of documents from the ERIC
system.

1804. Honig, Alice S. Language learning, language development: a bibliography. ERIC Clearinghouse on Early Childhood
Education, 1975. 72p. ED 105961.

Contains references relating to the young child and his
speaking and understanding of language.

1805. DeVito, Joseph A. Speech and language acquisition and
development: a bibliography. New York, Speech Communication
Association, 1973. 21p. ED 087046.

Over 500 citations date from 1957. Not annotated.

1806. Andersen, Elaine S. A Selected bibliography on language input to young children. ERIC Clearinghouse on Languages
and Linguistics, 1975. 22p. ED 104177.

Includes descriptive annotations of 31 papers and reports.

1807. DeVito, Joseph A. Speech and language: development and
acquisition: a bibliography. New York, Speech Communication
Association, 1970. 30p. ED 045638 (MF)

423 books and articles date from 1937. Not annotated.

LANGUAGE INSTRUCTION See also BILINGUAL EDUCATION and
        ENGLISH INSTRUCTION and ENGLISH (SECOND LANGUAGE)

1808. James, Charles J. A Selective bibliography of doctoral
dissertations in modern language education. ERIC Clearinghouse
on Languages and Linguistics, 1972. 36p. ED 069187.

    Includes 1841 entries dating from 1961. Not annotated.

1809. Birdsong, David. American doctoral dissertations in
foreign language education, 1965-1974: an annotated bibliography. ERIC Clearinghouse on Languages and Linguistics, 1976.
58p. ED 125269.

    Excludes bilingual education and English as a second lang-
    uage.

1810. Birkmaier, Emma Marie and Dale L. Lange. A Selective
bibliography on the teaching of foreign languages, 1920-1966.
New York, American Council on the Teaching of Foreign Languages, 1968. 43p. ED 024293.

1811. Miller, Helen B. and Lorraine A. Strasheim. An annotated bibliography of integrated FLES teaching materials.
Bloomington, University of Indiana, Indiana Language Program,
1969. 96p. ED 038077.

    Designed to help elementary school teachers and adminis-
    trators select classroom materials in French, Spanish,
    and German.

1812. Petty, Walter T. A Summary of investigations relating
to the English language arts, elementary and secondary. Champaign, IL, National Council of Teachers of English, 1968. 56p.
ED 015921.

    Annotates 151 articles from the English Journal and Elem-
    entary English.

1813. Rice, Frank A. Study aids for critical languages. Washington, DC, Center for Applied Linguistics, 1966. 39p. ED
014072.

    Includes 275 unannotated citations covering 80 of the less
    common modern foreign languages taught in the United States.

1814. Paquette, F. Andre. Required and suggested readings of
181 MFL methods courses. New York, Modern Language Association of America, 1965. 22p. ED 023325.

    337 entries treat language teaching and learning, linguis-
    tics, and related topics. Most are in English.

1815. Galt, Alan. Slides and the foreign language teacher:
a bibliography. 1977. 26p. ED 135213.

    Lists 275 items dealing with the use of audiovisuals.

1816. Malkoc, Anna M. Programmed instruction in foreign languages: a selective listing of ERIC documents. 1971. 48p.
ED 136583.

   The annotated bibliography dates from 1967 and includes
   English, French, German, Italian, and Russian as foreign
   languages.

1817. Audiovisual aids in language teaching, with special reference to English as a foreign language. London, British Council, English Teaching Information Centre, 1977. 7p. ED 152
099.

   Lists 69 books, articles, and films published since 1970.
   Not annotated.

1818. Pulliam, Robert. Automatic speech recognition in the
teaching of second languages: an annotated bibliography. Fair-
fax, VA, Pulliam and Associates Research Consultants, 1970.
27p. ED 039515.

   Contains 73 entries for using automatic speech recognition
   in programmed instruction, computer assisted instruction,
   or task simulation devices.

1819. Michel, Joseph. A Suggested bibliography for foreign
language teachers. Austin, University of Texas, Foreign Language Education Center, 1971. 38p. ED 047581.

   This selected classified bibliography cites publications
   for all instructional levels. Includes the philosophy and
   psychology of language, and the physiology of speech.

1820. Petrov, Julia A. and Kathleen McLane. Foreign language,
area, and other international studies: a bibliography of research and instructional materials completed under the National
Defense Education Act of 1958, Title VI, Section 602. Washington, DC, Bureau of Postsecondary Education (DHEW/OE), 1977.
75p. ED 136625.

   An annotated list for scholars, specialists, and planners.

1821. Languages for the world of work: an annotated bibliography. Salt Lake City, Olympus Research Corporation, 1975.
384p. ED 149606.

   A multimedia bibliography concerning training in languages
   for entering the world of work.

1822. Harris, Brian and M. Somcynsky. Bibliography: trans-
formational grammar and the teaching of second languages.
Ottawa University, 1973. 33p. ED 112642.

   Includes unannotated books and articles. Most are in English, but some are in French or German.

1823. Keesee, Elizabeth. References on foreign languages in

the elementary school. Washington, DC, Office of Education
(DHEW), 1963. 52p. ED 038045.

Covers French, Spanish, German, Russian, Italian, and Hebrew.

1824. Johnson, Dora E. Languages of Southeast Asia and the
Pacific: a survey of materials for the study of the uncommonly
taught languages. Arlington, VA, Center for Applied Linguistics, 1976. 73p. ED 132860.

Included for each of 170 languages are ,teaching materials,
readers, grammars, and dictionaries. Annotations are descriptive rather than critical.

1825. Advisory list of instructional media for languages.
Raleigh, North Carolina State Department of Public Instruction,
1977. 62p. ED 149750.

For primary through high school grades, the annotated bibliography includes books, films, kits, games, recordings,
and slide sets.

1826. Nieman, Linda W. A Selective bibliography on the individualization of foreign language instruction. 1976. 14p.
ED 132867.

The bibliography, part of a doctoral thesis, cites over
140 books and articles on the theories and goals of foreign language teaching and individualized instruction
techniques and programs.

1827. Source materials for teachers of foreign languages.
Revised ed. Washington, DC, National Education Association,
1974. 50p. ED 094590 (MF)

A wide variety of resources are included in this annotated
bibliography.

1828. Johnson, Dora E. Languages of Eastern Europe and the
Soviet Union: a survey of materials for the study of the un-
commonly taught languages. Arlington, VA, Center for Applied
Linguistics, 1976. 54p. ED 130537.

Under each language heading the items are arranged as
teaching materials, readers, grammars, and dictionaries.
Annotated.

1829. Bradford, Suzanne. Foreign language games. Maryland
Foreign Language Association, 1974. 13p. ED 125243.

An annotated list of 29 games that can be used in the
classroom.

1830. Languages of Western Europe: pidgins and creoles (European based): a survey of materials for the study of the uncommonly taught languages. Arlington, VA, Center for Applied

Linguistics, 1976. 44p. ED 130538.

This annotated bibliography focuses on materials for the English speaking adult learner, and under each language heading includes teaching materials, readers, grammars, and dictionaries.

1831. Gilman, Robert. Some suggested references for the busy foreign language teacher: how to make the most of day-to-day language activities. 1974. 29p. ED 109919.

An annotated list of bibliographies and reference works for the teaching of Spanish, Portuguese, and English to speakers of Spanish or Portuguese.

1832. Oller, John W. Research with cloze procedure in measuring the proficiency of non-native speakers of English: an annotated bibliography. ERIC Clearinghouse on Languages and Linguistics, 1975. 32p. ED 104154.

Includes some of the arguments pro and con using the cloze procedure, and some articles and studies that give how-to recommendations.

1833. Wilkins, Ernest J. Foreign language instruction and career preparation: a selected annotated bibliography. ERIC Clearinghouse on Languages and Linguistics, 1977. 31p. ED 138113.

1834. Birdsong, David. Computer assisted and programmed instruction in foreign languages: a selected annotated bibliography. ERIC Clearinghouse on Language and Linguistics, 1977. 24p. ED 138087.

The ERIC documents date from 1971 and include theory and application, and description of teaching materials.

1835. Bockman, John F. Reference and research materials for language teachers. Tucson, AZ, Public Schools, 1969. 49p. ED 037142.

Includes 767 unannotated entries under 63 subject classifications. Most are documents from the ERIC system.

1836. Brown, Judith. The Peace Corps and the development of foreign language instructional materials: an annotated bibliography. Washington, DC, Center for Applied Linguistics, 1969. 57p. ED 034176.

The 304 entries are grouped into five major geographic areas of the world and concern over 100 languages that the Peace Corps has been involved with since 1961.

1837. Blass, Brigit A. A Provisional survey of materials for the study of neglected languages. Washington, DC, Center for Applied Linguistics, 1969. 422p. ED 044683 (MF)

Contains over 2000 entries on 382 languages and dialects.

1838. Crymes, Ruth. A Bibliographical introduction to sentence combining. 1974. 20p. ED 115130.

An annotated list of the technique for teachers of English.

1839. Thogmartin, Clyde. A Bibliography of empirical investigations of certain aspects of foreign language teaching and learning, 1925-1975. 1975. 67p. ED 115128.

Includes 647 unannotated citations drawn mostly from American and British journals. Also includes dissertations, ERIC documents, and an author index.

1840. Survey of materials in the neglected languages. Washington, DC, Center for Applied Linguistics, 1968. 476p. ED 020510.

Includes study aids for those languages not commonly taught in the United States, and is intended for the adult learner whose native language is English.

1841. Foreign language testing. London, Centre for Information on Language Teaching, 1969. 28p. ED 040615.

Nearly 200 citations include bibliographies of tests, and books and articles on the theory and practice of language testing. Not annotated.

1842. Perren, G. E. Foreign language testing: specialised bibliography. London, Centre for Information on Language Teaching, 1977. 72p. ED 163807.

An annotated list of books and articles on testing skills in foreign languages which includes a brief selection of published tests.

LANGUAGE LABORATORIES See also INSTRUCTIONAL MATERIALS CENTER

1843. Keck, Mary E. and William F. Smith. A Selective annotated bibliography for the language laboratory, 1959-1971. ERIC Clearinghouse on Languages and Linguistics, 1972. 50p. ED 065006.

163 books, articles, and reports are provided for planning and installing, and administering and operating a language laboratory.

1844. Hefworth, John B. The Language laboratory: a bibliography. Manchester, England, Public Library, 1966. 21p. ED 011436.

Annotates 230 books and articles dating from 1955.

LATIN

1845. Norton, Mary E. A Selective bibliography on the teaching of Latin and Greek, 1920-1969. New York, Modern Language
Association of America, 1971. 47p. ED 046311.

The 1943 entries include linguistics, sociocultural heritage, values and rationale of the classics, audiovisual
aids, methods, testing, bibliographies, and dictionaries.
Not annotated.

1846. Austin, R. G. A Bibliography of Virgil. Oxford, England, Joint Association of Classical Teachers, 1968. 8p. ED
044988.

The 250 unannotated entries include books and articles
about Virgil and his poetry, and list various editions,
translations, and commentaries.

1847. Colebourn, R. and Marigold Cleeve. Suggestions for the
classical shelves of a school library. Oxford, England, Joint
Association of Classical Teachers, 1968. 14p. ED 044989.

Lists 550 entries for students and teachers of Latin,
Greek, and other ancient civilizations.

1848. Norton, Mary E. A Bibliography on the value of the
classics. 1970. 7p. ED 044058.

Annotates 100 references reflecting the values of Latin
study published over the past 50 years.

1849. Kobler, John F. A Bibliography of spoken Latin. 1966.
9p. ED 013565.

Annotates books, articles, and AV programs dating back to
1868, although most has been published since 1950 that is
included here.

LATIN AMERICA

1850. Jamieson, Alfred. A Selective annotated guide to materials on Latin America suitable for use at the secondary
school level. Albany, New York State Education Department,
1971. 62p. ED 061112.

Includes audiovisual materials and other bibliographies
dating from 1960.

1851. Farrell, Robert V. and John F. Hohenstein. Latin America: books for high schools: an annotated bibliography. New
York, Center for Inter-American Relations, 1969. 33p. ED
059120.

After examining over 1200 books, 171 were selected for
this list. Reading level is indicated. The general section
is followed by a country bibliography for each nation.

1852. Shepard, Marietta D. Selection aids on Latin America for primary and secondary school libraries. Washington, DC, Pan American Union, 1968. 20p. ED 019178.

Several bibliographies are included, especially for the humanities and social sciences.

1853. Seidel, Robert N. and Robert MacCameron. Abroad with translators: annotated bibliographies with introductory essays on Latin American literature and society for the English language reader and student. 1977. 42p. ED 149357.

The bibliographies are grouped by country including Puerto Rico. Biographical notes on prominent authors of each country are also included.

1854. Latin America: a selected functional and country bibliography. Washington, DC, Foreign Service Institute, 1971. 55p. ED 076490.

Topics covered are history, economics, politics, government, and international relations. Not annotated.

1855. Wilgus, Karna S. Latin America books: an annotated bibliography for high schools and colleges. New York, Center for Inter-American Relations, 1974. 82p. ED 093730 (MF)

Cites 479 books in English for the student and for the teacher. Includes material on Chicanos and Puerto Ricans.

1856. Levy, Kurt L. Book list on Latin America for Canadians. Ottawa, Canadian Commission for UNESCO, 1969. 54p. ED 044 057.

The books are in English or French and are on history, travel, culture, literature, religion, art, music, economics and politics. Not annotated.

1857. Jamison, Edward A. Introduction to Latin America: a manual for an interdisciplinary course: an annotated bibliography. Eau Claire, University of Wisconsin, 1976. 218p. ED 127231 (MF)

A teacher's manual of resources in English for the college level. Most items were produced in the 1960's and 1970's.

1858. Hawkins, John N. Teacher's resource handbook for Latin American Studies: an annotated bibliography of curriculum materials. Los Angeles, UCLA, Latin American Center, 1975. 230p. ED 133239 (MF)

Includes 1347 multimedia resources for K-12. The entries are arranged by grade and cover the Carribean, Central and South America.

LAW ENFORCEMENT

1859. Training law enforcement personnel. Washington, DC,
Adult Education Association of the USA, 1971. 29p. ED 054
400.

    This annotated bibliography contains 36 items, some of
    which are on police-community relations.

LAW INSTRUCTION

1860. Russell, Charles H. Liberal education and the law: a
bibliography. New York, Columbia University, Teachers College,
1957. 27p. ED 055561.

    An annotated bibliography on preparing for the study of
    law.

1861. Carsello, Carmen J. Law in the classroom: an annotated
bibliography. Chicago Circle, University of Illinois, 1978.
62p. ED 154480.

    Includes 236 entries relevant to the discussion of school
    law.

1862. Davison, Susan E. Gaming: an annotated catalogue of
law related games and simulations. Chicago, American Bar
Association, 1975. 39p. ED 114307.

    125 items are on the Constitution, the Bill of Rights, the
    political process, current issues, and basic concepts.

1863. Davison, Susan E. Bibliography of law related curriculum materials: annotated. Second ed. Chicago, American
Bar Association, 1976. 123p. ED 125946.

    For elementary and secondary levels, over 1000 materials
    are listed dealing with the philosophy, substance, and
    pedagogy of law related education.

1864. Davison, Susan E. Media: an annotated catalogue of law
related audiovisual materials. Chicago, American Bar Association, 1975. 88p. ED 107553.

    Over 400 films, filmstrips, videotapes, audio cassettes,
    and kits are described for elementary or secondary educa-
    tion.

LEAD POISONING

1865. Lin-Fu, Jane S. Selected bibliography on lead poisoning in children. Rockville, MD, Health Services and Mental
Health Administration, 1971. 35p. ED 068362.

    Over 200 unannotated items are cited dating from 1942.

Most of the papers noted are from the pediatric literature and are all in English. Some papers on experiments in laboratory animals are cited.

LEADERSHIP

1866. Leadership effectiveness: the best of ERIC. ERIC Clearinghouse on Educational Management, 1978. 5p. ED 149416.

Eleven recent abstracts of ERIC documents on the leadership role of the school administrator.

1867. Leadership styles: the best of ERIC. ERIC Clearinghouse on Educational Management, 1975. 5p. ED 099953.

Includes 24 articles and documents from the ERIC system on leadership in relation to personnel qualities, behavior theories, organizational influence, and the changing administrator role.

1868. House, Robert J. A 1976 theory of charismatic leadership. 1976. 38p. ED 133827.

This presented paper reviews the traditional literature on charisma as well as selected social psychology literature.

1869. Success prediction: a DDC bibliography. Alexandria, VA, Defense Documentation Center, 1972. 185p. ED 078206.

Abstracts for 145 technical reports dating from 1949 include development of individuals during military training, peer evaluation, biographical inventory, and the validity of success prediction tests.

LEARNING DISABILITIES

1870. Learning disabilities: research studies and program considerations. Arlington, VA, Council for Exceptional Children, 1969. 32p. ED 036026.

139 abstracts include diagnosis, teaching methods, physical aspects, perceptual problems, and treatment procedures.

1871. Learning disabilities: teaching methods and curriculum. Reston, VA, Council for Exceptional Children, 1977. 18p. ED 146738.

65 abstracts are included, 1974-1976.

1872. Learning disabilities: identification and assessment. Reston, VA, Council for Exceptional Children, 1977. 18p. ED 146736.

Contains 65 annotated entries.

1873. Learning disabilities - research: a selective bibliography. Reston, VA, Council for Exceptional Children, 1973.
26p. ED 090707.

Covers identification, reading difficulties, and parent
attitudes, and other topics in 100 annotated entries dating from 1963.

1874. Learning disabilities - programs. Arlington, VA, Council for Exceptional Children, 1971. 25p. ED 051596.

The 96 abstracts include conference papers, articles,
texts, and program guides.

1875. Learning disabilities - programs: a selective bibliography. Arlington, VA, Council for Exceptional Children, 1972.
28p. ED 065961.

100 abstracts are included dating from 1960.

1876. Learning disabilities - programs: a selective bibliography. Reston, VA, Council for Exceptional Children, 1973.
28p. ED 085922.

Includes 90 abstracts dating from 1964 through 1973.

1877. Learning disabilities - programs: 1977 topical bibliography. Reston, VA, Council for Exceptional Children, 1977.
18p. ED 146737.

Includes 65 annotated entries dated 1974 through 1976.

1878. Mangrum, Charles T. A Citation bibliography of selected sources on dyslexia and learning disabilities. ERIC Clearinghouse on Reading, 1968. 78p. ED 020865.

1400 books, articles, and papers are included in this unannotated list that dates back to 1868.

1879. McMurray, J. G. Learning disabilities: theory, assessment, and remediation: a bibliography. London, University of
Western Ontario, 1976. 140p. ED 140521.

1880. Learning disabilities: a first reading list. Springfield, IL, Instructional Materials Center, 1973(?) 30p. ED
141985.

An unannotated list of books and articles for parents and
professionals.

1881. Spiegel, Dixie Lee and Margaret Sherry. Learning disability or reading disability: an annotated bibliography for
coming together. Madison, WI, Public Schools, 1976. 46p.
ED 144037.

Designed to help reading specialists and learning disabilities specialists learn more about one another's disci-

pline. Provides an overview of the controversy; labels
and services; language, linguistics, and reading; cognition and reading; tools for identifying learning or reading problems; and educational strategies.

1882. Lee, Grace E. and Allen Berger. Learning disabilities
with emphasis on reading: an annotated bibliography. Newark,
Del., International Reading Association, 1978. 58p. ED 161
012.

Includes 250 entries dealing with affective, cognitive,
linguistic, neurological, and perceptual processes related
to reading and learning disabilities, and their diagnosis,
remediation, and treatment.

1883. Leitch, Linda J. Learning disabilities: review of the
literature and selected annotated bibliography. Montreal,
McGill University, Faculty of Education, 1973. 60p. ED 094
540.

Reviews information on diagnosis, teacher qualification
and training, the learning environment, curriculum, perception, and integration. The bibliography contains 80
references.

1884. Dyslexia: a selective bibliography. Reston, VA, Council for Exceptional Children, 1976. 23p. ED 129016.

Annotates 95 documents and articles published since 1966.

1885. Slow learners. Arlington, VA, Council for Exceptional
Children, 1971. 21p. ED 054574.

Contains 83 annotated references on academic achievement,
curriculum, disadvantaged youth, educable mentally retarded, ability grouping, instructional materials, motivation,
giftedness, underachievement, vocational education, and
teaching methods.

1886. Anderson, Sarah M. and Gloria Gominiak. The Child and
the learning environment: an annotated bibliography on diagnosis and prescription in learning. Buffalo, State University
of New York, Educational Research and Development Complex,
1974. 14p. ED 098754.

The 42 entries date from 1922 to 1973.

1887. Individual learning disabilities: a bibliography. Greeley, CO, Rocky Mountain Educational Laboratory, 1968. 53p.
ED 034340.

This unannotated multimedia bibliography contains 351 articles, 148 books, 37 tests, 36 videotapes, 28 audiotapes,
12 films, and 11 other bibliographies.

1888. Button, Linda. ITPA bibliography for teachers of the
learning disabled. Greeley, CO, Rocky Mountain Special Educa-

tion Instructional Materials Center, 1973. 74p. ED 082427.

Annotates 378 instructional materials to be used with the subtests of the Illinois Test of Psycholinguistic Abilities (ITPA) for education of learning disabled children at all age levels.

LEARNING RESOURCE CENTERS See INSTRUCTIONAL MATERIALS CENTER

LEARNING THEORIES

1889. Piagetian theory, research and practice: an abstract bibliography. ERIC Clearinghouse on Early Childhood Education, 1977. 95p. ED 135454.

All annotated entries are taken from RIE and CIJE from 1975 through 1976.

1890. Stern, Carolyn. Problem solving and concept formation: an annotated bibliography. Los Alamitos, CA, Southwest Regional Laboratory for Educational Research and Development, 1968. 120p. ED 111515.

Contains 350 entries concerned with young children. Many of the early articles by Jean Piaget are included.

1891. Staats, Arthur W. and Carl G. Carlson. Classical conditioning of emotional responses (meaning, attitudes, values, interests) and effects on social behavior: a bibliography. Honolulu, University of Hawaii, Department of Psychology, 1970. 21p. ED 043214.

Includes 81 books and papers published since 1957 relevant to the subject of verbally-elicited responses. 24 of the entries are authored by Staats.

1892. Thomas, Susan B. Malnutrition, cognitive development, and learning. Urbana, University of Illinois, College of Education, 1972. 126p. ED 069401.

A comprehensive annotated bibliography on the effects of nutrition on learning. Animal research has been omitted.

1893. Klausmeier, Herbert J. Concept learning: a bibliography, 1950-1967. Madison, University of Wisconsin, Research and Development Center for Cognitive Learning, 1969. 177p. ED 035954.

Includes an unannotated list of articles from 51 journals, in addition to publications of the Center. ED 036865 is a 62 page supplement, and ED 067606 is a 50 page second supplement.

1894. Klimoski, Richard J. An Annotated bibliography on so-

cial reinforcement: evaluative abstracts of research and theory. Brooks AFB, TX, Air Force Human Resources Laboratory,
1974. 270p. ED 097871.

Covers the period 1964 to 1972, and contains 234 studies
in diverse psychological and educational contexts.

1895. Wildemuth, Barbara M. Mastery learning and mastery
testing: an annotated ERIC bibliography. ERIC Clearinghouse
on Tests, Measurement, and Evaluation, 1977. 65p. ED 138646.

Contains 136 entries.

1896. Clark, Richard E. Sources of information about apti-
tude-treatment interactions. Washington, DC, Association for
Educational Communications and Technology, 1975. 16p. ED
116627 (MF)

The emphasis is on research and development of theoretical models, but many sources deal with application of ATI
theory to actual teaching and learning situations. Dating
from 1953, the bibliography lists 58 books and dissertations, and 116 articles and papers.

1897. Farley, Frank H. Individual differences, learning, and
instruction: a selected bibliography. Madison, University of
Wisconsin, Research and Development Center for Cognitive Learning, 1972. 59p. ED 064646.

The bibliography is not annotated.

1898. Humphreys, Les. Interdisciplinarity: a selected bibliography for users. 1975. 17p. ED 115536.

Developmentally and conceptually organized, this bibliography is based on the author's experience with implementing the unified education concept through the team taught
Unified Studies Program at Boston State College. Not annotated.

1899. Stolurow, Lawrence M. Psychological and educational
factors in transfer of training: bibliography of studies.
University of Illinois, Bureau of Educational Research, 1966.
168p. ED 010113.

Contains 1775 titles dating from 1890. Most are empiri-
cally based research, and some animal experiments are included. Not annotated.

LEGAL AID

1900. Conner, Ronald C. Legal information sources: an annotated bibliography. Arlington Heights, IL, Memorial Library,
1979. 28p. ED 180469.

Describes legal reference materials in 12 categories.

LIBRARIES AND LIBRARIANSHIP   See also   INSTRUCTIONAL MATERIALS
        CENTERS

1901.   Corum, Edythe. Reference librarianship and the small
library: a selected survey. Clarion State College (Penn.),
1978. 12p. ED 183338.

    This unannotated list, related to rural library service,
    contains 164 entries dating from 1970 that deal with ref-
    erence service.

1902.   Loertscher, David V. Budgeting for school media centers: an annotated bibliography. ERIC Clearinghouse on Information Resources, 1975. 26p. ED 115263.

    Includes philosophical and practical statements from the
    library and audiovisual fields in 70 books and articles.

1903.   Brose, Friedrich K. Junior college libraries: a checklist of about 750 published and unpublished sources. 1970.
62p. ED 045077.

    Excludes AV programs, but includes library technician pro-
    grams. Not annotated.

1904.   A Selected bibliography on library development and management for junior college libraries and administrators. Chicago, Association of College and Research Libraries, 1968.
45p. ED 031238.

    The unannotated entries date from 1955, and relate to the
    planning or establishment of new library facilities.

1905.   Library surveys and development plans: an annotated
bibliography. ERIC Clearinghouse on Library and Information
Science, 1969. 43p. ED 031609.

    Includes 104 library surveys and development plans at the
    state and national level published since 1965.

1906.   Skurdenis, Julie. Libraries and librarians: the next
generation. 1977. 12p. ED 138259.

    Partially annotated; deals with the future and trends in
    library automation, reader services, and the new copy-
    right law. 66 entries.

1907.   Crettol, Marie. Libraries and instructional materials
centers. 1975. 22p. ED 109802.

    Annotates 15 publications concerned with use and design.

1908.   A Short bibliography on library/media leadership. ERIC
Clearinghouse on Information Resources, 1975. 50p. ED 107288.

    An annotated list drawn from RIE and CIJE.

1909. Library materials collection building: problems and possibilities. University of Iowa, School of Library Science, 1977. 29p. ED 139400.

Includes articles which offer guidelines and techniques for collection development. Not annotated.

1910. Library management in the 1970's: summary of issues and selected bibliography. Washington, DC, Association of Research Libraries, 1977. 20p. ED 139429.

Annotates 41 items published since 1969 on management of human resources, administrative systems and procedures, research and development, and organizational change.

1911. Buckingham, Betty Jo. Selection bibliography: a bibliography of selection sources for school library media centers. Third ed. Des Moines, Iowa State Department of Public Instruction, 1976. 36p. ED 130678.

The annotated list is for print and nonprint materials for preschool through college levels.

1912. Stevens, Nicholas G. Adult, continuing, and inservice education and the library in higher education: a bibliographic checklist. Kutztown State College (Penn.), Educational Development Center, 1973. 280p. ED 095860.

1913. Freeman, Patricia. Index to research in school librarianship, 1960-1974. 1976. 50p. ED 119741.

A topical bibliography; not annotated.

1914. Baker, Leigh R. Librarianship in Papua New Guinea: a checklist, 1961-1977. 1977. 10p. ED 158739.

Includes 121 articles, papers, and reports.

1915. Kovacic, Mark. The Organization and function of gift and exchange programs in eighteen selected US academic libraries. 1978. 91p. ED 175397.

This report, sponsored by the Council on Library Resources, includes an extensive unannotated bibliography.

1916. New special libraries: a summary of research. Chicago, Special Libraries Association, 1979. 65p. ED 175395.

Annotates books and articles for a management audience.

1917. Myers, Margaret and Betty C. Sellen. Women in librarianship, 1920-1975: bibliography. Chicago, American Library Association, 1975. 22p. ED 112903 (MF)

243 journal articles are annotated.

1918. Klempner, Irving M. Audiovisual materials in support

of information science curricula: an annotated listing with
subject index. Second ed. ERIC Clearinghouse on Information
Resources, 1977. 76p. ED 148365.

Includes 451 AV aids.

1919. Minor, Barbara B. An Alerting service bibliography on
libraries, media, and educational technology. ERIC Clearinghouse on Information Resources, 1977. 21p. ED 148376.

Annotates 90 publications which were selected for their
usefulness and general interest.

1920. Laubacher, Marilyn R. An Alerting service bibliography
on libraries, media, and educational technology. ERIC Clearinghouse on Information Resources, 1979. 34p. ED 184553.

Lists 119 current publications received for review at the
ERIC Clearinghouse.

1921. Abbott, George L. Card catalogs: alternative futures.
a selected bibliography on closing card catalogs and alternative catalog formats with separate sections on AACR2 and PRE-
CIS. Syracuse, NY, Information Yield, 1979. 27p. ED 181908.

An unannotated list of 227 entries.

1922. Rao, Pal V. Academic library and its external relations: a selective bibliography. 1979. 22p. ED 181925.

Annotates 19 books and articles dating from 1967; this is
followed by a list of 56 items without annotations.

1923. Jameson, Andrew. The Organization of audiovisual materials: a bibliography. Portsmouth Polytechnic (England), 1971
(?) 7p. ED 060733.

Includes 77 items with brief annotations.

1924. Wakefield, Howard E. The Design and construction of
libraries and study facilities: an annotated reference list.
ERIC Clearinghouse on Educational Facilities, 1968. 30p. ED
024254.

These documents from the ERIC system cover all levels of
education.

1925. Perica, Esther. Public relations: a bibliography. 1976.
9p. ED 136783.

For public, academic, school, and special libraries. Lists
118 books and articles dating from 1963. Not annotated.

1926. Lopez-Munoz, Joanna. Bibliography on public service in
academic libraries. Orono, University of Maine, 1977. 87p.
ED 136756.

Includes 1120 journal articles published since 1968.

1927. Weiss, Kay. The Impact of nonverbal communications on the public services functions of libraries. 1976. 9p. ED 153659.

Annotates 21 books and articles to help library personnel develop their perceptions of body language, thereby helping them respond more appropriately to user queries.

1928. Allen, Annette C. School libraries/media centers: a selected bibliography. 1977. 12p. ED 145844.

Includes evolution of the media center concept, standards, evaluations, and research supporting the concept. 119 articles, books, and dissertations are in the list. Not annotated.

1929. Hill, Phyllis M. The Teacher's library. Washington, DC, National Education Association, 1977. 149p. ED 144935 (MF)

Devoted to the subject of establishing a school library; separate bibliographies are included.

1930. Libraries and study facilities: a selected bibliography. ERIC Clearinghouse on Educational Facilities, 1970. 27p. ED 041377.

Contains sections on library planning, carrels and study facilities, library automation and technology, resource and instructional materials centers, and building equipment and materials selection.

1931. Rike, Galen E. Statewide library surveys and development plans: an annotated bibliography, 1956-1967. Urbana, University of Illinois, Library Research Center, 1968. 110p. ED 023439.

Lengthy annotations are provided for 132 references arranged by state.

1932. Boelke, Joanne. Library technicians: a survey of current developments. ERIC Clearinghouse for Library and Information Science, 1968. 12p. ED 019530.

This review article includes 43 annotated references.

1933. Perkins, Ralph. Book selection media: a descriptive guide to 170 aids for selecting library materials. Champaign, IL, National Council of Teachers of English, 1967. 192p. ED 017506.

Intended for all age groups, and includes six indexes.

1934. Gates, Connie and Gaby Hendley. Losses in school library media centers: a survey and annotated bibliography. 1979. 24p. ED 184540.

1935. Goudeau, John M. State library history bibliography
series: South Carolina, Mississippi, and Minnesota. Tallahassee, Florida State University, School of Library Science,
1973. 88p. ED 094680.

These three separate bibliographies were originally
issued in the Journal of Library History.

1936. Lopez, Manuel D. Bibliography of the history of libraries in New York State. 1976. 88p. ED 145818.

This supplementary volume covers the years 1968-1972. It
is not annotated.

1937. Zubatsky, David S. The History of American colleges
and their libraries in the 17th and 18th centuries: a bibliographical essay. Urbana, University of Illinois, Graduate
School of Library Science, 1979. 69p. ED 183151.

Some entries consider the nature of the collections in the
individual libraries. Annotated.

1938. Kurtzman, Denise B. The Publications of B. Lamar Johnson, 1932-1974: an annotated bibliography. 1975. 56p. ED
111468.

This is a comprehensive list of a prominent leader in the
field of education, particularly in promoting innovative
and experimental library and instructional programs, and
in the development of the community junior college.

1939. Chepesiuk, Ronald J. Frances Lander Spain: an annotated bibliography, 1940-1971. 1977. 26p. ED 134218.

132 references on Dr. Spain's role in American librarianship.

1940. McAlister, Annette M. Juvenile correctional institutions library service: a bibliography. 1976. 5p. ED 148314.

Contains 35 books, articles, and reports on adult and
juvenile library service in correctional institutions.

1941. Recommended collections for prison law libraries. Chicago, American Association of Law Libraries, 1974. 12p. ED
092085.

Unannotated. Provides a minimum list and an expanded version.

1942. LeDonne, Marjorie. Survey of library and information
problems in correctional institutions. Berkeley, University
of California, Institute of Library Research, 1974(?) 33p.
ED 095845.

Covers the fields of criminology, sociology, education,
law, and librarianship, 1969-1973. Not annotated.

1943.   Akey, Sharon Ann.   An Annotated bibliography of recent prison library literature.   San Jose, CA, State University, Department of Librarianship, 1974.   40p.   ED 094784.

   This master's thesis contains 155 entries on California prison libraries, prison libraries in general, and prison law libraries.

1944.   Copenhaver, Christina and Joanne Boelke.   Library service to the disadvantaged: a bibliography.   ERIC Clearinghouse on Library and Information Sciences, 1968.   18p.   ED 026103.

   Includes 365 references to books, articles, theses, and pamphlets published since 1960 on the culturally, educationally, and economically disadvantaged. Not annotated.

1945.   Hughes, Jane B.   Rural library service.   Clarion State College (Penn.), 1979.   25p.   ED 183339.

   An unannotated subject bibliography of over 800 entries dating from 1930.

1946.   Davila, Daniel.   Library service for the Spanish-speaking user: source guide for librarians.   Bronx, NY, Hostos Community College, 1976.   46p.   ED 135400.

   Includes 269 references dating from 1950. Partially annotated.

1947.   Connor, Jean L.   A Selected bibliography on multitype library service, 1970-1975.   ERIC Clearinghouse on Information Resources, 1976.   24p.   ED 122826.

   Annotates 76 references on national, interstate, and individual library cooperation.

1948.   Boelke, Joanne.   Library service to the physically and visually handicapped: a bibliography.   ERIC Clearinghouse on Library and Information Sciences, 1969.   18p.   ED 031615.

   Covers state and local programs, and annotates 119 books, articles, bibliographies, reports, and pamphlets dating from 1964.

LIBRARY SCIENCE

1949.   Lieberman, Irving.   A Working bibliography of commercially available audiovisual materials for the teaching of library science.   Second ed.   ERIC Clearinghouse on Information Resources, 1979.   120p.   ED 180502.

   Annotates multimedia resources for all aspects of library instruction.

1950.   A Selected bibliography of documentation and informa-

tion science. Cleveland, Case Western Reserve University,
Center for Documentation and Communication Research, 1969.
21p. ED 038998.

Covers basic research, experimentation and application,
interdisciplinary aspects, and education in librarianship.
Not annotated.

1951. Matijevic, Nicolas. A Bibliography of library science
in Argentina. Bahia Blanca, Argentina, Universidad Nacional
del Sur, 1969. 364p. ED 038889.

A comprehensive unannotated bibliography of 2500 items
in Spanish which have been published up to 1967.

1952. Brown, K. R. Library, documentation, and archive ser-
ials. Fourth ed. The Hague, Netherlands, International Federation for Documentation, 1975. 209p. ED 112925 (MF)

Lists 950 titles from 79 countries, and other international
organizations.

1953. Kusnerz, Peggy Ann and Marie Miller. Audiovisual techniques and library instruction. Ann Arbor, University of Michigan, Library Extension Service, 1975. 33p. ED 118106.

A bibliography of printed material dating from 1960.

1954. Lemke, Antje B. Art and museum librarianship: a syllabus and bibliography. Syracuse University, School of Library
Science, 1973. 69p. ED 092124.

1955. May, Myron Jack. Audiovisual materials for teaching of
library science: an evaluation of 100 selected titles produced
from 1968 to 1973. Muncie, IN, Ball State University, Department of Library Science, 1974. 54p. ED 100315.

1956. Michael, Mary Ellen and Cathleen Palmini. A Selected
bibliography on continuing education 1965 to date. Urbana,
University of Illinois, Library Research Center, 1973. 41p.
ED 095919.

Includes books, articles, and ERIC documents for the field
of librarianship.

LIBRARY NETWORKS

1957. Glitz, Beryl. Networks: a bibliography. 1977. 43p.
ED 139428.

An unannotated list of books, reports, and articles on
library networks.

1958. A Selective annotated bibliography on library networking. ERIC Clearinghouse on Information Resources, 1975. 27p.

ED 115219.

Includes 150 entries most of which are drawn from the ERIC
system of documentation.

1959. Files, Patricia. Federal information systems: a selected annotated list of documents available from ERIC. ERIC
Clearinghouse on Information Resources,1976.   18p. ED 125527.

This paper includes studies, descriptions, and publications of several federal systems including ERIC, the Government Printing Office, National Technical Information
Service, the Library of Congress, and the National Commi-
sion on Libraries and Information Science.

LIGHTING

1960. The Luminous environment for education: a selected bibliography. ERIC Clearinghouse on Educational Facilities, 1970.
49p. ED 037993.

This literature survey is on lighting design for educational facilities.

1961. Hartman, Michael. The Luminous environment of the
classroom: a selected and annotated bibliography. ERIC Clearinghouse on Educational Facilities, 1968. 17p. ED 024250.

List 62 articles for designers and architects on lighting
design for classrooms.

LINGUISTICS See also BLACK ENGLISH and LANGUAGE INSTRUCTION

1962. Jokovich, Nancy and Sophia Behrens. A Bibliography of
American doctoral dissertations in linguistics, 1968-1974.
ERIC Clearinghouse on Languages and Linguistics, 1977. 153p.
ED 140615.

The 2271 entries are part of an update series to ED 016
966 which is the main bibliography covering 1900 to 1964.

1963. Moore, Mary Jo. A Preliminary bibliography of American
English dialects. Washington, DC, Center for Applied Linguistics, 1969. 61p. ED 033327.

The 804 items listed cover social dialects, the disadvantaged, Black English, and the teaching of standard English to speakers of non-standard dialects.

1964. Nuessel, Frank H. A Bibliography of generative-based
grammatical analyses of Spanish. 1973. 29p. ED 094568.

Includes 168 books, articles, and dissertations dating

from 1960. ED 101594 and ED 129096 are supplements of 21 and 17 pages respectively. The former has 100 items and the latter has 82. None are annotated.

1965. Nuessel, Frank H. An Annotated, critical bibliography of generative-based grammatical analyses of Spanish: phonology and morphology. 1977. 133p. ED 148150.

Includes 116 books, articles, papers, and dissertations in English and Spanish. ED 181718 is a 16 page supplement of 95 entries issued in 1979.

1966. Linguistics: a bibliography of selected Rand publications. Santa Monica, CA, Rand Corporation, 1971. 23p. ED 061790.

Over 100 items date from 1961 on theory, research, formal linguistics, and computational linguistics. Many documents are on the use of computers and machine translation. Several concern the analysis of Russian.

1967. A Bibliography of mostly generative synchronic phonological studies of TESOL languages. 1971. 38p. ED 057649.

An unannotated list of 400 works dating from 1924 deals with the phonology of about 30 languages whose speakers are frequently taught English.

1968. Shuy, Roger W. A Selective bibliography of social dialects. Washington, DC, Center for Applied Linguistics, 1968. 5p. ED 018800.

Includes 46 annotated references.

1969. Frink, Orrin. A Composite general graduate bibliography for linguistics. Athens, Ohio University, Occasional paper in Language, Literature, and Linguistics, 1966. 15p. ED 014258.

A recommended reading list of 131 items for students. Not annotated.

1970. Pietrzyk, Alfred. Selected titles in sociolinguistics: an interim bibliography of works on multilingualism, language standardization, and languages of wider communication. Washington, DC, Center for Applied Linguistics, 1967. 226p. ED 011120.

Abstracts are provided for most of the entries.

1971. Teoh, Irene. 1966 selected bibliography in linguistics and the uncommonly taught languages. ERIC Clearinghouse for Linguistics, 1967. 67p. ED 010693.

Unannotated. Contains 730 books, articles, and papers, nearly all in English, and a few published before 1966.

1972. Broz, James and Alfred S. Hayes. Linguistics and reading: a selective annotated bibliography for teachers of reading. Washington, DC, Center for Applied Linguistics, 1966. 29p. ED 010987.

Includes books, articles, and bibliographies published since 1942.

1973. Selected bibliography in linguistics with special emphasis on applied German linguistics. 1967. 65p. ED 011445.

809 books and articles published since 1885 are listed. Only a few are annotated; an author index is provided.

1974. Sajavaara, Kari and Jaakko Lehtonen. A Select bibliography of contrastive analysis. Finland, Jyvaskyla University Department of English, 1975. 126p. ED 136547.

This is part of a Finnish-English contrastive project for Finnish students and teachers.

1975. O'Deirg, Iosold. Language and linguistic theses in Irish university libraries. Dublin, Linguistics Institute of Ireland, 1977. 94p. ED 152116.

The 537 unannotated entries are listed by author and indexed by subject. They date from 1915.

1976. Moulton, William G. Linguistics and language teaching in the United States, 1940-1960. 1963. 30p. ED 038879.

An annotated bibliography is part of this historical study.

1977. Sheldon, Amy. Bibliography of psychological, linguistic, and philosophical research on the psychological reality of grammar. 1976. 13p. ED 134041.

The 160 books and articles deal with language usage, language acquisition, psycholinguistics, verbal behavior, psychology, and the philosophy of language. Not annotated.

1978. Pickett, Penelope O. A Selected bibliography on recent dialect studies. ERIC Clearinghouse on Languages and Linguistics, 1975. 27p. ED 111176 (MF)

An annotated list from the 1973-1974 issues of RIE.

1979. Filipovic, Rudolf. The Yugoslav Serbo-Croatian-English contrastive project. Washington, DC, Center for Applied Linguistics, 1972. 127p. ED 121080.

Annotates 116 American doctoral dissertations in contrastive linguistics.

1980. Grimes, Joseph E. and David J. Cranmer. Bibliography on discourse and related topics. Cornell University, 1972.

23p. ED 066959.

Lists over 350 books, articles, and papers written since 1912 on a wide variety of linguistic problems and issues.

1981. Ringbom, Hakan and Rolf Palmberg. Errors made by Finns and Swedish speaking Finns in the learning of English. Helsinki, Academy of Finland, 1976. 167p. ED 122628.

The volume concludes with a 444 item bibliography of error analysis, contrastive linguistics, language acquisition, language learning, and language testing.

1982. Zwicky, Arnold M. Forestress and afterstress, compounds and phrases. Columbus, Ohio State University, Department of Linguistics, 1973. 8p. ED 095721.

Includes 22 items published since 1914 on stress in noun compounds and phrases in English.

1983. Lotz, John. Preliminary bibliography on the syllable. 1966. 11p. ED 022165.

Over 200 books and articles are listed in many languages as well as English. The unannotated entries date from the late 19th century.

1984. Maddieson, Ian and Jack Gandour. An Annotated bibliography on tone. Los Angeles, UCLA Phonetics Laboratory, 1974. 187p. ED 101587.

Includes 550 entries on the phonetics and phonology of tone, studies on the physiology of phonation and pitch control, pitch perception, inherent pitch of vowels, and the interaction of tone with musical melody in tone languages.

1985. Ferguson, Charles A. and William A. Stewart. Linguistic reading lists for teachers of modern languages: French, German, Italian, Russian, Spanish. Arlington, VA, Center for Applied Linguistics, 1963. 120p. ED 130510.

An annotated collection of bibliographies designed as a basic professional reference library.

1986. Hammer, John H. and Frank A. Rice. A Bibliography of contrastive linguistics. Arlington, VA, Center for Applied Linguistics, 1965. 46p. ED 130509.

Lists 484 items on about 90 languages. Unannotated.

1987. Rice, Frank A. and Allene Guss. Information sources in linguistics: a bibliographical handbook. Arlington, VA, Center for Applied Linguistics, 1965. 52p. ED 130498.

Includes reference sources of many types arranged by subject. Most of the unannotated entries are in English.

1988. Dingwall, William O. <u>Transformational generative gram-</u><u>mar: a bibliography</u>. Arlington, VA, Center for Applied Ling-uistics, 1965. 92p. ED 130499.

Lists published works and conference papers on anthropolo-gical linguistics, contrastive analysis, computational linguistics, diachronic linguistics, dialectology, psycho-linguistics, and stylistics. Not annotated.

1989. Mieszek, Aleksandra. <u>Bibliography of English-Polish</u> <u>contrastive studies in Poland</u>. 1976. 42p. ED 130544 (MF)

Includes 403 works listed in both languages. The books, articles, papers, and dissertations are not annotated.

1990. Gadlin, Barry and Donald Nemanich. <u>Language</u>. 1974. 25p. ED 101342.

This is an article and a bibliography from the <u>Illinois</u> <u>English Bulletin</u>. The "Bibliography of linguistics and the English Language" is by Nemanich and covers history, teach-ing, child language, and several specific topics.

1991. Macken, Marlys A. <u>Readers, books, and articles on child</u> <u>phonology: a selected bibliography</u>. Stanford University, Cal-ifornia Committee on Linguistics, 1974. 13p. ED 100155.

Includes 29 annotated entries on normal (nondeviant) child phonology written in English.

1992. Zwicky, Arnold M. <u>Coivs</u>. Columbus, Ohio State Univer-sity, Department of Linguistics, 1973. 8p. ED 096826.

A literature survey of 25 entries related to coivs (con-nection-of-ideas verbs).

1993. Gage, William W. <u>Contrastive studies in linguistics</u>: <u>a bibliographical checklist</u>. Washington, DC, Center for Ap-plied Linguistics, 1961. 17p. ED 035324.

Contains 166 studies on many languages written in the Roman alphabet, and 37 studies printed in the Cyrillic alphabet.

1994. Zisa, Charles A. <u>Language classification and indexing</u>: <u>with an annotated bibliography</u>. Washington, DC, Center for Applied Linguistics, 1970. 24p. ED 044678.

The appended bibliography contains 32 entries.

1995. Becker, Judith A. <u>An Annotated bibliography of prag-</u><u>matics</u>. Minneapolis, University of Minnesota, Center for Re-search in Human Learning, 1979. 19p. ED 179091.

The briefly annotated entries exclude sociolinguistics and referential communication. The focus is on develop-mental pragmatics.

LISTENING

1996. Schubach, Deane Ford. Listening bibliography. College of the Virgin Islands, 1975. 10p. ED 119188.

Lists 100 unannotated references for all educational levels on listening and listening skills.

LITERACY EDUCATION

1997. Smith, Edwin H. A Revised annotated bibliography of instructional literacy material for adult basic education. Tallahassee, Florida State Department of Education, 1966. 53p. ED 010858.

1998. Ward, Betty A. and Edward W. Brice. Literacy and basic elementary education for adults: a selected annotated bibliography. Washington, DC, Department of Health, Education, and Welfare, 1961. 138p. ED 048559.

Earlier efforts to reduce illiteracy in the US are described, while other entries relate to special problems and programs.

1999. Fletcher, Philip R. Literacy training and the Brazilian political economy: an essay on resources. 1972. 14p. ED 070921.

An annotated bibliography is presented in essay form of sources concerning Brazil's literacy program for adults.

2000. Literacy documentation. Teheran, Iran, International Institute for Adult Literacy Methods, 1975. 195p. ED 121958.

Over 50 pages of bibliography concern literacy programs in underdeveloped countries.

2001. Nussbaum, Mary J. Adult literacy in the developing countries. 1971. 133p. ED 044638.

The 1777 unannotated items include statistics, teaching guides, media use, library services, and instructional methods among other topics.

LITERARY CRITICISM

2002. Drazan, Joseph G. and Paula Scott. Research Studies index: authors and subjects. Walla Walla, WA, Whitman College, Penrose Memorial Library, 1976. 52p. ED 139404.

Research Studies is a scholarly quarterly published at Washington State University (Pullman). Each author index

entry includes the title, volume number, and inclusive
pagination of the article for the complete run of the
journal from volume one through volume 43 (1929-1975).
About 560 articles are listed; most are literary criticism, but many others concern the Pacific Northwest in a
variety of disciplines.

LITERATURE

2003. Fritz, Alvin. American literature: selected basic reference works. Ann Arbor, University of Michigan Libraries,
1975. 27p. ED 154814.

   An annotated list for graduate students with an emphasis
   on bibliographies of criticism.

2004. George, Mary W. English literature: selected basic reference works. Ann Arbor, University of Michigan Libraries,
1975. 40p. ED 154813.

   An annotated list for graduate students with an emphasis
   on bibliographies of crtiicism.

2005. McNamee, Lawrence F. A Bibliography of all English and
American literature dissertations accepted by American, British, and German universities from 1865 to 1964 classified by
period and major authors. Commerce, TX, East Texas State University, 1966. 1423p. ED 010408.

   An unannotated aid for doctoral students.

LOUISIANA

2006. Bridges, Katherine. Bibliography of Northwestern State
University research papers relating to Louisiana, 1957-1969.
Natchitoches, LA, 1970. 69p. ED 044339.

   Includes 327 unannotated entries.

LUMBEE INDIANS

2007. Feehan, Paul G. A Bibliography of representative materials on the Lumbee Indians of Robeson County, North Carolina.
1978. 10p. ED 153660.

   Lists 33 books or monographs, 57 pamphlets and articles,
   and 16 dissertations and theses. Unannotated.

MCLUHAN, HERBERT MARSHALL

2008. Katula, Richard. A Selected bibliography of Herbert
Marshall McLuhan, 1911-1973. 1973. 24p. ED 093022.

An unannotated list of books, articles, and one movie by
and about McLuhan, as well as reviews of his books.

MAINSTREAMING   See also HANDICAPPED CHILDREN

2009. Regular class placement/special classes. Arlington, VA,
Council for Exceptional Children, 1971. 15p. ED 052567.

Contains 56 annotated references on the issue of class
placement for exceptional children.

2010. Howard, Norma K. Regular class placement of the exceptional child: an abstract bibliography. ERIC Clearinghouse on
Early Childhood Education, 1974. 57p. ED 097126.

The entries have been drawn from RIE and CIJE since 1970,
and relate to handicapped and gifted children, preschool
through the elementary grades.

2011. Peterson, Reece L. Mainstreaming: a working bibliography. Second ed. Minneapolis, University of Minnesota, Leadership Training Institute/Special Education, 1976. 35p. ED 127
745.

Contains over 500 citations on regular class placement
for handicapped students. Unannotated.

2012. Mainstreaming: program descriptions in areas of excep-
tionality: a selective bibliography. Reston, VA, Council for
Exceptional Children, 1976. 37p. ED 129004.

Annotates 210 documents published since 1961 on regular
class placement.

MANAGEMENT SYSTEMS, THEORIES, AND DEVELOPMENT

2013. Management information systems: analysis of literature
and selected bibliography. ERIC Clearinghouse on Educational
Administration, 1970. 14p. ED 043113.

This review analyzes literature dealing with applications
to educational management.

2014. Witt, Barbara. Management information systems. Monticello, IL, Council of Planning Librarians, 1974. 12p. ED 097
758.

Lists 150 unannotated citations to books and articles
dating from 1969.

2015. Management by objectives: the best of ERIC. ERIC Clearinghouse on Educational Management, 1976.   5p.   ED 122349.

   Summarizes 12 selections from RIE and CIJE.

2016.   Musgrave, Gerald L. and Richard S. Elster.   Management by objectives and goal setting.   Monticello, IL, Council of Planning Librarians, 1974.   41p.   ED 099978.

   Contains over 500 references to books, articles, and other documents. Not annotated.

2017.   ERIC abstracts: a collection of ERIC document resumes on management by objectives.   Washington, DC, American Association of School Administrators, 1973.   15p.   ED 091799.

   This annotated list is complete for all issues of RIE through August 1973.

2018.   Pressley, Milton M.   A Selected bibliography of readings in management theory and practice.   Monticello, IL, Council of Planning Librarians, 1974.   40p.   ED 099979.

   A topical unannotated bibliography.

2019.   Gast, Ilene.   Abstracts of selected management training evaluations.   Washington, DC, Civil Service Commission, Training Leadership Division, 1977.   39p.   ED 159186.

   Includes 28 abstracts of representative articles from journals in applied psychology and personnel management. The earliest is dated 1953.

2020.   Management development.   ERIC Clearinghouse on Adult Education, 1967.   15p.   ED 013430.

   This annotated bibliography contains 28 items in such areas as human relations and leadership training, program planning and evaluation, business games, and discussion group behavior.

2021.   Management development: current information sources. ERIC Clearinghouse on Adult Education, 1968.   23p.   ED 016927.

   Contains 33 annotated items which were published in 1966 and 1967.

2022.   Management development and supervisory training: current information sources.   ERIC Clearinghouse on Adult Education, 1969.   77p.   ED 033251.

   210 annotations are included.

2023.   Self development aids for supervisors and middle managers.   Washington, DC, Civil Service Commission, 1970.   202p. ED 052427.

   Includes annotated materials published through 1969.

2024. Kohn, Vera. A Selected bibliography on evaluation of management training and development programs. Hamilton, NY, American Foundation for Management Research, Inc., 1969. 25p. ED 034947.

Includes 61 annotated entries published since 1959.

MANPOWER See HUMAN RESOURCES and LABOR

MARINE SCIENCE See OCEANOLOGY

MARITIME HISTORY

2025. Heitzmann, William R. Two if by sea: America's maritime heritage and the social studies teacher. 1974. 32p. ED 109039.

The major portion of this presented paper is an annotated bibliography.

MARKETING

2026. Marketing and the low income consumer. Washington, DC, Bureau of Domestic Commerce (DOC), 1977. 71p. ED 147439.

Contains 326 classified and annotated entries.

2027. Stetz, Frank P. The Application of marketing science to educational settings: a bibliography. 1976. 33p. ED 146 592.

An unannotated list of articles, reports, and dissertations from the educational and psychological literature.

2028. Larson, Roger A. Marketing programs: an annotated bibliography. Minneapolis, University of Minnesota, General College, 1968. 20p. ED 021535.

The 30 entries on college marketing courses include books, theses, and articles.

MASLOW, ABRAHAM

2029. Bibliography: A. H. Maslow. Waltham, Mass., Brandeis University, 1972. 16p. ED 068432.

Listed in chronological order are 148 citations to Maslow's books and articles. His works arranged here date from 1932 to 1970.

MASS MEDIA   See   COMMUNICATION

MATHEMATICS AND MATHEMATICS EDUCATION   See also   COMPUTERS
   and   METRIC SYSTEM

2030. Schaaf, William L. A Bibliography of recreational mathematics. Fourth ed. Reston, VA, National Council of Teachers
of Mathematics, 1970. 160p. ED 121622 (MF)

   Lists partially annotated books and articles concerned
   with math games, puzzles, and amusements for the amateur
   and professional. This volume one is followed by a volume
   two of 204 pages (ED 040874), and a volume three of 187
   pages (ED 087631).

2031. Raab, Joseph A. Audiovisual materials in mathematics.
Washington, DC, National Council of Teachers of Mathematics,
1971. 95p. ED 058043 (MF)

   Includes 5000 current AV items under 18 subject headings.

2032. Bernbaum, Marcia. Number and concept development: an
abstract bibliography. ERIC Clearinghouse on Early Childhood
Development, 1971. 20p. ED 057921.

   The annotated entries are drawn from RIE and CIJE and
   focus on children's acquisition of math concepts.

2033. Geffen, Lawrence F. and Sandra J. Palmore. Selected
bibliography on mathematics for the blind. Ypsilanti, Eastern
Michigan University, 1969. 15p. ED 036018.

   137 references are provided. Some are annotated, and some
   are in languages other than English.

2034. An Annotated bibliography of children's literature related to the elementary school mathematics curriculum. Indianapolis, Indiana State Department of Public Instruction, 1979.
52p. ED 184887.

   Areas covered are sets and numbers, measurement and geom-
   etry, graphs, functions, and probability, calculators,
   computers, and biographies.

2035. Hewit, Frances and Richard C. Meckes. Bibliographies:
elementary school mathematics. Springfield, Illinois State
Superintendent of Public Instruction, 1966. 36p. ED 016611.

   Contains materials for teachers published since 1960, materials for parents, and a library booklist for K-6.

2036. Driscoll, Mark J. Elementary school mathematics annotated bibliography. St. Louis, Central Midwestern Regional
Educational Laboratory, 1979. 127p. ED 183378.

   Sex differences is one of the 17 topics included.

2037. Pikaart, Len. Bibliography of research studies in elementary school and preschool mathematics. Athens, University
of Georgia, 1966. 55p. ED 023464.

An unannotated subject list dating from the late 1950's.

2038. Clark, John and Vera Lovelass. Bibliographic guide for
advanced placement: mathematics. Albany, New York State Education Department, 1965. 16p. ED 020120.

Designed to aid in improving reference collection materials for advanced placement courses.

2039. Suydam, Marilyn N. Annotated compilation of research
on secondary school mathematics, 1930-1970. Two volumes. University Park, Pennsylvania State University, 1972. ED 062165
and ED 062166.

Volume one has 407 pages and contains 780 reports from the
ERIC system, and Volume two has 411 pages containing 770
doctoral dissertations completed in the United States.

2040. Woods, Paul E. Bibliographies: high school mathematics.
Springfield, Illinois State Superintendent of Public Instruction, 1966. 40p. ED 020115.

Contains recommended booklists for grades 7-12.

2041. Schaaf, William L. The High school mathematics library. Fifth ed. Washington, DC, National Council of Teachers
of Mathematics, 1973. 81p. ED 076428 (MF)

950 titles are listed; 200 are singled out as priority
purchases. Many entries are briefly annotated, and journal titles are included.

2042. Hardgrove, Clarence E. and Herbert F. Miller. Mathematics library: elementary and junior high school. Washington, DC, National Council of Teachers of Mathematics, 1973.
77p. ED 076407 (MF)

An annotated list that includes recreational reading.

2043. Sowder, Larry. A Review of research on solving routine
problems in pre-college mathematics. DeKalb, Northern Illinois University, 1979. 99p. ED 182175 (MF)

Reviews promising teaching practices with the "story"
problem, and others.

2044. Basic library list for four-year colleges. Second ed.
Berkeley, CA, Mathematical Association of America, Committee
on the Undergraduate Program, 1976. 111p. ED 144816 (MF)

Includes 700 titles arranged by topics, and also lists
journals, series, films, and some foreign language references.

2045.   Suydam, Marilyn N.   Compilation of research on college
mathematics education.   ERIC Information Analysis Center for
Science, Mathematics, and Environmental Education, 1975. 287p.
ED 121624.

Annotates research related to the teaching of college
mathematics, and includes 513 articles and 771 dissertations produced since 1900.

2046.   Chillrud, Dorothy N. and John J. Sullivan.   Books that
count: a bibliography.   Albany, New York State Education Department, 1973.   29p.   ED 085259.

An annotated guide for teachers and librarians for supple-
menting math programs and holdings. Elementary school level.

2047.   Suydam, Marilyn N.   Unpublished instruments for evaluation in mathematics education: an annotated listing.   ERIC
Information Analysis Center for Science, Mathematics, and Environmental Education, 1974.   264p.   ED 086518.

Includes 200 non-commercial investigator-developed tests
to assess math instruction, as reported in journals and
dissertations since 1964.

2048.   Zelenik, Mary E.   An Annotated bibliography of math materials.   Los Angeles, University of Southern California, Instructional Materials Center for Special Education, 1973. 52p.
ED 085950.

Contains about 500 entries suitable for preschool through
high school. Kits and manipulative aids are emphasized.

2049.   Cumulative index: the Arithmetic Teacher, 1954-1973.
Reston, VA, National Council of Teachers of Mathematics, 1974.
128p.   ED 111636 (MF)

This journal index for volumes 1-20 includes over 9000
entries indexed by author, title, and subject.

2050.   Advisory list of instructional media for mathematics.
Raleigh, North Carolina State Department of Public Instruction,
1977.   20p.   ED 149751.

The annotated multimedia materials are appropriate for
primary grades through high school, and are arranged by
type of material.

2051.   Sherling, Carole.   Annotated bibliography of mathematics curriculum, 1970-1978.   1978.   37p.   ED 171575 (MF)

For secondary schools; topics covered include goals, re-
forms, current issues, and calculators and computers in
the curriculum.

2052.   Greenwood, Jonathan.   Resources for individualizing mathematics. Salem, Oregon State Department of Education, 1973. 20p. ED 071918.

The annotated references cover program and course goals, diagnostic and achievement tests, teacher reference books, and activity sources. Also included are 21 articles from the Arithmetic Teacher which offer a rationale for the activity approach.

2053. Junge, Charlotte W. Mathematics for young children: a summary of research and related literature. Tallahassee, Florida State Department of Education, 1975. 33p. ED 120026.

Annotates 48 research reports on math teaching and learning of primary school children, and 102 additional unannotated papers.

2054. Graeber, Anna O. and Katherine B. Baxter. Math diagnosis and prescription literature search: final report. Philadelphia, Research for Better Schools, Inc., 1976. 42p. ED 139663.

Includes an annotated bibliography of selected documents.

2055. Schoen, Harold L. and Gloria L. Drapac. An Annotated bibliography of research on self-paced mathematics instruction (1965-1976). 1976. 55p. ED 128204 (MF)

Contains 148 papers reporting on the effectiveness of this method from the primary grades through college.

2056. Suydam, Marilyn N. A Categorized listing of research on mathematics education (K-12), 1964-1973. ERIC Information Analysis Center for Science, Mathematics, and Environmental Education, 1974. 364p. ED 097225.

Cites 3000 articles, dissertations, and ERIC documents.

2057. Begle, E. G. Ability grouping for mathematics instruction: a review of the empirical literature. Stanford University, Mathematics Education Study Group, 1975. 55p. ED 116 938.

Annotates 77 research reports concerning grades one to 12, and presents a list of findings and summary of research methods.

2058. Becker, Jerry P. Foreign and domestic journals in mathematical education. Revised ed. Reston, VA, National Council of Teachers of Mathematics, 1976. 111p. ED 123134.

Annotates 168 journal titles from 61 countries, and four journals of international organizations.

MEDIA SELECTION

2059. Dequin, Henry C. A Guide to selecting learning resource materials and equipment. Springfield, Illinois State Office of Education, 1978. 58p. ED 165806.

Annotates 54 selection tools and recommended lists. Includes discographies, and covers special education needs.

2060. Carter, Yvonne. Aids to media selection for students and teachers. Washington, DC, Bureau of Elementary and Secondary Education (DHEW), 1971. 89p. ED 053340.

This annotated bibliography presents selected book lists and periodicals which review books, AV materials, and multiethnic instructional materials dating from 1965.

2061. Moses, Kathlyn J. and Lois B. Watt. Aids to media selection for students and teachers. Revised ed. Washington, DC, Office of Education (DHEW), 1976. 127p. ED 127631.

Annotates reviewing journals and selection bibliographies.

2062. Simmons, Beatrice T. and Yvonne B. Carter. Aids to media selection for students and teachers. Washington, DC, Bureau of School Systems (DHEW), 1979. 105p. ED 181920.

This update of the previous entry annotates items published since 1976.

MEDICINE AND MEDICAL EDUCATION

2063. Minority groups in medicine: selected bibliography. Bethesda, MD, National Institutes of Health (DHEW), 1972. 21p. ED 099575.

Includes 146 books, reports, articles, and government documents on ethnic minorities in the health professions. Not annotated.

2064. Pijar, Mary Lou. Source book of educational materials for medical radiographers. Revised ed. Rockville, MD, Food and Drug Administration (DHEW), 1977. 79p. ED 160421.

An annotated bibliography in 12 sections of interest to those involved in diagnostic radiologic technology.

2065. Maatsch, Jack L. A Study of simulation technology in medical education: an annotated bibliography. East Lansing, Michigan State University, 1976. 96p. ED 148395.

Cites 224 publications dealing with the development, utilization, and evaluation of simulation technology with implications for medical education.

2066. The Foreign medical graduate: a bibliography. Washington, DC, Health Resources Administration (DHEW), 1972. 109p.

ED 080090.

On education of foreign medical graduates abroad, the flow of these graduates to the United States, and their training and utilization in American medicine.

2067. Zwell, Mary E. Training for family practice: a selected bibliography. University of Pittsburgh, Department of Psychiatry, 1970. 58p. ED 052677.

The partially annotated entries date from 1965.

2068. Lewis, Elizabeth M. An Exhibition of selected landmark books and articles in the history of military medicine, together with a graphic display of the wound man through history. West Point, NY, Military Academy Library, 1976. 46p. ED 156123 (MF)

Also contains a special list of works describing contributions of Army doctors to medicine and science.

2069. International migration of physicians and nurses: an annotated bibliography. Bethesda, MD, Health Resources Administration, 1975. 66p. ED 150943.

Includes books, articles, and reports dating from 1965.

2070. Heald, Karen A. and James K. Cooper. An Annotated bibliography on rural medical care. Santa Monica, CA, Rand Corporation, 1972. 39p. ED 078149.

Includes books and articles published since 1960 on need, demand, supply and distribution, and alternative approaches.

2071. Emergency health services selected bibliography. Bethesda, MD, Health Services and Mental Health Administration (DHEW), 1970. 165p. ED 062548.

Annotates books, articles, and visual aids on major and minor disasters.

MEMORY

2072. Hackbarth, Steven L. Semantic and acoustic properties of memory: an annotated, cross-referenced bibliography. Los Alamitos, CA, Southwest Regional Laboratory for Educational Research and Development, 1972. 212p. ED 108161.

Contains 441 article citations with annotations.

MENOMINEE INDIANS

2073. Stephens, Wayne E. Menominee Indian tribe of Wisconsin: Part I, Inventory of resources; Part II, annotated bibliography. Billings, MT, Bureau of Indian Affairs, 1975. 176p. ED 131992.

Includes over 400 entries on history and culture, resources and feasibility studies, legal matters, and other reports.

MENTAL HEALTH   See also   EMOTIONALLY DISTURBED

2074. Sive, Mary R. Mental health. Pearl River, NY, Informedia, 1979. 22p. ED 180471.

Lists 266 films, filmstrips, videotapes, slides, books, and pamphlets. Of these, 118 are suitable for high school, 8Q for elementary school, and 68 for professional use.

2075. Mental health. Arlington, VA, Council for Exceptional Children, 1971. 18p. ED 054578.

Annotates 66 documents related to children with emotional disturbances or other handicaps.

2076. An Annotated bibliography on mental health in the schools, 1970-1973. Bethesda, MD, National Institute of Mental Health, 1973. 35p. ED 091637.

Methodology and results are given for the 200 publications included. Only behavior modification is included as a form of treatment here.

2077. Planning for creative change in mental health services: a distillation of principles on research utilization. Bethesda, MD, National Institute of Mental Health, 1972. 555p. ED 068850.

The second of this two volume set is a bibliography with annotations.

2078. Active grants. Rockville, MD, Center for Minority Group Mental Health Problems, National Institute of Mental Health, 1978. 64p. ED 162004 (MF)

This document serves as an annotated bibliography of various programs, projects, and research being undertaken in the field of mental health throughout the United States.

2079. Comrey, Andrew L. A Sourcebook for mental health measures. Los Angeles, Human Interaction Research Institute, 1973. 435p. ED 096350.

1100 abstracts of tests and instruments are grouped into 45 categories. An author and title index is provided.

2080. Sharma, Prakash C. Problems, planning, and delivery of mental health services: a selected research bibliography.

Monticello, IL, Council of Planning Librarians, 1975. 25p.
ED 103567.

Includes 325 books and articles dated 1950 to 1973.

2081. Dykstra, Ralph R. and Peter J. Dirr. Drug and health
mediagraphy: mental health. Buffalo, State University of New
York, Educational Research and Development Complex, 1974. 113p.
ED 106993 (MF)

Lists 350 instructional materials for children and young
adults. Handicapped children are included.

2082. Annotated bibliography on inservice training for key
professionals in community mental health. Washington, DC,
Public Health Service (DHEW), 1969. 59p. ED 037355 (MF)

Includes 189 documents published since 1960.

2083. Annotated bibliography on inservice training for allied
professionals and nonprofessionals in community mental health.
Washington, DC, Public Health Service (DHEW), 1969. 55p. ED
035727 (MF)

Includes 169 entries published since 1960 for nurses,
teachers, school psychologists, clergy, social workers,
police, and volunteers.

2084. Annotated bibliography on inservice training in mental
health for staff in residential institutions. Bethesda, MD,
National Institute of Mental Health, 1968. 46p. ED 023990.

This bibliography of articles is from the American, Scandinavian, and Canadian literature.

2085. Annotated bibliography on inservice training in mental
health for staff in residential institutions. Washington, DC,
Public Health Service (DHEW), 1969. 32p. ED 035728 (MF)

This version of the preceding presents 86 classified entries.

2086. Klutch, Murray. Mental health manpower. San Francisco,
California Medical Association, 1967. 393p. ED 032380.

Part I is an annotated bibliography with commentary, and
Part II is a compilation of articles, surveys, and a review of applicable literature on recruitment, training,
and utilization.

2087. Coelho, George V. Mental health and social change: an
annotated bibliography. Rockville, MD, National Institute of
Mental Health, 1972. 467p. ED 074391.

Includes 730 abstracts dating from 1967.

MENTALLY HANDICAPPED

2088. <u>Recreation handbook for state and local unit recreation committees</u>. Arlington, TX, National Association for Retarded Citizens, 1973. 60p. ED 087181.

A descriptive list of 140 books and films on many kinds of indoor and outdoor recreations for the handicapped.

2089. Colella, Henry V. and John J. Gleason. <u>Selected bibliography of books, pamphlets, periodicals, and curriculum guides in work study for the educable retarded</u>. Boston University, School of Education, 1969. 19p. ED 036615.

Includes about 240 entries.

2090. <u>Social problem fiction: a source of help for retarded readers</u>. Iowa City, University of Iowa, Special Education Curriculum Development Center,1969. 316p. ED 030243.

Annotates over 500 major fiction books and basal readers with suggestions for their use. Reading levels are given.

2091. <u>Improving instruction for trainable mentally retarded: a working document</u>. Iowa City, University of Iowa, Special Education Curriculum Development Center, 1968. 90p. ED 029 404.

This selected bibliography lists 234 professional readings and curriculum guides. Not annotated.

2092. <u>Catalog of audiovisual aids for counselor training in mental retardation and emotional disability</u>. Devon, PA, Devereux Foundation, 1967. 110p. ED 013008.

Briefly annotates 341 films, and includes a subject index.

2093. Fearon, Ross E. <u>Mental retardation: catalog of library accessions</u>. 1966. 51p. ED 012997.

Lists about 570 items in the Farmington State College Library. The entries date from 1907 and are in Dewey Decimal Classification order.

2094. Cobb, Henry V. <u>The Predictive assessment of the adult retarded for social and vocational adjustment: a review of research</u>. Vermillion, University of South Dakota, 1966. 161p. ED 014171.

Annotates 532 references dating from 1912. The appendix lists 94 program summaries and reports.

2095. Blessing, Kenneth R. and Heinz Pfaeffle. <u>Bibliography on mental retardation</u>. Madison, Wisconsin State Department of Public Instruction, 1965. 51p. ED 011412.

Includes general literature, professional literature, and a curriculum section. The unannotated entries date from 1940.

2096. Altman, Reuben. <u>Bibliography of cooperative work/study</u>
<u>programs for the mentally retarded throughout the United States</u>
Austin, University of Texas, College of Education, 1970. 64p.
ED 040550.

Lists articles, bibliographies, state guidelines and cooperative agreements, agency publications, and conference
proceedings classified by state.

2097. Perlman, Joseph and Marvin Stober. <u>Program planning</u>
<u>guidelines: a review of research with implications for the ed-</u>
<u>ucation and training of the severely to profoundly mentally</u>
<u>retarded</u>. New York, City University Graduate School, 1976.
129p. ED 140518.

Annotates 164 citations in eight categories dating from
1969.

2098. Bialac, Verda. <u>The Severely and profoundly retarded</u>:
<u>a bibliography</u>. Olympia, Washington State Library, 1970. 29p.
ED 046203.

Medical literature is excluded, but the unannotated citations cover community programs, institutional services,
language, speech and hearing, mental processes, parents
and family, planning and legislation, recreation, self-
help, social and emotional development, and vocational rehabilitation.

2099. Horn, Fern M. and Anita O. Barsness. <u>Instructional ma-</u>
<u>terials for use with educable mentally retarded students en-</u>
<u>rolled in home economics classes</u>. Stevens Point, University
of Wisconsin, 1975. 312p. ED 112264.

A 68 page annotated bibliography covers child development,
personal development, clothing and textiles, consumer education, and foods and nutrition.

2100. <u>Reintegrating mentally retarded people into the commun-</u>
<u>ity: an annotated bibliography of print and audiovisual infor-</u>
<u>mation and training materials</u>. Reston, VA, Council for Excep-
tional Children, 1975. 31p. ED 112534.

Includes 123 sources dating from 1962 which document innovative efforts.

2101. Cook, Iva Dean. <u>Annotated bibliography of special ed-</u>
<u>ucation instructional materials</u>. Charleston, West Virginia
State Commission on Mental Retardation, 1974. 345p. ED 101
532.

Includes 900 commercially prepared materials for teaching
and training educable mentally retarded students.

2102. <u>Bibliography of materials for the secondary educable</u>
<u>mentally retarded</u>. Atlanta, Georgia State Department of Edu-
cation, Division of Special Education, 1974. 118p. ED 094514

Lists 500 instructional materials for use in the secondary
school programs.

2103. Malever, Michael and George Matyas. Project PRICE:
career education materials for educable retarded students.
Columbia, University of Missouri, College of Education, 1975.
45p. ED 118890.

PRICE stands for programming retarded in career education.
Age levels and brief annotations are given for the publications in three categories: daily living skills, personal
and social skills, and occupational guidance and preparation.

2104. Play and learn with toys: a bibliography of toys that
teach institutional children. Pierre, Redfield State Hospital
and the South Dakota State Library, 1976. 28p. ED 119740.

Describes toys and games appropriate for a library serving
the mentally retarded. Items are grouped under life skills,
concepts, communication skills, motor skills, and sensory
skills.

2105. Reiss, Philip. The Development of a social learning
curriculum for moderately retarded children: a working paper.
New York, Yeshiva University, Curriculum Research and Development Center in Mental Retardation, 1974. 323p. ED 100098.

1000 entries review the research on learning, language,
social behavior, and curriculum. Also includes parent aids,
Down's syndrome, and behavior modification.

2106. Cass, Michael and Jeffrey Schilit. An Annotated bibliography on the severely and profoundly mentally retarded. 1976.
58p. ED 129035.

The 250 entries include assessment, measurement, classical
conditioning, behavior modification, physical therapy, and
self-help skills, among other topics.

2107. Educable mentally handicapped - programs: a selective
bibliography. Reston, VA, Council for Exceptional Children,
1973. 25p. ED 090708.

Includes abstracts of 90 publications dating from 1960.
Some items treat work study curriculums, special teacher
education, and suggestions for public school counselors.

2108. Educable mentally retarded - programs/teaching methods.
Reston, VA, Council for Exceptional Children, 1976. 28p. ED
129017.

Annotates 100 publications dating from 1970.

2109. Mentally retarded - teaching methods and curriculum:
topical bibliography. Reston, VA, Council for Exceptional
Children, 1977. 17p. ED 146741.

Annotates 75 publications dated 1971-1976.

2110. <u>Mentally retarded - programs: 1977 topical bibliography</u>.
Reston, VA, Council for Exceptional Children, 1977. 20p. ED
146740.

Annotates 90 publications on programs for the mentally
retarded dated 1974-1976.

2111. <u>Educable mentally retarded - career education: a selective bibliography</u>. Reston, VA, Council for Exceptional Children, 1976. 20p. ED 129019.

Annotates 75 publications dated 1970-1975.

2112. <u>Educable mentally retarded - curriculum: a selective
bibliography</u>. Reston, VA, Council for Exceptional Children,
1976. 22p. ED 129018.

Includes abstracts of 90 publications dated 1970-1975.

2113. <u>Educable mentally handicapped - research: a selective
bibliography</u>. Reston, VA, Council for Exceptional Children,
1973. 26p. ED 090709.

Annotates 100 publications concerned with children and
youth published since early 1964. Covers special class
placement, self-concept, mathematics, and learning potential.

2114. <u>Educable mentally handicapped - research: a selective
bibliography</u>. Arlington, VA, Council for Exceptional Children, 1972. 31p. ED 065966.

Annotates 100 publications dating from 1958.

2115. <u>Trainable mentally handicapped - programs: a selective
bibliography</u>. Arlington, VA, Council for Exceptional Children,
1972. 20p. ED 069074.

Includes 55 abstracts of publications dated 1961 to 1971.

2116. <u>Trainable mentally handicapped - research: a selective
bibliography</u>. Arlington, VA, Council for Exceptional Children,
1972. 31p. ED 069075.

Includes 93 abstracts of publications dated 1958 to 1971.

2117. <u>Normalization - mentally retarded: a selective biblio-
graphy</u>. Reston, VA, Council for Exceptional Children, 1976.
28p. ED 129006.

Annotates 100 documents and journal articles dated 1968
to 1975.

2118. Schilit, Jeffrey. <u>The Secondary school level and adult
mentally retarded individual: an annotated bibliography</u>. Uni-

versity of Alabama, Department of Special Education, 1976.
91p. ED 127734.

Covers assessment, teaching methods, vocational rehabilitation, or community life in 350 articles dating from 1970.

2119. DeBusk, Christopher W. and Vincent P. Luchsinger. Vocational training and job placement of the mentally retarded:
an annotated bibliography. Lubbock, Texas Tech University,
Research and Training Center in Mental Retardation, 1974. 200p.
ED 096779.

Subjects include attitudes of parents and employers, behavior modification, economic factors, Federal programs, and
success prediction. 970 books and articles are listed
which were published between 1959 and 1972.

2120. McGovern, Kevin B. and Esther R. Brummer. Films in
mental retardation: a select annotated bibliography. Eugene,
University of Oregon, Rehabilitation and Research Training
Center in Mental Retardation, 1973. 41p. ED 109833.

Describes 33 16mm films which are on current treatment
strategies, programs, attitudes, concepts, or theories
on the rehabilitation of the retarded.

2121. Malever, Michael and George Matyas. Career education
materials for educable retarded students. Columbia, University of Missouri, Department of Counseling and Personnel Services, 1975. 45p. ED 116443.

Partially annotates 150 instructional materials and 50
other publications arranged according to each of 22 competencies.

2122. Mental retardation film list. Bethesda, MD, National
Library of Medicine, 1968. 65p. ED 035157.

The films are listed in two categories, those for the professional, and those most suitable for use by the general
public.

2123. Meyen, Edward L. Inservice training materials for
teachers of the educable mentally retarded. Iowa City, University of Iowa, Special Education Curriculum Development Center, 1968. 16p. ED 044837.

An annotated bibliography which provides age level, use
guidelines, and content summary.

2124. Peins, Maryann. Bibliography on speech, hearing, and
language in relation to mental retardation, 1900-1968. Washington, DC, Public Health Service, 1969. 164p. ED 044858(MF)

2125. Rondal, Jean A. and Renee N. Bibliography on speech
and language in mental retardation, 1900-1975. Minneapolis,
University of Minnesota, 1975. 60p. ED 108412.

Includes 750 unannotated references; some are on intervention studies, therapy, and training programs.

2126. Muthard, John E. Selected rehabilitation counseling
literature. Gainesville, University of Florida, College of
Health Related Professions, 1968. 142p. ED 042187.

Cites publications on placement, supervision, performance,
evaluation, personnel, psychology, testing, and other aspects of disability from the previous eight years. Also
includes annotated bibliographies on mental retardation
and sheltered workshops.

2127. Gardner, James M. Learning in mental retardation: a
comprehensive bibliography. Orient, OH, Orient State Institute, 1969. 62p. ED 042316.

Categories are applied behavior change, classical conditioning, discrimination, generalization, motor learning,
reinforcement, verbal learning, and miscellaneous. Not
annotated.

2128. Materials for secondary school programs for the educable mentally retarded adolescent. Boston University, New England Materials Instruction Center, 1970. 77p. ED 042310.

The items are related to work study programs and are
grouped according to academic areas. Briefly annotated.

2129. Goldstein, Ellen R. Principal sources for the study of
the mutability of intelligence and the epidemiology of mild
mental retardation. ERIC Clearinghouse on the Urban Disadvantaged, 1970. 71p. ED 042837.

An extensively annotated bibliography that includes studies on Blacks, East Tennessee mountain children, Scots,
Swedes, and the English.

MERIT RATING PROGRAMS

2130. Merit rating. Ottawa, Canadian Teachers Federation,
1971. 14p. ED 057433.

Includes 156 entries for books, articles, and theses published since 1961. Not annotated.

METEOROLOGY

2131. Roseman, Steven and Henry Ray. A Multimedia bibliography of weather materials for schools. Tempe, Arizona State
University, Laboratory of Climatology, 1977. 17p. ED 164415.

Lists 43 films and 47 books which include forecasting
techniques. For elementary and secondary levels.

METRIC SYSTEM

2132. Milek, John T. and Valerie Antoine. Bibliography of the metric system. Waukegan, IL, Metric Association, Inc., 1968. 88p. ED 078202.

An author list of 1196 articles. Unannotated; subject index included.

2133. Bibliography on the metric system: instructional materials. Indianapolis, Indiana State Department of Public Instruction, 1974. 35p. ED 137123.

This multimedia bibliography includes government publications and covers all grade levels. Not annotated.

2134. Some references on metric information. Washington, DC, National Bureau of Standards, 1973. 12p. ED 090025.

Lists publications of the American National Standards Institute and the US government. Not annotated.

2135. Wall, Celia. The Metric system: a bibliography of basic references. Memphis State University Libraries, 1976. 8p. ED 125915.

Briefly annotates 30 items.

2136. Metric conversion: an annotated bibliography for teachers. Washington, DC, National Education Association, 1974. 14p. ED 104722.

Includes books and articles, plus 30 films and videotapes for classroom use.

2137. Metric education: an annotated bibliography for vocational, technical and adult education. Columbus, Ohio State University, Center for Vocational and Technical Education, 1974. 154p. ED 115953.

Indicates educational level for the instructor guides, AV materials, and student resources.

2138. Bitter, Gary G. and Charles Geer. Materials for metric instruction. ERIC Information Analysis Center for Science, Mathematics, and Environmental Education, 1975. 85p. ED 115 488.

Briefly describes about 130 kits, films, and other miscellaneous materials.

MICHIGAN

2139. Selected list of recommended Michigan books and pam-

phlets. Lansing, Michigan State Department of Education, 1978.
15p. ED 160515.

Annotates 116 resources published during the 1960's and
1970's. Includes all subjects and some other bibliographies.

MICROFORMS

2140. Gleaves, Edwin S. and James R. Veatch. Microformula-
tion: a selective bibliography on microforms, 1970-1975. Nashville, TN, George Peabody College for Teachers, School of Library Science, 1975. 54p. ED 111408 (MF)

Presents listings on computer output microform (COM), and
the technical aspects of microreproduction technology.

MICROTEACHING

2141. Shore, Bruce M. Microteaching: a brief review. Montreal, McGill University, 1972. 31p. ED 066863.

Includes an extensive annotated bibliography which covers
applications to the subject matter and the skills involved.

2142. McKnight, Philip C. and Robert N. Bush. Microteaching:
a selected bibliography. ERIC Clearinghouse on Teacher Education, 1977. 46p. ED 141266.

Annotates articles and documents from the ERIC system.

2143. McKnight, Philip C. and David P. Baral. Microteaching
and the technical skills of teaching: a bibliography of research and development at Stanford University, 1963-1969.
Stanford University, School of Education, 1969. 9p. ED 030
621.

The 66 unannotated entries include dissertations, other
publications, and three films.

2144. Microteaching. Ottawa, Canadian Teachers Federation,
1969. 9p. ED 036480.

This unannotated bibliography covers the previous five
years and lists 82 books, articles and papers, plus four
theses.

2145. Cooper, James M. Microteaching: an annotated bibliography. ERIC Clearinghouse on Teacher Education, 1970. 14p.
ED 036466.

Lists 48 articles and papers dating from 1966.

MIDDLE AGE

2146. Committee on work and personality in the middle years
progess report. New York, Social Science Research Council,
1976. 48p. ED 135700 (MF)

Includes a 33 page list of papers on psychological, physical, occupational, medical, educational, and social aspects of the middle years.

MIDDLE EAST

2147. Harlow, Ann K. The Middle East: a bibliography. West
Point, NY, Military Academy Library, 1974. 139p. ED 156121
(MF)

A selective unannotated list of books from the Academy
library categorized by country following the general section.

2148. Stone, Frank A. Modern Middle Eastern fiction: an
approach to studying the area. Storrs, University of Connecticut, World Education Project, 1974. 16p. ED 091302.

Annotates fiction that has been translated into English
which can be used in humanities or social studies classes
at the secondary level.

2149. Maehr, Jane. The Middle East: an annotated bibliography of literature for children. ERIC Clearinghouse on Early
Childhood Education, 1977. 68p. ED 142278.

Includes folklore, fiction and nonfiction in English for
children aged five and older. Most books were published
since 1958.

2150. James, Eloise L. Far Middle East: an annotated bibliography of materials at elementary school level for Afghanistan,
Iran, and Pakistan. 1974. 126p. ED 104732.

This multimedia listing includes history and culture, customs, laws, religious beliefs, values, language, and social institutions.

2151. Griswold, William J. The Image of the Middle East in
secondary school textbooks. New York, Middle East Studies
Association of North America, 1975. 108p. ED 117013 (MF)

42 world history, social studies, and geography texts are
examined for errors in content, oversimplification, and
stereotyping. In addition, an annotated bibliography contains 62 critical references, and a list of recommended
textbooks.

2152. Hawkins, John N. and Jon Maksik. Teacher's resource
handbook for Near Eastern studies: an annotated bibliography
of curriculum materials, preschool through grade twelve. Los

Angeles, UCLA, Von Grunebaum Center for Near Eastern Studies, 1976. 111p. ED 133242 (MF)

The 828 multimedia entries are arranged by grade levels. Covers the Arab and non-Arab Middle East, North Africa, and the Sudan.

2153. Johnson, Dora E. Languages of the Middle East and North Africa: a survey of materials for the study of the uncommonly taught languages. Arlington, VA, Center for Applied Linguistics, 1976. 54p. ED 132834.

The annotated entries are grouped by language classification: Turkic, Iranian, Semitic, and Berber. Emphasis is on materials for the adult learner whose native language is English.

MIDDLE SCHOOLS

2154. Norman, O. Gene. Junior high school and middle school: a selected bibliography. Terre Haute, Indiana State University Library, 1979. 9p. ED 184218.

An unannotated topical bibliography on planning, guidelines, research, students, and curricula, among other subjects.

2155. Pansino, Louis P. The Middle school: a selected bibliography with introduction. Urbana, University of Illinois, Bureau of Educational Research, 1969. 8p. ED 029714.

Includes 51 books, articles, and reports taken from RIE and the educational literature. Not annotated.

2156. Piele, Philip. Selected bibliography of journal articles on the middle school. Eugene, University of Oregon, 1967. 6p. ED 017059.

In addition to the 35 articles, it lists 5 books and 21 other reports. Not annotated.

2157. Junior high and middle schools: bibliographies in education. Ottawa, Canadian Teachers' Federation, 1975. 30p. ED 105607.

An unannotated list of recent books, articles, theses, and dissertations.

2158. The Changing middle school: the best of ERIC. ERIC Clearinghouse on Educational Management, 1975. 5p. ED 114 905.

Annotates 14 articles and documents from RIE and CIJE.

2159. The Middle school: an organizational alternative. Austin, Texas Information Service, 1973. 41p. ED 084225 (MF)

Two selected ERIC bibliographies are included as well as an ERIC list of curriculum guides for the middle school, ages 10 to 13. Not annotated.

2160. The Middle school: a selected bibliography. University Park, PA, Pennsylvania School Study Council, 1967. 12p. ED 021315.

Contains 142 entries on the topic, plus 48 other references on related innovations. Some are annotated.

2161. Selected references: the middle school and junior high. Indianapolis, Indiana State Department of Public Instruction, 1978. 34p. ED 165335.

Includes books, articles, and pamphlets on the philosophy and rationale, the school plant, administration, teaching staff, curriculum, and guidance services.

2162. Benish, Jean. A Comprehensive middle school bibliography. Charleston, West Virginia State Department of Education, 1977. 185p. ED 165320.

Includes books, articles, pamphlets, ERIC documents, dissertations, theses, bulletins, and newsletters arranged under 13 topics that cover all aspects of the middle school concept. Not annotated.

2163. Bick, Lowell W. New concepts in design of middle schools. 1975. 27p. ED 109798 (MF)

Annotates 17 books and articles on building design.

MIGRANT EDUCATION

2164. Heathman, James E. Migrant education: a selected bibliography. ERIC Clearinghouse on Rural Education and Small Schools, 1969. 70p. ED 028011.

Nearly all of the 100 publications are in the ERIC system, and all are annotated. At least eight suuplements have been issued to append to this initial list. Each of them contains 100 or more entries and date through 1978. They are numbered: ED 040002, 055706, 075162, 087599, 101909, 139549, and 151109.

2165. Bibliography for migrant education programs. Washington, DC, Educational Systems Corporation, 1968. 114p. ED 030 052.

Annotates multimedia entries, and includes items on Puerto Ricans. It was designed to help consultants and project directors for migrant and seasonal farm worker programs under the Office of Economic Opportunity.

2166. Rugh, Patricia A. and Marlene L. Scardamalia. Learn-

ing problems of the migrant child: annotated bibliography.
Lewisburg, PA, Bucknell University, 1967. 15p. ED 036380.

Includes over 50 entries dating from 1957.

2167. Karr, Ken. A Selected bibliography concerning the education of Mexican-American migrant children. San Luis Obispo,
California State Polytechnic College, Education Department,
1969. 12p. ED 028014.

Includes 146 partially annotated citations, mostly dating
from the 1960's.

2168. An Annotated bibliography of migrant related materials.
Boca Raton, Florida Atlantic University, 1969. 143p. ED 030
523.

The 1000 entries cover health and occupational guidance,
and include many curriculum materials.

2169. Potts, Alfred M. Knowing and educating the disadvantaged: an annotated bibliography. Alamosa, CO, Adams State
College, 1965. 462p. ED 012189.

Includes a wide range of topics for migrant education and
the education of the economically disadvantaged.

2170. Selected references on migrant children's education.
National Committee on the Education of the Migrant Child, 1965.
4p. ED 020809.

Lists 23 references dating from 1954 with the emphasis on
educational programs at the state and local levels.

2171. Resources in migrant education. Geneseo, State University of New York, Migrant Center, 1978. 25p. ED 162800.

Annotates 206 publications including New York State Bureau of Migrant Education reports, and National Farmworker
Information Clearinghouse reports.

2172. Price, Daniel O. Rural-urban migration and poverty: a
synthesis of research findings with a look at the literature.
Austin, TX, Tracor, Inc., 1971. 325p. ED 114236.

This annotated bibliography contains 1139 articles, papers,
dissertations, and pamphlets. A topical index is included.

2173. A Teacher and teacher aide guide for programs for the
education of migrant children. Austin, Texas Education Agency,
1970. 33p. ED 049872.

Includes publications on philosophy, instructional programs, planning and preparation, nonverbal communication,
parent education, and the use of consultants.

2174. Migrant adult basic education project: annotated bibli-

ography. Albany, New York State Education Department, 1978.
70p. ED 164211 (MF)

Cites 397 high-interest, low-vocabulary materials and
teacher resource books for literacy instruction for migrant adults. Includes language arts, reading, math, social studies, survival skills, and consumer economics.

2175. Tuttle, Lester E. and Dennis A. Hooker. An Annotated
bibliography of migrant related materials. Third ed. Boca
Raton, Florida Atlantic University, 1969. 123p. ED 032171.

Instructional and reference materials are included in the
800 entries.

MILITARY SCIENCE

2176. Alger, John I. Antoine-Henri Jomini: a bibliographical
survey. West Point, NY, Military Academy Library, 1975. 46p.
ED 156117 (MF)

The writings of Jomini influenced military thought during
the 19th century. This review provides an accurate history
of his known published works. Titles and annotations are
in French with notes in English. Entries date from 1805.

2177. Aimone, Alan C. Bibliography of military history: a
selected and annotated history of reference sources. Third ed.
West Point, NY, Military Academy Library, 1978. 86p. ED 163
932 (MF)

This multimedia list includes order of battles, lineages,
statistics, guidebooks, customs, decorations, flags, in-
signias of ordinance, planes, ships, and vehicles.

2178. Montemerlo, Melvin D. and Michael E. Tennyson. Instructional systems development: conceptual analysis and comprehensive bibliography. Orlando, FL, Naval Training Equipment Center, 1976. 278p. ED 121356.

About 4000 entries were compiled as a first step in assessing the state of the art of the systems approach to military training. It is divided into 18 general sections.

MINNESOTA

2179. Bibliography of Minnesota materials. Revised ed. St.
Paul, Minnesota State Department of Education, 1977. 71p. ED
160478.

Briefly annotates 500 items for elementary and secondary
levels. Includes books, maps, calendars, films, filmstrips,
audiotapes, resource lists, and field trips.

MINORITY GROUPS   See also   ETHNIC GROUPS

2180. Schlee, Phillip. MRDAC resource library annotated bibliography. Manhattan, Kan., Midwest Race Desegregation Assistance Center, 1979. 42p. ED 184529.

   Includes 131 multimedia materials on minority groups, racial discrimination, and segregation. Use levels are indicated.

2181. Vivolo, Robert. ERIC references on urban and minority
education. New York, Columbia University, Institute for Urban
and Minority Education, 1977. 13p. ED 143720.

   Recent ERIC documents are listed on subjects such as bilingual education, school integration, education of specific minority groups, and problems of inner city schools.

2182. Schrader, Jerry G. and Marion Kent. Education of minorities and the disadvantaged: a partial annotated bibliography.
Madison, University of Wisconsin, Center for the Study of Minorities and the Disadvantaged, 1978. 328p. ED 152945.

   Entries are selected from the ERIC data system dating from
   1963, and cover such topics as academic achievement, admission criteria, achievement tests, affirmative action,
   bilingual education, compensatory education, curriculum
   development, financial support, and open enrollment.

2183. Red, White, and Black (and Brown and Yellow): minorities in America: a bibliography. Briarcliff Manor, NY, Com-
bined Paperback Exhibit, Inc., 1970. 32p. ED 039283.

   Lists about 600 books, art reproductions, films, filmstrips, and records for general reading purposes or classroom use. Most include aspects of history, sociology, and
   culture. Not annotated.

2184. Jayatilleke, Raja. The Law, the courts, and minority
group education. ERIC Clearinghouse on the Urban Disadvantaged,
1976. 41p. ED 128497.

   This annotated ERIC bibliography dates from 1970 to 1976.
   Covers educational legislation, school attendance legislation, integration litigation, and affirmative action.

2185. Jablonsky, Adelaide. Curriculum and instruction for
minority groups: an annotated bibliography of doctoral dissertations. ERIC Clearinghouse on the Urban Disadvantaged, 1975.
120p. ED 110587.

   Includes 79 entries dating from 1965 through 1973 on social studies, Black studies, math, science, music, art,
   drama, health, physical education, foreign languages, tutoring, individualized instruction, and vocational education.

2186. Jablonsky, Adelaide. <u>Social and psychological studies</u>
<u>of minority children and youth: an annotated bibliography of</u>
<u>doctoral dissertations</u>. ERIC Clearinghouse on the Urban Dis-
advantaged, 1975. 253p. ED 110589.

   Includes 182 entries dating from 1965 through 1973.

2187. Jablonsky, Adelaide. <u>Special programs and their effects</u>
<u>on minority children and youth: an annotated bibliography of</u>
<u>doctoral dissertations</u>. ERIC Clearinghouse on the Urban Dis-
advantaged, 1975. 130p. ED 109266.

   Covers Head Start, Follow Through, and other preschool and
   primary programs, and family and community influence,
   school achievement, and other studies. Entries date from
   1965.

2188. <u>Minority groups/disadvantaged youth: a selective bibli-</u>
<u>ography</u>. Arlington, VA, Council for Exceptional Children,
1972. 32p. ED 074685.

   Contains 100 abstracts of publications dating from 1960.

2189. Barabas, Jean. <u>The Assessment of minority groups: an</u>
<u>annotated bibliography</u>. ERIC Clearinghouse on the Urban Dis-
advantaged, 1973. 85p. ED 083325.

   Covers methods, effects, prediction, and reliability of
   tests, plus test construction and performance differences.

MOHAWKS

2190. Garrow, Larry. <u>A Selected bibliography of the Mohawk</u>
<u>people</u>. Minneapolis, National Indian Education Association,
1974. 53p. ED 093514.

   Annotates and arranges by subject 343 citations dating
   from 1762. The multimedia listing also includes materials
   on the Iroquois.

2191. Garrow, Larry. <u>Mohawk people, past and present: a list</u>
<u>of print and visual media on Mohawk history, culture, and cur-</u>
<u>rent events</u>. Minneapolis, National Indian Education Associa-
tion, 1974. 22p. ED 093513.

   Annotates 156 entries dating from 1847 on arts and crafts,
   government, relations with whites, language, Mohawk literature, and children's books.

MONGOLISM

2192. <u>Mongolism</u>. Arlington, VA, Council for Exceptional
Children, 1971. 12p. ED 050524.

Annotates 53 research reports, conference papers, journal articles, texts, and program guides.

MORMONS

2193. Christensen, Carol W. <u>Mormons and Mormon history as reflected in US Government documents, 1830 to 1907</u>. 1977. 53p. ED 146930.

Contains over 250 annotated sources including congressional publications, census reports, legislative publications, and court cases. Arranged chronologically.

MOTIVATION

2194. Galant, Richard and Nancy J. Moncrieff. <u>Counseling for achievement motivation: relevant resources in higher education</u>. ERIC Clearinghouse on Counseling and Personnel Services, 1974. 28p. ED 105362.

Annotates 107 ERIC documents, dissertations, and articles which review techniques to increase motivation at home and at school.

2195. <u>Improving employee performance</u>. Washington, DC, Civil Service Commission, 1972. 99p. ED 079520.

References cover morale and job satisfaction, motivation and productivity, job enlargement as a motivating device, creativity and innovative behavior, and the use of incentive awards for motivation. Annotated.

MULTICULTURAL EDUCATION   See   CULTURAL EDUCATION

MUSEUMS

2196. <u>Information about information: an annotated bibliography</u>. Washington, DC, George Washington University, Center for Museum Education, 1977. 34p. ED 137143.

The topics are related to museum education and include audiences, arts in education, the community, volunteers, evaluation, funding, history, museums and schools, touring, teaching, and interpretation.

MUSIC EDUCATION

2197. Collins, Thomas C. <u>A Survey of music education materials and the compilation of an annotated bibliography</u>. 1967.

162p.   ED 020194.

Lists over 1500 entries for elementary through college
level organized into 67 categories and selected by a committee of the Music Education Research Council.

2198. Wright, Stephanie G. Music: a vehicle for teaching
certain aspects of the elementary language arts. 1977. 31p.
ED 150599.

This paper reviews books and articles on the subject, and
includes a bibliography of examples that can be used with
children.

2199. Professional and instructional music materials for exceptional children. Albany, New York State Education Department, Division for Handicapped Children, 1972. 14p.   ED 071
259.

Annotates 88 items related to music education at the elementary and secondary levels

2200. Fink, Michael. Music analysis: an annotated bibliography. Los Alamitos, CA,Southwest Regional Library for Educational Research and Development, 1972. 25p.   ED 067359.

140 books, articles, and dissertations encompass trends
in music theory and K-16 music education since the late
19th century.

2201. Teaching woodwinds. Albany, New York State Education
Department, 1976. 160p.   ED 139704.

Arranged by type of instrument: flute, oboe, clarinet,
saxophone, and bassoon. Each section has an annotated bibliography in addition to the general bibliography of 59
entries.

2202. Words, sounds, and pictures about music: a multimedia
resource listing for teachers of music in grades K-6. Albany,
New York State Education Department, 1970. 225p.   ED 045686
(MF)

The annotated resources are for use by students or by
teachers.

2203. A Basic music library for schools offering undergraduate degrees in music. Washington, DC, National Association
of Schools of Music, 1967. 58p.   ED 082633.

Lists books and reference books, 25 periodical titles,
and a section of study scores.

2204. Brook, Barry S. Musicology and the computer: musicology 1966-2000: a practical program. New York, American Musi-
cological Society, 1970. 285p.   ED 081187 (MF)

Contains a bibliography of 617 entries. Not annotated.

2205. Sjolund, James and Warren Burton. Music of minority groups. Olympia, Washington State Office of Public Instruction, 1969. 11p. ED 042842 (MF)

This is the first in a series on minority group music. It is on the Black American and dates from 1926 including in its bibliography children's books, reference books, films and filmstrips, recordings and anthologies.

MUSIC THERAPY

2206. Music the healer: a bibliography. Olympia, Washington State Library, 1970. 35p. ED 046204.

An unannotated list of journal material dealing with music as a therapeutic tool. Categories include children, geriatrics, handicapped, emotionally disturbed, mentally retarded, music in prisons, psychotherapy, and music therapists.

MYTHOLOGY

2207. Smith, Ron. A Guide to post-classical works of art, literature, and music based on myths of the Greeks and Romans. 1975. 40p. ED 112438 (MF)

650 works are listed without annotations.

NARCOTICS See DRUGS

NATURAL HISTORY

2208. Loggins, Donald. Bibliography on the natural history of an urban area: New York City. Monticello, IL, Council of Planning Librarians, 1976. 15p. ED 137072 (MF)

Relates to the environment, biology, botany, zoology, and natural resources of the city. Most of the unannotated entries were published in the previous 20 years.

NATURAL RESOURCES

2209. Hoadley, Irene B. Natural resources bibliography. Columbus, Ohio State University Libraries, 1970. 254p. ED 040 872.

This annotated list from the social scientists point of view is international in scope. Also covers human, cultural and scientific resources.

NAVAJOS

2210. Kari, James. Navajo language bibliography. Albuquerque, University of New Mexico, Navajo Reading Study, 1973.
42p. ED 127065.

The 478 references published since 1829 cover grammatical
research, dictionaries, vocabularies, taxonomies, texts,
culture, and sociolinguistic research. Not annotated.

2211. Russell, Noma. A Bibliography of selected materials
on the Navajo and Zuni Indians. Gallup, NM, Gallup-McKinley
County Schools, 1974. 88p. ED 124367 (MF)

Fiction is included in the 896 citations on the two tribes.
The unannotated multimedia list dates from 1928.

2212. Navajo and Zuni: a bibliography of selected materials.
Gallup, NM, Gallup-McKinley County Schools, 1975. 166p. ED
165921.

This expanded edition of the previous entry includes 1500
items. Not annotated.

2213. Correll, J. Lee. Navajo bibliography with subject index. Revised ed. Window Rock, AZ, Navajo Tribe, 1969. 398p.
ED 050862.

Includes 5640 references published since 1638, and covers
historical, ethnographic, biographic, technical, popular,
and fictional works as well as archival and congressional
materials, books, pamphlets, government documents, and
items from Navajo tribal files. Not annotated.

2214. Spolsky, Bernard. Analytical bibliography of Navajo
reading materials. Revised ed. Albuquerque, NM, Bureau of
Indian Affairs, 1970. 108p. ED 043413.

Annotates 141 items published from 1897 to 1970. The English language materials were developed to teach Navajo
children about their own culture, and the Navajo language
materials were developed as part of a literacy program
for Navajos in their native language.

NEAR EAST See MIDDLE EAST

NEEDS ASSESSMENT

2215. Needs assessment: human services bibliography series.
Washington, DC, Project Share (DHEW), 1976. 76p. ED 129959.

Includes methodologies and evaluates results of various
studies. Annotated.

2216. ERIC literature search on needs assessment. Chelmsford, Mass., Merrimack Education Center, 1974. 20p. ED 100382.

Annotates 75 documents on educational needs.

2217. Needs assessment: the best of ERIC. ERIC Clearinghouse on Educational Management, 1976. 5p. ED 125069.

Includes twelve annotations of recent documents on the needs assessment process.

NEGOTIATIONS See COLLECTIVE BARGAINING

NETHERLANDS

2218. Lagerwey, Walter. Guide to Netherlandic studies: bibliography. Grand Rapids, Mich., Calvin College, 1964. 178p. ED 010348.

On language, literature, history, and culture. Unannotated; some films are included.

NEW YORK STATE

2219. Bielinski, Stefan. Research and publications in New York State history. Albany, New York State Museum, 1977. 124p. ED 150080.

Annotated entries include books, leaflets, graduate theses, journal and magazine articles. All are history-related works which were either published, completed, or in progress during 1976.

NEWSPAPERS See also JOURNALISM

2220. Fikes, Robert. Newspaper indexes, guides, directories, and union lists. San Diego State University Library, 1978. 17p. ED 156152.

This annotated bibliography lists 52 United States and foreign items held in the libraries at San Diego State.

NONFORMAL EDUCATION

2221. Paulston, Rolland G. Research on nonformal education: an annotated bibliography of bibliographies. University of Pittsburgh, School of Education, 1972. 28p. ED 057337.

Includes 62 items on various aspects of nonformal programs.

2222. <u>Nonformal education</u>. Washington, DC, Agency for International Development, 1975. 79p. ED 132657.

This annotated bibliography lists 195 publications, several of which are ERIC documents. The focus is on definition and scope, delivery systems, and target areas.

2223. Paulston, Rolland G. <u>Non-formal education: an annotated international bibliography</u>. University of Pittsburgh, International and Development Education Program, 1972. 346p. ED 125959.

Includes 875 books, articles, papers, reports, speeches, dissertations, and bibliographies published between 1910 and 1972. Concentrates on theory and practice in developing and developed nations.

2224. Colletta, Nat J. <u>Non-formal education in anthropological perspective</u>. East Lansing, Michigan State University, Institute for International Studies in Education, 1971. 31p. ED 068428.

Annotates 120 books, articles, and government documents published since 1913. The selected anthropological materials relate to the influence of culture on the learning process.

2225. Colletta, Nat J. <u>Non-formal educational programs in different geographical areas of the world</u>. East Lansing, Michigan State University, Institute for International Studies in Education, 1971. 19p. ED 103313.

Includes 147 unannotated books, articles, and reports on programs in all areas of the world except the United States.

2226. Colletta, Nat J. <u>Selected topics in non-formal education</u>. East Lansing, Michigan State University, Institute for International Studies in Education, 1971. 17p. ED 103314.

The unannotated list deals with programs in rural reconstruction, agricultural extension, community development, media, literacy, industrial and military education, continuing education, and human resources planning.

2227. Mannan, M. A. <u>The Economic aspects of non-formal education: a selected annotated bibliography</u>. Washington, DC, Agency for International Development, 1975. 90p. ED 110709.

Includes 303 references.

NONGRADED SCHOOLS

2228. McLoughlin, William P. <u>The Nongraded school: an annotated bibliography</u>. Albany, New York State Education Department,

1967. 35p. ED 026289.

372 items include books, articles, dissertations, guides, brochures, and handbooks.

2229. Shinn, Byron M. A Bibliography with selected annotations on nongraded elementary schools. Urbana, University of Illinois, Bureau of Educational Research, 1967. 21p. ED 015 024.

The books and articles describe and evaluate nongraded school programs.

2230. Kuzsman, Francis and Teresa MacIsaac. A Teacher's guide to nongrading. Antigonish, Nova Scotia, St. Francis Xavier University, 1969. 138p. ED 053106.

The guide includes an extensive bibliography on nongraded schools. Unannotated.

2231. Nongrading: an annotated bibliography. Toronto, Ontario Institute for Studies in Education, 1970. 37p. ED 071148.

Includes books, articles, research reports, dissertations, and AV items from Canadian and US sources.

2232. Taylor, Ruth. The Nongraded school: an annotated bibliography. Toronto, Ontario Institute for Studies in Education, 1973. 47p. ED 079862.

This is an update of the previous entry and includes materials issued during 1970-1972.

2233. Alpert, Selma. The Nongraded school: an annotated bibliography. 1972. 11p. ED 072868.

Thirty recent references are grouped under the headings theoretical, practical, and research.

NONVERBAL COMMUNICATION See also COMMUNICATION

2234. Arnold, William E. Nonverbal communication: a bibliography. 1977. 102p. ED 165204.

The books, articles, and dissertations cover the following topics: body language, sensory perception, communication behavior, facial cues, empathy, deception, signaling, nonverbal marital interaction, animal language, hostility, deference and demeanor, style of dress, social values, and sex related cues.

2235. Thornton, Barbara L. Bibliography for a research of the literature in nonverbal communication and its applications as related to the study of Black American nonverbal communication. 1972. 16p. ED 070108.

Includes 230 entries dating back to 1932.

NORTH CAROLINA

2236. Advisory list of instructional media for the study of
North Carolina. Raleigh, North Carolina State Department of
Public Instruction, 1977. 31p. ED 149759.

An annotated list for K-12. ED 175413 is a 13 page supplement issued in 1978.

NORTHWEST, PACIFIC

2237. Drazan, Joseph Gerald. The Pacific Northwest: a bibli-
ography of books having self-contained indexes. Walla Walla,
WA, Whitman College, Penrose Memorial Library, 1980. 166p.
ED 191471.

Designed to supplement and augment Charles W. Smith's
Pacific Northwest checklist (3rd ed, 1950), this bibliography is a comprehensive list of books that have their
own indexes and are concerned with the Pacific Northwest
as a whole or such parts of it as Alaska, British Columbia,
Idaho, Montana, Oregon, Washington, and the Yukon. This
list cites 1244 English language titles published through
1978, and includes a subject index.

NUCLEAR ENERGY

2238. A Bibliography of basic books on atomic energy. Washington, DC, Atomic Energy Commission, 1971. 64p. ED 059896.

Annotates 60 elementary books, and 70 more classified as
advanced. ED 107519 is a 79 page update issued in 1974.

2239. Books on atomic energy for adults and children. Oak
Ridge, TN, Atomic Energy Commission, 1969. 53p. ED 042653.

Annotates over 100 books with grade levels indicated.

2240. Kuhns, Helen F. Nuclear energy for water desalting: a
bibliography. Oak Ridge, TN, Atomic Energy Commission, 1967.
34p. ED 055814.

Includes abstracts of 215 publications.

NURSING

2241. Selected bibliography on associate degree nursing pro-

grams and nursing education in junior and community colleges.
New York, National League for Nursing, 1968. 5p. ED 028264.

An unannotated list of books, articles, dissertations,
and pamphlets dating from 1951.

2242. Selected bibliography on associate degree programs in
nursing. New York, National League for Nursing, 1969. 11p.
ED 034027.

An annotated subject bibliography of 99 entries, mostly
journal articles published since 1966.

2243. Schwirian, Patricia M. Prediction of successful nursing performance. Bethesda, MD, Health Resources Administration (DHEW), Division of Nursing, 1976. 306p. ED 150444 (MF)

398 studies were reviewed for this project and are listed
in the bibliography.

2244. Hanchett, Effie S. The Problem oriented system: a literature review. Washington, DC, Public Health Service (DHEW),
1977. 190p. ED 152255.

The bibliography of 680 entries is on the nursing process
and the problem oriented medical record (POMR), including
the computerized POMR.

2245. Nurse practitioners & the expanded role of the nurse:
a bibliography. Hyattsville, MD, Health Resources Administration (DHEW), Division of Nursing, 1978. 253p. ED 164511.

Most citations date from 1970 and cover continuing education, acceptance of practitioners, patient and physician
attitudes toward practitioners, and evaluation of their
use for cost effectiveness.

2246. Research in nursing, 1955–1968. Washington, DC, Public
Health Service (DHEW), 1970. 96p. ED 066592.

Summarizes 182 projects supported by the research grants
program of the Division of Nursing.

2247. Perry, Lesley. The Nurse as a primary health care pro-
vider, and the nurse practitioner: an annotated bibliography.
Rochester, NY, Community Planning Committee on Nursing Education, 1971. 119p. ED 099572.

The final 19 pages of this study is the bibliography.

2248. Ewens, Wilma A. Bibliography of nursing monographs,
1970–1978. Washington, DC, George Washington University Medical Center, 1978. 56p. ED 181907 (MF)

An unannotated list divided into five broad subject areas.

NUTRITION

2249. A Nutrition education bibliography for teachers of all subjects and grade levels. Revised ed. Kingston, PA, Luzerne Intermediate Unit 18, 1978. 21p. ED 164967 (MF)

This 207 multimedia list is designed to help provide for nutrition education implementation into the existing curriculum.

2250. Secondary teaching materials and teacher references. Berkeley, CA, National Nutrition Education Clearinghouse, 1972. 13p. ED 063113.

An unannotated list of 100 multimedia resources.

2251. Annotated bibliography, grades K-6. Boston, Massachusetts Department of Education, Bureau of Nutrition Education and School Food Services, 1976. 26p. ED 152713.

Books, films, and filmstrips on nutrition education are annotated for elementary school use.

2252. Preschool, primary and intermediate teaching materials and teacher references. Berkeley, CA, National Nutrition Education Clearinghouse, 1972. 17p. ED 078934.

Includes three separate lists by level on nutrition education multimedia resource materials.

2253. Springer, Ninfa S. Nutrition and mental retardation: an annotated bibliography, 1964-1970. Ann Arbor, University of Michigan, Institute for the Study of Mental Retardation, 1970. 67p. ED 046019.

The journal articles included cover malnutrition and its effects, nutrient metabolism, and techniques in feeding and therapeutic nutrition for the mentally retarded.

2254. Erickson, Joan G. Nutritional disorders and the development of young children: a bibliography. ERIC Clearinghouse on Early Childhood Education, 1976. 34p. ED 129473.

The 300 references relate to mental/intellectual/cognitive development from the fetal stage through early childhood. Covers ecological studies, vitamin and mineral deficiencies, food additives, and the correlation between socioeconomic status and nutritional problems.

2255. Food and nutrition supplementary resources: a selective annotated bibliography for elementary schools, K-6. St. Paul, Minnesota State Department of Education, Child Nutrition Section, 1977. 17p. ED 142305.

Topics include folktales and fiction, exercise and weight control, plant and animal food, technology of food, food experiments, food customs, gardening, world hunger, and consumerism. The materials were selected to implement, enrich, and support elementary curricula.

OBSERVATION TECHNIQUES

2256. Abramson, Theodore and Helen Spilman. Observation instruments and methodology and their application in the classroom: an annotated bibliography. New York, City University,
Office of Teacher Education, 1971. 31p. ED 062277.

Includes 157 books, papers, and reports on the development and use of observation techniques, instruments, and
methods.

OCCUPATIONAL GUIDANCE See also GUIDANCE

2257. Tyson, Kenneth L. Resource guide to selected materials
for the vocational guidance of slow learners. 1968. 29p. ED
030921.

A multimedia bibliography that includes professional resources and classroom materials in addition to listing
other bibliographies.

2258. Galant, Richard and Nancy J. Moncrieff. Vocational
counseling of disadvantaged students. ERIC Clearinghouse on
Counseling and Personnel Services, 1974. 14p. ED 105367.

Includes 76 ERIC documents and dissertations on guidance
practices at the elementary and secondary school level.

2259. Introducing children to the world of work. Salem, Oregon State Department of Education, 1971(?) 20p. ED 052377.

Lists 101 annotated resources for elementary levels.

OCCUPATIONAL INFORMATION See also CAREER EDUCATION

2260. McCracken, David. Work experience for broadening occupational offerings: a selected bibliography for use in program
development. Columbus, Ohio State University, Center for Vocational and Technical Education, 1969. 14p. ED 034062.

The 40 entries cover the need, descriptions, and evaluations of work experience programs. Unannotated.

2261. Professional and managerial occupations. Milwaukee,
Curative Workshop Research Department, 1964. 109p. ED 027552.

An unannotated list of literature other than books.

2262. Overs, Robert P. and Deutsch, Elizabeth C. Sociological studies of occupations: a bibliography. Washington, DC,
Manpower Administration (DOL), 1965. 91p. ED 015333.

Includes 777 books, articles, and graduate theses published since 1896 which present information from a personal and social point of view.

2263. Tarrier, Randolph. Sources of occupational information. Columbus, Ohio State Department of Education, 1968. 82p. ED 024810.

Annotated and arranged by source.

2264. Jacobsen, R. Brooke. The Family and occupational choice: an annotated bibliography. Eugene, University of Oregon, 1966. 45p. ED 020411.

Includes 68 entries by author dating from 1935.

2265. Kovlesky, William P. and George W. Ohlendorf. Bibliography of literature on status projections of youth: occupational aspirations and expectations. Texas A & M University, 1967. 58p. ED 020380.

The 621 unannotated citations date from 1938 and include articles, bulletins, reports, and unpublished material.

2266. Cooperative diversified occupations: job information resource guide for vocational educators: a cross-reference of jobs and resources. Millersville (Pennsylvania) State College, 1977. 113p. ED 155378.

Contains 132 publications with descriptive information on specific jobs. Annotated.

2267. Slick, James M. Career bibliography: a guide to free and inexpensive occupational information. University Park, Pennsylvania State University, Career Development and Placement Center, 1977. 176p. ED 140065.

Identifies over 2000 sources of information which offer about 5000 job-related publications. 522 occupations are included in this unannotated list.

2268. Archer, Joann R. and M. Joyce Giorgia. Bibliography of the Occupational Research Division, Air Force Human Resources Laboratory. Lackland AFB, TX, 1974. 37p. ED 105200.

Includes technical reports and other publications of the Division produced since 1957. Not annotated.

2269. Guide to local occupational information. Washington, DC, Manpower Administration (DOL), 1969. 151p. ED 039340.

Developed from selective studies made by state employment services for use in designing training programs, and for counseling in public employment offices and schools.

2270. Wieckhorst, Janice. Bibliography of occupational information. Cedar Falls, University of Northern Iowa Library, 1974. 88p. ED 103763.

Includes books, articles, pamphlets, and government publications describing individual careers, job hunting techniques, and the world of work.

2271. Smith, Gerard C. Counselor's guide to manpower information: an annotated bibliography of government publications.
Washington, DC, Bureau of Labor Statistics, 1968. 105p. ED
037559 (MF)

2272. Maddox, Marion E. An Annotated bibliography for occupational surveys. Little Rock, Arkansas State Department of
Education, 1969. 23p. ED 043753.

Concerned with planning, organizing and conducting surveys
to determine training and manpower needs. The 90 entries
include articles and government publications dating from
1928 to 1969.

OCEANOLOGY

2273. Schlenker, Richard M. and Linda L. A Bibliography of
marine education bibliographies for all educational levels.
1977. 13p. ED 149952.

Briefly annotates film lists and book lists.

2274. Cohen, Maxwell. 1960-1969 cumulative index of articles
related to oceanography and limnology education in the Science
Teacher. Washington, DC, National Science Teachers Association, 1970. 13p. ED 040072 (MF)

2275. Schlenker, Richard M. Recent articles, activities, and
other documents in the marine education field. 1977. 11p.
ED 148607.

Annotates 35 items from the previous two years for students at the elementary and secondary school levels.

2276. Schlenker, Richard M. Education and the world ocean:
a partial bibliography for marine educators. Orono, University of Maine, Sea Grant Program, 1978. 168p. ED 161674.

This is meant to be a cross-disciplinary bibliography,
and includes several marine science curriculum guides.

2277. Schlenker, Richard M. A Partial bibliography for pre-
college marine science educators. Orono, University of Maine,
Sea Grant Program, 1976. 101p. ED 137130.

Includes career education, methods, conference reports,
curriculum, texts, and equipment. Annotated.

2278. Schlenker, Richard M. Precollege marine science education 1973 through 1976. 1976. 39p. ED 129581.
This literature search yeilded 67 articles. Unannotated.

2279. Schlenker, Richard M. Marine science education materials and their usefulness. 1976. 54p. ED 128208.

Includes brief annotations of 289 items for elementary and secondary school levels.

2280. Reading in marine science: a partially annotated bibliography for young readers, nonprofessionals, and teachers. Corvallis, Oregon State University, Department of Oceanography, 1968. 28p. ED 046743.

Contains about 300 entries in the following categories: history, exploration, biological, chemical, geological, and physical oceanography.

2281. Elardi, James. Ocean careers: a survey of opportunities and requirements. Albany, New York Sea Grant Institute, 1975. 34p. ED 155017.

Includes an annotated bibliography of both print materials and films.

OHIO

2282. Rees, Louise F. Survey of libraries in Northwest Ohio and related workshops: holdings of Ohio titles by subject heading. Bowling Green State University, 1974. 256p. ED 101671.

This is a union list of materials about Ohio held by the public libraries of five counties. Not annotated; arranged under 99 subject terms.

OIL See PETROLEUM INDUSTRY

OPEN EDUCATION See also NONGRADED SCHOOLS

2283. Shaffer, Earl R. Open education: a CUNY union list. City University of New York, 1977. 30p. ED 145853.

An unannotated list of 188 items published since 1964. Materials on the British primary schools are included.

2284. Dirr, Peter J. Open education: a bibliography. 1974. 8p. ED 105676.

An unannotated list of 91 books, articles, and ERIC documents dating from 1965.

2285. Hawkridge, David G. The Open university: a selected bibliography. Milton Keynes, England, Open University Press, 1975. 58p. ED 114040 (MF)

Includes over 130 books, articles, and dissertations.

2286. Howard, Norma K. Open education: an abstract bibliography. ERIC Clearinghouse on Early Childhood Education, 1973.
43p. ED 075099.

The focus of this list of ERIC documents is on preschool,
kindergarten, and the elementary levels. ED 096019 is a
95 page supplement with 172 annotated entries.

2287. Doob, Heather S. Summary of research on open education.
Washington, DC, Educational Research Service, 1974. 47p. ED
087093 (MF)

Contains 201 entries for published and unpublished materials on the development of open education in the United
States and Great Britain.

2288. Tallboy, Felicity. Open education: review of the literature and selected annotated bibliography. Montreal, McGill
University, Faculty of Education, 1973. 110p. ED 097962.

Also covers the open area school and team teaching in the
list of books, articles, conference papers, and doctoral
dissertations.

2289. Cockburn, Ilze. The Open school: an annotated bibliography. Toronto, Ontario Institute for Studies in Education,
1973. 41p. ED 082292.

Part I is on open education; part II is on the open plan
school.

2290. McDiarmid, Mary S. An Annotated bibliography on the
British infant school. 1972. 13p. ED 072866.

Some of the 56 books are annotated; the 35 articles are
not.

2291. Allen, Harvey A. The British are coming: an annotated
bibliography on open education. 1972. 10p. ED 083255.

The books and articles included represent a small sample
of the available literature.

2292. SEF annotated bibliography on informal education. Toronto, Metropolitan School Board, Study of Educational Facilities, 1972. 24p. ED 063619.

On British and American systems; covers methodology, criticism, teacher education, research and evaluation, and
other bibliographies.

2293. Stevens, Jody L. Differentiated staffing: nongraded,
continuous progress, open concept schools: a comprehensive
bibliography. Houston, TX, University of Houston, Bureau of
Educational Research and Services, 1972. 65p. ED 066811.

Includes 4000 unannotated sources.

OPEN.PLAN SCHOOLS

2294. McGrady, Donna S. Open space elementary schools: an
annotated bibliography. Terre Haute, Indiana State University,
Curriculum Research and Development Center, 1973. 24p. ED
072544.

   Attempts to bring together most of what has been written
   since 1968.

2295. Open area schools: bibliographies in education. Ottawa,
Canadian Teachers Federation, 1971. 12p. ED 128890.

   An unannotated list of books, articles, and theses published between 1965 and 1970.

2296. A Short annotated list of information on open area
schools in Canada. Toronto, Canadian Education Association,
1973. 9p. ED 128891.

   Includes 50 publications issued between 1970 and 1973.
   The journal articles are not annotated.

OPERATIONS RESEARCH

2297. Neroda, Edward W. Operations research: an elementary
guide to the literature. Monticello, IL, Council of Planning
Librarians, 1973. 23p. ED 105624.

   An annotated survey of bibliographic sources.

2298. Case, C. Marston and Stephen C. Clark. A Bibliographic
guide to operations analysis of education. Washington, DC,
National Center for Educational Statistics, 1967. 22p. ED
025851.

   An unannotated list of 155 books, articles and other studies on systems analysis and program planning in education.

OPINION RESEARCH

2299. Bibliography of publications, 1941-1960. Chicago, National Opinion Research Center, 1969. 100p. ED 031741.

   Subjects include health and welfare, occupations and professions, political affairs, education, community affairs,
   and religion. Methodology and theory are included, too.
   ED 039572 is a 123 page supplement covering the years 1961-
   1969.

ORGANIZATIONAL CHANGE See also CHANGE

2300. Baldridge, J. Victor. Organizational change processes:
a bibliography with commentary. Stanford University, Center
for Research and Development in Teaching, 1970. 19p. ED 036
908.

On organizations in general. Not annotated.

OUTDOOR EDUCATION See also RECREATION

2301. Fulton, Eulyne and Charlotte Ann Loomis. Outdoor education: a selected bibliography. ERIC Clearinghouse on Rural
Education and Small Schools, 1970. 78p. ED 037285.

Includes 134 instructional materials, teaching guides, and
other ERIC documents on outdoor education, recreation, and
conservation education published between 1952 and 1969.
Annual supplements to this initial volume are: ED 055702
(264p.), ED 073903 (174p.), ED 087582 (136p.), ED 101907
(126p.), ED 136971 (111p.), ED 149884 (118p.), and ED 164
168 (54p.).

2302. Swan, Malcolm. Research in outdoor education: summaries of doctoral studies. Washington, DC, AAHPER Publications,
1978. 134p. ED 161608 (MF)

This second volume contains 121 dissertations, and supplements the 1973 edition which is available as ED 088636.

2303. Selected bibliography for outdoor education. Washington, DC, American Association for Health, Physical Education,
and Recreation, 1967. ED 022603.

The 61 books and articles also cover camping, conservation,
and recreation. The unannotated entries date from 1940.

2304. Kuester, Dorothy L. Bibliography of materials selected
for children's use in an outdoor education program. Washington, DC, American Association for Health, Physical Education,
and Recreation, 1967. 10p. ED 039958.

Annotates 94 entries under 14 subject headings. All listings are for books which have been published since 1918.

2305. Bibliography of studies and research in camping and outdoor education, and supplement. Martinsville, IN, American
Camping Association, 1964. 87p. ED 035499.

Presents over 1000 partially annotated items published
between 1909 and 1964.

2306. Suggested bibliography for outdoor education and camping. Branchville, New Jersey State School of Conservation,
1967. 5p. ED 035492.

Subjects include conservation education, aquatics, riding,

rifle, archery, arts and crafts, nature study, Indian lore, and therapeutic camping.

2307. Outdoor education research: a reference catalog. Washington, DC, Department of the Interior, Bureau of Outdoor Recreation, 1970. 120p. ED 045351 (MF)

Describes 371 current or completed projects related to environmental quality.

2308. Johnson, Hugh A. Outdoor recreation: publications and articles by the Economic Research Service, 1962-1969. Washington, DC, Department of Agriculture, Economic Research Service, 1970. 10p. ED 045246.

Includes 101 articles, reports, and speeches. Unannotated.

2309. Rillo, Thomas J. A Bibliography of articles pertaining to school camping and outdoor education. 1965. 19p. ED 042 544.

Includes 408 unannotated entries dating from 1928.

OUTWARD BOUND

2310. Shore, Arnold. Outward Bound: a reference volume. Greenwich, CT, Outward Bound, Inc., 1977. 594p. ED 165926.

Section IV is an extensive bibliography of related research organized under three headings: education, psychology, and corrections. The annotated bibliography includes well over 1000 citations dating from the early 1900's to 1977.

PARAPROFESSIONALS See also TEACHER AIDES

2311. Michael, Elizabeth B. The Use of educational paraprofessionals: a selected annotated bibliography. ERIC Clearinghouse on Early Childhood Education, 1972. 16p. ED 059785.

Lists over 100 entries.

2312. Grambs, Jean D. Paraprofessionals and teacher aides: an annotated bibliography. ERIC Clearinghouse on Teacher Education, 1970. 45p. ED 036482.

The 167 entries focus on job training and career education.

2313. Feldman, Richard. An Annotated bibliography on auxiliary personnel in education. New York, Bank Street College of Education, 1969. 100p. ED 025487.

Surveys the literature since 1960 on paraprofessional

school personnel and their training. The 283 entries cover preschool through secondary levels.

2314. Wolters, Virginia and Colin Cameron. Paraprofessionals, subprofessionals, and nonprofessionals: a selected annotated bibliography. Madison, University of Wisconsin, Institute for Research on Poverty, 1969. 22p. ED 038514.

The 157 citations date from 1962 and include articles, reports of conferences, and demonstration projects.

2315. Galant, Richard and Nancy J. Moncrieff. Support personnel. ERIC Clearinghouse on Counseling and Personnel Services, 1974. 21p. ED 105368.

Includes 78 articles, dissertations, and ERIC documents which focus on programs that have trained and utilized paraprofessionals, K-16. Annotated.

2316. Delworth, Ursula. Paraprofessionals in psychology: an annotated bibliography. 1971. 22p. ED 051533.

This paper was presented at the Rocky Mountain Psychological Association annual convention and lists over 30 books and articles.

2317. Paraprofessional school personnel: bibliographies in education. Ottawa, Canadian Teachers Federation, 1970. 33p. ED 048102.

Includes volunteers and nonprofessionals. The bibliography lists 438 books, articles, pamphlets, dissertations, and parts of books. Not annotated. ED 085352 is a 25 page supplement issued in 1973 that contains 142 books and papers, 146 articles, and eleven theses.

PARENT EDUCATION

2318. Kremer, Barbara. Parent education: abstract bibliography. ERIC Clearinghouse on Early Childhood Education, 1971. 39p. ED 056782.

The articles and documents from the ERIC system suggest specific activities for stimulating children at home. Included in addition are sections on running a day care center, and studies concerned with the Appalachian Educational Laboratory projects.

2319. Parent education/parent counseling: a selective bibliography. Arlington, VA, Council for Exceptional Children, 1972. 32p. ED 069070.

Includes 98 abstracts of documents published since 1952 primarily for parents of handicapped children.

2320. Parent education. Council for Exceptional Children,

1971. 20p. ED 053513.

These 92 annotated references are for or about parents of gifted and handicapped children.

2321. Parent, home, and family life education. ERIC Clearinghouse on Adult Education, 1970. 87p. ED 039376.

This annotated bibliography contains 149 entries on family life, home economics, roles, and needs; 56 of the items concentrate on parent child relationships and the teaching role of parents.

2322. The Role of parents as teachers. Philadelphia, Recruitment Leadership and Training Institute, 1975. 100p. ED 121 482.

2323. Television for effective parenthood: literature search and existing materials assessment. Charleston, WV, Appalachia Educational Laboratory, 1976. 242p. ED 132973.

Annotates 89 items including audiovisual materials.

2324. Parent involvement in school programs: bibliographies in education. Ottawa, Canadian Teachers Federation, 1971. 33p. ED 054270.

An unannotated list of books, articles, theses, and ERIC documents from the previous five years.

2325. Parenting in 1975: a listing from PMIC. Austin, TX, Southwest Educational Development Laboratory, 1975. 175p. ED 110156.

For parents and those working with parents, topics include child abuse, discipline, group relations, health and safety, sex education, and social and emotional development. Not annotated; audiovisuals are included. ED 130783 is a 169 page continuing bibliography titled Parenting in 1976.

PARENT SCHOOL RELATIONSHIP

2326. Howard, Norma K. Working with parents in the primary school. ERIC Clearinghouse on Early Childhood Education, 1974. 62p. ED 094883.

This annotated bibliography of ERIC documents covers parent participation, parent-teacher cooperation, and parent involvement in the decision-making process.

2327. Parent evaluation of schools: the best of ERIC. ERIC Clearinghouse on Educational Management, 1978. 5p. ED 150674.

Annotates eleven documents and articles which deal with ways for parents to evaluate schools and how the results can be utilized to improve school quality.

2328. Greenwald, Meryl A. <u>Parents and schools: an annotated</u> <u>bibliography</u>. New York, City University, Center for Advanced Study in Education, 1977. 29p. ED 156980.

Covers parents' knowledge of schools, communication between parents and schools, parent and community involvement in school decision-making and planning, and legal issues.

2329. Galant, Richard and Nancy J. Moncrieff. <u>Parent coun-</u> <u>seling</u>. ERIC Clearinghouse on Counseling and Personnel Ser- vices, 1974. 23p. ED 105364.

Annotates 87 documents, articles, and dissertations which cover ways in which the school can involve parents in the education and social development of the child.

PAROLE

2330. Dyer, Robert L. and James H. Harris. <u>A Partially anno-</u> <u>tated bibliography on prediction of parole success and delin-</u> <u>quency</u>. Fort Knox, KY, Human Resources Research Organization, 1972. 187p. ED 113635.

A literature review with particular reference to military prisoners.

PEACE CORPS

2331. Wight, William L. <u>Guidelines for Peace Corps cross-</u> <u>cultural training: annotated bibliography</u>. Estes Park, CO, Center for Research and Education, 1970. 117p. ED 059940.

Contains over 100 entries for trainers and trainees.

PENNSYLVANIA

2332. Weight, Glenn S. <u>Pennsylvania in autobiography</u>. Har- risburg, Pennsylvania State Library, 1967. 25p. ED 016665.

Includes 228 autobiographies by Pennsylvanians which were published prior to 1960. It does not include fictional ac- counts, diaries, journals or brief sketches from collec- tive biographies.

2333. Bodnar, John E. <u>Ethnic history in Pennsylvania: a sel-</u> <u>ected bibliography</u>. Harrisburg, Pennsylvania State Historical and Museum Commission, 1974. 50p. ED 098111.

Books and articles published between 1835 and 1974 are listed for high school and college students. The unanno- tated list refers to 23 separate ethnic groups.

PERCEPTUAL DEVELOPMENT

2334. Annotated bibliography on perceptual-motor development. Washington, DC, American Association for Health, Physical Education, and Recreation, 1973. 122p. ED 075399 (MF)

   Covers auditory perception, body image and movement, depth and distance perception, and feedback and regulation of movement behavior among other topics. Includes films.

2335. Perceptual-motor development. Arlington, VA, Council for Exceptional Children, 1971. 23p. ED 052574.

   Annotates 96 articles, texts, and research reports.

2336. Bibliography on cognition. Harvard University, 1966. 15p. ED 011316.

   Includes 120 unannotated references on cognitive development, perceptual skills, logical thinking, and concept formation and problem solving.

PERFORMANCE BASED EDUCATION

2337. Walonick, David. Competency-based education: a selected annotated bibliography. Minneapolis, St. Mary's Junior College, 1978. 31p. ED 151058.

   The 29 entries date from 1974 and deal with testing, instruction, student learning evaluation, curriculum development, and unit mastery learning.

2338. Chase, Cheryl. Competency based education: an information package. Denver, Colorado State Department of Education, 1977. 40p. ED 146709.

   The bibliography in section 2 is compiled from the ERIC data system.

2339. Competency based education: the best of ERIC. ERIC Clearinghouse on Educational Management, 1977. 5p. ED 133836

   Includes 12 annotated reports from Oregon, California, and Ohio.

2340. Cox, Helen. Competency based education: a bibliography. University of Wisconsin Library, 1976. 24p. ED 126048.

   The unannotated bibliography lists materials published from 1970 to 1976.

2341. Competency based education: an annotated bibliography. Charleston, West Virginia State Department of Education, 1974. 52p. ED 112244.

144 entries are grouped into these areas: agricultural education, allied health occupations education, business and office education, home economics education, and trade, industrial, and technical education. The purpose was to train vocational education teachers in competency based curriculum models.

2342. Competency based education resource guide. Redwood City, CA, San Mateo County Superintendent of Schools, 1977. 22p. ED 139822.

The focus is on California and its Hart Bill which establishes high school graduation standards of proficiency in basic skills. Emphasis in this list is on reading, math, and language arts.

2343. Pitman, John C. Bibliography of CBTE-CBC materials available through the state departments of education in the 50 states. Durham, NH, New England Program in Teacher Education, 1974. 17p. ED 142553.

An unannotated list of documents on competency based teacher education, and competency based certification.

2344. Competency based teacher education and evaluation: a selective bibliography. Reston, VA, Council for Exceptional Children, 1976. 24p. ED 129003.

Annotates 85 documents and journal articles published from 1955 to 1975.

PERSONALITY

2345. Personality. ERIC Clearinghouse on Early Childhood Education, 1968. 29p. ED 024475.

An annotated bibliography of 15 entries on basic temperamental and motivational traits, attitude, and ego functioning.

PERSONNEL EVALUATION

2346. Wallace, Richard E. Personnel evaluation: a bibliography of articles, audiovisual materials, and books. 1978. 79p. ED 152306.

Prepared for a library personnel evaluation institute. Most entries date from 1967 to 1977.

2347. Thiemann, Francis G. Selected bibliography on succession in complex organizations. Eugene, University of Oregon, 1967. 9p. ED 017062.

Lists 84 books, articles and dissertations dating from 1948.

2348. The Library: planning, organizing and evaluating training programs: personnel bibliography. Washington, DC, Civil
Service Commission, 1966. 91p. ED 029202.

Annotated.

PETROLEUM INDUSTRY

2349. Donavan, Patricia. A Bibliography of pro- and anti-di-
vestiture arguments. Chicago, Standard Oil Company of Indiana,
1977. 7p. ED 145476.

On divestiture by major oil companies; the list includes
government documents, hearings, Congressional Record sections, and information from the American Petroleum Institute, in addition to books, articles, and newspaper accounts.

PHILIPPINES

2350. Summaries of studies in agricultural education in the
Philippines, 1930-1959: an annotated bibliography. Laguna,
University of the Philippines, College of Agriculture, 1968.
49p. ED 049365.

This bibliography of research includes 54 entries. ED 049
366 is a 59 page bibliography on the same topic covering
the years 1960-1968. It has 77 entries.

PHILOSOPHY

2351. Smith, Marilyn K. A Bibliography of philosophy. West
Point, NY, Military Academy Library, 1972. 77p. ED 156119.

The unannotated bibliography emphasizes Western philosophical thought.

2352. Hannaford, William E. A Short bibliography of philosophy books for public libraries. 1977. 22p. ED 149764.

The annotated list covers the entire history of philosophy
and represents major philosophers and movements.

PHYSICAL EDUCATION See also RECREATION

2353. Advisory list of instructional media for health, safety,
and physical education. Raleigh, North Carolina State Department of Public Instruction, 1977. 45p. ED 149748.

An annotated multimedia list for all K-12 levels.

2354. Physical education and recreation. Arlington, VA,
Council for Exceptional Children, 1971. 19p. ED 051593.

Relates to handicapped and gifted children, and contains
73 annotated research reports, conference papers, texts,
journal articles, and program guides.

2355. Physical education and leisure time: a selective bibliography. Reston, VA, Council for Exceptional Children, 1973.
23p. ED 090705.

Includes 95 abstracts of publications dating from 1962 to
1973 for handicapped children and youth. Covers camping,
art projects, and the Special Olympics, among other topics.

2356. Eshelby, Don. Physical education: a bibliography of
selected documents from ERIC. Grand Forks, University of North
Dakota, 1970. 16p. ED 043405.

An unannotated list of 100 ERIC documents dated 1967 to
1969.

2357. Physical education and recreation: a selective bibliography. Arlington, VA, Council for Exceptional Children, 1972.
23p. ED 065960.

Annotates 70 publications for handicapped children dating
from 1965 to 1971.

2358. Rizzitello, Theresa G. An Annotated bibliography on
movement education. Washington, DC, American Alliance for
Health, Physical Education, and Recreation, 1977. 52p. ED
144936 (MF)

Includes 173 entries on theory and practice under the
headings of basic movement, dance/drama, gymnastics, and
sports.

2359. Movement education. ERIC Clearinghouse on Teacher Education, 1976. 25p. ED 120105.

An annotated bibliography of general and theoretical publications, and programs and guides. Views movement education as a singular program, and as offered in conjunction
with physical education.

2360. McGuire, Raymond and Pat Mueller. Bibliography of references for intramural and recreational sports. 1975. 101p.
ED 129825.

Includes 1596 articles that relate to the administration
of sports programs. Unannotated; indexed and arranged by
32 subject terms.

2361. A Selected bibliography for programing physical education and recreational activities for the mentally retarded.
Washington, DC, National Education Association, 1966. 19p.

ED 011426.

Includes 93 annotated references for teachers, parents, and counselors. The books, pamphlets, and articles date from 1937 to 1966.

2362. Fonger, Sandra. The Compilation of a selected bibliography of relevant theses and research in international comparative physical education and sport in the USA and Canada. 1972. 14p. ED 115611.

Contains 187 unannotated entries and is divided into master's theses, doctoral dissertations, and miscellaneous.

2363. Mutimer, Brian. Canadian graduating essays, theses, and dissertations relating to the history and philosophy of sport, physical education, and recreation. 1975. 15p. ED 126092.

Also includes biographies and other bibliographies. Not annotated.

2364. Buell, Charles. Bibliography on physical education. Philadelphia, Association for Education of the Visually Handicapped, 1974. 8p. ED 100092.

Annotates 75 books, articles, films, and videotapes for use in programing activities for the visually impaired. The publications are available in Braille and large type.

2365. Social sciences of sport. ERIC Clearinghouse on Teacher Education, 1976. 71p. ED 128293.

Covers sport history, psychology, sociology, and philosophy in the annotated entries drawn from RIE and CIJE.

2366. Truckey, Clarence A. Physical education facilities. 1975. 29p. ED 109803 (MF)

Annotates 21 books and articles dealing with school athletic facilities.

2367. Smoll, Frank L. Areas and facilities for physical education and recreation: an interpretive bibliography. ERIC Clearinghouse on Educational Facilities, 1970. 100p. ED 035 266.

Annotates publications from the ERIC system on indoor and outdoor facilities.

PLANNING   See also   EDUCATIONAL PLANNING   and   URBAN PLANNING

2368. Mazziotti, Donald F. Advocacy planning: a selected bibliography. Monticello, IL, Council of Planning Librarians, 1972. 16p. ED 106966.

The unannotated list of articles dates from 1965 and relates to urban and regional planning in social work, architecture, geography, and law.

2369. Booher, David E. Citizen participation in planning:
selected interdisciplinary bibliography. Monticello, IL, Council of Planning Librarians, 1975. 22p. ED 105628.

The unannotated list is compiled from planning literature,
economics, political science, psychology, public administration, and sociology.

2370. Miller, Donald H. Planning evaluation: a selective
bibliography on benefit-cost, goal achievement, and related
analytical methods. Monticello, IL, Council of Planning Librarians, 1975. 39p. ED 122347.

Unannotated; contains a number of British planning documents.

2371. Williams, Hugh E. General systems theory, systems anal-
ysis, and regional planning: an introductory bibliography.
Monticello, IL, Council of Planning Librarians, 1970. 33p.
ED 101429.

2372. Ray, William W. A Bibliography of dissertations, theses, and thesis alternatives in planning, 1965-1970. Monticello, IL, Council of Planning Librarians, 1971. 74p. ED
106952.

Contains an unannotated list of 1095 research topics completed in this field in the six year period.

2373. Catanese, Anthony J. Systemic planning: an annotated
bibliography and literature guide. Monticello, IL, Council
of Planning Librarians, 1969. 15p. ED 101420.

Provides a general guide to the literature of systems analysis, cybernetics, decision theory, and work programing.

POETRY

2374. Gidden, Nancy Ann. Multimedia bibliography: the search.
1974. 16p. ED 098581.

Annotates 42 items which may be used in teaching contemporary poetry.

POLICE

2375. Miller, Martin G. A Bibliography on police and community relations. East Lansing, Michigan State University, National Center on Police and Community Relations, 1966. 109p.

Includes police administration, police image, impact of civil rights movement, minorities and race relations, social change, the role of the news media, prejudice, violence, juvenile delinquency and youth problems, and children's books on the life and job of police officers.

2376. A Bibliography on police administration. Evanston, IL, Northwestern University, 1968. 31p. ED 055170.

An annotated bibliography compiled by the transportation library.

POLISH STUDIES

2377. Stambler, Moses. A Student's bibliography of current, accessible, English language materials on Polish education. New Haven, Southern Connecticut State College, 1977. 16p. ED 149023.

An unannotated list of 14 books and 128 articles.

2378. Galeski, Boguslaw. Rural sociology in Poland. Warsaw, Polish Academy of Sciences, 1976. 117p. ED 135578 (MF)

Contains a bibliography of 38 items which are dated 1957 to 1975.

2379. Wozniak, Albin S. Guide and bibliography for integrating Polish studies into the public school curriculum. 1976. 36p. ED 156795.

The unannotated list is on the Polish-Americans, their cultural and social roots, their history, literature, and arts, and ethnic identity.

POLLUTION See also AIR POLLUTION etc.

2380. Kiraldi, Louis and Janet L. Burk. Pollution: a selected bibliography of US Government publications on air, water, and land pollution, 1965-1970. Kalamazoo, Western Michigan University, Institute of Public Affairs, 1971. 80p. ED 058 080.

POLITICAL SCIENCE

2381. Hedstrom, Judith E. Selective bibliography in political science resources. ERIC Clearinghouse for Social Studies/ Social Science Education, 1977. 42p. ED 150031.

An annotated bibliography of materials that date from 1968 to 1977 for grades 7 to 12.

2382. Dubois, Carol J. and Mona Buckley. Politics in the age
of homespun: a bibliography. Oneonta, State University of New
York, 1968. 47p. ED 018320.

    Annotates 25 references on the New York political scene
    around the 1840's.

2383. Nagle, Richard W. Films for history and political science. Fourth ed. Pennsylvania State University, Audiovisual
Services, 1976. 123p. ED 134510.

    Lists 1200 films on many aspects of the broad subjects of
    history and political science. Unannotated; most were pro-
    duced within the previous 15 years.

2384. Beaubien, Anne K. American politics and government:
selected basic reference works. Ann Arbor, University of Michigan Libraries, 1977. 22p. ED 153628.

    An annotated guide designed to aid graduate students.

2385. Thornton, Barbara C. A Partially annotated political
communication bibliography. 1974. 63p. ED 111755.

    On facets of the election process and interaction between
    political parties and the voter. Includes books, articles,
    pamphlets, dissertations, and government publications da-
    ting from 1960.

2386. Heikoff, Joseph M. Urban politics: selected readings
related to planning. Monticello, IL, Council of Planning Librarians, 1971. 18p. ED 101433.

    Lists books and articles dealing with the structures and
    processes of local politics in the US, especially as they
    relate to urban planning. Unannotated.

2387. Reynolds, William M. Political reform: ERIC first analysis, 1974-1975: national high school debate resolutions
and resources on political reform: a reading list. ERIC Clearinghouse on Reading and Communication Skills, 1974. 81p. ED
096700.

    Includes 186 annotated books, articles, and government
    documents.

2388. ERIC abstracts: a collection of ERIC document resumes
on politics and power structure: influence on education. Washington, DC, American Association of School Administrators,
1969. 24p. ED 036891.

    Contains 31 annotated entries.

2389. Melrood, Margot. A Bibliography on decentralization.
Milwaukee, University of Wisconsin, Institute of Governmental
Affairs, 1970. 35p. ED 042846.

    This annotated bibliography deals with decentralization

as a structural feature of the local political system, examines the process of local citizen participation, and focuses on community control in the decentralization of education and the formation of community corporations.

POPULATION EDUCATION

2390. Carey, George W. and Julie Schwartzberg. Teaching population geography. New York, Teachers College Press, 1969. 134p. ED 065290.

Includes an annotated bibliography of over 300 references.

2391. Burleson, Noel-David. The Time is now: population education: a commentary and annotated bibliography. Harvard University, Graduate School of Education, 1969. 36p. ED 054020.

Contains 72 reports, papers, and articles, plus teacher's guides and model curricula.

2392. Marshall, Judith. Bibliography of population education. Chapel Hill, University of North Carolina Population Center, 1971. 13p. ED 062192.

Lists 115 items including books, pamphlets, papers, articles, case studies, dissertations, and bibliographies. Not annotated.

2393. Fowler, Kathryn M. Population: the human dilemma: an NSTA environmental materials guide. Washington, DC, National Science Teachers Association, 1977. 99p. ED 176984 (MF)

Annotates over 100 popular books on the subject for K-12.

2394. Burleson, David. The Twenty-one essential readings in population education. Chapel Hill, University of North Carolina Population Center, 1970. 12p. ED 050004.

Covers national and international family planning education in the annotated textbooks, articles, and government documents.

2395. Fowler, Kathryn M. Population growth: the human dilemma. Washington, DC, National Science Teachers Association, 1977. 93p. ED 160528 (MF)

Annotates over 100 books about population growth for students in K-12 and their teachers.

2396. Population and family education teaching materials: a bibliography. Bangkok, Thailand, UNESCO, 1973. 74p. ED 087 674.

Concentrates on family life and sex education in this recent list of annotated publications.

2397. Leighton, Andrew J. Population education: a selective annotated bibliography for United States schools. Revised ed. New York, Population Council, 1976. 17p. ED 125978.

Includes general works, opinionated works about population problems, and information about the United Nations World Population Conference.

2398. Smith, Suzanne M. An Annotated bibliography of small town research. Madison, University of Wisconsin, Department of Sociology, 1970. 142p. ED 042562.

Emphasis is on writings with a demographic or ecological perspective, and covers rural-urban differences and the urbanization process. The books, articles, and bulletins date from 1900.

2399. Casey, Ann D. General reference sources for accessing Census Bureau data: an annotated bibliography. Washington, DC, Bureau of the Census, 1979. 15p. ED 175479.

Describes catalogs, guides, and indexes to facilitate use of census documents.

PORTUGUESE

2400. Hoge, Henry W. Portuguese language teaching materials. Milwaukee, University of Wisconsin, Language and Area Center for Latin America, 1966. 15p. ED 033326.

Annotates 70 items.

2401. Hoge, Henry W. A Selective bibliography of Luso-Brazil-ian linguistics. Madison, University of Wisconsin, 1968. 87p. ED 050646.

Lists 1100 unannotated references that were compiled in connection with a research project titled "The syntax of Contemporary Brazilian Portuguese".

2402. Bibliography of instructional materials for the teach-ing of Portuguese. Sacramento, California State Department of Education, 1976. 63p. ED 134006.

An annotated multimedia bibliography containing bilingual and bicultural materials.

PORTUGUESE AMERICANS

2403. Pap, Leo. The Portuguese in the United States: a bib-liography. Staten Island, NY, Center for Migration Studies, Inc., 1976. 89p. ED 139727 (MF)

Contains 800 books and articles including some fiction.

Most entries are in English or Portuguese, but a few are
in German, French, or Spanish.

POVERTY

2404. O'Neill, Mara. Poverty related topics found in dissertations: a bibliography. Madison, University of Wisconsin,
Institute for Research on Poverty, 1976. 77p. ED 135540.

   Cites 322 doctoral dissertations written between 1970 and
   1974. Annotated.

2405. Thompson, Ernestine H. Poverty: an annotated bibliography for adult basic education teachers. Athens, University of
Georgia, College of Education, 1970. 72p. ED 058535.

   Contains 205 entries on the psychology of poverty, its
   dynamics, urbanization, and abolition.

2406. Maida, Peter R. and John L. McCoy. The Poor: a selected bibliography. Washington, DC, Department of Agriculture,
Economic Research Service, 1969. 59p. ED 029740.

   Arranged by subjects, this unannotated bibliography contains 652 books and articles published between 1945 and
   1968 dealing with all aspects of poverty. Includes an author index.

2407. Elkin, Anna. A Guide to current resources for antipov-
erty programs: a selected bibliography. New York, Federation
Employment and Guidance Service, 1966(?) 56p. ED 011028.

   An unannotated list on the economic, training, and vocational problems of the disadvantaged.

2408. Oster, Sharon. A Review of the definition and measurement of poverty. Washington, DC, Department of Health, Education, and Welfare, 1976. 712p. ED 141424.

   Part I is a summary review, and Part II is the annotated
   bibliography compiled from an exhaustive literature search
   in the fields of economics, sociology, and political science.

2409. Poverty, rural poverty, and minority groups living in
rural poverty: an annotated bibliography. Lexington, KY, Institute for Rural America, 1969. 165p. ED 041679.

   Includes over 1000 publications, the majority of which
   were. published in the 1960's. Major classifications are
   income, health, housing, education, and sociological characteristics. Separate sections pertain to Appalachia, migrants, American Indians, Chicanos, and Blacks.

2410. Cameron, Colin. Statistics of poverty: a bibliography.

Madison, University of Wisconsin, Institute for Research on
Poverty, 1977.   176p.   ED 154066 (MF)

2411.   Cameron, Colin.   Attitudes of the poor and attitudes
toward the poor: an annotated bibliography.   Madison, University of Wisconsin, Institute for Research on Poverty, 1975.
181p.   ED 110532.

Includes books, articles, dissertations, and accounts from
newspapers dating from 1965 to 1973. ED 148967 is a 163
page supplement issued in 1977.

2412.   Rural poverty: an annotated and referenced bibliography.
1966.   47p.   ED 032163.

About 200 books and articles published through 1966 are
listed. Covers demographic aspects of poverty, education
and youth, social structure and status, values, economic
aspects, and poverty programs and policies.

2413.   Fowler, Kathryn M.   Hunger: the world food crisis: an
NSTA environmental materials guide.   Washington, DC, National
Science Teachers Association, 1977.   65p.   ED 142394.

The annotated bibliography is for teachers and students,
preschool through grade 12. Films are included.

PREGNANCY

2414.   Baizerman, Michael.   Pregnant adolescents: a review
of literature with abstracts, 1960-1970.   University of Pittsburgh, 1971.   81p.   ED 065800.

Mostly articles are included. They demonstrate the size
and kind of problem, and not with evaluative research.

2415.   Galant, Richard and Nancy J. Moncrieff.   Counseling
the pregnant teenager.   ERIC Clearinghouse on Counseling and
Personnel Services, 1974.   12p.   ED 105359.

This annotated bibliography reviews 42 documents on several school system's attempts to provide medical, psychological, and educational support for this group in order
to prevent their dropping out of school.

PRESCHOOL EDUCATION   See also   CHILDHOOD EDUCATION and INFANTS

2416.   Preschool and early childhood education.   Arlington, VA,
Council for Exceptional Children, 1969.   29p.   ED 036024.

Includes 108 abstracts of program descriptions, curriculum
information, and research reports primarily concerning
handicapped children.

2417. Strully, Cynthia F. <u>Test analyses: screening and ver-</u>
<u>ification instruments for preschool children</u>. Harrisburg,
Pennsylvania State Department of Education, 1977. 290p. ED
135856.

   Developed to enable personnel to determine the appropri-
   ateness of a test in relation to a child. No endorsements
   of the 68 preschool tests are made. Annotated.

2418. <u>Preschool education: a bibliography</u>. New York, Yeshiva
University, 1967. 11p. ED 012293.

   The more than 130 unannotated citations relate to the disadvantaged child, and include books, articles, speeches,
   dissertations, program reports, and proposals.

2419. <u>Preschool education: an annotated bibliography, 1971-</u>
<u>1977</u>. Strasbourg, France, Council of Europe, Committee for
General and Technical Education, 1978. 13p. ED 154936.

   Consists of reports on the Council of Europe symposiums
   on preschool education, and summaries of papers related
   to the symposiums.

2420. Scott, Deborah. <u>The Junior kindergarten: an annotated</u>
<u>bibliography</u>. Toronto, Ontario Institute for Studies in Edu-
cation, 1974. 31p. ED 093485.

   Canadian material is included as much as possible. The
   junior kindergarten does not deal with the question of
   day care centers or private nursery schools.

2421. Lutsky, Judi. <u>Head Start and Follow Through, 1972-1974</u>:
<u>an ERIC abstract bibliography</u>. ERIC Clearinghouse on Early
Childhood Education, 1974. 61p. ED 097131.

   Cites 123 ERIC documents with evaluations and program descriptions.

PRESIDENTS (COLLEGE)

2422. Jackson, Malan. <u>The College president: a selected bib-</u>
<u>liography</u>. 1969. 16p. ED 034531.

   This unannotated list covers all aspects of the president's
   job, and includes community college presidents.

2423. Roueche, John E. and Natalie Rumanzeff. <u>The College</u>
<u>president: a bibliography</u>. Los Angeles, UCLA, 1968. 16p. ED
019966.

   Part I contains 70 references concerning the college presidency, and part II contains 24 references specifically
   related to the junior and community college presidency.
   Partially annotated.

PRINCE EDWARD ISLAND

2424. MacDonald, Allan F. and Harold J. O'Connell. Selected annotated bibliography of recent research on rural life on Prince Edward Island. Charlottetown, Prince Edward Island University, 1972. 75p. ED 080262.

Annotates 80 research reports dating from 1960.

PRINCIPALS

2425. Wilson, Alfred P. The Principalship: a selected bibliography. Revised ed. 1978. 39p. ED 147997 (MF)

Lists over 400 books and articles on the elementary and secondary public school principal and the functions of the office. Not annotated.

2426. Dohan, Margaret. Principals and vice-principals. Ottawa, Canadian Teachers Federation, 1978. 54p. ED 168163 (MF)

This bibliography lists materials published since 1975, and includes 215 books, 437 articles, and six theses. Not annotated. ED 114995 is a 33 page bibliography of the same title for items published prior to 1975. It has over 200 entries.

2427. The Assistant principal: a collection of ERIC document resumes. Washington, DC, National Association of Secondary School Principals, 1973. 18p. ED 073563.

Includes 42 annotated entries on the role of the assistant principal in relation to the curriculum, discipline, management, scheduling, staff relations, and student activities.

2428. Inservice education for administrators: a collection of ERIC document resumes. Washington, DC, National Association of Elementary School Principals, 1974. 16p. ED 089391.

This annotated bibliography is designed to improve the skills of elementary and secondary school principals as instructional leaders.

PRIVATE SCHOOLS

2429. Zeidner, Nancy. Private elementary and secondary education: a bibliography of selected publications, 1950-1974. Washington, DC, Council for American Private Education, 1976. 104p. ED 140498.

Includes church-related schools, religious instruction,

and alternative and free schools. 866 entries are annotated.

PROBLEM SOLVING

2430. Problem solving and concept formation: annotated listing of national and international curricular projects at the
early childhood level. Inglewood, CA, Southwest Regional Educational Laboratory, 1968. 17p. ED 029685.

Contains 50 citations.

2431. Cantwell, Zita M. Annotated bibliography of literature
related to adult problem solving. New York, City University,
Brooklyn College, 1977. 446p. ED 159429.

Includes models and specific applications, personal correlates, environmental correlates, evaluation and measurement, and materials for developing problem solving skills
and strategies.

2432. Klausmeier, Herbert J. Concept learning and problem
solving: a bibliography, 1950-1964. Madison, University of
Wisconsin, Research and Development Center, 1965. 87p. ED
010201.

Includes articles selected from 46 relevant journals.

PROGRAM EVALUATION

2433. Evaluation bibliography. Atlanta, Georgia State Department of Education, Educational Testing Service, 1979. 16p.
ED 181567.

Contains 47 annotated references for planning and implementing a comprehensive evaluation of a school program.

2434. ERIC abstracts: a collection of ERIC document resumes
on program evaluation. Washington, DC, American Association
of School Administrators, 1973. 28p. ED 091800.

Provides specific instruments and procedures for evaluation of educational programs. Several bibliographies and
documents on theoretical concerns of program evaluation
are also included.

2435. Ewy, Robert W. and Cheryl Chase. Program and product
evaluation: an information packet. Denver, Colorado State Department of Education, 1977. 31p. ED 147934.

Section II is an annotated bibliography of evaluation materials. Some are basic to any evaluation activity, and
others relate specifically to education.

2436. Barlow, Diana L. and Geoffrey Y. Cornog. A Bibliography in program evaluation. Springfield, IL, Sangamon State University, Public Sector Program Evaluation Center, 1974. 171p. ED 104920.

Lists over 500 books, articles, and other monographs related to the topic for government and education. Includes methodology, case studies for community action, personnel training, planning, and vocational rehabilitation.

2437. Hiemstra, Roger P. Program planning and evaluation: a bibliography. Lincoln, University of Nebraska, Department of Adult and Continuing Education, 1971. 22p. ED 056285.

Cites 229 books and journal articles. Not annotated.

PROGRAMMED INSTRUCTION

2438. Cayton, Paul W. Graduated reading list for users of programmed instruction. Elmore, Ala., Rehabilitation Research Foundation, Draper Correctional Center, 1971. 18p. ED 059440.

Includes 38 annotated entries on theory, management, motivation, and evaluation.

2439. Programmed instruction in business and industry. ERIC Clearinghouse on Adult Education, 1970. 47p. ED 035789.

Contains 97 annotated entries dating from 1960, and includes program descriptions and research and evaluation.

2440. Programmed instruction: a selective bibliography. Arlington, VA, Council for Exceptional Children, 1972. 23p. ED 074687.

Includes 70 abstracts of documents dated 1962 to 1972; many are related specifically to the handicapped.

2441. Roberts, A. Hood. Selected bibliography in programmed instruction. Washington, DC, Center for Applied Linguistics, 1966. 24p. ED 010878.

Annotates books, articles, documents, and unpublished papers from the period 1960-1966.

2442. Bjerstedt, Ake. Programmed instruction: a selective bibliographic guide. Malmo, Sweden, School of Education, 1966. 23p. ED 130658.

The briefly annotated entries include films and filmstrips and cover theory, research, and production techniques.

PSYCHOLOGY

2443. Teaching of psychology in the elementary school: research studies, 1964-1971. Washington, DC, American Psychological Association, 1971. 10p. ED 052074.

Lists 24 entries on teaching psychology, and in a separate bibliography lists 115 references on teaching behavioral sciences.

2444. Bryson, Carolyn Q. and Joseph N. Hingtgen. Early childhood psychosis: infantile autism, childhood schizophrenia, and related disorders: an annotated bibliography, 1964 to 1969. Indianapolis, University of Indiana Medical Center, 1972. 135p. ED 067804.

Contains 424 books, articles, conference papers, and research reports which pertain to theory, research, and treatment.

2445. Carroll, John B. Bibliography of selected publications and miscellaneous papers. 1968. 23p. ED 022182.

Lists over 200 writings by Carroll dating from 1938 in the areas of educational psychology, programmed instruction, psycholinguistics, reading, and aptitude testing.

2446. Beaubien, Anne K. Psychology: selected basic reference works. Ann Arbor, University of Michigan Libraries, 1977. 36p. ED 154818.

Designed as an annotated library guide for graduate students.

2447. Pedrini, D. T. and Bonnie C. Fixation: a bibliography. 1972. 4p. ED 076898.

Entries date from the middle 1930's.

2448. Pedrini, D. T. and Bonnie C. Projection: a bibliography. 1972. 12p. ED 076897.

The unannotated entries date from the late 1920's.

2449. Pedrini, D. T. and Bonnie C. Denial: a bibliography. 1972. 5p. ED 076922.

The unannotated entries date from the late 1920's.

2450. Pedrini, D. T. and Bonnie C. Rationalization: a bibliography. 1972. 4p. ED 076920.

2451. Pedrini, D. T. and Bonnie C. Repression: a bibliography. 1972. 12p. ED 076921.

2452. Pedrini, D. T. and Bonnie C. Regression: a bibliography. 1974. 10p. ED 089166.

The unannotated entries date from the middle 1920's.

2453. Pedrini, D. T. and Bonnie C. <u>Defense mechanisms: dis-</u>
<u>cussions and bibliographies</u>. 1973. 86p. ED 084344.

The unannotated list covers denial, displacement, substi-
tution, sublimation, fixation, identification, introjec-
tion, incorporation, internalization, intellectualization,
obsessive ideation, compulsion, projection, rationalization, reaction formation, regression, and repression.

2454. Pedrini, D. T. and Bonnie C. <u>Defense mechanisms: a</u>
<u>bibliography</u>. Omaha, University of Nebraska, 1967. 8p. ED
067578.

2455. Pedrini, D. T. and Bonnie C. <u>Displacement, substitu-</u>
<u>tion, sublimation: a bibliography</u>. Omaha, University of Neb-
raska, 1972. 7p. ED 067579.

The unannotated entries date from the middle 1930's.

2456. Pedrini, D. T. and Bonnie C. <u>Identification, introjec-</u>
<u>tion, incorporation, internalization: a bibliography</u>. Omaha,
University of Nebraska, 1967. 15p. ED 067580.

These unannotated entries on defense mechanisms date from
the 1920's.

2457. Pedrini, D. T. and Bonnie C. <u>Reaction formation: a</u>
<u>bibliography</u>. Omaha, University of Nebraska, 1965. 3p. ED
067581.

2458. Pedrini, D. T. and Bonnie C. <u>Intellectualization, ob-</u>
<u>sessive ideation, compulsion: a bibliography</u>. 1972. 4p. ED
065822.

2459. Ysseldyke, James E. and Herschel Pickholtz. <u>Doctoral</u>
<u>dissertations in school psychology, 1967-1973</u>. 1973. 56p.
ED 096800.

An unannotated list of 645 dissertations.

2460. Chovan, William L. <u>Perspectives on school psychology</u>:
<u>selected readings and bibliography, 1960-1970</u>. Cullowhee, NC,
Western Carolina University, 1970. 20p. ED 102487.

Includes books, articles, pamphlets, and bulletins from
various state departments of education.

2461. Taylor, Thomas C. <u>Bibliography of publications related</u>
<u>to the bio-rhythm theory</u>. 1976. 10p. ED 138241.

An unannotated list of 113 sources dating from 1904. Includes scientific papers, journal articles, and newspaper
accounts.

2462. Witkin, Herman A. <u>Field-dependence-independence and</u>
<u>psychological differentiation: a bibliography through 1972</u>.
Princeton, NJ, Educational Testing Service, 1973. 248p. ED
087790.

Contains 1508 conceptual papers and research of an empirical nature. The references date from 1948. ED 103459 is a 115 page supplement published in 1974 which contains 392 entries. ED 144946 is a second supplement of 126 pages issued in 1976, and ED 163029 is a third supplement of 125 pages issued in 1978.

PUBLIC FINANCE

2463. An Annotated bibliography of benefits and costs in the public sector. Philadelphia, Research for Better Schools, Inc, 1968. 254p. ED 026744.

Lists 2700 books, articles, and pamphlets from all over the world on public expenditure decision making. Not annotated, but subdivided into 33 categories followed by an author index.

PUBLIC RELATIONS

2464. ERIC abstracts: a collection of ERIC document resumes on public relations in education. Washington, DC, American Association of School Administrators, 1969. 36p. ED 036890.

Covers school-community relations and human services.

2465. Public relations programs: the best of ERIC. ERIC Clearinghouse on Educational Management, 1978. 5p. ED 151 895.

Annotates eleven articles and documents from the ERIC collection.

PUBLISHING

2466. Penchansky, Mimi. Publishing: alternatives and economics. New York, City University Library Association, 1974. 23p. ED 110057.

An annotated bibliography on small publishers, underground presses, book distribution, little magazines, feminist publishing, university presses, and copyright.

PUERTO RICO AND PUERTO RICANS

2467. Zirkel, Perry A. A Bibliography of materials in English and Spanish relating to Puerto Rican students. Hartford, Connecticut State Department of Education, 1971. 51p. ED 057142.

This multimedia bibliography is concerned with improving the educational opportunities for Puerto Rican students.

2468. Bourne, Dorothy D. and James R. Bibliography. 1966. 10p. ED 019333 (MF)

A partially annotated list of materials on socioeconomic change in Puerto Rican communities, primarily rural.

2469. Cordasco, Frank M. and Leonard Covello. Studies of Puerto Rican children in American schools: a preliminary bibliography. New York, Puerto Rico Commonwealth, 1967. 25p. ED 021910.

Many of the unannotated entries are written in Spanish.

2470. Dossick, Jesse J. Doctoral research on Puerto Rico and Puerto Ricans. 1967. 34p. ED 020215.

An unannotated list of dissertations written since 1900. About one-third of them are related to the field of education.

2471. Jablonsky, Adelaide. The Education of Puerto Rican children and youth: an annotated bibliography of doctoral dissertations. ERIC Clearinghouse on the Urban Disadvantaged, 1974. 39p. ED 094054.

Includes comparative studies with other ethnic groups.

2472. Wall, Muriel. Audiovisual aids to enrich the curriculum for the Puerto Rican child in the elementary grades. New York, City University, Hunter College, 1971. 33p. ED 049659.

Annotates over 60 records and tapes, plus additional lists of appropriate films and filmstrips.

2473. Borinquen: a bilingual list of books, films, and records on the Puerto Rican experience. Third ed. New York, Public Library, 1974. 41p. ED 101036.

An unannotated list of materials in Spanish and English selected by a staff committee of the NYPL.

2474. Bobson, Sarah. The Education of Puerto Ricans on the mainland: an annotated bibliography. ERIC Clearinghouse on the Urban Disadvantaged, 1975. 90p. ED 110586.

The 442 documents include general information, and teaching and resource materials.

2475. Estrada, Josephine. Puerto Rican resource units. Albany, New York State Education Department, 1976. 89p. ED 128505.

This annotated bibliography was developed for use in migrant education programs, but its units can serve as a resource for use in bilingual, social studies, or cross-cultural programs at the elementary and secondary levels.

2476. Herrera, Diane. *Puerto Ricans in the United States: a review of the literature.* Austin, TX, Dissemination Center for Bilingual Bicultural Education, 1973. 400p. ED 108488.

Some of the 2155 entries are annotated, and part I is a listing of other bibliographies. This review also includes resources on the Chicano and other minority groups.

QUESTIONNAIRES

2477. Dyer, Robert. *Questionnaire construction manual: literature survey and bibliography.* Fort Hood, TX, Army Research Institute for the Behavioral and Social Sciences, 1976. 465p. ED 147359.

Over 500 references are included in this comprehensive collection of journal articles, books, and reports in the fields of psychology, education, sociology, marketing, and the military.

RACISM

2478. *Bibliography on racism.* Rockville, MD, National Institute of Mental Health, Center for Minority Group Mental Health Programs, 1972. 199p. ED 075523.

This is an annotated bibliography on the relationship between racism and mental health.

RADIOCARBON DATING

2479. Fortine, Suellen. *Radiocarbon dating: an annotated bibliography.* 1977. 64p. ED 146931.

Includes journal articles, conference proceedings, and reports reflecting the most important and useful sources of the previous 25 years.

READING

2480. Laffey, James L. *Reports on reading and the disadvantaged - secondary level.* ERIC Clearinghouse on Reading, 1968. 85p. ED 016146.

Includes abstracts of 121 projects and reports relating to educational programs for the disadvantaged.

2481. Forinash, Melissa R. Reader development: filmstrips: an annotated bibliography. Free Library of Philadelphia, 1973. 51p. ED 083410.

   A critically evaluated collection of filmstrips for use with young adults and adults with special emphasis on the needs of the under-educated and the disadvantaged.

2482. Dyslexia. Arlington, VA, Council for Exceptional Children, 1971. 20p. ED 054579.

   Annotates 84 references to texts, articles, research reports, and teaching and program guides concerning reading difficulties.

2483. Craig, E. L. The Right to read. 1971. 17p. ED 052 916.

   Presents an overview of the work on underachievement in reading, with emphasis on the socially handicapped and related inner-city problems. The 200 unannotated entries include books, articles, conference proceedings, speech excerpts, and teacher's guides.

2484. Hahn, Christine T. Measuring attitudes toward reading: an annotated ERIC bibliography. ERIC Clearinghouse on Tests, Measurement, and Evaluation, 1977. 21p. ED 151423.

   Contains 30 items on the development and use of tests and procedures for evaluating student attitudes toward reading.

2485. Crawley, Sharon J. The Reading interests of elementary school pupils: a summary and bibliography. 1977. 9p. ED 145 416.

   Includes a 48 item unannotated bibliography.

2486. Dyer, Esther R. Children's reading interests: a chronological bibliography, 1889-1974. 1977. 17p. ED 150567.

   An unannotated list of books, articles, and dissertations on their preferences in relation to such factors as reading achievement and personality.

2487. Trela, Thaddeus M. and George J. Becker. Case studies in reading: an annotated bibliography. Newark, Del., International Reading Association, 1971. 16p. ED 076935.

   Includes descriptions of individual diagnosis and remediation of reading problems experienced by students at all levels.

2488. Johns, Jerry L. Assessing reading behavior: informal reading inventories: an annotated bibliography. Newark, Del., International Reading Association, 1977. 37p. ED 133703.

   Lists master's theses and doctoral dissertations in addition to other materials.

2489. A Banquet of books: an assortment of engrossing books for all ages and reading levels. Winnipeg, Manitoba Department of Education, 1975. 216p. ED 117681.

An annotated bibliography to assist teachers and librarians in selecting books for reluctant readers. Includes picture books, fiction, science fiction, biography, sports, science, and others.

2490. Mar, Judy. Bibliography on reading. Los Angeles, University of Southern California, Instructional Materials Center for Special Education, 1973. 58p. ED 085928.

Annotates 275 reading programs and instructional materials for handicapped and nonhandicapped children.

2491. Cotner, Susan. Leisure reading selection guide for public libraries and adult education programs. Morehead State University, Appalachian Adult Education Center, 1973. 140p. ED 087396.

Designed to aid in selecting reading materials for undereducated adults.

2492. Jablonsky, Adelaide. Reading and language arts curriculum for minority groups: an annotated bibliography of doctoral dissertations. ERIC Clearinghouse on the Urban Disadvantaged, 1975. 148p. ED 110593.

The 119 entries date from 1965, and include Black English, Black literature, and bilingualism.

2493. Fairbanks, Marilyn M. and Dorothy A. Snozek. Selected annotated bibliography relative to college reading-study skills program objectives and evaluation. 1975. 8p. ED 132562.

Includes 18 items: articles, dissertations, and ERIC documents.

2494. Reading methods and problems: a selective bibliography. Arlington, VA, Council for Exceptional Children, 1972. 32p. ED 072588.

Contains 100 abstracts dating back to 1943.

2495. Berger, Allen and James D. Peebles. Rates of comprehension: an annotated bibliography. Newark, Del., International Reading Association, 1976. 49p. ED 128761.

Covers tachistoscope and controlled pacing, paperback scanning, flexible rates of comprehension, retention of gains, perception, studying, conditioning, sex differences, and measurement. Contains 82 entries.

2496. Green, Richard T. Comprehension in reading: an annotated bibliography. Newark, Del., International Reading Association, 1971. 23p. ED 074480.

The eight sections cover cloze, critical reading, creativity, language, readability, skills, theory, and thinking.

2497. Bibliography of materials published about the Edison responsive environment learning system: the "talking typewriter". New York, Responsive Environment Corporation, 1968. 8p. ED 028648.

The annotated bibliography concerns the use of this system to aid reading skills among the disadvantaged and handicapped, and the benefits it has had on slum children, deaf children, illiterate adults, slow learners, and preschool children.

2498. Raygor, Alton and Dale E. Bennett. A Guide to high school and college reading tests. Minneapolis, University of Minnesota, 1965. 58p. ED 013702.

Includes 51 survey-type group reading tests, and briefly summarizes and reviews them for reliability, validity, and content.

2499. Farr, Roger. Measurement of reading achievement: an annotated bibliography. ERIC Clearinghouse on Reading, 1971. 96p. ED 049906 (MF)

Focuses on the assessment of reading behavior for researchers and test developers. The articles, dissertations, and conference proceedings date back to 1950.

2500. Gyarfas, Ed. Test collection bibliographies - reading tests: grades 4-6. Princeton, NJ, Educational Testing Service, 1975. 14p. ED 104908.

Annotates currently available tests to assess reading skills or to diagnose reading difficulties.

2501. Diagnostic tests in reading: an annotated bibliography. Albany, New York State Education Department, 1970. 61p. ED 073426.

2502. Wilson, Jean A. Books for you: a reading list for senior high school students. Urbana, IL, National Council of Teachers of English, 1971. 343p. ED 083595.

Over 2000 recommended titles in 45 categories. Brief commentaries are provided; author and title indexes are included.

READING INSTRUCTION

2503. Williams, Richard P. Bibliography for teaching read-

ing in the secondary school. Las Cruces, New Mexico State University, Bureau of Educational Research, 1968. 78p. ED 027
156.

The unannotated list of 955 citations is in eleven categories. The publications date from 1903.

2504. Narang, H. L. Teaching reading in the secondary school:
a bibliography. 1976. 16p. ED 132524.

Includes books, articles, and ERIC documents that cover
the content areas. Unannotated.

2505. Hill, Walter and Norma Bartin. Reading programs in secondary schools: an annotated bibliography. Newark, Del., International Reading Association, 1971. 14p. ED 071057.

The emphasis is on documents which identify trends and
patterns in the field, and concern the underlying philos-
phy, evaluation and status, and administration and organization of secondary reading programs.

2506. O'Neil, Eva. Annotated bibliography of secondary school
materials for the remediation of reading. Salem, Oregon Association for Supervision and Curriculum Development, 1973. 39p.
ED 078378 (MF)

An evaluative bibliography limited to four basic areas:
decoding, comprehension, vocabulary, and recreational
reading.

2507. Remedial reading: a mediagraphy of selected educational
recordings on the college level. Albany, State University of
New York, Center for Educational Communications, 1970. 21p.
ED 073423.

Includes 60 sets for community college level use.

2508. Ford, David and Eunice Nicholson. Adult basic reading
instruction in the United States: an annotated bibliography.
1967. 28p. ED 017832.

Contains readers and professional level publications.

2509. Brake, Rachel G. and Richard D. Elder. Language arts
tools: an annotated bibliography of materials for use in the
teaching of reading. Detroit, Wayne County Board of Education,
1967. 149p. ED 017426.

The items are listed in nine categories with reading and
interest level given.

2510. Harris, Larry A. International Reading Association
conference proceedings reports on elementary reading. ERIC
Clearinghouse on Reading, 1967. 1135p. ED 013197.

Includes the text of the important papers published each

year since 1960. 345 papers in 16 categories are presented.

2511. Summers, Edward G. <u>International Reading Association conference proceedings reports on secondary reading</u>. ERIC Clearinghouse on Reading, 1967. 612p. ED 013185.

Includes the important papers on junior and senior high school reading published each year in the proceedings since 1960.

2512. Romer, Robert D. <u>Teaching reading in the elementary school: selected references</u>. Los Angeles, City Schools, 1966. 149p. ED 018348.

Briefly annotated entries to provide educators with background knowledge on the many different aspects of elementary reading instruction.

2513. <u>Cover to cover: a literature course, grades 5 and 6</u>. National Council for Chicano Sociolinguistic Research, 1975. 100p. ED 118119 (MF)

"Cover to Cover" is a 32 program educational TV series to encourage reading for pleasure. The annotated bibliography lists all the featured and suggested books from the program series.

2514. Hutcheson, Pat Penn. <u>Language development and reading: perspectives on the linguistically different learner: an annotated bibliography</u>. Washington, DC, Manpower Administration, 1972. 138p. ED 134943.

Includes books and articles on the nature of nonstandard dialects and the way they may contribute to reading failure in the children who speak them.

2515. Narang, H. L. <u>Canadian doctoral dissertations in reading education: an annotated bibliography</u>. 1971. 29p. ED 063604.

Contains 27 entries dating back to 1928.

2516. <u>Advisory list of instructional media for reading</u>. Raleigh, North Carolina State Department of Public Instruction, 1977. 23p. ED 149754.

An annotated list for primary through senior high school grade levels. Includes books, recordings, kits, slide sets, games, films, and workbooks with recordings.

2517. Koenke, Karl. <u>A Minimal professional library in elementary reading instruction: a survey</u>. 1977. 10p. ED 151761.

Includes 118 titles selected by reading program directors to serve as a guide for starting a personal professional level library. Not annotated.

2518. Kerstiens, Gene. *Junior-community college reading/ study skills: an annotated bibliography.* Newark, Del., International Reading Association, 1970. 45p. ED 075787.

Includes books, articles, dissertations, and conference proceedings on program descriptions and evaluation, status and reaction surveys, centers and other facilities, methods and techniques, and testing.

2519. Sartain, Harry W. *Individualized reading: an annotated bibliography.* Newark, Del., International Reading Association, 1970. 18p. ED 075788.

Contains 84 entries in four categories including arguments for and against, suggestions on materials, and program descriptions.

2520. Eller, William and Judith G. Wolf. *Critical reading, a broader view: an annotated bibliography.* Newark, Del., International Reading Association, 1969. 16p. ED 076966.

Covers the process of, research on, and the teaching of critical reading.

2521. Spache, George D. *Sources of good books for poor readers: an annotated bibliography.* Newark, Del., International Reading Association, 1969. 11p. ED 080943.

Includes 70 source bibliographies.

2522. Durkin, Dolores. *Reading and the kindergarten: an annotated bibliography.* Newark, Del., International Reading Association, 1969. 9p. ED 080944.

Contains 34 items on whether or not reading should be taught in kindergarten, and if so, how the instruction should be conducted. Opposing and varying points of view are presented.

2523. Fern, Leif and Amelia Martucci. *Reading and the denied learner: an annotated bibliography.* Newark, Del., International Reading Association, 1969. 33p. ED 079692.

The role of language development and its influence on reading is the focus.

2524. Ford, David H. and Mildred A. Fitzgerald. *Contingency management and reading: an annotated bibliography.* Newark, Del., International Reading Association, 1973. 28p. ED 079 696.

2525. Laffey, James L. *Methods of reading instruction: an annotated bibliography.* ERIC Clearinghouse on Reading, 1971. 88p. ED 047930 (MF)

The list is divided into sections for elementary, secondary, and college-adult. Entries date from 1959.

2526. Slick, Myrna. Recreational reading materials for special education students. 1969. 37p. ED 046173.

An annotated list for the educable mentally retarded. This is a part of a master's degree project.

2527. Mortensen, Erik. Computer-based information search and analysis of references to the initial teaching alphabet. New York, Initial Teaching Alphabet Foundation, 1977. 267p. ED 149286.

Compiled from searches of the ERIC system, Psychological Abstracts, Exceptional Child Education Abstracts, and Language and Language Behavior Abstracts.

2528. Koenke, Karl. Reading instruction in the content area. ERIC Clearinghouse on Reading and Communication Skills, 1978. 41p. ED 149303.

An annotated bibliography for content area teachers who want to integrate reading skills instruction with their subject areas.

2529. Fay, Leo and Lee Ann Jared. Reading in the content fields: an annotated bibliography. Revised ed. Newark, Del., International Reading Association, 1975. 20p. ED 110958.

2530. Moya, Phyllis E. and Naomi Reeve. Teaching reading to the Spanish speaking pupil: an annotated bibliography. 1975. 19p. ED 111575.

Includes about 80 books and articles published since 1940.

2531. Hillerich, Robert L. Critical reading: an annotated reference list and skills chart. 1978. 12p. ED 163455.

Techniques are included in the 74 books, articles, and dissertations listed.

2532. Winkeljohann, Rosemary. A Selective bibliography of ERIC abstracts for the teacher of reading, 1966-1974. ERIC Clearinghouse on Reading and Communication Skills, 1976. ED 127597 through ED 127605.

These nine separate annotated bibliographies cover the following topics: Reading process, 280 entries (147p.), Methods in teaching reading, 190 entries (101p.), Reading readiness, 131 entries (75p.), Reading difficulties, 115 entries (66p.), Reading materials, 245 entries (120p.), Adult education, 201 entries (102p.), Tests and evaluations, 231 entries (118p.), Reading in the content area, 94 entries (51p.), and Teacher education, 109 entries (62p.). Each document has author and subject indexes.

2533. Browning, Carole L. A Selected bibliography for non-middle-class children, grades 1-3. 1974. 42p. ED 097659.

The annotated bibliography identifies reading materials
which meet the needs of the culturally disadvantaged child.

2534. Trends and practices in secondary school reading. 1970.
224p. ED 036669.

This is a companion bibliography to A. S. Artley's report
of the same title. It annotates articles, dissertations,
conference proceedings, and other materials.

2535. Fay, Leo. Organization and administration of school
reading programs: a bibliography in the reading research pro-
file series. ERIC Clearinghouse on Reading, 1971. 63p.   ED
046677.

The annotated entries date from 1950 and cover classroom
organization, special programs and services, and school
administration of programs.

2536. Harris, Larry A. and E. Marcia Kimmel. For the reading
teacher: an annotated index to "Elementary English", 1924-70.
Urbana, IL, National Council of Teachers of English, 1972.
78p. ED 066728.

The bibliography lists only those articles from the journal that might be of interest to someone in the area of
reading.

2537. Summers, Edward G. Twenty year annotated index to the
"Reading Teacher". Newark, Del., International Reading Association, 1969. 149p. ED 031608 (MF)

Includes all 816 articles from the 20 volumes organized
under 18 categories. Over half of the entries deal specifically with reading instruction, development of reading
skills, and instructional materials.

2538. Norris, Mildred W. and John H. Messerli. Sights, sounds
and senses in step with reading: fifth grade. Cedar Rapids,
Iowa, Joint County System, 1969. 40p. ED 045295.

This unannotated bibliography lists books, films, filmstrips, and records to enrich a reading program. They are
divided into easy, average, and difficult categories.

2539. Moe, Alden J. A Bibliography for word freaks. 1976.
5p. ED 123614.

This is a 41 item bibliography of word lists and reading
and writing vocabularies for children and adults. Not annotated.

2540. McKenna, Michael C. and Richard D. Robinson. An intro-
duction to the cloze procedure: an annotated bibliography.
Newark, Del., International Reading Association, 1980. 41p.
ED 184087.

The entries include background reviews, statistical and

constructional issues, the psychology of cloze, contextual phenomena, cloze as a teaching device, foreign language applications, and cloze and maze.

READING RESEARCH

2541. Boyce, Max W. A Comprehensive bibliography of the cloze procedure. 1974. 31p. ED 099830.

A 300 item unannotated bibliography prepared in Australia. It includes books, articles, papers, and dissertations. ED 127580 is a 16 page supplement of 152 entries.

2542. Riley, Pamela M. The Cloze procedure: a selected annotated bibliography. 1973. 40p. ED 106749 (MF)

Includes methodology and rationale, cloze as a measure of readability and as a teaching technique, cloze in English as a second language, and cloze in languages other than English.

2543. Annotated list of PhD dissertations in reading, 1916-1969. University of Chicago, Department of Education, 1970. 23p. ED 045307.

Annotates 72 dissertations done at the University of Chicago.

2544. Fay, Leo. Doctoral studies in reading, 1919-1960. Bloomington, Indiana University, School of Education, 1964. 90p. ED 011486.

Lists over 700 studies classified under 34 subject headings with an author index.

2545. Summers, Edward G. Recent doctoral dissertation research in reading. ERIC Clearinghouse on Reading, 1967. 221p. ED 012693.

Includes 379 studies completed since 1960 with analytical abstracts prepared by other professionals. ED 028055 is a 178 page supplement published in 1969 that contains 344 annotated entries.

2546. Narang, H. L. Research in reading education in Canada: a bibliography of master's theses and doctoral dissertations. 1971. 11p. ED 075798.

An unannotated author list.

2547. Narang, H. L. Canadian master's theses in reading education: an annotated bibliography. 1974. 78p. ED 097663.

Includes 131 entries dating from 1922 in author order with a subject index.

2548. Smith, Carl B. and Nancy Roser. Research on elementary reading: critical ind interpretive reading. Bloomington, Indiana University, 1969. 60p. ED 030779.

An annotated list of studies that date back to 1900.

2549. Miller, ChloeAnn. Research on elementary reading: interests and tastes. Bloomington, Indiana University, 1970. 129p. ED 042593.

Part I annotates studies dating from 1950 to 1969. Part II includes studies done prior to 1950.

2550. Dunn, Mary K. and James L. Laffey. Research on reading: word lists. Bloomington, Indiana University, 1969. 56p. ED 030778.

Annotates 51 studies published since 1950, and 76 others published prior to 1950.

2551. Dunn, Mary K. and Larry A. Harris. Research on elementary reading: oral reading. Bloomington, Indiana University, 1969. 82p. ED 033265.

The annotated entries date back to 1900.

2552. Dunn, Mary K. and Larry A. Harris. Research on elementary reading: word recognition. Bloomington, Indiana University, 1969. 119p. ED 028310.

The annotated entries are in two parts, 1900-1949, and 1950-1969.

2553. Trull, Ronald L. Research on elementary reading: comprehension. Bloomington, Indiana University, 1970. 142p. ED 038553.

Includes annotated studies dating back to 1900.

2554. Burton, Jane and Larry A. Harris. Research on elementary reading: reading readiness. Bloomington, Indiana University, 1969. 124p. ED 029163.

Annotates studies dating back to 1900.

2555. Summers, Edward G. An Annotated bibliography of selected research related to teaching reading in the secondary school, 1900-1960. University of Pittsburgh, School of Education, 1963. 192p. ED 010757.

Contains 1110 studies in 35 categories. ED 010758 is a 34 page supplement bringing the list up to 1964.

2556. Summers, Edward G. Published research literature in reading, 1950-1963. ERIC Clearinghouse on Reading, 1967. 398p. ED 012834.

Annotate 1913 studies. ED 013969 is a 180 page supplement

with 849 annotated entries for 1964–1966.

2557. Laffey, James L. <u>Research on reading in the content fields: mathematics, science, and social studies</u>. ERIC Clearinghouse on Reading, 1968. 128p. ED 024538.

Includes three separate annotated bibliographies.

2558. Seels, Barbara and Edgar Dale. <u>Readability and reading: an annotated bibliography</u>. Revised ed. Newark, Del., International Reading Association, 1971. 20p. ED 075789.

Contains 125 references; most are dated from 1965 to 1970.

2559. Vernon, Magdalen D. <u>Visual perception and its relation to reading: an annotated bibliography</u>. Newark, Del., International Reading Association, 1973. 19p. ED 076959.

The entries were compiled from major educational and psychological journals and cover development, ability, and sequential memory.

2560. Daly, Brian. <u>Reading while listening: an annotated bibliography of materials and research</u>. University of Leeds (England), Institute of Education, 1975. 37p. ED 146633 (MF)

Citations cover empirical studies, theoretical issues, and descriptions and assessments of methods.

2561. Fay, Leo. <u>Reading research: methodology, summaries, and application: an annotated bibliography</u>. ERIC Clearinghouse on Reading, 1971. 76p. ED 049023 (MF)

Includes dissertations, conference proceedings, journal articles, and ERIC documents. The entries date from 1950.

2562. <u>The Reading process: a selective review of the literature</u>. Baltimore, Maryland State Department of Education, Division of Research, 1975. 48p. ED 114770.

The topics for K-12 cover learning to read, the value of reading, the nature and purpose of language, and developing cognitive structure and comprehension processes.

2563. Verna, Gary. <u>Response learning, mediation, and intersensory integration: an annotated bibliography</u>. Los Alamitos, CA, Southwest Regional Laboratory for Educational Research and Development, 1971. 45p. ED 110920.

Includes 106 articles that are relevant to word identification activity.

2564. Graham, Steve and Floyd Hudson. <u>Oral reading miscues or errors: a bibliography of research</u>. Lawrence, University of Kansas, 1978. 15p. ED 159604.

Includes 154 books, articles, dissertations, federal reports, and other research projects.

2565. Pedrini, Bonnie C. and D. T. Bibliography for the prediction of college grades from reading scores. 1972. 8p. ED
068028.

An unannotated list of books, articles, and government
publications dating from the 1920's.

2566. Blachowicz, Camille. Visual literacy and reading: an
annotated bibliography. 1973. 15p. ED 126952.

Includes nonverbal communication, and explores the possible relationship between the development of visual skills
and verbal skills.

2567. Kuchenbecker, Shari Y. Component skills in the word
decoding task for the beginning reader: an annotated cross-
referenced bibliography. Los Alamitos, CA, Southwest Regional
Laboratory for Educational Research and Development, 1972.
137p. ED 106769.

Contains 233 items on auditory and visual discrimination,
integration, blending, and the cognitive processing of
information.

2568. Fairbanks, Marilyn M. A Bibliography of studies relative to the teaching of vocabulary, grades five through adult.
1975. 17p. ED 132561.

This paper, which was presented to the National Reading
Conference, annotates 47 studies.

2569. Weintraub, Samuel. Vision-visual discrimination: reading research profiles. ERIC Clearinghouse on Reading, 1973.
80p. ED 073437.

This annotated bibliography contains both opinion and research articles dealing with various aspects of vision.

2570. Reading diagnosis and remediation: a companion bibliography to Ruth Strang's monograph. ERIC Clearinghouse on Reading, 1972. 276p. ED 058019.

This bibliography contains complete citations and abstracts
for all references made by Strang in her 1968 book Reading
diagnosis and remediation published by the International
Reading Association. This list also includes pertinent literature which has appeared since then.

2571. Laffey, James L. Research on reading from "Research in
Education". Bloomington, Indiana University, 1969. 400p. ED
032453.

617 annotated entries are included from the 1967 and 1968
issues of RIE.

2572. Shepardson, Marie E. Final analysis and annotated bibliographies. Eugene, University of Oregon, Center for Educa-

tional Policy and Management, 1977.   188p.   ED 142189.

Three papers analyze available material. Each is followed by a bibliography. They are: basic skills, mathematics; basic skills, reading; and competency based education.

RECREATION

2573. Eshelby, Don. Recreation: a bibliography of selected documents from ERIC. Grand Forks, University of North Dakota, College of Education, 1970. 32p. ED 039997.

Over 200 citations are collected from the 1967-1969 issues of RIE. They are categorized by activities, facilities, finances, legislation, programs, and reading.

2574. Van der Smissen, Betty. A Bibliography of research related to recreation. 1962. 122p. ED 080484.

The 921 partially annotated citations refer only to theses and dissertations dating from the early 1920's to 1962. Camping and outdoor recreation are not included.

2575. Community recreation and community recreation/education. ERIC Clearinghouse on Teacher Education, 1977. 88p. ED 133 301.

The annotated entries were drawn from issues of RIE and CIJE.

2576. Althoff, Sally. A Selected annotated bibliography on recreation. ERIC Clearinghouse on Teacher Education, 1974. 66p. ED 090142.

The entries were compiled from a search of the ERIC system, both RIE and CIJE. Part II of this document is available as ED 090143. It is related to physical education, and was compiled by Marvin Eyler (72p.).

REDUCTION IN FORCE

2577. Reduction in force: the best of ERIC. ERIC Clearinghouse on Educational Management, 1977. 5p. ED 143101.

Most of the 13 articles and documents annotated deal with the impact of declining enrollments on school staffs.

REFERENCE BOOKS

2578. Specialist's choice: important reference works in the mid 1970's. Washington, DC, District of Columbia Library Association, 1975. 47p. ED 126887.

The entries are divided into 57 subject categories and date from 1970 to 1975.

2579. Advisory list of instructional media: reference books. Raleigh, North Carolina State Department of Public Instruction, 1977. 12p. ED 149756.

This annotated list is for K-12 school media collections.

REHABILITATION

2580. Mann, Joe and Jim Henderson. Catalog of audiovisual materials related to rehabilitation. Auburn University, Alabama Rehabilitation Media Service, 1971. 353p. ED 061511.

This classified annotated list was collected from over 200 AV catalogs.

2581. Mohler, Irvin C. and Donald F. Bowers. Publications of the rehabilitation research and training centers: a bibliography. Washington, DC, George Washington University, 1973. 236p. ED 080751.

An annotated compilation of the publications issued from the 19 centers of the Social and Rehabilitation Service (DHEW).

2582. Johnson, Carolyn and Marjorie Kravitz. Halfway houses: a selected bibliography. Germantown, MD, Aspen Systems Corporation, 1978. 46p. ED 155350.

The 72 annotated entries cover the issues in halfway house operation, evaluation, and innovations. Books, articles, films, technical reports, and government publications are listed.

2583. Rehabilitation research and demonstration grants: an annotated listing. Washington, DC, Social and Rehabilitation Service (DHEW), 1968. 243p. ED 041122.

Lists 5555 grants and projects authorized from 1955 to 1968.

2584. Jackson, Dorothy G. Research 1970: an annotated list of research and demonstration grants, 1955-1968. Washington, DC, Social and Rehabilitation Service (DHEW), 1970. 268p. ED 043762.

This document lists 1997 projects adminstered by branches of the Social and Rehabilitation Service.

2585. Sussman, Marvin B. Rehabilitation occupations for the disadvantaged and advantaged: annotated bibliography. Cleveland, Case Western Reserve University, Department of Sociology, 1971. 53p. ED 066563.

Includes books, articles, pamphlets and other publications on the use of paraprofessionals.

2586. Sussman, Marvin B. Selected references on paraprofessionalism and rehabilitation counseling: rehabilitation occupations for the disadvantaged and advantaged. Cleveland, Case Western Reserve University, Department of Sociology, 1971. 53p. ED 056268.

Annotates 118 publications.

RELIGION

2587. Johnson, Benton. Religion and occupational behavior: an annotated bibliography. Eugene, University of Oregon, Center for Research in Occupational Planning, 1966. 26p. ED 025591.

Speculative works are limited in this list of 56 publications dating from 1951.

2588. McDonald, Richard R. Glossolalia: a selected bibliography. 1975. 23p. ED 119464.

The entries date from 1964, and are drawn from behavioral and psychological literature. Dissertations are included. Not annotated.

2589. Pitts, V. Peter. Concept development and the development of the God concept in the child: a bibliography. Schenectady, NY, Character Research Press, Union College, 1977. 67p. ED 135487 (MF)

Includes 600 unannotated references on the development of children's conceptions and artistic representations of God.

RESEARCH METHODS AND CENTERS

2590. Wolcott, Harry F. Field study methods for educational researchers: a bibliography. Eugene, University of Oregon, Center for Advanced Study of Educational Administration, 1972. 19p. ED 089445.

Annotates 100 items, the majority of which are from the field of anthropology.

2591. Linking schools and state education departments to research & development agencies: analysis of literature and selected bibliography. ERIC Clearinghouse on Educational Administration, 1970. 14p. ED 043118.

The 43 entries refer to regional laboratories, the ERIC
system, and other cooperative projects.

2592. McFarland, Dalton E. Research methods in behavioral
sciences: a selected bibliography. Monticello, IL, Council
of Planning Librarians, 1974. 23p. ED 106908 (MF)

The unannotated list includes books and articles, each in
a separate section.

2593. Farr, Richard S. and Suzanne Pingree. Research utilization: an annotated bibliography. ERIC Clearinghouse on Educational Media and Technology, 1970. 72p. ED 039777.

Includes 202 books and articles.

2594. Fivars, Grace. The Critical incident technique: a bibliography. Palo Alto, CA, American Institutes for Research in
the Behavioral Sciences, 1973. 39p. ED 091501.

Over 600 studies in which applications of the technique
were used are cited in this bibliography. It covers the
areas of industry, education, health, and community service.

RESIDENCE HALLS See DORMITORIES

RESIDENTIAL SCHOOLS

2595. Brandon, George L. Research visibility: exemplary programs and residential schools. Washington, DC, American Vocational Association, 1969. 16p. ED 033245.

Includes twelve research reviews, and 22 additional references.

REVOLUTION

2596. Revolution and intervention: a bibliography for classroom use. Denver, Center for Teaching International Relations,
1970. 43p. ED 075289.

Lists over 400 books and articles dating from 1917 on aspects of international revolution for use in secondary
social studies programs.

REVOLUTIONARY WAR (US) See also COLONIAL HISTORY

2597. Gee, Thomas C. Factual literature about the American
Revolution: the intermediate grades. 1976. 8p. ED 122301.

Briefly annotates 30 books, 23 of which are about individual figures of the period.

2598. York, Grace Ann. The American Revolution, 1763-1783: selected reference works. Ann Arbor, University of Michigan Libraries, 1976. 34p. ED 154816.

For the most part American sources are annotated, but some British sources are included.

ROLE MODELS

2599. Thomas, Susan B. Modeling and imitation learning in young children: an abstract bibliography. ERIC Clearinghouse on Early Childhood Education, 1973. 76p. ED 077600.

Covers aggression, values, attitudes, and sex role behaviors. The entries are drawn drom RIE and CIJE.

RURAL DEVELOPMENT

2600. Bibliography on rural and community development. ERIC Clearinghouse on Rural Education and Small Schools, 1976. 61p. ED 135550.

Annotates 36 entries from RIE and CIJE issues dated 1973 to 1975.

2601. Rural development literature: an annotated bibliography, 1969-1975. State College, Miss., Southern Rural Development Center, 1976. 86p. ED 156407.

Over 350 entries cover fire and emergency services, housing, health care, vocational education, recreation, local government, and taxation. ED 157648 is a 47 page supplement of 150 annotated items for 1976-1977.

2602. Duncan, James A. The Role of universities in developmental programs - the land grant idea: annotated bibliography of selected readings. Madison, University of Wisconsin, Department of Agriculture and Extension Education, 1967. 18p. ED 017841.

Land grant colleges of the United States can be an example for rural development in new nations.

2603. Summers, Gene F. Rural industrial development bibliography. Madison, University of Wisconsin, Center of Applied Sociology, 1975. 23p. ED 135571.

The 186 documents relate to the impact of new industry on demographic, economic, and social dimensions of rural community life in the USA. Unannotated entries date from 1945.

2604. Selvik, Arne and Gene F. Summers. Social impacts of
nonmetro industrial growth: annotated bibliography of U.S.
case studies. State College, Miss., Southern Rural Development Center, 1977. 65p. ED 156405.

Annotates over 150 journal articles dating from 1965.

2605. Voth, Donald E. Citizen participation in rural development: a bibliography. State College, Miss., Southern Rural
Development Center, 1977. 493p. ED 156408.

Covers citizen participation in neighborhoods, community
development, poverty programs, education, and health care.
Of the 2310 citations, only 530 are annotated. Most are
from the 1960's and 1970's.

2606. Cosby, Arthur G. and G. Richard Wetherill. Resources
in evaluation for rural development: a bibliography. State
College, Miss., Southern Rural Development Center, 1977. 100p.
ED 157649.

Annotates over 500 citations; most are from the 1960's
and 1970's.

2607. Wheelock, Gerald C. and Pushpa Sapra. Educational needs
projection and rural development: a bibliography. State College, Miss., Southern Rural Development Center, 1978. 171p.
ED 158928.

Contains 739 citations for ERIC documents and doctoral
dissertations (1965-1975).

2608. Smith, Eldon D. Industrialization of rural areas: a
bibliography. State College, Miss., Southern Rural Development Center, 1976. 155p. ED 158907.

Many of the 750 entries are annotated, and date from 1960
to 1975.

2609. Documents on rural development and rural education.
Bangkok, Thailand, UNESCO, 1970. 28p. ED 069964.

Annotates 284 documents located in the UNESCO regional
office in Bangkok.

2610. Holmquist, Garth and Jack L. Hervey. Rural manpower:
an annotated bibliography. East Lansing, Michigan State University, Rural Manpower Center, 1968. 44p. ED 037265.

The 300 citations date back to 1945, and include practical
as well as theoretical research. Books, articles, speeches,
government publications, and other materials are listed.

2611. Johnson, Deborah K. and Collette Moser. Rural manpower:
a select annotation of theses and dissertations completed at
Michigan State University. 1974. 15p. ED 100571.

Migratory labor and demographics are topics in the 50 selected for inclusion.

2612. Parker, Carrie G. A Bibliography of rural development:
listings by topic. Clemson University, Department of Agricultural Economics and Rural Sociology, 1976. 85p. ED 127100.

> Covers leadership, rural-urban relationships, agriculture,
> community development, and human resource development. The
> 776 journal articles are not annotated.

2613. Hoskins, Myrna S. A Synthesis of evaluative research
literature for rural development in the southern region: a
preliminary bibliography. State College, Miss., Southern Rural Development Center, 1976. 64p. ED 129522.

> 117 of the 560 annotated references are case studies. The
> focus is on non-economic topics from the period 1950-1975.

2614. Rogers, David L. An annotated bibliography of rural
development research in the North Central region. Ames, Iowa,
North Central Regional Center for Rural Development, 1975.
233p. ED 108839 (MF)

> Annotates 475 references from the period 1967 to 1974.
> Many are publications from the Agricultural Experiment
> Stations in the area.

2615. Harrington, Clifford R. and Leslie C. Hyde. Community
resource development: a preliminary bibliography of extension-
related material in the Northeast. Ithaca, NY, Northeast Regional Center for Rural Development, 1973. 14p. ED 108773.

> Includes 103 unannotated references for the 12 states in
> the Northeastern region. The period covered is 1966-1973.

RURAL EDUCATION

2616. Wurster, Stanley R. and James Heathman. Rural education and small schools: a selected bibliography. ERIC Clearinghouse on Rural Education and Small Schools, 1969. 183p.
ED 033257.

> Over 300 publications are annotated, all of which are
> compiled from the ERIC system from 1965 to 1969.

2617. Rural education and small schools: a bibliography. ERIC
Clearinghouse on Rural Education and Small Schools, 1970-1972.
ED 055695, ED 065256, and ED 081532.

> These three documents are annual supplements to the prev-
> ious entry. Respectively, they contain 510, 423, and 275
> annotated entries.

2618. Rural education: a selected bibliography with ERIC abstracts. ERIC Clearinghouse on Rural Education and Small

Schools, 1974. 453p. ED 097186.

Includes 335 citations from RIE, and 149 from CIJE. Annual supplements through 1977 are ED 107429, ED 125808, and ED 144772. Respectively, they contain 196, 267, and 180 annotated entries.

2619. Small schools: a selected bibliography with ERIC abstracts. ERIC Clearinghouse on Rural Education and Small Schools, 1974. 43p. ED 097185.

Covers public, private, or parochial schools located in rural or urban settings. The 30 entries are taken from RIE and CIJE from the period 1967-1974. ED 107416, ED 125 807, and ED 141059 are annual supplements of 64 pages, 64 pages, and 59 pages, respectively.

2620. Kniefel, David R. and Tanya S. Annotated bibliography and descriptive summary of dissertations and theses on rurality and small schools. ERIC Clearinghouse on Rural Education and Small Schools, 1970. 51p. ED 039962.

Annotates 76 entries from Dissertation Abstracts, 1965-1969.

2621. Cushman, M. L. Selected bibliography on rural education. 1967. 7p. ED 036346.

Includes 90 books and articles dated from 1929 to 1967. Not annotated.

2622. Buser, Robert L. and William L. Humm. Problems of nonurban education: a bibliography. King of Prussia, PA, Montgomery County Schools, 1969. 5p. ED 028888.

Includes 56 articles and reports dated from 1963 to 1968. Not annotated.

2623. Edington, Everett D. and Lewis Tamblyn. Research abstracts in rural education: rural, small schools, Indian education, migrant education, Mexican American education, outdoor education. ERIC Clearinghouse on Rural Education and Small Schools, 1968. 75p. ED 025357.

Includes 94 entries published between 1959 and 1968.

2624. Bohrson, Ralph G. Bibliography: rural education and the small school. Denver, Colorado State Department of Education, 1962. 14p. ED 020047.

Contains 176 books and articles published between 1912 and 1961. Not annotated.

2625. Rural education: a select bibliography. Paris, UNESCO, 1975. 12p. ED 135534 (MF)

Some of the 120 titles listed are in French or Spanish.

Aspects of rural education in developing nations is the focus of these entries that date from 1967 to 1975.

2626. Swick, Kevin J. and Lawrence L. Henley. The Rural and small school: a comprehensive information booklet. Springfield, Illinois Local Control of Schools Association, 1975. 17p. ED 110265.

Annotates 31 books and articles on finances, program quality, staff development, community control, and facilities.

2627. Poliakoff, Lorraine. Some selected topics: part 5 of a bibliographic series on meeting special educational needs. ERIC Clearinghouse on Teacher Education, 1970. 21p. ED 044 385.

Almost half of these 69 ERIC documents deal with rural education and migrant concerns.

2628. Clarenbach, Kathryn F. Educational needs of rural women and girls. Washington, DC, National Advisory Council on Women's Educational Programs, 1977. 66p. ED 136997.

This report includes an annotated bibliography of 74 items.

2629. Educating the teacher for rural areas: a selected topics bibliography of ERIC documents. ERIC Clearinghouse on Rural Education and Small Schools, 1977. 120p. ED 153759.

Includes 167 annotated entries dating from the 1960's and 1970's.

2630. Social studies in rural areas: a selected topics bibliography of ERIC documents. ERIC Clearinghouse on Rural Education and Small Schools, 1977. 36p. ED 153761.

Annotates 40 entries from RIE and CIJE, 1963-1976.

2631. Styler, W. E. A Bibliographical guide to adult education in rural areas, 1918-1972. Hull University (England), Department of Adult Education, 1973. 51p. ED 074340.

Annotates books and articles dealing with the topic in Great Britain.

RURAL YOUTH

2632. Charles, Edgar B. Youth in rurality: a bibliography. ERIC Clearinghouse on Rural Education and Small Schools, 1967. 19p. ED 025337.

An unannotated list of 200 books, pamphlets, and documents dating back to 1949 that focus on education, mental health, vocational aspirations, functions of the church, and economic variables.

2633. Kuvlesky, William P. and Nelson L. Jacob. Educational status projections of rural youth: annotations of the research literature. Texas A & M University, Department of Agricultural Economics and Sociology, 1968. 76p. ED 026189.

The 49 annotated research reports published between 1947 and 1968 are designed to point out areas of conflicting findings.

2634. Educational and occupational aspirations of rural youth: a selected topics bibliography of ERIC documents. ERIC Clearinghouse on Rural Education and Small Schools, 1977. 89p. ED 153772 (MF)

Annotates 116 items from the ERIC system covering racial differences, rural-urban differences, dropouts, career choice, social mobility, and employment opportunities.

2635. Rural youth expectations: a selected topics bibliography of ERIC documents. ERIC Clearinghouse on Rural Education and Small Schools, 1977. 42p. ED 153764 (MF)

Annotates 42 ERIC documents and articles on aspirations about education, occupation, residence, marriage, and procreation.

2636. Aspirations of rural youth: a selected topics bibliography of ERIC documents. ERIC Clearinghouse on Rural Education and Small Schools, 1977. 17p. ED 153760.

Annotates ten items published between 1966 and 1974. Includes rural-urban, male-female, and ethnic group comparisons.

2637. Socioeconomic and social aspects of rural youth: a selected topics bibliography of ERIC documents. ERIC Clearinghouse on Rural Education and Small Schools, 1977. 66p. ED 153762.

Annotates 80 entries dating from 1960 to 1976.

2638. Cosby, Arthur G. Development of human resource potentials of rural youth in the South and their patterns of mobility. Texas A & M University, Agricultural Experiment Station, 1973. 13p. ED 086386.

Includes 118 book chapters, articles, reports, and theses published from 1964 to 1973. Not annotated.

2639. Cosby, Arthur G. Youth status projections in the South: structured annotations of research literature from regional research project S-61. Texas A & M University, Agricultural Experiment Station, 1974. 99p. ED 100594.

Project S-61 is titled "Development of human resource potentials and mobility in the rural South". 60 references are included.

RUSSIA   See   USSR

RUSSIAN LANGUAGE

2640. Pockney, B. P. and N. S. Sollohub. Bibliography of
Russian teaching materials. Leeds, England, Nuffield Foundation, 1966. 48p. ED 039788 (MF)

 Annotates reference books, teaching aids, readers, grammars, vocabulary and phrase books, and audiovisual materials.

2641. Stankiewicz, Edward. Russian dialect project, volume
III: bibliography of Russian dialect studies. Washington, DC,
Institute of International Studies, 1968. 182p. ED 057670.

 Lists 1600 unannotated references in several linguistic
 categories. Includes an author index.

SABBATICAL LEAVES

2642. Jensen, Ida-Marie. Sabbatical leave: a selected bibliography. Logan, Utah State University Library, 1974. 31p.
ED 091986.

 The 60 entries include books, articles, and dissertations
 concerning various aspects of the subject. Not annotated.

SAFETY EDUCATION

2643. Thomas, John C. Safety in trade and industrial and
technical education. Lexington, University of Kentucky, Vocational Education Curriculum Development Center, 1974. 54p.
ED 098397.

 Includes a 25 page bibliography of books, articles, films,
 catalogs, documents, and other instructional aids. Not
 annotated.

2644. Bicycle safety education: a guide to resources and materials. Washington, DC, Lawrence Johnson and Associates,
1977. 77p. ED 147610.

 Contains curriculum guides, packaged programs, films,
 books, and public relations materials. Briefly annotated.

SCANDINAVIA

2645. Scandinavian mass communication research: publications

in English, French, and German. Aarhus, Denmark, Nordic Documentation Center for Mass Communication Research, 1978. 55p.
ED 162617 (MF)

Includes four separate lists for Norway, Denmark, Finland,
and Sweden. Annotated.

SCHOOL-COMMUNITY RELATIONS

2646. Fink, Ira S. and Joan Cooke. Campus/community relationships: an annotated bibliography. New York, Society for College and University Planning, 1972. 103p. ED 072720.

The articles and books deal with the effects of campus
growth and expansion, circulation and transportation, commercial services, research parks, and zoning on the community.

2647. Educational and social demands on the schools: analysis
of literature and selected bibliography. ERIC Clearinghouse
on Educational Administration, 1970. 17p. ED 043110.

This 65 item bibliography deals with the expectations and
demands of the public for their schools.

2648. Bowles, B. Dean and Charlotte Oinonen. School-community relations: a comprehensive bibliography. Madison, University of Wisconsin, Research and Development Center for Individualized Schooling, 1979. 268p. ED 177737.

Many of the entries are annotated and cover program, organization, activities, processes, political aspects, research, and a bibliography of bibliographies.

2649. Jackson, Kathleen O. Annotated bibliography on school-
community relations. ERIC Clearinghouse on Educational Administration, 1969. 25p. ED 030220.

Contains 79 citations for books, articles, pamphlets, and
dissertations dated 1964 to 1969. Covers school politics
and the community power structure, and schools and urban
problems.

2650. Templeton, Ian. Communicating with the public: analysis and bibliography. Washington, DC, National School Public
Relations Association, 1972. 16p. ED 071141.

Includes a 64 item bibliography intended for educational
administrators.

2651. Muxen, Marla J. and Michael L. Henniger. Community
involvement in the schools: an annotated bibliography, 1976-
1978. 1978. 25p. ED 165305.

Most of the list is derived from a search of RIE and CIJE.

2652. Davies, Dan and Ross Zerchykov. Citizen participation
in education: annotated bibliography. Second ed. Boston, Institute for Responsive Education, 1978. 399p. ED 157144 (MF)

Over 800 entries concern decision-making, policy development, and school governance in public schools and school
systems. Most of the books, articles, and documents were
published in the 1970's.

SCHOOL DECENTRALIZATION

2653. Christiansen, Dorothy. Decentralization: a bibliography. New York, Center for Urban Education, 1968. 17p. ED
025575.

Part I is a general bibliography on the issue; part II is
many articles from the New York Times during 1967 dealing
with the Bundy plan for decentralizing the schools in New
York City.

2654. Bibliography on school decentralization and community
control. Flushing, City University of New York, Queens College, 1970. 33p. ED 044460 (MF)

Emphasis is on the growing community-school movement, and
the New York City school strike. Unannotated.

SCHOOL INTEGRATION

2655. Racial desegregation and integration in our schools.
New York, Yeshiva University, 1966(?) 9p. ED 011910.

An unannotated list of over 140 published and unpublished
works produced during the 1960's concerning plans and methods of integration.

2656. St. John, Nancy and Nancy Smith. Annotated bibliography on school racial mix and the self-concept, aspirations,
academic achievement, and interracial attitudes and behavior
of Negro children. Harvard University, 1966. 83p. ED 011
331.

Contains 242 items produced since 1954. In subject categories with an author index.

2657. Hall, John S. Implementing school desegregation: a
bibliography. ERIC Clearinghouse on Educational Administration, 1970. 28p. ED 037825.

Some of the 183 books, articles, papers, and reports are
annotated. They were published mainly between 1966 and
1969, and cover legal background, school-community relations, implementation problems and techniques, and evaluation.

2658. ERIC abstracts: a collection of ERIC document resumes on impact of racial issues on educational administration. Washington, DC, American Association of School Administrators, 1970. 32p. ED 037824.

An annotated bibliography selected from RIE through 1969.

2659. Annotated bibliography and summaries of reference materials: school desegregation/integration notebook. New York, American Civil Liberties Union, 1977. 60p. ED 152905.

Covers general and legal references, important cases, busing, and "white flight".

2660. Jablonsky, Adelaide. School desegregation: an annotated bibliography of doctoral dissertations. ERIC Clearinghouse on the Urban Disadvantaged, 1973. 147p. ED 078098.

Includes dissertations produced from 1965 to 1972.

2661. Pettigrew, Thomas F. and Rae C. Kipp. Community case studies on school desegregation. Washington, DC, National Institute of Education, 1977. 114p. ED 149001.

Includes critical reviews of eleven studies in addition to an extensive bibliography, and a list of 40 communities which have experienced school integration.

2662. Bynum, Effie. Desegregation, preservice, and inservice training: an annotated targeted bibliography. New York, Columbia University, National Center for Research and Information on Equal Educational Opportunity, 1971. 7p. ED 049350.

This is a list of materials available through the ERIC system.

2663. Jablonsky, Adelaide. School desegregation and organization: an annotated bibliography of doctoral dissertations. ERIC Clearinghouse on the Urban Disadvantaged, 1975. 193p. ED 110585.

A comprehensive list of 128 dissertations done from 1965 through 1973.

SCHOOL LAW

2664. Nolte, M. Chester. Bibliography of school law dissertations, 1952-1968. ERIC Clearinghouse on Educational Administration, 1969. 43p. ED 027646.

503 dissertations are listed under 25 major subject headings. Not annotated.

2665. Norman, O. Gene. School law: a selected bibliography. Terre Haute, Indiana State University Library, 1977. 18p.

ED 140505 (MF)

Most of the entries are annotated reference sources and statutes.

SCHOOLS AND SCHOOLING

2666. Rubel, Robert. Crime and disruption in the schools: a selected bibliography. Germantown, MD, Aspen Systems Corporation, 1979. 103p. ED 180102.

This annotated list considers an overview of the problem, the students, some school programs, and facilities and their security.

2667. Runkel, Philip J. Bibliography on organizational change in schools: selected and annotated. Eugene, University of Oregon, Center for Educational Policy Management, 1974. 148p. ED 098678.

2668. Anderson, Robert H. Bibliography on organizational trends in schools. Washington, DC, National Education Association, 1968. 38p. ED 024125 (MF)

Includes 386 books, articles, pamphlets, and AV resources published between 1955 and 1968. Not annotated.

2669. Stanton, Jim. Resource guide and bibliography on school councils. Boston, Institute for Responsive Education, 1978. 104p. ED 157142 (MF)

Contains an annotated bibliography.

2670. Improving school climate: the best of ERIC. ERIC Clearinghouse on Educational Management, 1977. 5p. ED 146664.

Annotates 12 documents and articles from the ERIC system on school "climate" in relation to principal behavior, educational change, organizational development, and leader-staff relations.

2671. Guthrie, P. D. and Eleanor V. Horne. School readiness measures: an annotated bibliography. Princeton, NJ, Educational Testing Service, 1971. 26p. ED 056083.

The annotations of the tests give purpose, scope, scoring, and interpretation.

2672. Gislason, Barbara J. School readiness testing: a bibliography. ERIC Clearinghouse on Tests, Measurement, and Evaluation, 1975. 24p. ED 117196.

Includes 113 entries on when a child is ready to enter kindergarten. Not annotated. Dissertations, journal articles, and ERIC documents are listed.

2673. Vars, Gordon F. A Bibliography of research on the effectiveness of block-time programs. Kent State University, Bureau of Educational Research, 1970. 7p. ED 045540.

The 62 unannotated entries include comparative studies, normative studies, and summaries.

2674. Grose, Robert F. Academic calendars: a bibliography. Amherst College, Massachusetts, 1970. 42p. ED 053666.

Annotates books, articles, and empirical studies concerning the school calendar in higher education.

2675. Smith, Hollie. Class size: does it make a difference? Urbana, IL, National Council of Teachers of English, 1971. 20p. ED 058210.

This annotated bibliography of 34 entries is a review of research directed toward finding an optimum class size in relation to teacher work load and collective bargaining.

SCIENCE AND TECHNOLOGY

2676. Armstrong, M. A. Core bibliography on technology and social change in foreign cultures. Ames, Iowa State University, Engineering Research Institute, 1973. 143p. ED 112174.

Annotates several hundred books, plus selected US Government publications, and United Nations documents produced since 1950.

2677. Science and technology for international development: a selected list of information sources in the United States and bibliography of selected materials. Second ed. Ithaca, NY, Cornell University, Program on Policies for Science and Technology in Developing Nations, 1975. 122p. ED 118419.

An unannotated bibliography emphasizing technology transfer, industrialization, and small-scale industries.

2678. Terner, Janet. Biographical sources in the sciences. Washington, DC, Library of Congress, 1978. 26p. ED 164332.

Both historical and contemporary scientists are covered, with the emphasis on Americans. Unannotated.

2679. Science and society, history of science and mathematics education, science and mathematics history, general studies and surveys. ERIC Information Analysis Center for Science Education, 1970. 41p. ED 044271.

Includes 183 citations to ERIC documents.

2680. Moore, John A. Science for society: a bibliography.

Washington, DC, American Association for the Advancement of
Science, 1970. 52p. ED 039205.

An unannotated booklist for secondary school teachers and
students which includes all aspects of science and technology.

2681. Stonehouse, Marie L. Science and technology: a purchase guide for branch and public libraries. Pittsburgh, Carnegie Library, 1978. 57p. ED 163922.

Includes about 1000 titles.

2682. Caldwell, Lynton K. Science, technology, and public
policy: a selected and annotated bibliography, Volume 2, articles in journals. Washington, DC, National Science Foundation,
1969. 549p. ED 045366 (MF)

Lists 2700 articles from 50 English language periodicals
dating from 1946 to 1967.

SCIENCE EDUCATION   See also   MATHEMATICS EDUCATION

2683. Advisory list of instructional media for science. Raleigh, North Carolina State Department of Public Instruction,
1977. 87p. ED 149757.

Annotates books, films, filmstrips, kits, and slide sets
for K-12.

2684. English for science and technology. London, British
Council, English Teaching Information Center, 1977. 16p. ED
152100.

Lists 180 unannotated books and articles dealing with scientific and technological English for the second language
learner.

2685. Pacesetters in innovation. ERIC Information Analysis
Center for Science Education, 1970. 67p. ED 050937.

Contains 211 citations of planning and development grant
documents related to science and/or mathematics education.

2686. Theiss, Frances C. Science and mathematics for young
children: an annotated bibliography. ERIC Information Analysis Center for Science Education, 1970. 42p. ED 050938.

Updates, but does not replace a 1969 bibliography, ED 033
259. Covers activities, concepts, goals, curriculum, Head-
start, perception, problem solving, Piaget, and Montessori.

2687. Shea, Dick. Instructional materials for science. Los
Angeles, University of Southern California, Instructional Materials Center for Special Education, 1974. 50p. ED 091892.

Includes 207 multimedia materials for use with K-12 normal or handicapped children. Annotated.

2688. Wall, Charles A. Individualizing science instruction: a bibliography of readings. Athens, University of Georgia, Department of Science Education, 1972. 9p. ED 069498.

The 90 unannotated entries cover audio-tutorial systems, computer-assisted instruction, programmed materials, independent study, teaching by contract, other experimental projects, and measurement and evaluation.

2689. The ASEP bibliography. Toorak, Victoria, Australian Science Education Project, 1975. 62p. ED 113176 (MF)

ASEP has developed 41 separate science units; this bibliography includes the science materials relating to these curricula.

2690. Helgeson, Stanley. Science education: a dissertation bibliography. Ann Arbor, MI, University Microfilms International, 1978. 83p. ED 161667 (MF)

A subject/author listing of 3200 available doctoral dissertations dating from 1950 to 1975.

2691. Course and curriculum improvement materials: mathematics, science, social sciences - elementary, intermediate, and secondary. Washington, DC, National Science Foundation, 1976. 61p. ED 162913.

An annotated multimedia bibliography.

2692. Sciences: a select list of US Government produced audiovisual materials. Washington, DC, National Archives and Records Service, National Audiovisual Center, 1978. 53p. ED 158968 (MF)

Covers aerospace technology, astronomy, biology, chemistry, electronics and electricity, energy, environmental studies, geology, mathematics, computer sciences, oceanography, physics, and meteorology.

2693. Olson, Nancy B. Rocks, minerals, plants, wildlife: a preliminary bibliography of identification media for use in Minnesota schools. 1970. 46p. ED 100643.

This unannotated bibliography is part of a master's degree project at Mankato State College.

2694. Connelly, F. Michael and Richard W. Binns. Logical reasoning in science education, and an annotated bibliography. ERIC Information Analysis Center for Science, Mathematics, and Environmental Education, 1974. 48p. ED 097198.

Includes doctoral dissertations, and articles from educational and research journals, and curriculum newsletters.

2695. Stanhope, Roy. <u>Some aspects of secondary school science in Australia</u>. North Ryde, Australia, Macquarie University, 1976. 128p. ED 130863.

Includes an annotated bibliography of articles from the <u>Australian Science Teachers Journal</u>, 1955-1973.

2696. Theiss, Frances C. <u>Science and mathematics for young children: an annotated bibliography</u>. ERIC Information Analysis Center for Science Education, 1969. 33p. ED 033259.

Lists journal articles and dissertations from 1964 to 1969 with one section devoted to bibliographies. ED 050938 updates, but does not replace, this list.

2697. <u>Instructional procedures</u>. ERIC Information Analysis Center for Science Education, 1968. 66p. ED 026277.

Includes 217 references related to instructional procedures in science education.

2698. <u>Teacher education</u>. ERIC Information Analysis Center for Science Education, 1968. 34p. ED 026278.

Includes 100 citations related to teacher education in science education. Speeches, manuals, research reports, and other materials are listed.

2699. <u>Instructional equipment and materials</u>. ERIC Information Analysis Center for Science Education, 1969. 88p. ED 032442.

Contains 366 unannotated references.

2700. <u>Curriculum</u>. ERIC Information Analysis Center for Science Education, 1969. 125p. ED 032443.

Includes 460 references related to curriculum development in science and mathematics education.

2701. <u>Achievement</u>. ERIC Information Analysis Center for Science Education, 1968. 27p. ED 026281.

Includes 76 references related to student achievement in science education.

2702. <u>Teacher resource materials</u>. ERIC Information Analysis Center for Science Education, 1968. 93p. ED 026282.

Includes 332 citations to teacher resource materials for science education.

2703. <u>Science and society, history of science education, science history, general studies and surveys</u>. ERIC Information Analysis Center for Science Education, 1968. 32p. ED 026283.

Includes 98 references to materials for use in science education teaching.

2704. Legislative acts and reports, administration and supervision, science facilities. ERIC Information Analysis Center
for Science Education, 1968. 16p. ED 026284.

Includes 36 references on these topics related to science
education.

2705. Evaluation and educational objectives, learning theories and processes, research methodology. ERIC Information
Analysis Center for Science Education, 1968. 49p. ED 026285.

Includes 184 citations on these topics related to science
education.

2706. Teacher characteristics and student characteristics.
ERIC Information Analysis Center for Science Education, 1969.
25p. ED 026286.

Includes 67 references related to science education.

SCIENCE FICTION

2707. Sween, Roger. Bibliography of science fiction. Wisconsin Council of Teachers of English, 1974. 29p. ED 133739.

Lists 280 science fiction novels, short stories, and anthologies, 19 magazines devoted to the genre, and 43 films.
Nine basic reference works are also included.

SELF CONCEPT See also VALUES EDUCATION

2708. Kremer, Barbara. Self-concept development: an abstract
bibliography. ERIC Clearinghouse on Early Childhood Education, 1972. 28p. ED 063015.

This list was compiled from a search of RIE and CIJE. It
covers self-concept formation and implications for education, enhancing self-image in preschoolers, and self-concept and racial attitudes.

2709. Bobson, Sarah. Self concept: an annotated bibliography
of selected ERIC references. ERIC Clearinghouse on the Urban
Disadvantaged, 1973. 88p. ED 076729.

The focus is on self concept in relation to academic
achievement. The entries are from the 1971 and 1972 issues
of RIE.

2710. Stern, Carolyn and Maryann Luckenbill. The Study of
self concept in children: an annotated bibliography. Los
Angeles, UCLA, Early Childhood Research Center, 1972. 88p.
ED 076247.

Contains over 100 entries; most are annotated.

2711. Coller, Alan R. and P. D. Guthrie. Self-concept measures: an annotated bibliography. Princeton, NJ, Educational Testing Service, 1971. 11p. ED 051305.

These 27 instruments from the Head Start collection are appropriate for preschool through third grade level.

2712. Howard, Norma K. Self concept: an abstract bibliography. ERIC Clearinghouse on Early Childhood Education, 1974. 58p. ED 091085.

Includes 165 entries from the 1970 to 1974 issues of RIE. Covers sex differences, socioeconomic status, personality development, parent-child relationship, student-teacher relationship, ethnic and racial attitudes, special education, and tutorial programs.

2713. Matthews, Bruce E. Adventure education and self concept: an annotated bibliography with appendix. 1976. 26p. ED 160287 (MF)

Adventure education is described as "those programs and experiences in which elements of high excitement and controlled risk are inherent". Includes 150 citations to books, articles, dissertations, and ERIC documents. Not annotated.

2714. Schachter, Jaqueline. Self-image books as "soul food". 1977. 13p. ED 163520.

Fiction and nonfiction are included in this list intended for bibliotherapy. Headings are: overcoming physical disabilities, courage, friendship, family living, and growing up. Arranged by reading level.

2715. Farrah, George A. An Annotated bibliography of research concerning the self-concept and motivation inventory (SCAMIN). 1977. 21p. ED 164436.

The research concerns motivation in both students and teachers.

2716. Rosen, Pamela. Self-concept measures: Head Start test collection. Princeton, NJ, Educational Testing Service, 1973. 8p. ED 086737.

Includes 44 items for preschool through third grade that were published between 1963 and 1972. Annotated.

2717. Rosen, Pamela. Measures of self-concept, grades 4-6. Princeton, NJ, Educational Testing Service, 1973. 6p. ED 083320.

An annotated bibliography of 31 tests.

2718. Rosen, Pamela. Self-concept measures: grade 7 and above. Princeton, NJ, Educational Testing Service, 1973. 7p.

ED 083319.

An annotated bibliography of 34 tests.

SENIOR CITIZENS   See   GERONTOLOGY

SEX DISCRIMINATION

2719. Mills, Gladys H. Bibliography: equal educational opportunity, myth or reality? Denver, Education Commission of the
States, 1975. 41p. ED 110538.

   The focus is on sex and race discrimination. Not annotated.

2720. Title IX: selected resources. Washington, DC, National
Foundation for the Improvement of Education, 1976. 14p. ED
125465.

   Annotates 57 resources which provide information on Title
   IX of the 1972 Education Amendments and to give assistance
   in the implementation of its regulatory requirements. The
   purpose of Title IX is to prohibit sex discrimination a-
   gainst students and employees of education programs and
   activities receiving federal funds.

2721. Schlee, Phillip F. MSDAC resource library annotated
bibliography. Manhattan, Kans., Midwest Sex Desegregation
Assistance Center, 1979. 23p. ED 184530.

   67 multimedia materials are annotated for use in public
   schools.

2722. Lockheed, Marlaine E. Sex discrimination in education:
a literature review and bibliography. Princeton, NJ, Educational Testing Service, 1977. 90p. ED 144976.

   Includes an unannotated bibliography of 1000 entries.

2723. Advisory list of instructional media for reduction of
sex bias. Raleigh, North Carolina State Department of Public
Instruction, 1977. 29p. ED 149755.

   The annotated list is for K-12, and includes biographies,
   history, biology of sex roles, sociology, and other curriculum materials.

2724. An Annotated bibliography of resources for eliminating
sex bias and role stereotyping in vocational education. Atlanta, Georgia State Department of Education, 1979. 79p. ED
178754.

   Covers textbook bias, women in the labor force, males in
   nontraditional roles, parental involvement, guidance and
   counseling, legislation, and statistics.

2725. Kane, Roslyn D. Sex discrimination in education: a
study of employment practices affecting professional personnel.
Washington, DC, National Center for Education Statistics, 1976.
258p. ED 132744.

This volume two of the study is the annotated bibliography
of materials used to do the research. Major research studies and primary source materials are included.

2726. Olin, Ferris. Fair play: a bibliography of non-stereotyped materials. Rutgers University, Training Institute for
Sex Desegregation of the Public Schools, 1976. 83p. ED 162
021 (MF)

An annotated multimedia list for K-12. Volume two contains
86 pages and is available as ED 162022.

2727. Hulme, Marylin A. Sourcebook for sex equality: inservice training: an annotated listing of materials and media for
affirmative action inservice training. Rutgers University,
Training Institute for Sex Desegregation of the Public Schools,
1978. 25p. ED 162024.

2728. Wheeler, Helen R. Alice in wonderland, or, through the
looking glass: resources for implementing principles of affirmative action employment of women. 1975. 14p. ED 110776.

Annotates 64 books, articles, films, tapes, and slides.

2729. Russ, Anne J. Sex-role stereotyping in occupational
education: a selected bibliography for educators. Ithaca, NY,
Cornell Institute for Occupational Education, 1978. 20p. ED
163198 (MF)

Annotates 64 references published since 1970.

SEX EDUCATION

2730. A Broadly representative bibliography of materials on
sex education. Lansing, Michigan State Department of Education, 1969. 20p. ED 030925.

An unannotated list for teachers and administrators interested in initiating or improving a local sex education
program.

2731. Gordon, Sol. Sex education and the library: a basic
bibliography for the general public with special resources for
the librarian. ERIC Clearinghouse on Information Resources,
1979. 46p. ED 180504.

Includes the history of sexual attitudes, pornography,
molestation, sexuality and the handicapped, special parent situations, sexual identity and sensitivity. The items
are for children, parents, teachers, and administrators.

2732. Watt, Lois B. Family life and sex education: a bibliography. Washington, DC, Office of Education, 1966. 9p. ED
024958.

Includes textbooks and teacher resources. Not annotated.

2733. Some guides for sex education and marriage preparation.
Toronto, United Church of Canada, 1968. 38p. ED 023997.

Lists annotated reading materials for children, youth,
adults, and parents, and for those planning and leading
study courses.

2734. Dusseau, Joanne. Sex education: a survey of the problem. Burlingame, California Teachers Association, 1970. 58p.
ED 038715.

Covers historical background, arguments for teaching the
subject, suggestions for a curriculum, controversial issues, and evaluation. Not annotated.

2735. Wolf, Goldye. Sexuality for the young: a bibliography.
1974. 13p. ED 094293.

The purpose of this annotated bibliography is to expand
the meaning of sexuality to include concepts such as feelings, friendships, and relationships. The books are for
elementary school age children and teenagers.

2736. Annotated guide to venereal disease instructional materials available in Canada. Ottawa, Department of National
Health and Welfare, 1975. 43p. ED 131018.

A multimedia bibliography classified according to age
group and suitability.

2737. Sexuality resource guide and supplement. Denver, Colorado State Library, 1975. 28p. ED 130465 (MF)

Contains 300 entries intended for those working with the
developmentally disabled. Includes books, articles, films,
and tapes. Not annotated.

2738. Sex education: a selective bibliography. Reston, VA,
Council for Exceptional Children, 1976. 30p. ED 129007.

Includes 135 annotated publications concerning handicapped
children and sex education. The entries date from 1962 to
1975.

2739. Oberteuffer, Delbert. Growth patterns and sex education: an updated bibliography, preschool to adult. Kent, OH,
American School Health Association, 1972. 61p. ED 097315.

This annotated list includes AV material for students,
teachers, and parents, in addition to articles, dissertations, and curriculum guides.

SEX ROLE

2740. Sells, Lucy W. Current research on sex roles. Sociol-
ogists for Women in Society, 1972. 79p. ED 117029.

The annotated bibliography covers media, the women's movement, affirmative action, minorities, family, sexuality,
deviance, politics, culture, religion, and history.

2741. Katz, Lilian G. Sex role socialization in early childhood: an annotated bibliography. ERIC Clearinghouse on Early
Childhood Education, 1977. 76p. ED 148473.

Contains 321 references published between 1970 and 1977,
and covers the influence of media, school, and family.

2742. Howard, Norma K. Sex differences and sex role development in young children: an abstract bibliography. ERIC
Clearinghouse on Early Childhood Education, 1975. 33p. ED
105991.

Cites recent ERIC documents on behavioral differences
between young girls and boys in such areas as moral judg-
ment, school readiness, self esteem, motor performance,
aggression, locus of control, and social development.

2743. Bibliography of non-sexist materials: annotated bibliography of non-sexist picture books. New York, Women's Action
Alliance, Inc., 1976. 23p. ED 150989.

The first part lists films, filmstrips, books, games, toys
and dolls. The second part lists 37 picture books for
children. A final section lists books, articles, and reports on the subject of sex roles.

2744. Nelson, Audrey A. Sex and proxemics: an annotated bibliography. 1978. 27p. ED 154454.

Over 90 titles date from 1965 to 1978, and focus on the
sex differences and similarities in two proxemic variables: physical distance and orientation of the body.

SEX STEREOTYPES

2745. Sex-stereotyping in child care. New York, Women's Action Alliance, Inc., 1973. 14p. ED 093476.

An unannotated multimedia bibliography of non-sexist instructional materials for preschool children.

2746. Hanson, Gordon. A Guide to assessing minority and sex
role stereotyping in elementary and secondary schools. Revised
ed. Madison, Wisconsin Department of Public Instruction,
1978. 88p. ED 159300.

This is a resource guide and annotated bibliography for educators, and includes books, articles, and testing instruments.

2747. Stakelon, Anne E. and Joel H. Magisos. Sex stereotyping and occupational aspiration: an annotated bibliography. Columbus, Ohio State University, Center for Vocational Education, 1975. 49p. ED 118926.

The 88 entries include articles and ERIC documents.

2748. Motomatsu, Nancy R. A Selected bibliography of bias-free materials: grades K-12. Olympia, Washington State Office of the Superintendent of Public Instruction, 1976. 23p. ED 127408.

Includes textbooks and other instructional materials which present a positive image of both sexes. The unannotated list contains fiction and nonfiction, and indicates reading levels.

2749. Pugliese, Pamela P. and Donald R. Chipley. Sexual bias in children's books: annotated bibliography and comparative study. 1976. 39p. ED 139007.

The significant findings are given in the annotations of 33 studies.

SHAKESPEARE, WILLIAM

2750. Claener, Anne. Shakespeare: a student's guide to basic reference sources. Montreal, McGill University Library, 1977. 8p. ED 151863.

The annotated entries are grouped by type of reference book.

2751. Mullin, Michael. Shakespeare on film in the classroom. 1974. 12p. ED 109682 (MF)

This paper presents an annotated list of 13 films.

SIGN LANGUAGE

2752. Deuchar, Margaret. A Selected bibliography on sign language studies. ERIC Clearinghouse on Languages and Linguistics, 1976. 8p. ED 121098.

Annotates 24 theoretical and historical studies, and some textbooks.

2753. A Selected annotated bibliography: books, films, and teaching media on sign language. Silver Spring, MD, National

Association of the Deaf, 1970. 23p. ED 039694.

   Contains 22 books and nine films.

2754. Manual communication bibliography. Silver Spring, MD,
National Association of the Deaf, 1970. 6p. ED 039695.

   Includes 33 unannotated titles.

SIGNS (GRAPHIC)

2755. Directional and informational signs for educational facilities: a selected bibliography. ERIC Clearinghouse on Educational Facilities, 1970. 14p. ED 040511.

SIMULATION   See also   GAMES

2756. Kidder, Steven J. Simulation games: practical references, potential use: selected bibliography. Baltimore, MD,
Johns Hopkins University, Center for the Study of Social Organization of Schools, 1971. 26p. ED 054486.

   Discusses several recently published books, and provides
   an unannotated list of 113 other publications.

2757. Twelker, Paul A. A Basic reference shelf on simulation
and gaming. ERIC Clearinghouse on Educational Media and Technology, 1970. 18p. ED 041487.

   An annotated guide to the literature that also provides
   other bibliographies.

2758. Coombs, Don H. Simulation and gaming: the best of ERIC.
ERIC Clearinghouse on Information Resources, 1976. 28p. ED
126891.

   Annotates 101 references published between 1972 and 1975
   that include theory and research and other materials related to a variety of subject areas.

SLAVIC LANGUAGES

2759. Birkenmayer, Sigmund S. A Selective bibliography of
works related to the teaching of Slavic languages and liter-
atures in the United States and Canada, 1942-1967. New York,
American Council on the Teaching of Foreign Languages, 1968.
41p. ED 025988.

   Includes annotated books, articles, and reports on linguistics, teacher education, curricular problems, and the
   physiology and psychology of language learning.

SLIDES (PHOTOGRAPHY)

2760. Hess, Stanley W. An Annotated bibliography of slide library literature. Syracuse University, School of Information Studies, 1978. 50p. ED 181926 (MF)

Covers post-1960 imprints, and deals with the care and administration of slide collections, including their indexing, cataloging, control, and acquisition.

2761. Freudenthal, Juan R. The Slide as a communication tool: a selected annotated bibliography. Second ed. Boston, Simmons College, School of Library Science, 1974. 17p. ED 098 966.

The 80 entries cover visual literacy, and the organization and maintenance of slide collections.

SMALL SCHOOLS See RURAL EDUCATION

SMOKING

2762. Guthrie, P. D. Measures pertaining to health education: smoking, an annotated bibliography. ERIC Clearinghouse on Tests, Measurement, and Evaluation, 1972. 20p. ED 060042.

Describes instruments pertaining to smoking attitudes, behaviors, knowledge, and correlates.

SOCIAL CHANGE

2763. Whitaker, William H. Social movements: a general annotated bibliography. Monticello, IL, Council of Planning Librarians, 1970. 5p. ED 101426.

The unannotated list does not include specific movements or episodes.

2764. Bibliography on planned social change, with special reference to rural development and educational development. Minneapolis, University of Minnesota, Department of Political Science, 1967. 3 Volumes. ED 040108 to ED 040110.

Volume I includes about 900 articles in 691 pages. Volume II contains books and monographs, but excludes dissertations. Volume III lists government reports, United Nations documents, and conference proceedings. The entries in all the volumes are annotated. Volume II has 215 pages, and Volume III has 198 pages.

2765. Akin, Joy. Selected bibliography of centrally planned

social change in the Soviet Union. Monticello, IL, Council
of Planning Librarians, 1970. 17p. ED 062618.

The annotated entries cover education, collective farms,
trade unions, and other organizations.

2766. Farrell, Joseph P. A Selective annotated bibliography
on education and social development. Syracuse University, Center for Development Education, 1966. 136p. ED 048019.

Most of the 700 entries are annotated. Covers social change
theory, the formation of elites, the role of the mass media, political development, social mobility, educational
planning, and social development.

SOCIAL INDICATORS

2767. Putting social indicators to work: an annotated bibliography. Sacramento, California State Office of Planning and
Research, 1977. 74p. ED 166074.

Annotates 134 resources about their use in national, state,
county, and city profiles.

2768. McVeigh, Thomas. Social indicators: a bibliography.
Monticello, Il, Council of Planning Librarians, 1971. 47p.
ED 106951.

The annotated entries cover surveys of health, education,
welfare, housing, urban development, relevant legislation,
and societal models.

2769. Social indicators: human services bibliography. Washington, DC, Project Share (DHEW), 1978. 76p. ED 160501.

The 60 annotated references are designed to help social
service administrators and planners identify and priori-
tize human needs as they are designing social service programs.

2770. Moos, Rudolf and Wendy Max. The Social climate scales:
an annotated bibliography. Stanford University, Department
of Psychiatry and Behavioral Science, 1977. 101p. ED 156714.

Over 60 projects are described that used the scales in
treatment, institutional, school, and community settings.

SOCIAL PROBLEMS

2771. Education for a global society: a resource manual for
secondary education teachers. Philadelphia, Jane Addams Peace
Association, 1976(?)   53p. ED 142481 (MF)

Includes over 400 books, articles, and other materials

under the headings peace, economic equity, social justice,
and ecological balance.

2772. Steinwachs, Barbara. A Selected list of urban, environ-
mental, and social problem gaming/simulations. Revised ed.
Ann Arbor, University of Michigan Extension Service, 1976. 25p.
ED 121593.

   Most of the citations are applicable at the secondary
   school and adult level.

2773. Covert, Nadine. Alternatives: a filmography. New York,
Educational Film Library Association, Inc., 1974. 13p. ED
101672.

   Annotates over 120 films that deal with alternatives in
   education, lifestyles, work, religion, and politics. Specifically covers communes, day care, changing family structure, and racial problems.

2774. Sacco, Margaret. A Bibliography of books dealing with
the problems of older children, grades 3-12. 1975. 16p. ED
114081.

   This conference paper annotates books for this age group
   on several social problems, including racial inequality,
   poverty, desertion, broken homes, drugs, alcohol, sex,
   mental illness, and death.

SOCIAL STRUCTURE

2775. Oberle, Wayne H. A Bibliographical guide to structural
development. Texas A & M University, Department of Agricultural Economics and Rural Sociology, 1972. 87p. ED 074375.

   The unannotated bibliography presents literature on the
   relationship of social structures to societal development.

SOCIAL STUDIES

2776. Resource materials for secondary social studies: an
annotated list of selected titles for the basic program. Edmonton, Alberta Department of Education, 1975. 78p. ED 130
926.

   This multimedia bibliography includes materials that were
   published in the 1970's.

2777. Resource materials for elementary social studies: an
annotated list of selected titles for the basic program. Edmonton, Alberta Department of Education, 1975. 53p. ED 130
925.

   A multimedia list of 1970's materials.

2778. Pike, Mary L. and Louise Lusignan. Update 76: selected recent works in the social sciences. New York, Special Libraries Association, 1976. 34p. ED 127245.

Lists 25 current reference and acquisitions tools for the social sciences for each of 40 subject areas.

2779. Hadjisky, Maryellen G. Peace education in the primary grades: the young world citizen: a bibliography and sample activities, K-3. Detroit, Wayne State University, Center for Teaching about Peace and War, 1973. 19p. ED 096229.

Includes annotated multimedia resources for the student and teacher.

2780. Huus, Helen. Children's books to enrich the social studies for the elementary grades. Revised ed. Washington, DC, National Council for the Social Studies, 1966. 213p. ED 067352 (MF)

Annotates 630 social studies books published between 1935 and 1964 intended for teachers and librarians.

2781. Bishop, John E. Curriculum materials. Washington, DC, National Council for the Social Studies, 1978. 58p. ED 164 407 (MF)

A guide to about 200 curriculum materials that were exhibited at the 1978 annual conference.

2782. Torres, Don. Potpourri: a guide to the new social studies. Boston, Massachusetts State Department of Education, 1970. 35p. ED 044328.

Includes several bibliographies organized around such topics as the definition of the new social studies, instructional objectives, teaching strategies, evaluation, and materials for reference.

2783. Advisory list of instructional media for social studies. Raleigh, North Carolina State Department of Public Instruction, 1977. 134p. ED 149758.

An annotated multimedia list for grades K-12.

2784. McPhie, Walter E. Dissertations in social studies education: a comprehensive guide. Washington, DC, National Council for the Social Studies, 1964. 111p. ED 080426 (MF)

The dissertations are arranged in 26 categories, and were published between 1934 and 1962.

SOCIOLOGY

2785. LeBeau, Bryan. Films for sociology. Pennsylvania

State University, Audiovisual Services, 1973. 210p. ED 134 511.

This catalog contains over 1000 16mm films for students, teachers, and researchers. Most of them were produced in the previous 15 years.

2786. Davis, Ethelyn. Teaching sociology: a bibliography. Second ed. Washington, DC, American Sociological Association, 1977. 120p. ED 141255.

Annotates 351 entries in 19 categories for teaching at the college level.

SOUTHWEST UNITED STATES

2787. Bockman, John F. Lives and thoughts of all peoples of all times from the Gila River to the Rio Yaqui: a source bibliography for regional language and culture instructional materials. Tucson, AZ, Public Schools, 1971. 71p. ED 051692.

Includes over 900 unannotated references to books, articles, and manuscripts which focus on the people of the Southwestern area of the USA.

SPACE SCIENCES

2788. Rodgers, Kay. Unidentified flying objects: a selected bibliography. Washington, DC, Library of Congress, 1976. 21p. ED 138464.

A general, selective, unannotated list of English language materials published since 1969.

2789. Aerospace bibliography. Sixth ed. Washington, DC, National Aerospace Education Council, 1972. 115p. ED 096097.

This is an annotated NASA bibliography of books, articles, and other educational materials related to space flight and space sciences.

SPANISH

2790. De la Portilla, Marta and Thomas Colchie. Textbooks in Spanish and Portuguese: a descriptive bibliography, 1939-1970. ERIC Clearinghouse on Languages and Linguistics, 1972. 126p. ED 060761.

Includes those published in the United States for the high school and college student whose native language is English. Both sections contain Latin American materials, too.

2791. Tome, Martha V. <u>Proyecto Leer Bulletin</u>. Washington, DC, Books for the People Fund, Inc., 1972. 26p. ED 083839.

This bulletin number eleven lists educational materials for students of Spanish, and for the Spanish speaking. Puerto Ricans are included as well as many subjects of contemporary interest. It also lists over 100 films and filmstrips for children and adults.

2792. Taylor, Jose G. <u>Bilingual books, translations, and recommended books in Spanish</u>. Los Angeles Public Library, 1978. 19p. ED 151136.

Cites 123 books published since 1960 in two sections: K-3, and older children.

2793. Rosen, Pamela and Eleanor V. Horne. <u>Tests for Spanish speaking children: an annotated bibliography</u>. Princeton, NJ, Educational Testing Service, 1971. 14p. ED 056084.

Includes measures for intelligence, personality, ability, and achievement.

2794. Ehrlich, Alan. <u>Tests in Spanish and other languages and nonverbal tests for children in bilingual programs: an annotated bibliography</u>. New York, City University, Hunter College, Bilingual Education Applied Research Unit, 1973. 23p. ED 078713.

2795. Buell, Kenneth. <u>An Annotated list of tests for Spanish speakers</u>. Princeton, NJ, Educational Testing Service, 1973. 26p. ED 079393.

Topics for tests include verbal achievement, aptitude/ability, mathematics and science, intelligence, personality, personnel/industrial, and miscellaneous.

2796. Lopez Morales, Humberto. <u>Spanish in Cuba: bibliographies</u>. 1968. 27p. ED 046313.

Commentaries on bibliographies, dictionaries, glossaries, readers, and linguistic studies are provided.

2797. <u>Teaching materials for Spanish: supplementary materials and readers</u>. London, Centre for Information on Language Teaching, 1978. 62p. ED 165452.

Includes phrase books, vocabularies, and readers readily available in the United Kingdom.

2798. Sharples, Hedley. <u>Bibliography of Spanish teaching materials</u>. Leeds, England, Nuffield Foundation, 1968. 98p. ED 043260.

An annotated multimedia guide for teachers. The ten categories include materials for Spain and Latin America.

2799. Gonsalves, Julia. <u>Bibliography of Spanish materials</u>

for children: kindergarten through grade six. Sacramento, California State Department of Education, 1971. 48p. ED 048797.

Annotates more than 400 items for students and teachers,
and for native speakers of Spanish. Includes materials on
language and culture.

2800. Bibliography of audiovisual instructional materials for
the teaching of Spanish, kindergarten through grade twelve.
Sacramento, California State Department of Education, 1975.
129p. ED 119508 (MF)

An annotated list for all academic areas, plus driver education, vocational education, and physical education.

2801. Teschner, Richard V. Spanish and English of United
States Hispanos: a critical, annotated, linguistic bibliography. Washington, DC, Center for Applied Linguistics, 1975.
382p. ED 108515.

Includes 675 items on the speech and language behavior of
Chicanos, Puerto Ricans, Cubans, Islenos, Peninsulares,
and Sephardic Jews.

2802. Bibliography of Spanish materials for students, grades
seven through twelve. Sacramento, California State Department
of Education, 1972. 110p. ED 082575.

Annotates materials in the content areas, plus vocational
education, industrial arts, reference books, and Spanish
textbooks.

2803. Bibliography of literature books related to Spanish
history and culture. Detroit Public Schools, 1969. 17p. ED
032958.

Includes 90 annotated entries.

SPEECH

2804. Starr, Douglas P. A Selected annotated bibliography
on speech ghostwriting: its principles, practices, and ethics.
1972. 27p. ED 070131.

These 80 references are from the author's doctoral dissertation.

2805. Bartlett, John B. Bibliography in oral interpretation
of the non-speech journals, 1973-1974. New York, Speech Communication Association, 1973. 19p. ED 084569.

The eight categories contain 198 annotated entries.

2806. Logue, Cal M. Georgia public address as a research
area: a bibliography. 1973. 79p. ED 114893.

Pertains to the history and criticism of public address in Georgia. Includes dissertations, books, and other materials.

SPEECH HANDICAPPED

2807. Speech handicapped research: a selective bibliography. Reston, VA, Council for Exceptional Children, 1973. 32p. ED 085918.

Includes abstracts of 100 studies dated 1960 to 1972.

2808. Speech handicapped programs: a selective bibliography. Reston, VA, Council for Exceptional Children, 1973. 18p. ED 085941.

Includes abstracts of 60 programs dating from 1963 to 1972.

2809. Healey, William C. Administrative guide in speech correction. 1965. 58p. ED 013010.

Includes 152 clinical and educational references on aphasia, articulation, cerebral palsy, cleft palate, hearing loss, stuttering, and voice problems.

SPEED READING

2810. Berger, Allen. Speed reading: an annotated bibliography. Newark, Del., International Reading Association, 1970. 43p. ED 074481.

Includes 150 references from the previous 40 years. Some are theoretical discussions.

SPORTS See PHYSICAL EDUCATION

SRI LANKA

2811. Goonetileke, H. Mass communication in Sri Lanka: an annotated bibliography. Singapore, Asian Mass Communication Research and Information Centre, 1978. 87p. ED 165173 (MF)

The 362 entries are grouped into 20 sections, and include published and unpublished materials.

STAFF DEVELOPMENT

2812. Perry, Ione L. and Leslee J. Bishop. Staff development:

<u>sources and resources</u>. Athens, University of Georgia, Center for Curriculum Improvement and Staff Development, 1974. 100p. ED 141890.

Annotates over 300 publications related to programing for staff development.

2813. Nicholas, Russell C. <u>Staff development: a guide to selected resources of information on improving the staff of educational institutions</u>. Cupertino, CA, De Anza College Learning Center, 1977. 45p. ED 140444.

Lists over 600 unannotated references from <u>Education Index</u>, RIE, and CIJE. All entries are dated 1970 through 1976.

2814. <u>Personnel development for career education: a selected annotated bibliography</u>. Columbus, Ohio State University, Center for Vocational and Technical Education, 1973. 379p. ED 098446.

Includes books, parts of books, dissertations, and journal articles for the years 1970-1973.

STAFF UTILIZATION

2815. McKenna, Bernard. <u>A Selected annotated bibliography on differentiated staffing</u>. ERIC Clearinghouse on Teacher Education, 1969. 16p. ED 033898.

Includes 31 entries, nine of which are available as ERIC documents.

2816. Ross, Marlene. <u>Preparing school personnel for differentiated staffing patterns: a guide to selected documents in the ERIC collection, 1966-1968</u>. ERIC Clearinghouse on Teacher Education, 1969. 74p. ED 028155.

The 114 documents cover the roles of the various personnel in a school system, in addition to programmed instruction, team teaching, curriculum organization, and innovation.

2817. Piele, Philip K. <u>New sets of jobs for school personnel</u>: <u>analysis of literature and selected bibliography</u>. ERIC Clearinghouse on Educational Administration, 1970. 18p. ED 043112.

This review analyzes the trend toward differentiation of secondary school instructional staffs to include teacher aides, technical assistants, and staff specialists in addition to professional teachers. 96 entries are included.

2818. <u>Differentiated staffing: an annotated bibliography</u>. Toronto, Ontario Institute for Studies in Education, 1971. 24p. ED 071149.

Deals mainly with the role of the professional in a differentiated staffing arrangement. Includes books, theses, articles, pamphlets, and research reports.

2819. Differentiated staffing: bibliographies in education. Ottawa, Canadian Teachers' Federation, 1970.   12p.   ED 045608.

Contains 113 unannotated entries concerned mainly with professional staff. The materials include books, parts of books, papers, articles, and theses dated from 1965 to 1970. ED 085353 is a 15 page supplement issued in 1973 with 74 books, and 93 articles.

2820. Jones, John E. Bibliography and reference information on differentiated staffing. Eugene, University of Oregon, Center for Educational Policy and Management, 1975.   54p.   ED 114922.

Lists 355 citations published from 1964 through 1974. Many are from the ERIC system and Education Index. Not annotated.

2821. Georgiades, William. Selected annotated bibliography relating to new patterns of staff utilization. Salem, Oregon State Department of Education, 1965.   109p.   ED 012506.

Includes team teaching and flexible scheduling among other topics.

2822. Staff differentiation: an annotated bibliography. San Raphael, CA, Marin County Superintendent of Schools, 1970. 21p.   ED 043591.

Includes 62 items dated from 1966 to 1970, and lists 31 projects which received federal funding. ED 100918 is a 12 page supplement containing 18 annotated entries.

STATE EDUCATION AGENCIES

2823. Buser, Robert L. and William L. Humm. State education agencies: a bibliography. 1969.   14p.   ED 034297.

Lists 151 items covering the literature from 1952 through 1968. Not annotated.

2824. Linking schools to state education departments: analysis of literature and selected bibliography. ERIC Clearinghouse on Educational Administration, 1970.   19p.   ED 043117.

Includes an 85 item bibliography of recent literature. Not annotated.

STORYTELLING

2825. For storytellers and storytelling: bibliographies, ma-

terials, and resource aids. Chicago, American Library Association, 1968. 35p. ED 028797.

This multimedia listing deals with the art of storytelling
and provides a variety of resource material for the story-
teller.

STRESS

2826. Frederick, A. B. The Tension literature. 1975. 21p.
ED 115638 (MF)

An annotated bibliography of physiological, psychological,
and philosophical books, articles, and films on stress
from a paper that was presented to the 2nd annual meeting
of the American Association for Advancement of Tension
Control.

2827. Gmelch, Walter H. Beyond stress to effective management. Eugene, Oregon School Study Council, 1977. 74p. ED
140440.

Provides an overview of the most recent ideas on psychological stress and ways to reduce it, with particular a-
ttention to the impact of stress on administrative personnel.

2828. Coping with stress: the best of ERIC on educational management. ERIC Clearinghouse on Educational Management, 1980.
5p. ED 182801.

Deals with causes and how to manage stress, how to recog-
nize stressors, how to make life style changes, and stress
prevention. Includes twelve annotated entries.

STUDENTS

2829. Hall, John S. Selected bibliography on student activism in the public schools. ERIC Clearinghouse on Educational
Administration, 1969. 11p. ED 027644.

Includes 86 unannotated citations to books, pamphlets, and
articles, most published since 1967. Topics cover dissent,
demonstrations, personal appearance, drugs and alcohol,
discipline, and student government.

2830. Rinnander, Elizabeth. About the students: a brief highlighting important literature since 1973 on student characteristics, and the development of programs to meet student needs.
ERIC Clearinghouse for Junior College Information, 1977. 22p.
ED 140929.

Annotates 39 references to published and unpublished materials.

2831. Galant, Richard and Nancy J. Moncrieff. <u>Students as</u>
<u>resources</u>. ERIC Clearinghouse on Counseling and Personnel
Services, 1974. 32p. ED 105365.

   101 ERIC documents, journal articles, and dissertations
   review different ways in which students can be utilized
   as volunteers in school and in the community.

2832. James, Edmund. <u>Student relations: ARIS annotated bib-</u>
<u>liography</u>. Columbus, Ohio Education Association, Association
Referral Information Service, 1970. 21p. ED 078310.

   Covers student unrest, school dropouts, pupil self-esteem,
   school desegregation, and drug abuse.

2833. <u>Student activities in secondary schools: a bibliography</u>.
Washington, DC, National Association of Secondary School Principals, 1974. 95p. ED 089188 (MF)

   Most of the 450 references are annotated and were published
   in the previous ten years.

2834. Jayatilleke, Raja. <u>Grouping practices</u>. ERIC Clearinghouse on the Urban Disadvantaged, 1976. 17p. ED 128494.

   An annotated bibliography of ERIC documents on student
   grouping, by age grade, ability, and other factors. Flexible schedules are covered in conjunction with the topic.

2835. Whitson, Helene. <u>Strike: a chronology, bibliography,</u>
<u>and list of archival materials concerning the 1968-1969 strike</u>
<u>at San Francisco State College</u>. 1977. 86p. ED 158735.

   Includes monographs, theses, dissertations, journal articles, and state and federal documents. The archival items
   are held at San Francisco State College Library and include newspapers, photos, tapes, posters, and other materials.

2836. Rosen, Pamela. <u>Attitudes toward school and school ad-</u>
<u>justment, grades 4-6</u>. Princeton, NJ, Educational Testing Ser-
vice, 1973. 8p. ED 083321.

   An annotated bibliography of 31 tests.

2837. Rosen, Pamela. <u>Attitudes toward school and school ad-</u>
<u>justment, grades 7-12</u>. Princeton, NJ, Educational Testing
Service, 1973. 7p. ED 083323.

   An annotated bibliography of 53 tests.

STUDENTS' RIGHTS

2838. Caruso, Robert G. <u>Bibliography on campus judiciaries,</u>
<u>student conduct and discipline</u>. Washington, DC, American Col-

lege Personnel Association, 1975. 36p. ED 118166.

Includes 474 unannotated entries for books, articles, and
dissertations. Most are dated 1968-1972.

2839. Dunlap, Riley E. and Dennis L. Peck. Student activism:
a bibliography of empirical research. Monticello, IL, Council
of Planning Librarians, 1974. 27p. ED 105627.

Deals with radical activists, conservative activists, and
Black student protests. Also covers student, faculty, and
public attitudes toward protest.

2840. ERIC abstracts: ERIC document resumes on student rights
and responsibilities. Washington, DC, American Association
of School Administrators, 1976. 34p. ED 120893.

A search of RIE using the terms student rights, court
cases, and school law found 63 entries through July 1975.

2841. Hutchinson, Myra. Student rights and school discipline:
bibliography. Ann Arbor, University of Michigan, Project for
the Fair Administration of Student Discipline, 1975. 64p. ED
126385.

An annotated bibliography that dates from 1968 to 1975.

2842. Williams, Junious and Charles B. Vergon. Student rights
and responsibilities: a legal-educational bibliography. Ann
Arbor, University of Michigan, Program for Educational Opportunity, 1974. 148p. ED 100059.

The 22 major categories include due process, corporal pun-
ishment, student records, police in schools, searches,
pregnant students, married students, dress, demonstrations,
freedom of association, freedom of speech, and others.

2843. Tice, Terrence N. Student rights, decision-making, and
the law. ERIC Clearinghouse on Higher Education, 1976. 107p.
ED 135269.

Contains 327 entries along with subject, author, and case
indexes, and provides a review of the literature since
1960.

2844. Tice, Terrence N. Decision-making and the law in higher education: emphasis on student rights: essay and bibliography. 1974. 50p. ED 099063.

The annotated bibliography contains 181 items covering
college law, faculty rights, students in collective bargaining, community college situations, and the legal background.

2845. Galant, Richard and Nancy J. Moncrieff. School discipline and student rights. ERIC Clearinghouse on Counseling
and Personnel Services, 1974. 20p. ED 105358.

Includes 79 ERIC abstracts, dissertations, and journal articles covering the defined civil rights of students at the high school and college level, in addition to recent legal pronouncements.

2846. Kopita, Ronald R. <u>School discipline and student rights</u>. ERIC Clearinghouse on Counseling and Personnel Services, 1973. 63p. ED 082104.

Includes 92 ERIC abstracts, and other articles and dissertations.

SYSTEMS ANALYSIS

2847. <u>Systems analysis in education: bibliographies in education</u>. Ottawa, Canadian Teachers' Federation, 1971. 30p. ED 058171.

Covers the previous five years and includes 188 books, 163 articles and excerpts from books, and 23 theses. Not annotated.

TALENTED   See   GIFTED

TAXATION

2848. White, Anthony G. <u>Urban property taxation</u>. Monticello, IL, Council of Planning Librarians, 1973. ED 130406 through ED 130408 (MF)

Volume one covers administrative aspects in 15 pages, volume two is on land and location (14p.), and volume three is on rejection and reformation (11p.). Not annotated.

TEACHER AIDES

2849. Metzner, Seymour and Jeffrey Neuman. <u>The Teacher auxiliary - aide or maid: an analysis with annotated bibliography</u>. 1967. 28p. ED 015171.

Covers past and present techniques and programs, and presents current trends.

2850. <u>Teacher aides: bibliographies in education</u>. Ottawa, Canadian Teachers' Federation, 1970. 15p. ED 037406.

The period covered is the previous ten years, and it includes 166 articles, 42 books and papers, and three theses.

2851. <u>Teacher aides and nonprofessional personnel: a selec-</u>

tive bibliography. Arlington, VA, Council for Exceptional
Children, 1972. 32p. ED 072594.

The 100 abstracts are dated from 1965 to 1971, and are
pertinent to those who work with handicapped children.

TEACHER EDUCATION

2852. Mathieson, Moira B. and Rita M. Tatis. Social change
and teacher education: an annotated bibliography. ERIC Clearinghouse on Teacher Education, 1970. 29p. ED 043558.

Includes 137 research reports, program descriptions, articles, addresses, and conference papers, mostly from the
previous three years.

2853. Sacay, Valerie H. Teachers and teaching: annotated
bibliographies on selected topics. New York, Brooklyn College,
1975. ED 111776 through ED 111778.

Volume one is on teacher candidates and has 122 entries
in 144 pages; volume two is subtitled "Analyzing teacher
attitudes toward students and behavioral interaction in
the classroom", and has 127 entries in 159 pages; volume
three is on characteristics, attitudes, and values of
teachers and contains 142 items in 159 pages.

2854. Tarling, Mary E. Teacher training bibliography. Los
Angeles, University of Southern California, Instructional Materials Center for Special Education, 1972. 71p. ED 077926.

Annotates 527 items, and includes packaged programs and
guides, bibliographies and newsletters.

2855. Wilson, David A. An Annotated bibliography of published
works from R&D Center for Teacher Education. Austin, University of Texas, Research and Development Center for Teacher Education, 1969. 138p. ED 033096.

The 112 entries cover administration, personalization,
assessment, the teaching laboratory, and team teaching.

2856. Teacher education: 1977 topical bibliography. Reston,
VA, Council for Exceptional Children, 1977. 21p. ED 146746.

Annotates 80 entries related to special education for the
years 1974-1976.

2857. Clothier, Grant. Preparing teachers for urban schools:
an annotated bibliography for teacher education. ERIC Clearinghouse on Teacher Education, 1969. 43p. ED 033094.

The 187 entries, related to psychological and sociological
literature, include some nonprint materials.

2858. Training teachers for inner city schools: bibliographies in education. Ottawa, Canadian Teachers' Federation, 1971. 10p. ED 058172.

The 90 unannotated entries are from the previous 5 years.

2859. Crisp, Raymond D. KWIC-index bibliography of selected references on the preparation of secondary school English teachers. Urbana, Illinois State-wide Curriculum Study Center, 1969. 144p. ED 031488 (MF)

Includes 906 entries. Not annotated.

2860. Schaefer, James. A Bibliography of references used in the preparation of nine model teacher education programs. ERIC Clearinghouse on Teacher Education, 1969. 97p. ED 031 460.

The 1372 entries are in four sections: the nature and training of teachers, education and educational practices, educational psychology, and educational technology. The items were published between 1916 and 1969, and are not annotated.

2861. Cottrell, Donald P. Selected bibliography on the accreditation of teacher education. ERIC Clearinghouse on Teacher Education, 1970. 22p. ED 036467.

Annotates 83 books and articles from the previous 15 years. Some are factual, and some are opinionated.

2862. Suchara, Helen T. Cooperative teacher education: school-college relations in developing school personnel. Washington, DC, National Education Association, 1969. 26p. ED 028154.

Annotates 93 documents dating from 1960 that cover team teaching, student teaching, internship programs, and supervisory personnel.

2863. Lindsey, Margaret. Annotated bibliography on the professional education of teachers. Association for Student Teaching, 1969. 183p. ED 029855 (MF)

Section I contains 466 print materials in five categories. Section II presents 164 references to nonprint items, including films, records, and tapes.

2864. Sandefur, J. T. and Alex A. Bressler. Classroom observation systems in preparing school personnel: an annotated bibliography. ERIC Clearinghouse on Teacher Education, 1970. 10p. ED 036483.

Includes 39 books, articles, reports, and manuals dating from 1943 to 1969.

2865. Ross, Marlene. Preparing school personnel for an open society: a guide to selected documents in the ERIC collection, 1966-1968. Washington, DC, National Education Association,

1969. 98p. ED 028156.

Covers school integration, teaching minorities and disadvantaged, teaching English as a second langugage, teaching migrants and rural youth, teaching superior students,
and teaching on the college level. Annotates 166 documents.

2866. Ross, Marlene. Structured practice in preparing school
personnel: a guide to selected documents in the ERIC collection, 1966-1968. ERIC Clearinghouse on Teacher Education,
1969. 68p. ED 026349.

Covers microteaching, use of television, inservice programs, simulation, role playing, sensitivity training,
and instruments for analysis of classroom behavior, among
other topics. 100 books, articles, and papers dating
from 1959 to 1968 are included.

2867. Teacher education and media: a selective and annotated
bibliography. Washington, DC, American Association of Colleges
for Teacher Education, 1964. 55p. ED 021471 (MF)

2868. Smith, Holly D. and Daniel J. Dieterich. A Selected
annotated bibliography on teacher preparation and certification. Urbana, IL, National Council of Teachers of English,
1971. 19p. ED 058208.

Contains 103 entries, and covers both traditional and innovative methods and criteria.

2869. Evertts, Eldonna L. Selected annotated bibliography:
English, English education, and certification. Champaign, IL,
National Council of Teachers of English, 1968. 38p. ED 022
778.

Provides 61 evaluative references on the historical development and current status of teacher preparation and certification.

2870. McGuire, Carson. Behavioral science memorandum number
ten. Austin, University of Texas, Research and Development
Center for Teacher Education, 1966. 36p. ED 023121.

This issue annotates 137 books, articles, and other publications related to teacher education.

2871. Science education information report: teacher education.
ERIC Information Analysis Center for Science Education, 1969.
36p. ED 032441.

Lists 113 unannotated entries related to science and mathematics education, including textbooks, manuals, and research reports.

2872. Cruickshank, Donald R. and Frank W. Broadbent. Simulation in preparing school personnel: a bibliography. ERIC
Clearinghouse on Teacher Education, 1970. 13p. ED 036465.

This unannotated list includes 130 books, articles, reports, papers, and theses. Most were published in the
1960's, but a few date back to 1953.

2873. Kovac, Roberta J. and Michael A. Pollack. Simulation/
gaming in teacher education: an annotated bibliography of selected sources for use in the development of teacher training
programs. Bloomington, University of Indiana, School of Education, 1975(?) 40p. ED 112836.

    Includes 23 simulations or games, and 134 other referen-
    ces on the subject.

2874. Westby-Gibson, Dorothy. Inservice education: perspectives for educators. Far West Laboratory for Educational Research and Development, 1967. 82p. ED 015161.

    Covers the 1950 to 1967 period, and includes in its lit-
    erature 184 entries.

2875. Edelfelt, Roy A. Inservice teacher education: sources
in the ERIC system. ERIC Clearinghouse on Teacher Education,
1975. 17p. ED 099308.

    256 documents were reviewed, and 30 of them were selected
    for annotation in this bibliography. They are all from
    1973 and 1974.

2876. Glazer-Waldman, Hilda R. Teaching internships: an annotated bibliography. St. Louis, Evaluative Research Associates,
Inc., 1978. 19p. ED 162963.

    The entries date from 1964 to 1977, and cover student
    teaching and teacher education programs, inservice pro-
    grams, and studies of effective teaching.

2877. Bjerstedt, Ake and Evy Gustafsson. Towards intergroup
and global solidarity via teacher training: teacher training
as a vehicle in fostering intercultural awareness, intergroup
understanding, and global solidarity: a collection of abstracts. Malmo, Sweden, School of Education, 1978. 112p.
ED 166069.

    Includes over 100 items available from the ERIC system,
    1966-1976.

2878. Poliakoff, Lorraine. Preparing school personnel: early
childhood education. ERIC Clearinghouse on Teacher Education,
1970. 12p. ED 043581.

    The 25 citations refer to teacher training for kindergar-
    ten and nursery situations, and Head Start programs.

2879. Olmsted, Lucia. Teacher Corps teacher education materials bibliography: the Bambi collection. Emporia, Kansas
State Teachers College, 1972. 75p. ED 092544.

    Includes materials for training teachers, teacher certifi-

cation, management materials, community-based education
materials, team teaching, differentiated staffing, and
materials relating to ethnic studies.

2880. Alternatives: an annotated bibliography of selected
topics related to alternative and inservice education. Washington, DC, Teacher Corps, Office of Education, 1976. 63p.
ED 131042.

Over 500 recent journal articles are listed under 38 subject headings.

2881. Ross, Naomi V. Community college teacher preparation
programs in the United States: a bibliography with introductory notes. Pennsylvania State University, Center for the
Study of Higher Education, 1972. 30p. ED 100409.

This annotated bibliography contains books, articles,
dissertations, and speeches from the 1950's to 1972.

2882. Ewens, Bill. Preparing graduate students to teach: a
selected annotated bibliography. Washington, DC, American
Sociological Association, 1977. 33p. ED 139713.

Includes 110 citations, most published since 1970.

2883. Cockburn, I. Elementary teacher education/certifica-
tion: an annotated bibliography, 1963-1973. Toronto, Ontario
Institute for Studies in Education, 1974. 54p. ED 099385.

Includes books, articles, reports, dissertations, tapes,
and other bibliographies.

2884. Howard, Norma K. Education of preschool and elementary
teachers:an abstract bibliography. ERIC Clearinghouse on Early
Childhood Education, 1974. 68p. ED 097130.

The 130 ERIC documents include inservice training.

2885. Elliott, Peggy G. Field experiences in preservice
teacher education. ERIC Clearinghouse on Teacher Education,
1978. 96p. ED 159138.

An annotated list of documents and articles from RIE and
CIJE, 1968 to 1977.

2886. Pre-service teacher education in Canada: bibliographies
in education. Ottawa, Canadian Teachers' Federation, 1969.
26p. ED 034726.

The 358 items in this bibliography include books, parts
of books, papers, articles, and 51 theses. Most of the
material was published in the previous ten years.

2887. Professional education: a selective bibliography. Arlington, VA, Council for Exceptional Children, 1972. 32p.
ED 072592.

Includes 100 abstracts concerning the teaching of handicapped children. Publication dates range from 1943 to 1971.

2888. Performance-based teacher education: an annotated bibliography. Washington, DC, American Association of Colleges for
Teacher Education, 1972. 64p. ED 065477.

Covers the kinds and nature of performance based education,
its improvement and assessment, and teacher certification.
Contains 189 entries.

2889. Performance-based teacher education: publications and
sources of information for educators. New Haven, CT, Education Improvement Center, 1973. 37p. ED 083181.

The annotated bibliography covers programs, criteria, and
evaluation.

2890. Gebhard, Ann O. and Patricia K. Waelder. Annotated
bibliography for planning, implementing, and assessing a competency-based teacher preparation program in English education, 1961-1975. 1976. 27p. ED 126088.

2891. Pascale, Pietro J. Competency-based teacher education:
an annotated bibliography. 1974. 71p. ED 095115.

Includes 158 entries dating from 1952 to 1974.

2892. Kay, Patricia M. and John E. Schoener. Program evaluation for competency based teacher education: a brief review
of literature and an annotated bibliography. New York, City
University, Center for Advanced Study in Education, 1975. 74p.
ED 164615.

The 150 entries in four sections deal with theoretical and
philosophical issues, models and strategies, teacher assessment, development of competency based programs and
modules, and descriptions of existing programs.

2893. Clarke, Dennis. Competency based vocational teacher
education: an annotated bibliography. Athens, University of
Georgia, Division of Vocational Education, 1974. 98p. ED
110627.

The 331 entries include many ERIC documents.

2894. Benedict, Marjorie A. Competency-based teacher education: a bibliography of bibliographies. Albany, State University of New York, Teacher Education Developmental Service,
1975. 6p. ED 118565.

Most of the unannotated citations are dated post-1970.
Some are ERIC documents.

TEACHER EVALUATION

2895. Blount, Gail. Teacher evaluation: an annotated bibliography. Toronto, Ontario Institute for Studies in Education,
1974. 43p. ED 093033.

Covers the purposes, the criteria, and the evaluators. A
final section includes listings that deal with the subject
from an essentially Canadian point of view.

2896. Teacher evaluation: bibliographies in education. Ottawa, Canadian Teachers' Federation, 1975. 31p. ED 110447.

The topics deal with performance based teacher education,
accountability, effective teaching, and staff development.
This unannotated bibliography includes 150 books, 209 articles, and eleven theses.

2897. Rosen, Pamela. Assessment of teachers. Princeton, NJ,
Educational Testing Service, 1973. 11p. ED 083322.

This annotated test bibliography includes 53 items.

2898. Baral, Laurie R. The Evaluation of teachers: ERS annotated bibliography. Washington, DC, Educational Research Service, 1974. 22p. ED 089478 (MF)

A 125 item list taken from the issues of RIE and CIJE.

2899. De Wolf, Virginia A. Student ratings of instruction
in postsecondary institutions: a comprehensive annotated bibliography of research reported since 1968. Seattle, University of Washington, Bureau of Testing, 1974. 86p. ED 093248.

Includes 220 journal articles, but does not cover theory
or evaluations.

2900. Coley, Richard J. Student evaluation of teacher effectiveness. ERIC Clearinghouse on Tests, Measurement, and Evaluations, 1975. 65p. ED 117194.

The 163 annotated entries are drawn from RIE, CIJE, and
the psychological literature. They are not limited to any
educational level or curriculum area.

2901. Scott, Craig S. and Gaylord Thorne. Assessing faculty
performance: a partially annotated bibliography. Monmouth,
Oregon State System of Higher Education, Teaching Research
Division, 1974. 20p. ED 093187.

Contains 139 recent references to books and articles.

2902. Harrison, Patrick and Lillian Edmonson. An Annotated
bibliography of the evaluation of college and university teaching effectiveness. San Diego State University, 1975. 15p.
ED 111772.

Most of the information included is from the student point
of view. Contains books, articles, and ERIC documents.

2903. Leigh, Terry. <u>A Selected and annotated bibliography</u>
<u>on evaluating performance of college faculty members</u>. Lexing-
ton, University of Kentucky, 1969. 30p. ED 035376.

    The 56 entries deal with methods, procedures, and problems
in faculty evaluation by students, peers, and administrators. The items date from 1961 to 1968.

2904. Kay, Patricia M. <u>Performance based certification</u>. New
York, City University, Office of Teacher Education, 1971.
62p. ED 056991.

    This annotated bibliography contains 115 citations dating
from 1957 to 1971, and covers teacher selection, observation, measurement, and research on teacher characteristics.

TEACHER IMPROVEMENT

2905. Gaff, Sally S. <u>Resource notebook</u>. Washington, DC,
Project on Institutional Renewal through the Improvement of
Teaching, 1976. 139p. ED 130591.

    Prepared as a guide to resources on several topics related
to the subject. Includes annotated bibliographies.

2906. Perlman, Daniel H. <u>Bibliography on the improvement of</u>
<u>teaching and learning</u>. Chicago, Roosevelt University, 1970.
6p. ED 055554.

    The 74 references are books and documents related to high-
er education. Not annotated.

2907. Hatch, Winslow R. and Ann Bennet. <u>Effectiveness in</u>
<u>teaching: new dimensions in higher education</u>. Washington, DC,
Office of Education, 1966. 36p. ED 145738.

    Covers directed learning, problem oriented approaches to
teaching, class size, and general methods.

2908. Webber, Robert. <u>Improving college teaching: an anno-</u>
<u>tated bibliography</u>. New Rochelle, NY, Change Magazine, 1976.
16p. ED 148221.

    The 105 references deal with group teaching, teaching sty-
les, learning contracts, faculty development, theories of
instruction, instructional technology, teacher evaluation
and accountability, motivation, innovation, individualized
instruction, and teacher characteristics.

TEACHERS

2909. <u>Evaluation of student teachers: bibliographies in edu-</u>
<u>cation</u>. Ottawa, Canadian Teachers' Federation, 1977. 82p.

ED 137226.

Annotates books, articles, and documents from the previous five years.

2910. A Bibliography of demand and supply of education personnel. Washington, DC, National Center for Education Statistics, 1975. 46p. ED 103367.

This annotated list covers all levels of education for the years 1970-1973.

2911. Tracz, George S. Annotated bibliography on determination of teachers' salaries and effective utilization of teacher manpower. Toronto, Ontario Institute for Studies in Education, 1971. 19p. ED 056374.

Most of the citations are included in the literature survey to ascertain the relevance of mathematical techniques to the determination of teacher salaries.

2912. Crum, Mary F. Teacher centers. Washington, DC, Bureau of Occupational and Adult Education (DHEW), 1977. 51p. ED 134556.

This bibliography is compiled from the previous five years of RIE and CIJE.

2913. Haynes, Donald. The American Federation of Teachers: a short annotated bibliography. Washington, DC, American Federation of Teachers, 1976. 11p. ED 164512.

Provides an overview and history, and covers collective bargaining and political action for social policies, and case studies of strikes and their consequences. Also includes discussion of the question of a merger with the National Education Association. Citations date from 1936 to 1976.

2914. Gage, N. L. Paradigms: an annotated bibliography with special reference to research on teaching. Stanford University, Center for Educational Research, 1977. 45p. ED 152779.

Includes 189 citations to journal articles and documents.

2915. Nerenz, Anne G. and Constance K. Knop. The Supervision of teachers: a selected annotated bibliography. ERIC Clearinghouse on Teacher Education, 1979. 36p. ED 166169.

Provides references to theoretical models and practical styles. Entries date from 1965 to 1979.

2916. Teacher characteristics, student characteristics. ERIC Information Analysis Center for Science Education, 1969. 21p. ED 030782.

Includes 49 unannotated entries.

2917. Spencer, Mima. Bibliography: teacher characteristics.
ERIC Clearinghouse on Early Childhood Education, 1969. 51p.
ED 029716.

Most of the 82 annotated entries refer to preschool or
primary levels.

2918. Balzer, A. L. A Review of research on teacher behavior relating to science education. Association for the Education of Teachers in Science, 1973. 522p. ED 087638.

The 1300 studies included were produced between 1960 and
1971.

2919. Flaxman, Erwin. A Selected bibliography on teacher
attitudes. ERIC Clearinghouse on the Urban Disadvantaged,
1969. 23p. ED 027357.

Annotates studies on racial and social attitudes of the
middle-class urban teacher related to student performance.
Also includes reports of inservice programs conducted to
change negative teacher attitudes.

2920. Stern, Carolyn and Evan R. Keislar. Teacher attitudes
and attitude change. Los Angeles, UCLA, Teacher Education
Laboratory, 1975. 68p. ED 109074.

This is volume three, a comprehensive bibliography for
the study presented in volumes one and two which are a-
vailable as ED 109072 and ED 109073. Much of the bibliography was compiled from RIE; it also includes dissertations, and psychological literature.

2921. Pincus, Richard E. and Judith W. Baum. Classified bibliography of journal articles on school personnel, 1966. New
York, City University, Division of Teacher Education, 1967.
35p. ED 015883.

The 480 unannotated items were compiled from a search of
150 journals issued during 1966.

TEACHING LOAD

2922. Teacher workload. Ottawa, Canadian Teachers' Federation, 1971. 33p. ED 054060.

This unannotated bibliography covers assignment and distribution, class size and pupil-teacher ratio, hours of
work, and morale. It includes 467 references to books,
papers, and articles dating from 1954 to 1970.

2923. Moll, Marita. Teacher workload: bibliographies in education. Ottawa, Canadian Teachers' Federation, 1978. 73p.
ED 161827.

This annotated bibliography updates the previous entry by

listing materials from 1968 to 1976. It includes articles
in both English and French.

2924. Bibliographies of research in the teaching of English.
Champaign, IL, National Council of Teachers of English, 1961.
49p. ED 043617.

A collection of annotated bibliographies that includes
studies on teaching loads of English teachers, among other
topics.

TEACHING METHODS

2925. Training methodology: an annotated bibliography. Washington, DC, Public Health Service (DHEW), 1969. ED 034032
through ED 034035 (MF)

Part I: background theory and research contains 310 references in 98 pages. Part II: planning and administration
contains 447 references in 128 pages. Part III: instructional methods and techniques contains 345 references in
109 pages. Part IV: audiovisual theory, aids, and equipment contains 332 references in 89 pages. All are annotated.

2926. Tamminen, Paul G. A Guide to resources for undergraduate academic reform. Washington, DC, American Council on
Education, 1970. 15p. ED 044086.

This special report is a bibliography for the study of
undergraduate learning, curriculum, and instruction.

2927. Instructional procedures. ERIC Information Analysis
Center for Science Education, 1970. 96p. ED 047933.

Contains 428 citations related to teaching methods in science and mathematics. Not annotated.

2928. Diagnostic teaching: a selective bibliography. Arlington, VA, Council for Exceptional Children, 1972. 19p. ED
069071.

Annotates 48 publications dealing with handicapped children and special education. The references are dated 1965
to 1971.

2929. Johnson, James R. and William W. Wilen. Questions and
questioning: research studies. 1974. 9p. ED 099279.

The entries are dated from 1912 to 1973; most are doctoral dissertations.

2930. Korn, Max. Bibliography: precision teaching. Toronto,
National Institute on Mental Retardation, 1974. 6p. ED 096
807.

Covers behavior modification and teaching methods with
handicapped students. The 84 unannotated entries include
books, articles, and dissertations.

2931. Bibliography on verbal learning. Harvard University,
1966. 6p. ED 011305.

The 50 unannotated references date from 1960 to 1965.

TEAM TEACHING

2932. Smith, Donna M. and Judith P. Fitch. Team teaching
bibliography. Minneapolis, Upper Midwest Regional Educational
Laboratory, 1969. 103p. ED 035098.

Includes 120 ERIC documents, 130 books and pamphlets, 7
films, 700 journal articles, and 120 other reports, papers,
studies, and theses. Not annotated. Most all were published
since 1950.

2933. Davis, Harold S. Team teaching: a selected annotated
bibliography. Educational Research Council of Greater Cleveland, 1967. 56p. ED 023159.

Includes over 300 entries published since 1958 for elementary and secondary levels. Some films are also listed.

2934. Team teaching: bibliographies in education. Ottawa,
Canadian Teachers' Federation, 1971. 38p. ED 055044.

Contains 554 references to books, parts of books, papers,
articles, and theses. All were published between 1960 and
1971. Not annotated.

TECHNICAL EDUCATION   See   VOCATIONAL EDUCATION

TECHNOLOGY   See   SCIENCE AND TECHNOLOGY

TELECOMMUNICATIONS   See   COMMUNICATIONS

TELEVISION   See also   CABLE TV   and   EDUCATIONAL TELEVISION

2935. Clark, Richard E. Children's television: the best of
ERIC. ERIC Clearinghouse on Information Resources, 1978.
76p. ED 152254.

Annotates research reviews, position papers, and planning
documents from the ERIC system, 1974-1977. The 100 entries
cover effects of TV on the learning of social behaviors,
and using TV in the classroom, among other topics.

2936. Children and television: an abstract bibliography.
ERIC Clearinghouse on Early Childhood Education, 1975. 61p.
ED 113058.

Areas covered include the effects of programing and com-
mercials on children's creativity, reading, social behavior, and susceptibility to stereotypes, and the role of
parents and teachers in mediating between television and
young viewers. The 127 entries are from RIE and CIJE, 1971
through 1974.

2937. CTW research bibliography: research papers relating to
the Children's Television Workshop and its experimental educational series: "Sesame Street" and "The Electric Company",
1968-1976. New York, Children's Television Workshop, 1976.
23p. ED 133079.

The annotated entries also include other theoretical and
scholarly discussions of research topics within the scope
of media and children.

2938. Atkin, Charles K. Television and social behavior: an
annotated bibliography of research focusing on television's
impact on children. Rockville, MD, National Institute of Mental Health, 1971. 153p. ED 056478.

The annotated portion includes 300 references; an unannotated supplement includes 250 more.

2939. Schramm, Wilbur. The Effects of television on children
and adolescents: an annotated bibliography with an overview
of research results, reports, and papers on mass communication.
UNESCO, 1964. 55p. ED 017197.

Citations include effects on leisure time and learning,
and psychological implications.

2940. Adler, Richard P. Research on the effects of television advertising on children: a review of the literature and
recommendations for future research. Washington, DC, National
Science Foundation, 1977. 230p. ED 145499.

In addition to the bibliography, evaluations of 21 other
studies are appended.

2941. Elsas, Diana. Children and film/television. Washington, DC, American Film Institute, 1977. 10p. ED 153653 (MF)

A bibliography and filmography for elementary and secondary levels. Annotated.

2942. Elsas, Diana. Film/television: a research guide. Washington, DC, American Film Institute, 1977. 29p. ED 153616.

Annotates a variety of television and film reference books,
guides, and indexes, plus some dissertations.

2943. Elsas, Diana. Film and television periodicals in Eng-

lish. Washington, DC, American Film Institute, 1977. 13p.
ED 153648 (MF)

Annotated, but not meant to be comprehensive.

2944. Elsas, Diana. Film/television grants, scholarships, and
special programs. Washington, DC, American Film Institute,
1977. 23p. ED 153617.

Includes an annotated bibliography.

2945. Bierschenk, B. Television as a technical aid in education and in educational and psychological research: a bibliography. Malmo, Sweden, School of Education, 1971. 29p. ED
049644.

Primarily composed of dissertations and ERIC documents.

2946. Kiefl, J. B. Notes and sources for the content analysis of television. 1978. 43p. ED 158732.

An extensive unannotated bibliography that includes sam-
pling and measurement.

2947. An Annotated gathering of the best of ERIC on research
on television. ERIC Clearinghouse on Information Resources,
1976. 16p. ED 125528.

The 32 documents include an overview, children and television, project reports, cable television, and bibliographies.

TENNESSEE

2948. A Bibliography of materials on the upper Cumberland
region. Livingston, TN, Upper Cumberland Project, 1967. 5p.
ED 020067.

The unannotated list includes 17 books, 34 master's theses,
and other materials published between 1941 and 1966.

TENURE

2949. Jensen, Ida-Marie. Tenure: a selected bibliography.
Logan, Utah State University Library, 1974. 31p. ED 091986.

Includes books, articles, dissertations on the various
aspects of tenure. Not annotated.

TERRORISM

2950. Boston, Guy D. Terrorism: a selected bibliography.

Washington, DC, National Institute of Law Enforcement and Criminal Justice, 1977.   62p.   ED 152663.

   Annotates 85 items that include concepts of violence, and terrorist philosophy and motivation.

TESTS AND TESTING

2951.   Backer, Thomas E.   A Directory of information on tests. ERIC Clearinghouse on Tests, Measurement, and Evaluation, 1977. 42p.   ED 152802.

   Includes an annotated bibliography.

2952.   Porter, Deborah E. and Barbara Wildemuth.   State assessment and training programs: an annotated ERIC bibliography. ERIC Clearinghouse on Tests, Measurement, and Evaluation, 1976. 85p.   ED 141389.

   Part I includes 39 documents and articles describing the design and implementation of programs. Part II is a state-by-state listing of 150 technical reports by those who have or have had testing programs.

2953.   Bye, Thomas J.   Tests that measure language ability: a descriptive compilation.   Berkeley, CA, Unified School District, 1977.   91p.   ED 181083.

   Includes 40 commercial and non-commercial tests.

2954.   Bibliography on testing and measurement.   Harvard University, 1966.   10p.   ED 011304.

   80 unannotated tests dating from 1960 are listed. Subjects include school readiness, criterion measures, personality measurement, statistical trends, and reliability.

2955.   Vollbrecht, Michele T.   Grade equivalent scores: an annotated bibliography.   ERIC Clearinghouse on Tests, Measurement, and Evaluation, 1977.   19p.   ED 141386.

   Includes 23 documents and journal articles which describe the derivation, use, and misuse of grade equivalent scores.

2956.   Wildemuth, Barbara.   Test anxiety: an extensive bibliography.   ERIC Clearinghouse on Tests, Measurement, and Evaluation, 1977.   114p.   ED 152860.

   Contains ERIC documents, dissertations, and articles from the psychological and sociological literature.

2957.   Wissman, Dale J.   Audiovisual proficiency testing: annotated bibliography.   Brooks AFB, TX, Air Force Human Resources Laboratory, 1977.   18p.   ED 152807.

   Relates to the AV testing of job proficiency.

2958. Passmore, David L. References to the Rasch one para-
meter logistic measurement model. 1973. 10p. ED 078018.

The 96 unannotated entries include both theoretical and
empirical studies.

2959. Test bias: a bibliography. ERIC Clearinghouse on Tests,
Measurement, and Evaluation, 1971. 12p. ED 051312.

Lists books, articles, research reports, and reference
works. Not annotated.

2960. Pasanella, Ann K. Bibliography of test criticism. New
York, College Entrance Examination Board, 1967. 56p. ED 039
395.

Annotates 47 scholarly items from the previous ten years.

2961. Berger, Allen. Thirty-five annotated references to
writings related to test-taking appearing between 1935 and
1970. 1970. 11p. ED 044263.

Prepared for a seminar of college directors of reading
centers at the International Reading Association convention, 1970.

2962. Evaluation bibliography: parent, child decision makers.
Chapel Hill, University of North Carolina, Technical Assistance Development System, 1973. 42p. ED 081789.

An annotated list of tests for children and parents to
measure language, cognition, self-help, social-affective,
visual-motor, and physical health.

2963. Cornish, Richard D. Annotated bibliography of MMPI research among college populations, 1962-1970. Madison, University of Wisconsin Counseling Center, 1971. 16p. ED 069755.

Includes 49 articles on the Minnesota Multiphasic Personality Inventory.

2964. Rosenthal, Elsa J. and Albert E. Beaton. Annotated
bibliography. New York, College Entrance Examination Board,
1976. 14p. ED 148879 (MF)

Cites 32 reports and other publications pertaining to national declines in abilities and in test scores. The references date back to 1961.

2965. Cook, John J. Test anthology: fugitive and standardized
tests. Madison, Wisconsin State Department of Public Instruction, 1971. 257p. ED 069051.

Annotates 300 tests intended for special education.

2966. Berger, Barbara. An Annotated bibliography of measurements for young children. New York, Center for Urban Educa-

tion, 1969. 53p. ED 068519.

For preschool and kindergarten levels. Most of these are not commercially produced.

2967. Annotated bibliography on applied performance testing. Portland, OR, Northwest Regional Education Laboratory, 1975. 61p. ED 121821.

Includes publications on the development and applications of applied performance testing in many subject areas.

2968. Hawisher, Margaret F. Competency testing: annotated bibliography. 1979. 38p. ED 181084.

Includes overviews, basic skills, compensatory education, cost effectiveness, curriculum, district programs, and graduation requirements. Legal aspects and handicapped students are also covered.

2969. Jackson, Michael and Barbara Battiste. Competency testing: an annotated bibliography. 1978. 30p. ED 167503.

All entries are dated 1976-1978. Includes program descriptions.

2970. Keller, Claudia M. Criterion referenced measurement: a bibliography. ERIC Clearinghouse on Tests, Measurement, and Evaluation, 1972. 14p. ED 060041.

References date from 1965 to 1972. The entries are from RIE, CIJE, and the library collection at Educational Testing Service.

2971. Hsu, Tse-chi and M. Elizabeth Boston. Criterion-referenced measurement: an annotated bibliography. University of Pittsburgh, Learning Research and Development Center, 1972. 25p. ED 068531.

The 52 items included date from 1913 to 1971, and annotate published and unpublished material.

2972. Hahn, Christine. Domain referenced testing: an annotated ERIC bibliography. ERIC Clearinghouse on Tests, Measurement, and Evaluation, 1977. 22p. ED 152803.

The 32 items are not limited to any educational level or subject area.

2973. Ellsworth, Randolph A. and Carleen Franz. Bibliography on criterion referenced measurement. 1975. 24p. ED 115699.

Includes 262 unannotated references. All entries contained in numbers 2970 and 2971 (above) are listed in this bibliography.

2974. Knapp, Joan. A Collection of criterion-referenced tests.

ERIC Clearinghouse on Tests, Measurement, and Evaluation, 1974. 13p. ED 099427.

Annotates 21 tests.

2975. Nondiscriminatory testing: a selective bibliography. Reston, VA, Council for Exceptional Children, 1976. 27p. ED 129005.

Contains 79 abstracts of documents and journal articles dated 1962 to 1975. ED 146742 is a 13 page supplement published in 1977 which has 50 citations.

2976. Cameron, Colin. Discrimination in testing: bibliography. Revised ed. Madison, University of Wisconsin, Institute for Research on Poverty, 1973. 146p. ED 086736.

Emphasis is on discrimination in the employment and ability testing of adults, rather than academic testing. Over 1000 books and articles are listed which date from 1942 to 1973.

2977. Lippey, Gerald. Bibliography on computer-assisted test construction. San Jose, CA, IBM Corporation, 1973. 5p. ED 095909.

Includes 64 references. Not annotated.

2978. Stetz, Frank P. Selected references concerning objective-based assessment: a bibliography. New York, Psychological Corporation, 1975. 55p. ED 126118.

This bibliography is divided in two parts: references dealing with instructional objectives, and those which deal with criterion referenced testing. Not annotated.

2979. Rosen, Pamela. Test collection bibliographies: criterion-referenced measures. Princeton, NJ, Educational Testing Service, 1973. 18p. ED 104910.

An annotated list of recent tests.

2980. Court, J. H. Researchers' bibliography for Raven's progressive matrices and Mill Hill vocabulary scales. Flinders University of South Australia, School of Social Sciences, 1972. 170p. ED 073161.

Some of the entries have clinical interest, anthropological interest, or vocational interest. Includes textbooks and normative data. Annotated.

2981. Kopita, Ronald R. Tests and testing programs. ERIC Clearinghouse on Counseling and Personnel Services, 1973. 28p. ED 082115.

Emphasis is on tests for counseling. Includes 167 ERIC documents, dissertations, and articles.

2982. Galant, Richard and Nancy J. Moncrieff. Testing and
testing programs. ERIC Clearinghouse on Counseling and Personnel Services, 1974. 31p. ED 105369.

Includes 153 ERIC documents, journal articles, and dissertations primarily intended for the counselor.

TEXTBOOK SELECTION

2983. Textbook selection and controversy: the best of ERIC.
ERIC Clearinghouse on Educational Management, 1976. 5p. ED
119287.

Summarizes eleven publications selected from RIE and CIJE.

THEATRE ARTS

2984. Claener, Ann. English and American theatre and drama:
a student's guide to reference sources. Montreal, McGill University Library, 1977. 28p. ED 149378 (MF)

Includes a variety of annotated reference materials.

2985. Norris, Lynne. A Theatre movement bibliography. Washington, DC, University and College Theatre Association, 1978.
23p. ED 154468.

The partially annotated list covers anatomy, kinesiology,
combat and martial arts, mime, movement notation systems,
and movement techniques and theories.

2986. Frankel, Edith. Drama: a guide to theater materials
in the Frederick W. Crumb Memorial Library, State University
College, Potsdam, New York. 1978. 128p. ED 154823.

This annotated library guide deals with general and specific aspects of the theatre.

2987. Adler, Richard R. and Lawana Trout. Creative dramatics:
a selected bibliography. Champaign, National Council of Teachers of English, 1971. 7p. ED 058211.

Annotates 47 books and articles.

2988. Moe, Christian and Jay E. Raphael. A Bibliography of
theatrical craftsmanship. New York, Speech Communication
Association, 1974. 22p. ED 091774.

Covers administration and management of the theatre, act-
ing, directing, playwriting, design and technology, and
production. The bibliography is composed of articles from
major English language periodicals in the field. Not annotated.

2989. DeYoung, James L. A Bibliographic guide to all plays published in Theatre Arts Magazine from the Spring of 1948 to the last published issue in January 1964. 1964. 8p. ED 132 616.

Over 180 plays are listed by title.

2990. Marlor, Clark S. Readers' theatre bibliography, 1965-1969. New York, Speech Communication Association, 1973. 15p. ED 087048.

The first section is a list of books, articles, and dissertations. The second section is a listing of suggested plays, poetry, and prose materials for group reading.

2991. Mersand, Joseph. Guide to play selection: a selective bibliography for production and study of modern plays. Third ed. Urbana, IL, National Council of Teachers of English, 1975. 296p. ED 109696.

Lists over 400 anthologies of plays, and describes the production details for 850 plays.

2992. Wilkerson, Margaret B. Selected bibliography of Black theatre materials. 1976. 16p. ED 127650.

Includes a selection of plays and musicals, and provides a guide to reference works, dissertations, and periodicals.

2993. Tedesco, John L. A Select bibliography of plays written by Black American playwrights between 1955 and 1970. 1975. 8p. ED 103926.

The plays included were both published and produced in New York City, either on or off Broadway, or in one of the Black theatres.

2994. Weisfeld, Zelma H. Selected annotated bibliography on costume design and construction. ERIC Clearinghouse on Reading and Communication Skills, 1975. 8p. ED 103919.

Intended for use in secondary schools, colleges, and repertory and professional costume shops.

2995. Weisfeld, Zelma H. Selected annotated bibliography on costume history. ERIC Clearinghouse on Reading and Communication Skills, 1975. 9p. ED 102639.

Most of the books include illustrations.

THESAURI

2996. Pope, Nolan F. Thesauri used by SLA Documentation Division members. Special Libraries Association, 1977. 27p. ED 156188.

Cites 115 thesauri most frequently used.

TRACK AND FIELD

2997. Morrison, Ray Leon. An Annotated bibliography of track
and field books published in the United States between 1960
and 1974. San Jose State University, 1975. 115p. ED 147271.

A comprehensive list is the aim of this master's thesis.

TRADE EDUCATION   See   VOCATIONAL EDUCATION

TRAINING

2998. Planning, organizing, and evaluating training programs:
personnel bibliography series. Washington, DC, Civil Service
Commission, 1971. 144p. ED 085546.

Deals with sensitivity training, orientation training,
internships, work-study programs, games and simulation
techniques, programmed instruction, case study methods,
and role playing. Annotated.

2999. Valverde, Horace H. Annotated bibliography of the ad-
vanced systems division reports, 1950-1972. Wright-Patterson
AFB, OH, Air Force Human Resources Laboratory, 1973. 265p.
ED 075714.

Covers research and development in the area of training
techniques, and the psychological and engineering aspects
of training equipment.

3000. Stephenson, Robert W. and James R. Burkett. An Action
oriented review of the on-the-job training literature. Washington, DC, American Institute for Research in the Behavioral
Sciences, 1974. 169p. ED 110702.

Includes literature from both civilian and military
sources. Annotated.

3001. Gant, Charles R. Economics of on-the-job training:
annotated bibliography and literature review. Lowry AFB, CO,
Air Force Human Resources Laboratory, 1977. 35p. ED 156903.

Contains 88 annotated entries, and an additional four
pages of unannotated citations. Lists Rand reports, ERIC
documents, and other publications.

TRANSPORTATION

3002. Doctoral dissertations on transportation: a bibliogra-

phy. Evanston, IL, Northwestern University, 1971. 21p. ED
062550.

The 283 entries cover traffic analysis, urban travel, and
physical distribution, among other topics. Unannotated;
most are dated 1969-1970.

3003. Dubois, Carol J. and Mona Buckley. Transportation in
the age of homespun: a bibliography. Oneonta, State University of New York, 1967. 14p. ED 018322.

Covers canal and river travel, railroads, carriages, and
wagons. Cites 93 books, papers, and articles.

3004. Preparation for careers in transportation: teacher's
guide. Columbus, Ohio State Department of Education, 1973.
116p. ED 159310.

Includes an unannotated bibliography, and is intended for
teachers at the grade 11 and 12 level.

3005. Wood, Tom and Edwin T. Petrie. Orientation to careers
in transportation: teacher's guide. Columbus, Ohio State Department of Education, 1973. 86p. ED 159306.

Includes an unannotated bibliography of books, articles,
films, and government publications.

3006. Exploration of careers in transportation: teacher's
guide. Columbus, Ohio State Department of Education, 1973.
86p. ED 159308.

Intended for use by teachers at the grade 9 and 10 levels.
The bibliography includes films, books, articles, and government publications. Not annotated.

TRUSTEES

3007. Terrey, John N. A Trustee reading list: bibliographic
essay. ERIC Clearinghouse for Junior College Information,
1977. 43p. ED 143395.

Covers roles, relationships, governance, collective bargaining, planning, and budgeting at the community college
level.

3008. Perlman, Daniel H. Selected bibliography on trustees
and trusteeship. Chicago, Roosevelt University, 1970. 7p.
ED 055553.

Includes over 100 references to books, articles, and conference proceedings published since 1958. Unannotated.

TUTORING

3009. Wilkes, Roberta. Peer and cross-age tutoring and related topics: an annotated bibliography. Madison, University
of Wisconsin, Research and Development Center for Cognitive
Learning, 1975. 76p. ED 114372.

  Compiled from a search of educational and psychological
  literature from 1960 to 1973.

TWAIN, MARK

3010. Haviland, Virginia and Margaret Coughlan. Samuel Lang-
horne Clemens: a centennial for Tom Sawyer: an annotated, selected bibliography. Washington, DC, Library of Congress,
Children's Book Section, 1976. 66p. ED 137806.

  Lists editions of Twain classics most widely read by young
  people. Also includes foreign language editions, biocrit-
  ical works, and bibliographies.

UNEMPLOYMENT   See also   EMPLOYMENT

3011. Unemployment and retraining: an annotated bibliography
of research. Washington, DC, Office of Manpower, Automation,
and Training (DOL), 1965. 36p. ED 018642.

  Includes 57 research studies related to social-psychological factors in job training and hard-core unemployment.
  The publications date from 1931 to 1964.

3012. Cameron, Colin and Anita B. Menon. Hard-core unemployment: a selected, annotated bibliography. Madison, University
of Wisconsin, Institute for Research on Poverty, 1969. 29p.
ED 039323.

  The references include books, articles, and films on the
  sociology of the group, training programs, and business
  and the hard-core unemployed.

3013. Mesics, Emil and Samuel Marcus. The Hard-core unemployed: an annotated bibliography. Ithaca, NY, School of Industrial and Labor Relations at Cornell University, 1969. 5p.
ED 032424 (MF)

  Covers poverty, national policy, retraining programs,
  specific applications, and experiences with integrating
  the hard-core unemployed into work involvement. The 41
  entries date from 1964 to 1968.

UNGRADED SCHOOLS See NONGRADED SCHOOLS

UNION OF SOVIET SOCIALIST REPUBLICS

3014. Hawkins, John N. and Jon Maksik. Teacher's resource handbook for Russian and East European studies: an annotated bibliography of curriculum materials, preschool through grade twelve. Los Angeles, UCLA Center for Russian and East European Studies, 1976. 54p. ED 133240 (MF)

Contains 633 multimedia entries arranged by grade level.

3015. Apanasewicz, Nellie. Education in the USSR: an annotated bibliography of English language materials, 1965–1973. Washington, DC, Office of Education, 1974. 104p. ED 109929.

The 347 entries stress bilingual education, career education, early childhood education, and education for the handicapped, but other aspects of education are also covered.

3016. Ukrainian instructional aids. Edmonton, Alberta Teachers Association, 1976. 7p. ED 150874.

Annotates 25 items for instruction in Ukrainian language, culture, history, and literature. Also covers their migration to Canada.

UNITED NATIONS

3017. Teaching materials on the UN: an annotated bibliography for elementary and secondary schools. New York, United Nations Association of the USA, 1973. 21p. ED 099253.

Includes audiovisual materials.

UNITED STATES HISTORY   See also   COLONIAL HISTORY

3018. Orr, Oliver H. A Guide to the study of the United States of America: representative books reflecting the development of American life and thought: supplement, 1956–1965. Washington, DC, Library of Congress, 1976. 536p. ED 156575 (MF)

This is an annotated supplement to the 1960 edition.

3019. Wright, Esmond. The Special relationship: the United States as the British have seen it: a selective reading list by British Writers. London, National Book League, 1976. 42p. ED 142460 (MF)

Annotates 250 entries providing a sample of how British students of USA studies perceive the New World, dating from 1940. Also includes 29 early accounts of life in the 19th Century South and New England, and diaries of Civil War correspondants and travellers to the Western Territories.

3020. Dubois, Carol J. and Mona Buckley. Life in the age of homespun: a bibliography. Oneonta, State University of New York, 1968. 11p. ED 018323.

Contains 69 annotated entries which describe daily life in early US history.

3021. Marsh, Sheila J. U.S. history: a media bibliography. Sacramento, California State University Library, 1978. 34p. ED 183471.

Annotates 60 filmstrips, audiotapes, slides, and video-tapes produced since 1956.

3022. Ramos, June E. and Barbara Crevling. Selective biblio-graphy in United States history resources. ERIC Clearinghouse for Social Studies/Social Science Education, 1977. 42p. ED 150032.

For grades 7 through 12. Includes print and nonprint ma-terials, and 17 games and simulations.

3023. Brown, Ralph and Marian. American history booklist for high schools: a selection for supplementary reading. Washing-ton, DC, National Council for the Social Studies, 1969. 218p. ED 040114 (MF)

Annotates 2000 references, and classifies them by type and reading level.

UNIVERSITIES See HIGHER EDUCATION

URBAN EDUCATION

3024. Vivolo, Robert L. ERIC references on urban and minor-ity education. ERIC Clearinghouse on the Urban Disadvantaged, 1978. 13p. ED 162013.

Covers bilingual education, compensatory education, school integration, and problems of inner city schools. ED 173506 is a 1978 supplement of 13 pages.

3025. Poliakoff, Lorraine. Urban society. ERIC Clearing-house on Teacher Education, 1970. 26p. ED 044383.

Cites 111 ERIC documents on urban education that were announced in 1968 and 1969.

3026. Holland, Nora. A Selected bibliography on the education of urban American Indian and Mexican American children. ERIC Clearinghouse on the Urban Disadvantaged, 1969. 22p. ED 029 935.

Covers bilingual schooling, and the acculturation/assimi-lation process. Abstracts 36 documents.

3027.   Randolph, H. Helen. Urban education bibliography: an
annotated listing. New York, Center for Urban Education, 1968.
110p. ED 024474.

    Includes a classified annotated list of 1000 entries, and
    another list of 350 items which are not annotated.

3028. Bibliography on urban education: supplement to bibliography on disadvantaged. Harvard University, 1966. 24p. ED
011309.

    The 220 unannotated citations cover dropouts, low achiev-
    ers, culturally deprived, family environment, and school
    desegregation. The entries date from 1961 to 1965.

3029. Klebe, John A. and Stuart C. Smith. Selected bibliography on educational parks. ERIC Clearinghouse on Educational Administration, 1969. 11p. ED 030219.

    The 63 books and articles relate educational parks to the
    educational needs of urban students.

3030. ERIC abstracts: a collection of ERIC document resumes
on urban crises in educational administration. Washington,
DC, American Association of School Administrators, 1970. 38p.
ED 036893.

    Includes 57 citations.

3031. Instructional materials for urban schools: a bibliogra-
phy of multi-ethnic textbooks and supplementary materials. New
York, American Educational Publishers Institute, 1969. 65p.
ED 033992.

    Lists 1000 titles for preschool through grade 12.

URBAN PLANNING   See also   PLANNING

3032. Thornton, Barbara. Gaming techniques for city planning:
a bibliography. Monticello, IL, Council of Planning Librarians, 1971. 15p. ED 062617.

    Compiled especially from the fields of administration and
    education. Simulation and decision-making theory are also
    included. Not annotated.

3033. Armstrong, Philip A. Planning urban services: a bibliography on new directions. Santa Monica, CA, Rand Corporation,
1976. 16p. ED 151451.

3034. Mitchell, Bruce and Joan. Benefit-cost analysis: a
select bibliography. Monticello, IL, Council of Planning Librarians, 1972. 46p. ED 106959.

    The sources present theoretical and applied aspects.

3035. Kinton, Jack F. The American community: a multidisciplinary bibliography. Monticello, IL, Council of Planning Librarians, 1970. 56p. ED 101428.

Many of the unannotated entries deal with city and regional planning.

3036. Cherukupalle, Nirmala devi. Application of multivariate statistical methods to urban and regional planning. Monticello, IL, Council of Planning Librarians, 1970. 14p. ED 101425.

This partially annotated bibliography includes some textbooks.

3037. Bolton, Charles K. and Donald W. Lenz. A Selected bibliography on planned change and community planning practice: making things happen. Monticello, IL, Council of Planning Librarians, 1971. 23p. ED 106953.

3038. Jenkins, Thomas H. and Robert Seufert. Theory, research, policy, and action: a bibliography on planning and social analysis. Monticello, IL, Council of Planning Librarians, 1975. 31p. ED 122348.

Not annotated. Includes books, parts of books, articles, and papers.

3039. Burg, Nan C. Fiscal management and planning for local governments: a selected bibliography of recent materials. Monticello, IL, Council of Planning Librarians, 1973. 32p. ED 106968.

URBAN STUDIES

3040. Allen, Irving L. An Annotated and classified list of 16mm films on urban studies: new towns, urban problems, city and regional planning. Monticello, IL, Council of Planning Librarians, 1975. 33p. ED 115537 (MF)

Lists over 100 films produced since 1960.

3041. Bibliography on the urban crisis: the behavioral, psychological, and sociological aspects of the urban crisis. Chevy Chase, MD, National Clearinghouse for Mental Health Information, 1968. 164p. ED 022837.

Most of the unannotated references were published since 1954.

3042. Steinwachs, Barbara. A Selected list of urban, environmental, and social problem gaming/simulations. Ann Arbor, University of Michigan Extension Service, 1977. 27p. ED 135 667 (MF)

The entries are suitable for a variety of age groups and

educational purposes. Bibliographies are appended.

3043. Daly, Kenneth. Institutions of higher education and
urban problems: a bibliography and review for planners. Monticello, IL, Council of Planning Librarians, 1973. 261p. ED
086116.

Some annotations and an author index are included for this
six part bibliography.

3044. Carmack, Norma J. Information sources for research in
urbanology: a basic bibliography. San Antonio, TX, Trinity
University, 1978. 16p. ED 164688.

This annotated list includes indexes and abstracts, dissertations, reference books, statistics, government sources, and periodicals.

3045. Blumenfeld, Hans. The Trend to the metropolis: bibliography. Monticello, IL, Council of Planning Librarians, 1970.
11p. ED 101427.

Covers urbanization in Canada, rural-urban migration,
public finance, urban planning, population change, industrial location, social mobility, and theories of urbanization. Not annotated.

3046. Roles of cities in human services. Washington, DC,
Project Share (DHEW), 1976. 42p. ED 129958.

Annotations and an author index are included.

3047. Peterson, Emy M. New communities: a bibliography.
1975. 11p. ED 103506.

Annotates 22 books, and contains a list of 40 periodicals
that carry literature on new communities.

3048. Urban outlook: a selected bibliography of films, filmstrips, slides, and audiotapes. Washington, DC, Department
of Housing and Urban Development, 1969. 38p. ED 037078 (MF)

Over 200 titles are briefly annotated, and cover architecture, building standards, ghetto problems, urban planning, and redevelopment.

3049. Clark, Walter E. Community power and decision-making:
a selective bibliography. Monticello, IL, Council of Planning
Librarians, 1971. 28p. ED 058518.

Includes studies on the small and large community, comparative studies, and theoretical studies.

VALUES EDUCATION

3050. Superka, Douglas P. Values education sourcebook: con-

ceptual approaches, materials analyses, and an annotated bibliography. ERIC Clearinghouse for Social Studies/Social Science Education, 1976. 262p. ED 118465.

Over 400 references conclude this resource guide for
teachers and curriculum designers.

3051. Thomas, Walter L. A Comprehensive bibliography on the
value concept. Grand Rapids, MI, Northview Public Schools,
1967. 45p. ED 024064.

Not annotated.

3052. Burgess, Evangeline. Values in early childhood education. Washington, DC, National Education Association, 1965.
94p. ED 088565 (MF)

Includes studies of the effects of nursery school and kindergarten on children's social, personal, emotional, and
intellectual development. Other reports focus on race
awareness, dramatic play, and culturally disadvantaged
children. Some are annotated.

3053. Middleberg, Maurice I. Moral education and student
development during the college years: a selective annotated
bibliography. Tucson, University of Arizona, Program in Liberal Studies, 1977. 62p. ED 146882.

Includes 40 books and anthologies. Covers major theoretical and empirical findings in moral learning, development,
and education, and the effects of a college education on
student personality and values. All citations date from
1960 to 1975.

3054. Resource books for values education. Raleigh, North
Carolina State Department of Public Instruction, 1974. 5p.
ED 126389.

This annotated bibliography includes books on the philosophy, purpose, and methods of values education for
children, youth, and adults,

3055. Kuhmerker, Lisa. A Bibliography on moral development
and the learning of values in schools and other social settings. New York, Center for Children's Ethical Education,
1971. 45p. ED 054014.

Includes psychological and cultural approaches to the
learning of values. Books, articles, and theses are cited.

3056. Klafter, Marcia B. A Bibliography on moral/values education. Philadelphia, Research for Better Schools, Inc.,
1976. 106p. ED 129766.

Lists 1800 books, articles, and curriculum materials published between 1960 and 1975. Not annotated.

3057. Superka, Douglas P. and Patricia L. Johnson. Values

education: approaches and materials. ERIC Clearinghouse for
Social Studies/Social Science Education, 1975. 164p. ED 103
284.

> Summaries and analyses of 13 sets of materials are included
> in addition to 200 other resources, some of which are
> annotated.

3058. Curry, Charles. An Annotated bibliography of instructional materials which emphasize positive work ethics. Blacksburg, Virginia Polytechnic Institute, 1975. 122p. ED 115766.

> The 56 items deal specifically with developing pride in
> good workmanship, job attainment and holding power, occu-
> pational decision-making, self-image, ethical conduct,
> and reasons for working.

3059. Hill, Russell A. and Joan D. Wallace. Research studies
reporting experimental effects in the moral/ethical/values
domain: an annotated bibliography. Philadelphia, Research
for Better Schools, Inc., 1976. 163p. ED 134523 (MF)

> Over 1500 documents published since 1960 are included
> which deal with the training and acquisition of behaviors,
> skills, and dispositions that can be determined moral in
> themselves, or can contribute to moral behavior. The en-
> tries represent controlled experimental studies which de-
> scribe a treatment, and measure the results.

3060. Hearn, D. Dwain and Sandy Nicholson. Values, feelings,
and morals: part I, research and perspectives; part II, an
annotated bibliography of programs and instructional materials.
Washington, DC, American Association of Elementary, Kindergarten, and Nursery Educators, 1974. 175p. ED 095472 (MF)

> The multimedia bibliography is for children and teachers,
> and deals with the development of values and morals in
> children.

VANDALISM

3061. Vandalism prevention: the best of ERIC. ERIC Clearinghouse on Educational Management, 1976. 5p. ED 127658.

> Annotates 12 documents in the ERIC system.

3062. ERIC document resumes on school vandalism and violence.
Washington, DC, American Association of School Administrators,
1976. 23p. ED 131517.

> Annotates 35 items on the causes, prevention, solutions,
> security methods, and programs and responses advocated
> and used by various groups.

VENEZUELA

3063. Anderson, Teresa. <u>Rural development in Venezuela and</u>
<u>the Guianas: a bibliography</u>. Madison, University of Wisconsin
Land Tenure Center, 1972. 71p. ED 138417.

> Includes 930 items published between 1949 and 1972 on
> agrarian reform, economic affairs, human resources, pop-
> ulation studies, natural resources, social affairs, sci-
> ence and technology, politics and government, trade and
> commerce, and communication. Not annotated.

VIDEO CASSETTES

3064. Molenda, Michael. <u>Annotated bibliography on video</u>
<u>cassettes in education</u>. Greensboro, University of North Car-
olina, School of Education, 1972. 5p. ED 059608.

> Includes 25 articles from popular magazines dated 1970-
> 1972.

VIETNAM AND VIETNAMESE

3065. <u>Vietnam in children's books</u>. New York, United Nations
Children's Fund, 1975. 7p. ED 117269.

> Briefly annotates 25 nonfiction and 18 fiction and folk-
> lore titles. Also includes films and filmstrips. Subjects
> are cookery, customs, culture, Ho Chi Min, and history.

3066. <u>Vietnamese history, literature, and folklore</u>. Washington, DC, Center for Applied Linguistics, 1975. 6p. ED 116
480.

> Annotates 14 books in English including Zen poems, geo-
> graphy, politics, and customs.

3067. <u>Recreational reading in Vietnamese</u>. Arlington, VA,
Center for Applied Linguistics, 1976. 12p. ED 129063.

> Annotates titles of general interest, history, culture,
> poetry, short stories, and novels.

VIRGINIA

3068. <u>Virginiana: a bibliography of materials about Virginia</u>
<u>and by Virginians in the Educational Media Examination Center</u>.
Richmond, Virginia State Department of Education, 1976. 89p.
ED 147252 (MF)

> Lists over 1000 titles including city and county histor-
> ies, novels, biographies, and folklore. Many subjects are
> covered in this unannotated bibliography.

VISUAL LEARNING AND PERCEPTION

3069. Levie, W. Howard. Pictorial research in 1976. 1977.
30p. ED 143341.

This conference paper lists research articles from about
50 journals in psychology, educational psychology, and
communications. Most articles report research in which
pictorial materials were used as experimental stimuli.

3070. Polito, Ronald. Media education: an annotated bibliography. 1973. 20p. ED 134220.

Pertains to various aspects of visual communication and
their instructional implications, and contains 82 entries
for dissertations, articles, books, papers, and projects.

3071. Benning, Virginia E. An Annotated bibliography concerning visual literacy. 1973. 8p. ED 099845.

Topics include visual literacy and remedial and developmental reading, aspects of visual literacy in the classroom, photography and visual literacy, and visual literacy
and disadvantaged and disabled children. The 38 entries
include films and audiovisual instruction.

3072. Fork, Donald J. Visual literacy: a selected bibliography. 1975. 23p. ED 131838.

This conference paper lists about 300 books, articles,
and AV materials related to visual literacy and perception. Unannotated.

3073. Lyman, Bernard. Visual detection, identification, and
localization: an annotated bibliography. Alexandria, VA,
Human Resources Research Organization, 1968. 124p. ED 098
609.

Contains research on visual perception executed in laboratory situations, and includes 407 reports and studies
published from 1945 to 1964 in military and government
publications as well as many psychological journals.

3074. Donoghue, Beverly E. A Bibliography on cross-cultural
differences in visual perception. 1978. 36p. ED 156810.

Includes 533 books and journal articles. Not annotated.

VISUALLY HANDICAPPED

3075. Morris, June E. and Carson V. Nolan. Bibliography of
research on the visually handicapped, 1953-1971. Louisville,
KY, American Printing House for the Blind, 1972. 109p. ED
064851.

All 1300 studies are empirical in nature, and many relate
to legally blind subjects. Medical research on eye blind-
ness is excluded, however. Unannotated.

3076. Dimmick, Kenneth. Psychoacoustics: a selected bibliography. New York, American Foundation for the Blind, 1966.
29p. ED 011419.

Includes 346 unannotated entries related to sensory impairment, especially the partially sighted and the blind.
The books and articles date back to 1934.

3077. Horn, Thomas D. and Dorothy J. Ebert. Books for the
partially sighted child. Champaign, IL, National Council of
Teachers of English, 1965. 81p. ED 030634 (MF)

An annotated list selected for children in grades 1 to 8.
Fiction and nonfiction are included.

3078. Pamphlet library for working with multihandicapped,
visually impaired individuals. Boston Center for Blind Children, 1974. 17p. ED 094528.

Annotations are provided for 66 entries.

3079. Morris, June E. and Carson Nolan. Bibliography on tests
and testing of the blind. Louisville, KY, American Printing
House for the Blind, 1971. 32p. ED 064850.

The 420 entries date from 1920 to 1971 and cover theoretical and practical aspects of testing for the blind, and
its historical development.

3080. Ostberg, Ann-Mari and Bengt Lindqvist. Learning problems in connection with special information media for the visually handicapped: a selected bibliography. Uppsala University (Sweden), 1970. 56p. ED 048686.

Covers barriers to effective listening, critical listening, teleteaching, homebound instruction, note-taking,
rate-controlled speech, braille, form perception, and
tactile discrimination.

3081. Visually handicapped programs: a selective bibliography.
Reston, VA, Council for Exceptional Children, 1973. 27p. ED
085923.

Includes 100 abstracts dating from 1955 to 1972.

3082. Visually handicapped research: a selective bibliography.
Reston, VA, Council for Exceptional Children, 1973. 27p. ED
085924.

Includes 100 abstracts of publications that date from 1963
through 1972.

VOCABULARY DEVELOPMENT

3083. Fairbanks, Marilyn M. Annotated bibliography of experimental studies related to the teaching of vocabulary: intermediate to adult levels, 1950-1977. 1977. 18p. ED 134979.

   The 50 annotations give length and methods of instruction,
   evaluation instruments, and findings.

VOCATIONAL EDUCATION See also INDUSTRIAL ARTS EDUCATION
      and OCCUPATIONAL INFORMATION

3084. Songe, Alice. Vocational education: an annotated bibliography of selected references, 1917-1966. Washington, DC,
Office of Education, 1967. 44p. ED 050225 (MF)

   The books, articles, and dissertations listed trace the
   history of vocational education.

3085. Vocational education: a bibliography of research. Washington, DC, National Advisory Council on Vocational Education,
1971. 25p. ED 050287.

   Most of the entries are unpublished reports prepared under
   contract for DHEW, and relate to the national, state, and
   local level.

3086. Bibliography of vocational rehabilitation with emphasis
on work evaluation. University of Pittsburgh, Research and
Training Center in Vocational Rehabilitation, 1968. 109p. ED
030758.

3087. Training and technology project: listing of documents
and reports for training and technology. Knoxville, University of Tennessee, 1969. 30p. ED 033220.

   Lists 148 project reports from 1966 through 1968. Annotated.

3088. Pennsylvania's abstracts of research and related materials in vocational education. Harrisburg, Pennsylvania
Research Coordinating Unit for Vocational Education, 1969.
121p. ED 031604.

3089. Vocational education and work study programs. Arlington, VA, Council for Exceptional Children, 1969. 19p. ED
036025.

   Includes 55 annotated entries covering all aspects of vocational education and rehabilitation techniques with several handicapping conditions.

3090. Evaluation in vocational education: research summary.
Sacramento, California Coordinating Unit for Occupational Research and Development, 1967. 81p. ED 025587.

   The document also includes a bibliography of books, articles, dissertations, and research reports.

3091. A Bibliography of published and unpublished vocational and technical education literature. Chicago, Corplan Associates, 1966. 225p. ED 018531.

Includes over 1800 references dated from 1960 to 1965. A subject index is provided, as well as some annotations.

3092. Borosage, Lawrence. Research on vocational education in Michigan, 1937-1963. East Lansing, Michigan State University, Bureau of Educational Research, 1965. 53p. ED 016040.

341 studies are listed for agricultural education, business education, homemaking and family life, and industrial education.

3093. Trade, industrial, and technical education: RCU research summaries. Sacramento, California Coordinating Unit for Occupational Research and Development, 1967. 51p. ED 014566.

Includes 81 research studies completed between 1959 and 1966.

3094. Schroeder, Paul E. Vocational education for the handicapped: a bibliography of ERIC documents. Columbus, Ohio State University, Center for Vocational and Technical Education, 1973. 33p. ED 083480.

Annotates 37 items announced in RIE from 1970 to 1972.

3095. Thomas, Robert W. Research and development in vocational and technical education: non-metropolitan areas: survey of reported research. Ames, Iowa State University, 1968. 290p. ED 023891.

Lists 430 books on occupational training and career guidance, and vocational and technical education. Also includes a bibliography of journal articles that date from 1945 to 1965.

3096. Research in industrial education: summaries of studies, 1930-1955. Washington, DC, Government Printing Office, 1957. 532p. ED 042022 (MF)

Annotates 3800 studies. ED 042023 is a 152 page supplement that lists 433 doctoral dissertations on the subject.

3097. Streichler, Jerry. Review and synthesis of research in industrial arts education. Columbus, Ohio State University, Center for Vocational and Technical Education, 1966. 102p. ED 011564.

An unannotated list of dissertations, staff studies, articles, and speeches dating from 1960 to 1966.

3098. Tuckman, Bruce W. and Carl J. Schaefer. Review and

synthesis of research in trade and industrial education. Columbus, Ohio State University, Center for Vocational and Technical Education, 1966. 91p. ED 011560.

An unannotated list of books, articles, papers, and dissertations dating from 1954 to 1966.

3099. Larson, Milton E. Review and synthesis of research in
technical education. Columbus, Ohio State University, Center
for Vocational and Technical Education, 1966. 84p. ED 011559.

An unannotated list of 284 studies published from 1961 to
1966.

3100. Wallace, Harold R. Review and synthesis of research on
cooperative vocational education. Columbus, Ohio State University, Center for Vocational and Technical Education, 1970.
124p. ED 040274.

An unannotated bibliography of 279 dissertations, ERIC
documents, and journal articles dating from 1934 to 1969.

3101. Guiding students into vocational curricula: a bibliography. ERIC Clearinghouse on Counseling and Personnel Services, 1970. 10p. ED 039374.

An annotated list of books, articles, dissertations, and
ERIC documents dating from 1963 to 1970.

3102. Retaining students in training: a bibliography. ERIC
Clearinghouse on Counseling and Personnel Services, 1970. 9p.
ED 039373.

An annotated list of books, articles, dissertations, and
ERIC documents dating from 1962 to 1969.

3103. An Annotated bibliography of resources in the fields
of vocational-technical education and vocational guidance.
Concord, New Hampshire State Department of Education, 1970(?)
36p. ED 038513.

The 29 ERIC documents cover trade and industrial education,
the disadvantaged child, work experience programs, and
the dropout.

3104. Parsons, Edgar A. Assessment of need in programs of
vocational education for the disadvantaged and handicapped:
bibliography. Chapel Hill, NC, System Sciences, Inc., 1975.
74p. ED 136021.

This annotated bibliography is volume three of the final
report. It includes demonstration projects, research studies, curriculum development materials, inservice training
information, and program planning and development information.

3105. Hamlin, Roger E. Planning for vocational education: a selected bibliography. East Lansing, Michigan State University, Proaction Institute, 1977. 55p. ED 143840.

The annotate entries are from the literature of urban planning, labor market planning, management, and vocational education.

3106. Advisory list of instructional media for vocational education. Raleigh, North Carolina State Department of Public Instruction, 1977. 16p. ED 149760.

An annotated multimedia list for K-12.

3107. Finch, Curtis R. Reviews and bibliographies related to research in vocational-technical education: a selective bibliography with annotations. Pennsylvania State University, Department of Vocational Education, 1971. 22p. ED 052383.

Contains 74 entries.

3108. York, Edwin G. An Inventory of New Jersey research concerning vocational education: a list of projects and reports 1931-1969. Trenton, New Jersey Occupational Research and Development Branch, 1969. 123p. ED 040278.

Annotates 364 entries in 21 categories.

3109. Annotated bibliography of instructional materials in cooperative vocational education. De Kalb, Northern Illinois University, 1977. 155p. ED 146382.

Includes 536 items selected from over 700 publishers.

3110. Magisos, Joel H. and Anne E. Stakelon. Individualization and modularization of vocational education instructional materials: an annotated bibliography of publications and projects. Columbus, Ohio State University, Center for Vocational Education, 1975. 58p. ED 133573.

Contains 128 citations from RIE and CIJE.

3111. Magisos, Joel H. and Anne E. Stakelon. Adult vocational education: an annotated bibliography of publications and projects. Columbus, Ohio State University, Center for Vocational Education, 1975. 26p. ED 133575.

Contains 37 citations from RIE and CIJE.

3112. Magisos, Joel H. and Anne E. Stakelon. Special needs populations: annotated bibliographies on bilingual, correctional, migrant, and handicapped populations with unique vocational needs. Columbus, Ohio State University, Center for Vocational Education, 1975. 142p. ED 133607.

This bibliography was compiled from a search of RIE and CIJE.

3113. Magisos, Joel H. and Anne E. Stakelon. Post-secondary

vocational education: an annotated bibliography of publications and projects. Columbus, Ohio State University, Center for Vocational Education, 1975. 25p. ED 133574.

Includes 37 items from a search of RIE and CIJE.

3114. Songe, Alice H. Vocational education: secondary and post-secondary, 1967–1972: an annotated bibliography. Washington, DC, National Advisory Council on Vocational Education, 1972. 59p. ED 112124.

Contains books, articles, and dissertations on trends, management, legislation, and program improvement.

3115. York, Edwin G. A Compilation of resource lists for vocational educators: an annotated bibliography of bibliographies in vocational education, 1960–1969. Trenton, New Jersey State Department of Education, 1969. 198p. ED 049367.

579 bibliographies are listed under 22 general headings.

3116. Reynolds, William E. and Lonnie M. Hart. A National annotated bibliography of curriculum materials in vocational and career education. Springfield, Illinois State Board of Vocational Education and Rehabilitation, 1974. 829p. ED 090 442.

Contains 410 entries in an effort to help publicize the materials on a national scale.

3117. Smith, Brandon B. Selected bibliography: identifying, measuring, and utilizing societal information for vocational-technical education curriculum development. Madison, University of Wisconsin, 1968. 7p. ED 043759.

The 72 citations date from 1958 to 1968, and include articles, research reports, and university publications.

3118. Schroeder, Wayne E. Technical and vocational education planning: an international annotated bibliography of ERIC documents. Columbus, Ohio State University, Center for Vocational Education, 1976. 73p. ED 128652.

Includes 160 abstracts from RIE since 1970.

3119. Magisos, Joel H. and Paul E. Schroeder. Curriculum, demonstration, and installation studies: information sources. Columbus, Ohio State University, Center for Vocational and Technical Education, 1974. 22p. ED 106518.

Includes 19 annotated studies from RIE and CIJE.

3120. Magisos, Joel H. and Paul E. Schroeder. State administration of vocational education: information sources. Columbus, Ohio State University, Center for Vocational and Technical Education, 1974. 36p. ED 106519.

Includes 55 abstracts from RIE and CIJE since 1967.

3121. Magisos, Joel H. and Paul E. Schroeder. Local administration of vocational education: information sources. Columbus, Ohio State University, Center for Vocational and Technical Education, 1974. 29p. ED 106520.

Includes abstracts of 42 items from RIE and CIJE since
1965.

3122. Lambert, Roger H. A Bibliography of free loan materi-
als for trade and industrial education. Third ed. Madison,
University of Wisconsin, Vocational Studies Center, 1976. 45p.
ED 132276.

Annotations and grade levels are included.

3123. Sullivan, Peggy. A Bibliography of library materials
for vocational-technical programs in community colleges.
Eugene, University of Oregon, School of Librarianship, 1969.
66p. ED 034868.

The unannotated entries are listed in 23 instructional
categories.

3124. Four years of research, development, and training: a
bibliography. Washington, DC, Office of Education, Division
of Comprehensive and Vocational Education Research, 1968.
100p. ED 032432.

Cites the final reports of projects funded by the Division
from 1964 to 1968.

3125. Brandon, George L. Research visibility: report on vocational research. Washington, DC, American Vocational Association, 1970. 16p. ED 037576.

Reports on five research reviews and 14 other studies.

3126. Brandon, George L. Research visibility: comprehensive
planning. Washington, DC, American Vocational Association,
1969. 16p. ED 034060.

Includes 12 research reviews, and a bibliography of 28
other studies.

3127. Brandon, George L. Research visibility: vocational
education curriculum. Washington, DC, American Vocational
Association, 1970. 16p. ED 036641.

Includes 16 research reviews, and a bibliography of 56
additional studies.

3128. Law, Gordon F. Research visibility: vocational education for girls and women. 1968. 16p. ED 022063.

Includes 17 research reviews, and a bibliography 12 related studies.

3129. Vocational training: a selective bibliography. Arling-

ton, VA, Council for Exceptional Children, 1972. 31p. ED 069
072.

Includes 88 abstracts dated from 1962 to 1971 related to
the education of handicapped children.

VOLUNTEERS

3130. Adams, Ethel M. and Suzanne D. Cope. Volunteers: an
annotated bibliography. New York, United Community Funds and
Council of America, 1968. 31p. ED 029208.

The areas covered include the evolving role of volunteers,
organization, recruitment, motivation, placement, recognition, staff and volunteer relationships, training and
supervision, program standards, and evaluation. Also includes volunteers in the schools, hospitals, youth services, and case work.

3131. School volunteer programs: the best of ERIC. ERIC Clearinghouse on Educational Management, 1977. 5p. ED 132644.

Annotates 12 ERIC documents on administration, organization, concerns, and practices of school volunteer programs.

3132. Volunteer services system: annotated bibliography. Columbus, OH, Public Schools, 1975. 57p. ED 116291.

This handbook is intended to be of help to volunteer
staff in developing school programs and materials.

VOUCHER SYSTEMS

3133. Educational vouchers: the best of ERIC. ERIC Clearinghouse on Educational Management, 1978. 5p. ED 163663.

Annotates eleven ERIC documents. The promotion of freedom
of choice is covered, as is the effects on racial segregation, and the participation of sectarian schools. Houston's
magnet school program is highlighted.

WAR

3134. Dougall, Lucy. War, peace: film guide. Chicago, World
Without War Publications, 1973. 127p. ED 075310 (MF)

Annotates over 200 films and a large number of program resources. Topics include international law, nonviolent social change, world community, armaments and disarmaments,
roots of war, and the democratic processes.

WASTE DISPOSAL

3135. Himes, Dottie. Operation, maintenance, and management
of wastewater treatment facilities: a bibliography of technical documents. Washington, DC, Environmental Protection Agency, 1978. 25p. ED 160465.

Fourteen manuals are annotated.

3136. Solid waste management: a list of available literature.
Cincinnati, Environmental Protection Agency, 1972. 50p. ED
092350.

The 269 items include conference proceedings, results of
research, and demonstrations in progress.

3137. Fowler, John M. and Kathryn E. Mervine. No deposit -
no return: the management of municipal solid wastes. 1973.
84p. ED 085231.

Part two is an annotated bibliography of general references on management, policy, economics, and sources of waste.
Also covers collection and transportation, processing, in-
cineration, sanitary landfills, and recycling.

3138. Larsen, Julie T. Solid waste management: available in-
formation materials: total listing, 1966-1976. Washington,
DC, Environmental Protection Agency, 1976. 111p. ED 152497
(MF)

The unannotated list includes teaching materials, films,
exhibits, training programs, slide programs, and other
materials.

3139. Golueke, C. G. Solid waste management: abstracts and
excerpts from the literature. Rockville, MD, Public Health
Service, 1970. 467p. ED 087626.

Covers management, collection and transport, disposal,
salvage, environmental and public health, pollution, and
agricultural and food processing wastes.

WATER POLLUTION

3140. Bibliography of water quality research reports. Washington, DC, Environmental Protection Agency, 1972. 50p. ED
068275.

Over 600 published reports present information on the advancement of water pollution control technology and knowledge. The unannotated citations concern municipal, industrial, agricultural, mining, and other sources of pollution.

3141. Fowler, K. E. M. Water pollution: part I, municipal

wastewaters; part II, industrial wastewaters. Washington, DC,
Environmental Protection Agency, 1976. 190p. ED 152490.

Includes student readings, as well as textbooks and handbooks on wastewater management. Annotated.

3142. Mackenthun, Kenneth M. Nitrogen and phosphorus in water: an annotated selected bibliography of their biological
effects. Cincinnati, Public Health Service and Division of
Water Supply and Pollution Control, 1965. 140p. ED 044307
(MF)

Freshwater investigations predominate, but some marine
studies are included. Contains 181 citations of books, articles, and research reports dating from 1922 to 1965.

WATER RESOURCES

3143. Ralston, Valerie H. Water resources: a bibliographic
guide to reference sources. Storrs, University of Connecticut
Library, 1975. 122p. ED 119966.

Annotates 411 references, nearly half of which are government publications.

WELSH

3144. Jones, O. G. Teaching Welsh as a second language: a
bibliography. University College of Wales, 1962. 51p. ED
117961.

Annotates 136 items for teachers and students of Welsh.
About half of the titles are in English, the remainder in
Welsh.

WISCONSIN

3145. Blackshear, Orrilla T. Wisconsin authors and their
books, 1836-1975: a compilation. Madison, Wisconsin State
Department of Public Instruction, Division of Library Services,
1976. 659p. ED 176750.

The books of 5100 Wisconsin authors are listed in this
unannotated bibliography. Omits ephemeral publications,
and dissertations, sermons, state and federal documents.

WOMEN   See also CHICANAS

3146. Chrisman, Sara B. Women and American politics: a selected bibliography, 1965-1974. Rutgers University, Center for

the American Woman and Politics, 1974. 64p. ED 099247 (MF)

Covers voting behavior, political attitudes, participation, women in parties, and women's election campaigns. Many of the uanannotated entries are unpublished source materials.

3147. Eide, Margaret. Women and sports. Ypsilanti, Eastern Michigan University, 1978. 41p. ED 156631.

Deals with women in professional and amateur athletics, physical education and intramurals, the physiological and psychological aspects of women athletes, and equality for women in sport. Not annotated.

3148. Women's athletics. ERIC Clearinghouse on Teacher Education, 1976. 43p. ED 130991.

Annotates 90 articles and documents compiled from the ERIC system.

3149. Caliguri, Joseph P. and Jack P. Krueger. Women in management: bibliography. University of Missouri, School of Education, 1977. 44p. ED 148711.

Over 100 entries from journals, bibliographies, dissertations, research studies, and books are included. The focus is on sex discrimination, sex role stereotypes, affirmative action programs, attitudes of management, federal legislation, change strategies, career development, marital status, and leadership styles. The annotated items relate to education, business, and industry.

3150. Yarborough, JoAnne. Women in management: selected recent references. Washington, DC, Department of Labor Library, 1978. 34p. ED 164901 (MF)

The annotated books and articles date from 1975, and cover the development, training, and recruitment of women managers.

3151. Silver, Donna and Jane Magee. Women administrators in higher education: a selected bibliography. 1978. 27p. ED 151024.

The annotated entries are concerned with the history of women in academia, their current status, and future trends. Includes books, articles, ERIC documents, dissertations, conference proceedings, and government documents.

3152. Horton, Davis M. and Marjorie Kravitz. The Female offender: a selected bibliography. Germantown, MD, Aspen Systems Corporation, 1979. 56p. ED 176172.

The annotated entries concern women's crime and criminality. They were drawn from the data base of the National Criminal Justice Reference Service, 1965-1978.

3153. Women offenders: a bibliography. Olympia, Washington
State Library, 1970. 17p. ED 132448.

Over 180 unannotated citations are listed which originate
primarily from the several state agencies. The period covered is 1940 to 1970.

3154. Women in non-traditional occupations: a bibliography.
Washington, DC, Koba Associates, Inc., 1976. 194p. ED 133460.

Books, articles, dissertations, pamphlets, and government
documents are annotated, and concern professional and
nonprofessional employment.

3155. Walton, Whitney. Current sources on women and literature. Madison, University of Wisconsin Library, 1979. 55p.
ED 178957 (MF)

The 670 unannotated entries include books, articles, and
dissertations, and are essentially a listing of critical
works. Covers women authors, female characters in the
literature, and feminist analyses of works by men and women.

3156. Elsas, Diana. Women and film/television. Washington,
DC, American Film Institute, 1977. 12p. ED 153652.(MF)

Annotates books, articles, pamphlets, bibliographies, and
filmographies.

3157. Women in American agriculture: a selected bibliography.
Washington, DC, National Agricultural Library, 1977. 33p.
ED 157663.

Annotates over 250 entries dating from 1854 to 1977. They
cover women as landowners, farm managers, farm laborers,
and women in agricultural education and science.

3158. Bachmann, Gail. The Life and times of women: a bibliography of biographies for use in various secondary school curricular areas. 1977. 35p. ED 141247 (MF)

The 141 entries include background readings, bibliographies, 63 individual biographies, and several collective
biographies.

3159. Ryan, Florence H. When George Washington takes second
place. 1976. 19p. ED 132565.

Includes an unannotated seven page bibliography of biographies about women chosen to appeal to young girls.

WOMEN - EDUCATION

3160. Continuing education of women. ERIC Clearinghouse on

Adult Education, 1968. 80p. ED 028340.

    Contains 143 annotated entries dating from 1965 to 1968.
Covers sex differences in ability and achievement, social
role, employment interests, and women's education in foreign countries.

3161. Cirksena, Kathy. Continuing education, re-entry, and
the mature woman: annotated selected references and resources.
Bethesda, MD, Women's Educational Equity Communications Network, 1977. 26p. ED 155349.

    Includes 93 monographs, articles, papers, and bibliogra-
phies which provide overviews, counseling resources, program development, and specific programs.

3162. Continuing education of women. Washington, DC, Adult
Education Association, 1970. 76p. ED 042122.

    Annotates 150 entries.

3163. Elkin, Anna. The Emerging role of mature women: basic
background data in employment and continuing education: a selected annotated bibliography primarily of free and inexpensive
materials. New York, Federation Employment and Guidance Service, 1976. 27p. ED 123415.

    100 items are evaluated.

3164. Brandon, George L. Research visibility: educating women for the world of work. Washington, DC, American Vocational Association, 1970. 16p. ED 045849.

    Annotates 11 research reports, and lists an additional 22
studies. Some refer to the situation in England and France.

3165. Harris, Abigail M. ETS studies related to women and
education: annotated bibliography. Princeton, NJ, Educational
Testing Service, 1976. 93p. ED 138603.

    Some of the research is on identifying methods of deter-
mining and correcting for bias and sex differences in
testing.

3166. Barabas, Jean. Women: their educational and career
roles: an annotated bibliography of selected ERIC references.
ERIC Clearinghouse on the Urban Disadvantaged, 1972. 71p.
ED 067423.

    The entries are taken from RIE and CIJE, 1966-1971.

3167. Wheat, Valerie and Judi Conrad. Rural women and education: annotated selected references and resources. ERIC Clearinghouse on Rural Education and Small Schools, 1978. 30p.
ED 160334.

    Most citations are from the 1970's, but some date to 1939.

3168. Non-formal education and the role of women and families
in human resource development: topical acquisitions list. East
Lansing, Michigan State University, Non-formal Education Information Center, 1976. 32p. ED 132353.

3169. Williams, Kathleen L. Measures of educational equity
for women: a research monograph. Palo Alto, CA, American Institutes for Research in the Behavioral Sciences, 1977. 200p.
ED 152810.

  Annotates 61 measurement instruments.

3170. Cirksena, Kathy. Women's educational equity: annotated
selected references and resources. San Francisco, Far West
Laboratory for Educational Research and Development, 1977.
21p. ED 151281.

  Contains 88 references to programs, services, and materials available to overcome sexism.

3171. Elkin, Anna. Resources for the employment of mature
women and/or their continuing education: a selected bibliography and aids. New York, Federation Employment and Guidance
Service, 1966. 27p. ED 021179.

  Covers job hunting aids, volunteer work, continuing education, and correspondence study, among other topics. Annotated.

3172. Mills, Gladys H. Equal rights for women in education:
a bibliography. Denver, Education Commission of the States,
1973. 14p. ED 102439.

  Deals with affirmative action, continuing education and
  counseling, employment profiles, sex discrimination, and
  the status of women in higher education. Not annotated.

WOMEN - EMPLOYMENT

3173. Tack, Martha W. and Deborah T. Ashford. Dimensions on
women's employment in non-traditional female occupations: a
selected bibliography. 1975. 85p. ED 123490.

  Unannotated. Concerns nearly all occupations except homemaking, nursing, and pre-college teaching. Includes books,
  articles, reports, pamphlets, dissertations, and government documents.

3174. Samuels, Victoria. Nowhere to be found: a literature
review and annotated bibliography on white working class women.
New York, American Jewish Committee, 1975. 32p. ED 139858.

  Covers the literature of sociology, psychology, marketing,
  the mass media, and other fields.

3175. Bickner, Mei Liang. Women at work: an annotated bibli-

ography. Los Angeles, UCLA, Manpower Research Center, 1974.
437p. ED 095398.

Presents material from an economic and sociological perspective, as opposed to a political or psychological approach. Excludes dissertations and items published prior
to 1960.

3176. Kohen, Andrew. Women and the economy: a bibliography
and review of the literature on sex differentiation in the
labor market. Columbus, Ohio State University, Center for
Human Resource Research, 1977. 115p. ED 151274.

Includes 660 unannotated references to literature about
sex discrimination in the labor market, and a review of
research about male/female differences in earnings and
occupational assignments.

3177. Women and work in U.S. history: an annotated selected
bibliography. Washington, DC, Business and Professional Women's Foundation, 1976. 32p. ED 147253 (MF)

Cites research in the methods and theory of women's history. Covers sexual divisions in labor, women's role in
labor unionization, and experiences of various ethnic women. Most of the 105 references were published in the
1970's.

3178. Schroeder, Paul E. Women in the world of work: a bibliography of ERIC documents. Columbus, Ohio State University,
Center for Vocational and Technical Education, 1973. 29p. ED
083479.

Annotates 32 items dated 1970-1972.

3179. Hughes, Marija M. The Sexual barrier: legal and economic aspects of employment. 1970. 43p. ED 065701 (MF)

Includes books, articles, pamphlets, and government publications dating from 1959 on the laws and conditions governing the employment of women. ED 065702 and ED 065703
are supplements to the bibliography and contain 40 pages
and 79 pages respectively. The entries are annotated.

WOMEN'S STUDIES

3180. Bibliography of sources relating to women. Lansing,
Michigan State Department of State, 1975. 27p. ED 128683.

Annotates unpublished source materials relating to women
which are available in a number of archives in Michigan.

3181. Goodman, Sara. Resources on women. 1978. 81p.   ED
159098.

Includes 600 resources concerning many subjects related

women's studies. Some are annotated.

3182. Kusnerz, Peggy A. and Ann M. Pollack. Women: a select bibliography. Ann Arbor, University of Michigan, Library Extension Service, 1975. 46p. ED 112320.

A topical list of books, articles, films, and videotapes related to feminism and women's studies. Not annotated.

3183. Haller, Elizabeth S. Images of women: a bibliography of feminist resources for Pennsylvania schools. Harrisburg, Pennsylvania State Department of Education, 1973. 53p. ED 090470.

Annotates instructional materials which favorably portray women in non-traditional roles. Includes films, tapes, biographies, fiction, history, the arts, and psychology.

3184. Busby, Linda J. The Uses of media to improve the status of women on an international scale. 1977. 31p. ED 147 900.

This conference paper presents bibliographies on the status of women around the world, research reports on women in other countries, and a film list on women's roles in several other countries.

3185. Images of women: curriculum resources for teachers and students. New York, Informedia, 1978. 22p. ED 152325 (MF)

Includes 228 print and nonprint items, most of them for the secondary school level. The resources are designed to highlight the role of women outside the home.

3186. King, Judith D. Women's studies sourcebook: a comprehensive classified bibliography of books. 1976. 75p. ED 156616 (MF)

Over 1000 titles are listed in 51 categories ranging from abortion to the women's liberation movement. An author and title index is included. Not annotated.

3187. Froschl, Merle and Jane Williamson. Feminist resources for schools and colleges: a guide to curricular materials. Revised ed. Old Westbury, NY, Feminist Press, 1977. 73p. ED 154809.

A selective annotated bibliography of nonsexist books, articles, pamphlets, and other materials for teachers, students, librarians, and parents.

3188. Books on women in history: a selected listing. Austin, Texas Education Agency, 1973. 12p. ED 096231.

The annotated entries are on the roles and contributions of women in U.S. history for secondary level students and teachers. Most were published in the 1970's.

3189. Kelly, Joan. Bibliography in the history of European women. Bronxville, NY, Sarah Lawrence College, 1976. 136p. ED 155106 (MF)

The 1300 citations are unannotated. Most are in English, and were published in the 20th Century. Covers antiquity, the Middle Ages, the Renaissance and Reformation, early modern Europe, and the Nazi period. Women in the Soviet Union are also included.

3190. Rosenfelt, Deborah S. Strong women: an annotated bibliography of literature for the high school classroom. Old Westbury, NY, Feminist Press, 1976. 55p. ED 135675 (MF)

Includes anthologies, biographies, autobiographies, drama, novels, short stories, and poetry which emphasize the accomplishments of women.

3191. Wright, Maureen. Women's studies: a student's guide to reference sources. Montreal, McGill University Library, 1975. 14p. ED 117747.

Annotates 73 reference works with an emphasis on Canadian women.

3192. Samalonis, Bernice and Earl R. Shaffer. Some sources of bibliographies pertaining to women's studies. 1975. 22p. ED 106707.

An unannotated list of ERIC documents from the previous four years is presented in this conference paper.

3193. Freeman, Leah. The Changing role of women: a selected bibliography. Third ed. Sacramento, California State University, 1977. 196p. ED 176139.

Covers crime and rape, education, employment, family planning, history of women prior to 1900, juvenile books, literature and the arts, political activity and civil rights, sex roles and sexuality, health and psychology, and third world women.

3194. Special issues of periodicals about women of recent date. Madison, University of Wisconsin Library, 1979. 16p. ED 184501.

Lists 66 issues published from 1977 to 1979. Unannotated.

3195. Stineman, Esther. Basic reference and periodical resources to support women's studies: recommended list. Madison, University of Wisconsin Center System, 1978. 21p. ED 181927.

Annotates 67 reference works, and 13 periodicals.

3196. Valiant, Sharon. Crossing cultures - third world women: a book of materials, activities, and ideas for the classroom

teacher. Rutgers University, Training Institute for Sex Desegregation of the Public Schools, 1977. 33p. ED 162028 (MF)

Covers lifestyle, economics, handicrafts, and notable
women, among other topics.

3197. Dupont, Julie A. Women - their social and economic
status: selected references. Washington, DC, Department of
Labor Library, 1970. 46p. ED 049371.

Includes 396 citations in a general section, historical
section, and a group on the 19th and 20th Centuries. Not
annotated.

3198. Soltow, Martha J. Women in American labor history,
1825-1935: an annotated bibliography. East Lansing, Michigan
State University, School of Labor and Industrial Relations,
1972. 156p. ED 093744.

Includes books, articles, pamphlets, and government publications; excludes theses, dissertations, and state publications.

3199. Lee, Sylvia L. Implications of women's work patterns
for vocational and technical education: an annotated bibliography. Columbus, Ohio State University, Center for Vocat-
tional Education, 1967. 36p. ED 016826.

A subject bibliography of 80 items dating from 1963 to
1967.

3200. Dodds, Dorothy. Recommended non-stereotyped software
and educational materials. Tempe, Arizona State University,
College of Education, 1975. 10p. ED 121304.

Annotates 60 multimedia instructional materials which relate to the role of women in society.

3201. Friedman, Barbara. Women's work and women's studies,
1973-1974: a bibliography. New York, Barnard College, 1975.
381p. ED 130986 (MF)

Lists 4000 books, articles, pamphlets, and research papers
on a wide variety of topics related to women. Some are
annotated.

3202. Moser, Collette and Deborah Johnson. Rural women workers in the 20th Century: an annotated bibliography. East Lansing, Michigan State University, Center for Rural Manpower and
Public Affairs, 1973. 70p. ED 100570.

Includes books, articles, and research papers dating from
1875 to 1971. There are 338 entries.

WORD PROCESSING

3203. Potts, Peggy J. <u>Educators resource guide to WP mater-</u><u>ial for the classroom.</u> 1979(?) 25p. ED 184629.

Annotates multimedia items on word processing technology. Includes machine transcription programs, corporate reports, films, skill manuals, and workbooks.

WORK

3204. Fry, Ronald R. <u>Work evaluation: an annotated biblio-</u><u>graphy, 1947-1970.</u> Menomonie, WI, Stout State University, 1971. 97p. ED 062590.

Includes 403 annotations of articles, speeches, and other publications related to work as an evaluation tool.

3205. Schroeder, Paul E. <u>Attitudes toward work: a bibliogra-</u><u>phy of ERIC documents.</u> Columbus, Ohio State University, Center for Vocational and Technical Education, 1973. 38p. ED 083478.

45 selected documents from RIE (1970-1972) are listed in this annotated bibliography.

WORK EXPERIENCE PROGRAMS

3206. Banta, Trudy W. <u>Work education: a topical bibliography</u><u>of programs, procedures, and research.</u> Santa Monica, CA, Systems Development Corporation, 1973. 136p. ED 090414.

This unannotated literature review contains over 1600 listings.

3207. Herschbach, Dennis R. <u>Cooperative work experience: an</u><u>annotated resource guide.</u> University of Maryland, Department of Industrial Education, 1975. 219p. ED 134805.

Covers program operation and administration, classroom management, counseling, and career awareness. The 500 entries also cover personal adjustment and job training.

3208. Herschbach, Dennis R. <u>Cooperative work experience: an</u><u>annotated resource guide for teachers of the handicapped.</u> University of Maryland, Department of Industrial Education, 1976. 146p. ED 134806.

Includes over 300 entries which cover basic skills, job skills, life skills, and other topics.

WORLD AFFAIRS

3209. <u>Global education guidelines.</u> Lansing, Michigan State

Department of Education, 1977. 75p. ED 159106 (MF)

The bibliography, which comprises about half of the publication, annotates teacher resource material, and print and
nonprint materials for classroom use at all levels.

3210. Basa, Patricia and Tony Codianni. Global perspectives:
a bibliography. Bloomington, IN, Social Studies Development
Center, 1975. 45p. ED 114350.

The briefly annotated entries emphasize the interrelated-
ness of world problems and issues. They are designed to
help teachers find resources and suitable K-12 classroom
materials that introduce global perspectives into the curricula.

WRITING INSTRUCTION

3211. Collins, Terence and Suzanne Hofer. A Selected annotated bibliography of articles on interdepartmental responsibility for the teaching of writing skills. 1976. 13p. ED
139033.

The 37 articles and papers reviewed here suggest that the
standards for writing among college students are college-
wide responsibilities.

3212. Donovan, Robert B. Technical writing texts for secondary schools, two-year colleges, and four-year colleges. 1977.
14p. ED 150635 (MF)

This annotated bibliography was prepared for the National
Council of Teachers of English Committee on Technical and
Scientific Writing. It also includes a few anthologies
that may be used to supplement the texts.

3213. Bowman, Mary Ann. Books on business writing and technical writing in the University of Illinois Library. Urbana,
American Business Communication Association, 1975. 38p. ED
127624.

Books written in English between 1950 and 1973 are included in the two separate lists.

3214. Day, Robert and Gail C. Weaver. Creative writing in
the classroom: an annotated bibliography of selected resources, K-12. ERIC Clearinghouse on Reading and Communication
Skills, 1978. 122p. ED 161038.

Categories include theory and practice, results, and special resources for the 700 books and articles listed. The
entries date from 1950 to 1976.

3215. McCracken, H. Thomas. A Graduate program in English
education is more than courses. 1977. 39p. ED 146585 (MF)

Includes an annotated bibliography of over 100 books, articles, papers, and dissertations that deal with the evaluation of written composition.

3216. You've made the assignment: now what? An annotated bibliography on the process of teaching composition. Redlands, California Association of Teachers of English, 1977. 21p. ED 145467.

About the process and teaching of writing for kindergarten through college. Experimental research and methodology are included in the books, articles, and reports.

3217. Blackman, Carolyn M. A Bibliography of resources for beginning teachers of technical writing. 1977. 13p. ED 144 066.

The entries presented in this conference paper are not annotated.

YEAR ROUND SCHOOLS

3218. Whitney, Howard and Philip Piele. Annotated bibliography on year round school programs. ERIC Clearinghouse on Educational Administration, 1968. 10p. ED 023199.

The 45 entries discuss several plans including trimester programs, quarter system plans, and summer school. All were published since 1962.

3219. Pierce, Willitt S. and Robert C. Remstad. A Bibliography of references to the extended school year, year round school, and related topics. Burlington, Southeast Wisconsin Regional Education Center, 1972. 41p. ED 077129.

An unannotated bibliography presented in chronological segments. Some items date prior to 1950.

3220. Schwartzman, Paula and Bruce Campbell. Annotated bibliography: extended school year materials. Fifth ed. 1975. 177p. ED 104021.

Covers only programs in the United States in the books and articles listed. Some theses and filmstrips are also included.

3221. The Year-round school: a source book and review of the literature. Raleigh, North Carolina State Department of Public Instruction, 1973. 97p. ED 084673.

50 pages are devoted to the review summary of recent literature.

3222. ERIC abstracts: a collection of ERIC document resumes on the year-round school. Washington, DC, American Association of School Administrators, 1973. 24p. ED 091798.

This listing is comprehensive for all issues of RIE through July 1973.

3223. Campbell, Bruce. Annotated bibliography: extended school year materials. Trenton, New Jersey State Department of Education, 1972. 24p. ED 066799.

The 77 entries include books, articles, papers, reports, theses, filmstrips, and bibliographies.

3224. Smith, Paul J. A Review of literature pertaining to the year-round school and its implications for the Macomb Community Unit District Number 185, K-12. Macomb, IL, 1974. 70p. ED 120968.

Reviews material pertaining to the economic feasibility, public acceptance, and learning outcomes of such programs. Includes books, articles, and ERIC documents.

3225. Shepard, Morris A. Year-round schools: the importance of year-round schools. Cambridge, Mass., Abt Associates, 1975. 133p. ED 128875.

This volume two of a final report presents an extensive bibliography. It is not annotated.

3226. Gayden, Joyce and Barbara Thornton. Year-round schools: a chronological selected bibliography from 1907 to 1972. Columbia, SC, Richland County School District 1, 1972. 45p. ED 087140.

Lists 800 books, articles, newspaper accounts, pamphlets, and reports. Not annotated.

3227. The Extended school year: an information packet. Phoenix, Arizona State Department of Education, 1972. 72p. ED 072531.

Presents an extensive annotated bibliography which includes some filmstrips. Discusses the rationale for such a program, and describes basic types of ESY plans.

YOUTH See CHILDREN AND YOUTH

YUGOSLAVIA

3228. Early childhood education in Yugoslavia: a special issue of selected bibliography of Yugoslav educational materials. Belgrade, Yugoslav Institute for Educational Research, 1973. 25p. ED 097286.

Annotates journal articles, research, and excerpts from books published in the 1970's. Covers child care, nursery schools, and kindergartens.

Author Index

Elder, Richard, 2509

Elkin, Anna, 2407, 3163, 3171

Eller, William, 2520

Elliott, Pamela, 316

Elliott, Peggy, 2885

Elliott, Peter J., 484

Ellis, Willie, 116, 117

Ellison, John, 1035

Ellsworth, Randolph, 2973

Elnor, Nancy, 1485

Elsas, Diana, 524, 1177, 1375, 1376, 1377, 1378, 2941, 2942, 2943, 2944, 3156

Elster, Richard, 2016

Embree, A., 279

Emerson, George, 1356

Endo, Russell, 259

Epley, David, 72

Erbstoeszer, Marie, 1609

Erickson, Joan, 2254

Erskine, Richard, 289

Ertel, Kenneth, 1036

Escobar, Joanna, 1251

Eshelby, Don, 2573

Esp, Barbara, 135

Espejo, Cristina, 772

Estrada, Josephine, 2475

Evans, G. E., 197, 210

Evans, Gwynneth, 479

Everard, Kenneth, 460

Evertts, Eldonna, 2869

Ewens, Bill, 2882

Ewens, Wilma, 2248

Ewing, Gordon, 242

Ewy, Robert, 2435

Eyler, Marvin, 2576

Fabriele, Peter, 1593

Fairbanks, Marilyn, 2493, 2568, 3083

Falcione, Raymond, 774

Fanslow, Alyce, 1647

Farley, Frank, 1897

Farnan, John, 1254

Farr, Richard, 2593

Farr, Roger, 2499

Farrah, George, 2715

Farrell, Joseph, 2766

Farrell, Robert, 1851

Farrell, William, 1770

Fay, Leo, 2529, 2535, 2544, 2561

Fearon, Ross, 306, 1499, 2093

Feder, Helga, 1434

Feehan, Paul, 2007

Feeney, Joan, 606

Fehr, Helen, 146

Feingold, S. N., 539

Feldman, Marjorie, 1238

Hinds, Richard, 1145

Hingtgen, Joseph, 2444

Hinrichs, Roy, 1513, 1715

Hippler, Arthur, 1294, 1295

Hirshfeld, Marvin, 1039

Hlavsa, J., 925

Hoadley, Irene, 2209

Hobron, Robert, 979

Hodges, Jimmy, 349

Hofer, Suzanne, 3211

Hoffman, Fae, 496

Hoge, Henry, 2400, 2401

Hohenstein, John, 1851

Holcomb, Beverly, 1004

Holland, Nora, 3026

Hollister, Robert, 433

Holmberg, N., 477

Holmquist, Garth, 2610

Holmwood, Donald, 28

Holt, Carol, 658

Holtgrieve, Donald, 1426

Honig, Alice, 1369, 1720, 1804

Hooker, Charlotte, 1371

Hope, Henry W., 436

Hopper, Mark, 636

Horn, B. R., 1282

Horn, Fern, 1651, 2099

Horn, Thomas, 3077

Hornburger, Jane, 721

Horne, Eleanor, 648, 2671, 2793

Horton, Davis, 3152

Hoskins, Myrna, 2613

House, Robert, 1868

Houston, Helen, 372

Howard, Norma K., 650, 940, 957, 2010, 2286, 2326, 2712, 2742, 2884

Hoyt, Anne, 576

Hsu, Tse-chi, 2971

Huang, Che-tsao, 1165

Hubbard, Terry, 129

Hudson, Barclay, 1148

Hudson, Bennett, 757

Hudson, Floyd, 2564

Hughes, Jane, 1945

Hughes, Marija, 3179

Hulme, Marilyn, 2727

Humberg, Renae, 69

Hume, Mildred, 414

Humm, William, 2622, 2823

Humphreys, Les, 1898

Hunt, Irmgard, 1210

Hurlburt, Evelyn, 360

Hussey, Edith, 401

Hutcheon, N. B., 1793

Hutcheson, Pat, 2514

Hutchinson, Myra, 2841

Huus, Helen, 2780

Hyland, Anne, 615, 616

Hylton, V. W., 1324

Hyslop, David, 891

Ibarra, Herb, 355

Ingle, Henry T., 992

Inglehart, Babette, 1315

Isaacson, Arlene, 1048

Isler, Norman, 1091, 1119, 1133, 1628

Isquith, Robert, 1588

Jablonsky, Adelaide, 429, 598, 998, 1006, 1016, 1027, 1028, 1049, 1052, 1053, 2185, 2186, 2187, 2471, 2492, 2660, 2663

Jackson, Anne, 1320

Jackson, Clara O., 694

Jackson, Dorothy, 2584

Jackson, Kathleen, 2649

Jackson, Malan, 2422

Jackson, Michael, 2969

Jackson, Miles, 405

Jacob, Nelson, 2633

Jacobs, H. L., 1444

Jacobsen, R. B., 2264

Jaglinski, Carol, 185

Jakle, John, 1314

James, Edward, 2832

James, Eloise, 2150

James, H. Thomas, 432

Jameson, Andrew, 1923

Jamieson, Alfred, 1850

Jamison, Edward, 1857

Janeway, Sally, 1134

Jared, Lee, 2529

Jarrett, Gladys, 175

Jayatilleke, R., 142, 263, 841, 1667, 2184, 2834

Jelden, David, 1710

Jenkins, Hugh, 433

Jenkins, Thomas, 3038

Jensen, Ida-Marie, 1417, 2642, 2949

Jezierski, Kathleen, 521

Job, Amy, 764

Johns, Jerry, 2488

Johnson, B. Lamar, 1938

Johnson, Benton, 2587

Johnson, Carolyn, 2502

Johnson, Charles, 1162

Johnson, Claudia A., 649

Johnson, Deborah, 2611, 3202

Johnson, Dora, 266, 269, 1824, 1828

Johnson, G. W., 107

Johnson, Harry A., 681

Johnson, Hugh, 2308

Johnson, James R., 2929

Johnson, Norbert, 527

Johnson, Pam, 1487

Nolan, Carson, 3075, 3079

Nolte, Jane, 1453

Nolte, M., 2664

Norberg, Kenneth, 781

Norman, O., 2154, 2665

Norris, Lynne, 2985

Norris, Mildred, 2538

Norton, Mary E., 1845, 1848

Novak, Jan, 519

Nuessel, Frank, 1964, 1965

Nupoll, Karin, 612

Nussbaum, Mary, 2001

Nuttall, John, 902

Nyheim, Charlotte, 874

Nyka, James, 554

Oberle, Wayne, 2775

Oberteuffer, D., 2739

O'Connell, Dorothy, 1555

O'Connell, Harold, 2424

O'Deirg, I., 1975

Odland, Norine, 716, 725

Ogilvie, William, 808

Ohlendorf, George, 696, 2265

Ohliger, John, 41, 61, 67, 1729

Oinonen, C., 2648

O'Leary, Charles, 1789

Olin, Ferris, 2726

Oller, John, 1832

Olmsted, Lucia, 2879

Olsen, Diane, 187

Olson, LeVene, 493

Olson, Nancy, 2693

O'Neil, Eva, 2506

O'Neill, Mara, 2404

O'Neill, Peggy, 1325

Ong, Paul, 265

Onouye, Wendy, 1312

Orr, Oliver, 3018

Ortiz, Ana Maria, 593

Osborn, Lynn R., 209

Osman, David, 1184

Ostberg, Ann, 3080

Oster, Sharon, 2408

Ott, Helen K., 705

Overs, Robert, 2262

Owen, Harold J., 816

Padbury, Peter, 1413

Paden, John, 397

Palic, Vladimir, 1478

Palmberg, Rolf, 1981

Panday, N., 771

Pannell, Clifton, 1421

Pansino, Louis, 2155

Pap, Leo, 2403

Paquette, F., 1814

Paquette, Dan, 1310

Parker, Carrie, 2612

Subject Index

1088, 1130, 1145, 1684, 2370, 3034

Costume design, 2994, 2995

Counseling, 349, 494, 501, 513, 528, 546, 994, 1025, 1064, 1189, 1440, 1529, 2126, 2194, 2981

Counselors, 811, 2092

County government, 1476

Course organization, 2673

Court litigation, 2665

"Cover to Cover", 2513

Creative writing, 3214

Creativity, 312, 729, 1461, 1462, 1468, 1469

Crime, 2950

Criminal justice, 908, 930

Criminals, 3152, 3153

Criterion referenced tests, 2970-2974, 2978, 2979

Critical incident technique, 2594

Critical reading, 2520, 2531, 2598

Cross-cultural studies, 174

Cuba, 2796

Cubans, 619, 2801

Cultural
awareness, 2877
differences, 681, 3074
education, 1323-1325, 1329, 2331, 2787
exchange, 779, 782

Culturally disadvantaged, 1229

Cumberland region, 2948

Curriculum development, 509, 3117
guides, 1231

Cybernetics, 2373

Dance, 253, 2358, 2985

Data processing, 861

Day care, 662, 671, 940, 1720, 2318, 2773

Deaf, 1530-1532

Deaf education, 2753, 2754

Death, 1361, 1437, 1604, 1718

Debate, 2387

Decentralization, 2389, 2653, 2654

Decision making, 569, 1724, 2373, 2431

Defense mechanisms, 2453-2458

Demography, school, 1262-1264

Demonstration projects, 2583, 2584

Denial, psychological, 2449

Dental health, 1386, 1584

Deschooling, 1729

Developing nations, 52, 72, 822, 1001, 1087, 1144, 1375, 2001, 2676, 2677, 3196

Deviant behavior, 200

Diagnostic teaching, 1701, 1886, 2928

Dialect studies, 361, 365, 1963, 1968, 1978

Dictionaries, French, 1409

Differentiated staffing, 2293, 2816-2820, 2822